Exploring Government

Ray Notgrass

Cover and Interior Design by Mary Evelyn Notgrass

Pictured on the cover:
United States flag (Department of Defense)
Children in San Francisco, 1942
(Library of Congress Prints and Photographs Division)
United States Supreme Court Building (public domain image)
Washington, D.C. (Department of Defense)
Indiana State Capitol (Mary Evelyn Notgrass)
U.S. Air Force personnel outside the United States Capitol (Department of Defense)

Notgrass Company
370 S. Lowe Avenue, Suite A
PMB 211
Cookeville, Tennessee 38501

1-800-211-8793
books@notgrass.com
www.notgrass.com

ISBN: 978-1-933410-88-3

Published in the United States by Notgrass Company.

Dedication

I dedicate this curriculum to my sweet wife and life companion, Charlene.

God brought us together when we were both work-study students in the Political Science Department at college.

Your study and work in Urban Planning gave us both a sense of what government is and what it should be.

Your heart for God has helped us both see what people should be able to expect from leaders in government and from governmental policies.

We have seen people and events in government that have inspired us and that have discouraged us. We have learned not to put our trust in princes.

Your selfless service in carrying so much of our family's responsibilities has enabled this curriculum to be produced. I especially appreciate your work in laying out the text for *We Hold These Truths*. I could not have done this without you. You are as much a part of this publication as I am.

Many daughters have done nobly,
but you excel them all.
Proverbs 31:29

Table of Contents

Part 3—State and Local Government, Taxes, and Budgets

Part 4—Issues Facing American Government Today

Introduction

We must consider that we shall be as a city upon a hill,
the eyes of all people are upon us.

—John Winthrop,
from his sermon "A Model of Christian Charity," given in 1630
to those who were about to establish the Massachusetts Bay colony

When Governor John Winthrop led his small band of settlers to the shores of America, he understood that the entire world would be watching the outcome of this experiment in the wilderness. As it has turned out, it was not just the people of that generation who watched. For almost four hundred years, the world has studied the American experiment in governing. In many ways it has been a source of inspiration for learning how humans can live together in a civil society in peace and harmony.

It is our purpose in *Exploring Government* to educate, to inspire, and sometimes to warn you concerning the governments of the United States, the individual states, and our local communities. Special emphasis is placed on the Biblical basis for government and on understanding the U.S. Constitution. We hope that you will come to understand the background, basis, and operation of American government on all levels. We hope that you will remain prayerful, thoughtful, informed, and involved with regard to government throughout your life. We also hope that you will be a better Christian and a better citizen as a result of studying this material.

The curriculum has three parts: *Exploring Government*, a 75-lesson text; *We Hold There Truths*, a volume of historic documents, essays, and speeches that are to be read in conjunction with the lessons; and an optional *Quiz and Exam Book* that has review questions over the lessons and readings, quizzes, and exams. By working through the entire curriculum, we believe that you will gain a good understanding of the purpose and function of government.

We include historical information on government before the founding of the United States in 1776 and the formulation of the Constitution in 1787. Our purpose in doing this is to help you understand not only what government does but why our government came to be the way it is and why it does what it does. Ideas and events have causes. The American system did not just appear, nor was it inevitable. We have to understand why in order to understand what and how. When you understand why things happen (1) you learn something; (2) you are better able to discuss the subject with others, some of whom may not share your assumptions; and (3) you will be better able to bring about changes that need to take place.

We need to make two distinctions to help you understand what we present in the curriculum. First, there is a difference between government and politics. Government is not the same as politics and elections, although governments are formed by the political process and people in government can be and often are very political in their actions. Politics involves the electoral process, political parties, and trying to persuade voters about candidates and issues. Government officials often make decisions based on the political impact that those decisions will have (that is, how popular they will be with voters), not on whether the decisions are the best ones to make. Government, on the other hand, involves defending the nation, building roads, operating schools, collecting taxes, and other activities. Since politics and government are two different functions, this explains why sometimes politicians who win elections aren't good at governing and why the best government workers are not necessarily concerned about politics.

Second, we need to understand the difference between what is and what should be. The Bible sets forth what government should be. The U.S. Constitution, state constitutions, and local laws have established how things should operate in our country. However, centuries of history show us that government does not always do what it should do. For example, black Americans for many years did not have the equal protection under the law that is promised in the Constitution. What existed was not what should have existed. Also, the Federal government has in recent decades taken oversight of areas that were originally reserved to the states. It is not what should be, but it is nonetheless what is happening. When we describe what government does today, we do not mean to say that everything it does is right and what it should be doing. We try to point out discrepancies we see between what the founding documents say and what government actually does.

God, the Creator of government, has given us a wonderful system of government in our country. It has provided the most personal freedom and the best economic opportunity for the most people of any government in history, with the exception of the government that God gave to Israel in the Old Testament. Our government deserves our respect, our involvement, and our prayers.

At the same time, our governments (local, state, and national) have not always been the city upon a hill that they should have been. Sometimes what American governments have done has been embarrassing and wrong. Still, we have always been on the hill: able to be seen and judged by ourselves and by the citizens of the world. We should help our country to be an example of truth, love, righteousness, and compassion.

I want to express a special thanks to my daughter Mary Evelyn for her excellent graphic design of the cover and for her work in editing and laying out the text. I would also like to thank my daughter Bethany for her editing work. I appreciate my family's support, encouragement, and assistance for this project.

A note about capitalization: A friend who is an assistant district attorney taught me that the word Federal, when referring to the national government, should be capitalized. That has been our usage throughout this text. Capitalization of the word president is troublesome. Technically, it is to be capitalized when referring to a specific President and lower case when referring to the president in general. We have tried to follow this rule, but I offer my apologies for any inconsistencies.

Those of us who follow the Lord are citizens of the kingdom of God even as we live as citizens of the country in which He has placed us. God has already assured us that His kingdom will win in the end, regardless of the form that human governments take. May God bless us in doing good for His glory.

Ray Notgrass
Gainesboro, Tennessee
May 2008
ray@notgrass.com

How to Use This Curriculum

Exploring Government is designed as a one-semester high school course that provides a half-credit in Government. Each unit is intended to be studied for one week. With 75 lessons, the material can be completed in one semester even with field trips, testing days, and other activities.

What the student is to do each day and each week is clearly outlined. The Unit Introduction page gives a brief overview of the unit, the lessons in that unit, and a suggestion for an activity that is relevant to that unit. Most of these activities are writing ideas, but some take a different form. The activities are designed to help the student think about and interact with the ideas that he or she is studying. For the most part it will be best to do the activity toward the end of the unit.

The readings from the accompanying document book, *We Hold These Truths*, are assigned at the end of lessons, except that, when studying the Constitution, the student should read the relevant portion of that document before studying the lesson.

The optional *Quiz and Exam Book* provides review questions over the lessons and readings; a multiple-choice quiz at the end of each unit; and three short-answer exams, each of which covers five units. An answer key to all of these exercises is also included.

You should plan to allow one hour per day to complete a lesson, although using the *Quiz and Exam Book* and doing the activities might add a bit more time to that total.

Exploring Government

Ray Notgrass

Part 1

Backgrounds to
American Government

1 The Biblical Basis of Government

God gave the institution of government to mankind, and He rules over it. The influence of the Ten Commandments and the rest of the Bible on government and law in Western Civilization has been profound. The Scriptures teach us a great deal about what government should do and what kind of people the leaders of government should be. The practices of governments in Biblical times are described often in the Bible.

Lessons in This Unit

1—God Is the Author of Government
2—The Influence of the Law of Moses
3—Biblical Principles of Government
4—The Bible on Leadership
5—Government in the Bible

Activity Idea

What characteristics should a leader in government possess? Some suggested traits are: truthfulness, justice, fairness, honesty, understanding, compassion, self-discipline, knowing how to listen, a desire for peace, a willingness to work hard, a commitment to God's will, a commitment to doing what is right, an ability to encourage others, a knowledge of people, and a love for the poor. You might think of others. Write a two- to three-page essay on what you expect in a leader. You might select the five most important traits to emphasize. Give Biblical examples and cite verses to support your ideas. You might also describe a government leader whom you respect and tell why you do. The person can be historical or contemporary. He or she does not have to be a well-known figure. The person might be a local government official whom you know and admire.

If you are using the optional *Quiz and Exam Book*, answer the questions for each lesson after you have completed the lesson and read any assigned readings in *We Hold These Truths*. After you have completed Lesson 5, take the quiz for Unit 1.

Lesson 1—God Is the Author of Government

Any man who has been placed in the White House can not feel that it is the result of his own exertions or his own merit. Some power outside and beyond him becomes manifest through him. As he contemplates the workings of his office, he comes to realize with an increasing sense of humility that he is but an instrument in the hands of God.
—Calvin Coolidge, **Autobiography**

From community elders sitting in the city gate to the far-flung operations of the United Nations, government has been a part of man's existence from his earliest days to the present time. Government has taken many forms throughout the centuries, including absolute monarchs, participatory town meetings, government by the wealthy elite, and representative republics. Despite its many forms and the various functions that governments seek to carry out, the idea or institution of government has a single, clear beginning. Human government originated with God. It was His idea. It is intended to serve His purposes in the human realm.

Romans 13 contains the most direct and extensive statement in Scripture about the purpose of human government and the Christian's relationship to it. To understand this passage fully, we need to look at the historical context of the times and the literary context of the book of Romans as a whole (Romans 13 is included in the document book that accompanies this text).

Christians in the Roman Empire

At some point following the Day of Pentecost that came a few weeks after the resurrection of Jesus, someone carried the gospel message to Rome, the capital of the Roman Empire. Paul did not do this, since he wrote to Christians in Rome before he went there

The Colosseum in Rome

himself (Romans 1:10). It probably was not Peter either, though that tradition is strong in the minds of many people. The gospel might have been carried to Rome by the "visitors from Rome" who were in Jerusalem on Pentecost (Acts 2:10). These people were probably Jews who became Christians that day and who carried the message of the Messiah back to Rome. This Pentecost event took place around 30 AD.

These converted Jews would have gone back to their homes in the city of Rome. Rome had a Jewish section, where most Jews in the city lived because of Roman prejudice against their living elsewhere and because of the Jews' own desire for self-preservation. No doubt these new believers began telling their Jewish friends about the good news of Christ that they had come to believe. As was always the case in the ancient world, the proclamation of the gospel was met with acceptance by some and violent opposition from others. The Roman historian Suetonius tells us that the government of the emperor Claudius ordered all Jews to leave the city in 49 AD because of disturbances in the Jewish section related to "one called Chrestus." Chrestus was probably a Roman's misunderstanding of the name "Christus" or Christ. The edict of Claudius is mentioned in Acts 18:2 as the reason why Paul met Priscilla and Aquila in Corinth after that couple had been expelled from Rome.

Emperor Claudius

When Claudius died in 54 AD, his decree died with him; so many Jews who had formerly lived in Rome returned to their homes. These would have included Jewish Christians like Aquila and Priscilla. When these Christians returned to Rome after a five-year absence, they found a church that was ethnically Gentile. Gentile Christians and Jewish Christians often did not get along well in the early church, a situation which mirrored the conflict that Jews and Gentiles had in society at large (note how the same issue is addressed in Ephesians 2:11-22).

Paul's purpose in writing to the Christians in Rome around 55 AD was to encourage them to get along with each other (Romans 15:5-13). One issue he addressed in the letter was the Christian's relationship to the government. This was a major issue for the Christians in Rome. It is quite likely that the Jewish Christians in Rome had little respect for the Roman government. These Christians had, after all, given allegiance to the true Ruler of the universe and might not have felt any necessity to obey what a mere pagan emperor said. Besides, it was the Roman government that had carried out the execution of the Lord and that had ordered the Jews to leave Rome. By contrast, Gentile Christians might have had somewhat more loyalty to Rome than Jewish Christians had. Gentiles would not have been as likely to see allegiance to a temporal ruler as competing with loyalty to God. Jewish Christians and Gentile Christians might have used these different perspectives on government as another excuse to be in conflict with each other.

Thus the inspired apostle addressed the question of a Christian's relationship to government in the context of a dramatic issue that Christians in that time and place were actually facing. It is an issue that we continue to face today. Christians still have to deal with governments and government leaders who often do not act out of a desire to do God's will.

Government: God's Agent

Paul says that governmental authority is the creation of God (Romans 13:1). He goes on to say that government "is a minister of God to you for good" (Romans 13:4) and that "rulers are servants of God" (verse 6). This echoes what the Bible says in many places about God's sovereignty over human government. In His working with Israel, God at various times raised up Moses, Joshua, the judges, and eventually King Saul and then the dynasty of David. Isaiah described the pagan Persian emperor Cyrus as God's "anointed"; in other words, Cyrus was the leader whom God raised up to bring about His purposes in the world and especially for Judah (Isaiah 45:1). Daniel 2:21 proclaims that God "removes kings and establishes kings." In her song of rejoicing, Mary said that God "has brought down rulers from their thrones" (Luke 1:52). The pagan Roman governor Pontius Pilate claimed to have life-and-death authority over Jesus, but Jesus told Pilate that he would have no authority at all if it had not been given to him by God (John 19:10-11).

Of course, not every government leader or official always does God's will. Governmental authority is from God, but people in government are human sinners who sometimes abuse the authority that they have. Pontius Pilate, Genghis Khan, Louis XVI of France, Richard Nixon, and Bill Clinton all did wrong things while they served as governmental leaders. Agents of the Internal Revenue Service or of a local school district might do wrong as they carry out their responsibilities. Nevertheless, governmental authority is from God; and God holds sovereignty over all the governments of the world.

In Romans 13, Paul says that two important functions of government are to preserve order and to provide physical security for those living under it. Government carries out these functions by encouraging the doing of good and punishing those who do wrong (Romans 13:3-4). Restraining and punishing evil in society must be carried out by a recognized authority.

French Stained Glass Window

The alternatives are either that evil is not punished or that roving bands emerge and take justice into their own hands. Thus life with government is superior to the alternative, which is life with anarchy.

The Christian's Relationship to Government

Since governmental authority is from God, Paul told the Christians in Rome that God's people are to be in subjection to government (Romans 13:1). Whoever resists government is doing wrong because he or she is resisting God (Romans 13:2). Christians should do what is right, pay their taxes, and give honor to whom honor is due (Romans 13:3, 7). Paul's teaching in this passage is in accord with the overall teaching of Scripture, which is that Christians are to respect and obey the government under which they live. Jesus said that people should pay their taxes to Caesar and should not make doing so a test of faithfulness, as the Jewish leaders and rebellious Jewish zealots had done (Matthew 22:15-22). Peter told his readers to submit to kings and governors (1 Peter 2:13-17). When Paul was before the Jewish ruling council, he apologized for condemning the high priest, even though the high priest had ordered the apostle to be struck on the mouth, because Scripture says not to speak evil of a ruler of one's people (Acts 23:1-5). Paul urged believers to pray for "kings and all who are in authority" (1 Timothy 2:2).

This attitude of submission is commanded of Christians even though it was the Jewish governmental authorities of first century Israel who decided to do away with the innocent Son of God, and even though the Roman government endorsed and carried out His execution. Christians are to submit respectfully to government even though Peter and John were arrested and put in prison by government authorities (Acts 4:1-3). Paul suffered repeatedly at the hands of government officials (Acts 13:50, 14:5-7, 16:22-24, 18:12-17, 23:1-2; 2 Corinthians 11:24-25). Taxes that Christians paid funded governments that were officially pagan and that carried out activities that were often ungodly. Still, the basic teaching of Scripture is for Christians to respect and obey their government.

This is the Christian's responsibility even though our chief loyalty is to Another. Jesus—not Caesar, not the president, not the state, not any political party—is our Lord. A Christian's most important citizenship is in heaven (Philippians 3:20), regardless of the political subdivision in which a Christian resides and regardless of who might be the chief official of one's government. As Jesus put it, "My kingdom is not of this world" (John 18:36). Jesus' primary interest is not material or political but spiritual, the arena of the most important truths and the arena of eternal realities. Christians live in this world as aliens and strangers (1 Peter 2:11). In other words, we live here, but we don't belong here. Christians live

in a constant state of tension, being in the world but trying not to be part of the world. Nevertheless, we have a responsibility to the civil government because our obedience to it says something about who we are in Christ (1 Peter 3:13-16). We are to respect government because it is God's agent for maintaining order and because in doing so we demonstrate an attitude of trust in God regardless of one's physical circumstances.

Christians have no guarantee from God regarding the kind of government under which they will live or that only good people will hold government office. Still, a Christian can be faithful to God regardless of the form of government under which he lives. For the most part, it is easier to be a faithful Christian in the United States with its freedoms than in Communist China with its restrictions and oppressions. However, the threat of government persecution, such as that which exists in China, can produce Christians who are truly committed to following God faithfully, while the freedoms of the United States can result in lukewarm or cultural Christians who do not please God. Whatever the political situation might be, God is in charge. He knows each person's heart, and He also knows how each person is utilizing or abusing the freedoms and opportunities that he has.

Generally speaking, then, if you do what is right, you will have nothing to fear from the government. The exception that the Bible addresses involves a situation in which the governmental authority commands something that is a direct violation of what God commands. In such a situation, as Peter and the other apostles told the Jewish authorities, "We must obey God rather than men" (Acts 5:29). When Christians do not stand firm in the face of ungodliness, we cave in to the world and compromise our faith. Peter and the other apostles stood firm before the Jewish authorities and won a great victory (Acts 5:41). Stephen did not cave in to the governing authorities when he was arrested; and although he paid with his life, his stand for what was true and right won a victory in the Lord's eyes (Acts 7:54-60).

The fact that God raises rulers up and brings them to naught should tell us that when someone comes to power whom we do not support, it is not the end of the world. Christians can still be faithful and the kingdom of God can still be advanced. Moreover, that person will someday not be in power any longer; but Jesus will still be Lord.

As true as this is, Christians must be careful when assuming a stance of defiance against a government. It is not the position to take just because you don't like a particular law or a particular head of state. A Christian's first calling is to be faithful to Christ and to further His cause, and Christians will usually further the cause of Christ more by being obedient to governmental authority than by being disobedient and rebellious against it.

Obedience in a Representative Government

The most direct application of Paul's teachings about government would be in a situation involving a monarchy or an empire, since that was the form of government under which Paul wrote his letter. The Bible does not directly address what a Christian should do if he lives in a democracy or in a country with some form of representative government. In such cases we have to draw inferences from and make applications of the principles of Scripture.

If God is the author of government, then He is the author of republics and democracies just as much as He is the author of monarchies. Americans live under a government that officially guarantees freedom of speech and that is formed by free elections with political campaigns. Christians can respect those in government positions even while speaking and campaigning (respectfully) against them and their policies. Christians are to be zealous for good deeds (Titus 2:14) and are to be a positive influence in society. Jesus calls it being salt and light (Matthew 5:13-16). We can respect government authority even while working to make things better by campaigning for one candidate over others. This respectful but committed and prayerful dedication to what is good can bring about meaningful change in a society.

Government is from God. Christians are commanded in Scripture to be obedient to and respectful of governmental authority as God's agent, although in some circumstances Christians are forced to choose between obeying God and obeying men. The moral and spiritual tension of being in the world but not of the world, of trying to live for God in societies run by men, creates our need to understand the nature of government and to understand a Christian's relationship to and involvement with that government.

[Nebuchadnezzar] was given grass to eat like cattle,
and his body was drenched with the dew of heaven
until he recognized that the Most High God is ruler
over the realm of mankind
and that He sets over it whomever He wishes.
Daniel 5:21b

Reading

All readings assigned at the end of lessons are contained in the book *We Hold These Truths*, which accompanies this volume.

- Romans 13 (*We Hold These Truths* [abbreviated WHTT], p. 6)

- Preamble of the Frame of Government of Pennsylvania by William Penn (*WHTT*, p. 47)

Lesson 2—The Influence of the Law of Moses

Men must be governed by God or they will be ruled by tyrants.

—William Penn

American government, especially its practice of law, rests in large part on the law code given by God through Moses as recorded in the Old Testament. Our society has been strongly influenced by the Bible; and, for the most part, the founders of our system of government believed in God and in the inspiration and authority of the Bible. Of course, the Law of Moses is not the only influence on American law and government. English common law and other sources have also played important roles. Moreover, the Law of Moses does not have any specific guidelines dealing with many aspects of our system of government, such as the holding of elections or the separation of powers among three branches of government. Nevertheless, the Mosaic Law provides significant background for the system of law and government that we have in the United States.

Moses with the Ten Commandments

The Ten Commandments

The Ten Commandments stand at the head of the Law which God gave to Moses for the nation of Israel to observe. In these commandments we see the principles for life as God would have people live it. The following is a discussion of these principles as they are reflected in the Ten Commandments. (Exodus 20:1-17 is included in *We Hold These Truths*. Consult this passage as you read the following paragraphs.)

God is the basis for life. The Bible teaches that God is real, that He created everything, and that all people are accountable to Him for how they live. The existence of God and our dependence on Him are basic assumptions of American government (for further discussion of this topic, see Lesson 14). Any foundation for government and society other than these truths constitutes a faulty foundation because any government built on a lie is ultimately unreliable. Belief in God is essential for the proper working of any society.

Some things are holy. The worth of anything is determined by the Creator, not by popular opinion. The name of God, for instance, is to be treated as holy; that is, special and set apart. In addition, the Israelites were to keep the Sabbath day holy. Exodus 35:1-3 gives further detail on how the Israelites were to observe the Sabbath as a day of rest.

God extended the identity of holiness to people. Humans are a special part of God's creation, being made in His image (Genesis 1:26-27). God called on the people of Israel to

9

be holy because He is holy (Leviticus 11:44, 19:1-4). The New Testament teaches Christians to be holy in their lives because God considers them to be holy (1 Peter 1:15-16, 2:9). This distinctive worth and identity of humans is why taking a human life has always been seen as more serious than taking the life of a dog or a tree. Troubles arise in government and society when those who hold power no longer see persons as being holy in the eyes of God.

The Old Testament Sabbath was the seventh day of the week. At some point after the church began, some believers shifted this concept of a holy day and applied it to the first day of the week, when Christians held their meetings in honor of the resurrection of Christ, which happened on the first day of the week. However, the New Testament does not authorize a Christian Sabbath. In the first century AD, the first day of the week was just another work day in the secular world. Christians could not just decide to take the day off; instead, they often had to assemble early in the morning or in the evening. When Christians became numerous and powerful enough to have an influence on government, laws were frequently enacted that restricted certain activities on Sunday. For instance, for many years in many places liquor could not be sold on Sunday; and certain forms of entertainment could not be presented on the first day of the week. These were often called blue laws, a term first applied to Sunday regulations in 17th-century Connecticut. That colony's Sunday restrictions called for punishments that included whippings, which made the body black and blue. These laws have largely been repealed as our society has become more secular.

Honor family relationships. God told the people of Israel to respect their parents and to honor the marriage relationship. These aspects of the Ten Commandments are supported by other provisions in the Law of Moses (for example, Exodus 21:15, 17 and 22:16). This tells us that God sees the family as extremely important in human relationships and in the life of a nation. American law and government have traditionally supported the family, although recent changes have undermined the family in some ways, such as making a divorce easier to obtain and giving schools the authority for training and educating children. Any weakening of the family, either by accepted practice or by law, will weaken a society and its government.

Truthfulness is essential. Honesty is a crucial element of family and societal living. People must be able to trust one another for their society to operate well. This is especially true regarding testimony given in a legal proceeding (see Deuteronomy 19:16-20). It is also essential that people be able to trust the truthfulness of their government officials.

Life is sacred. God is the giver of life, so it is not within man's rights to take away another person's life in the act of murder. The community of Israel was empowered to put to death those who committed capital crimes, and on occasion the armies of Israel took the lives of its political and spiritual enemies with God's approval. However, these were divinely-ordained situations for the good of the community. Personal hatred resulting in murder violates the sanctity that God gives to human life.

The property of others is to be respected. Not only is it wrong to steal, but it is also wrong to covet (or to desire greatly) what belongs to another. The attitude of coveting leads to stealing. Coveting is the result of not appreciating and being thankful for what God has given to you and instead focusing on and being jealous of what God has given to another. God is the giver of all things, and everything ultimately belongs to Him; but the Law of Moses recognized personal property (note the provision in

Deuteronomy 19:14 against moving boundary stones). The Law provided what steps were to be taken if someone's property were damaged or stolen (see, for instance, Exodus 22:14).

The fact that a neighbor's wife is included in the Tenth Commandment does not mean that she was considered mere property. The ban on coveting a neighbor's wife relates to the sanctity of marriage and the family.

Imagine a situation in which the truths of the Ten Commandments are not honored by the government and where their violation is honored by society: God is rejected and ridiculed; the worth of persons is determined by popular opinion; life is seen as cheap and the result of mere materialistic forces; the family is downplayed and dismissed as unimportant; lies and deception are the rule of the day; property can be taken away by the whim of the government or stolen with impunity by any number of means. The result of such a society would be breakdown and chaos. Can you see how our society's ignoring of the truths of the Ten Commandments has contributed to the problems we have in our country?

*1889 Calligraphic Drawing
of the Ten Commandments*

Other Aspects of the Law of Moses

The Law of Moses called for justice to be applied fairly, regardless of the accused person's wealth or social status (Leviticus 19:15, Deuteronomy 24:17). Bribes were outlawed because they pervert justice (Exodus 23:8). An accused person was considered innocent until proven guilty (Numbers 5:11-28, Deuteronomy 13:12-15). Trials were to be fair (Exodus 22:7-9, Numbers 35:12). The testimony of more than one witness was required for conviction (Numbers 35:30, Deuteronomy 17:6 and 19:15). The judges who enforced the laws and ruled on a person's guilt or innocence had to be above reproach for the system to work (Deuteronomy 16:18-20). The goal of the Israelite court system was justice. Deuteronomy 16:20 begins literally, "Justice, justice, you shall pursue."

The Mosaic Law included other elements that were precedents for our system of justice, such as:

- making a distinction between murder and manslaughter (Exodus 21:12-14);

- the prohibition against kidnapping (Exodus 21:16);

- justice and fairness for workers (Leviticus 19:13);

- and the regulation of business (Leviticus 19:35-36).

One aspect of the Law that was different from our practice involved the method of punishing those who were guilty of crimes. Under the Law, wrongdoers paid fines (Exodus 21:33-34 and 22:1, 4, and 7), were subjected to beatings (Deuteronomy 25:1-3), and in some cases were put to death (Exodus 21:12 and Deuteronomy 24:7). Punishment was to be swift and sure. What the Old Testament Law did not call for were long prison terms. A person who was guilty of manslaughter could flee to a city of refuge and stay there until the death of the high priest, but that is the only example of anything like the long-term incarceration that is practiced today. A main feature of American justice is the handing out of prison terms to those convicted of crimes. Little is done in prisons to train inmates in a better way of living. As a result, the rate of recidivism (repeat offenders) under our system is quite high.

New York City Prison, c. 1904

In addition, the American justice system is encumbered by lengthy delays before trials, the practice of shortening prison sentences handed down by judges and juries, and the inconsistent application of the death penalty. It is widely agreed that the American justice system is not doing a good job of punishing the guilty, rehabilitating those who want to change, or discouraging the spread of crime.

Much of the Law of Moses related to the Old Testament system of priests and sacrifices, which Christ set aside when He made the ultimate and once-for-all sacrifice of Himself on the cross (see Hebrews chapters 8-10). The specific laws and general principles of the Law that we have emphasized in this lesson, however, have served as significant influences on our American legal system because they teach God's perspective on human life and human interaction. We will see in the next lesson more Biblical teachings that form the basis for American life and government.

> *Speak to all the congregation*
> *of the sons of Israel and say to them,*
> *"You shall be holy, for I the Lord your God am holy."*
> *Leviticus 19:2*

Reading

- Exodus 20:1-17 (*WHTT*, p. 3)

Lesson 3—Biblical Principles of Government

Our Constitution was designed only for a moral and religious people. It is wholly inadequate for the government of any other . . . . Free government rests upon public and private morality.

—John Adams

Although the Bible is not a textbook on government, it is the Textbook on life; and human government is part of life. We can learn a great deal in the pages of Scripture about what government and a citizen's attitude toward the government should be.

Personal Government

He who is slow to anger is better than the mighty,
And he who rules his spirit, than he who captures a city. (Proverbs 16:32)

One definition of the verb to govern is "to control, direct, or strongly influence the actions and conduct of" (*Webster's Seventh New Collegiate Dictionary*, 1965, s.v. "govern," p. 361). Before the term came to be used almost exclusively in relation to the sovereign authority of a country or political subdivision, people used the term in several different contexts. A person sometimes spoke of governing his emotions, for example. The King James Version of James 3:4 says that a large ship can be turned "with a very small helm, whithersoever the governor listeth" (the New American Standard translates this phrase, "by a very small rudder wherever the inclination of the pilot desires").

At the Wheel of an Oyster Barge, Alabama, 1911

Using the word in a personal sense, the most important human government is that which takes place within a person's own heart and mind. If a person chooses not to live by self-control and submission to the rule of God, his life will be a failure regardless of the form of political government under which he lives. He will not be a free man under God because he will be a slave to his passions and sins. Jesus asked, "For what is a man profited if he gains the whole world, and loses or forfeits himself?" (Luke 9:25). Ruling the entire world is not worth as much in God's eyes as being under the rule of God.

Because people do not practice good or consistent self-government (that is, the governing of themselves), society needs the institution of government for the common good.

Even so, the external controls of government cannot accomplish what a person should do within himself. For the institutions of government to work, individuals must practice self-government. This means that individuals must first respect God and then themselves. With that attitude, they will respect government, even if they differ with government officials over specific issues and policies (see Exodus 22:28).

The Purpose of Government: To Do Good

According to the Bible, government is to do good. Government leaders have a social responsibility to see that justice is provided for all and especially to those who do not have the money to get their way and to influence others. Isaiah proclaimed to both the rulers and the people of Israel:

> Cease to do evil,
> Learn to do good;
> Seek justice,
> Reprove the ruthless,
> Defend the orphan,
> Plead for the widow. (Isaiah 1:16b-17)

Later, Isaiah said,

> Woe to those who enact evil statutes
> And to those who constantly record unjust decisions,
> So as to deprive the needy of justice
> And rob the poor of My people of their rights. (Isaiah 10:1-2a)

The prophet Amos told the people of Israel, "Hate evil, love good, and establish justice in the gate" (Amos 5:15a). This is probably a reference to the gate as the place where the elders sat and where disputes were settled. Amos went on to say, "Let justice roll down like waters and righteousness like an ever-flowing stream" (Amos 5:24).

These passages teach us that (1) good is defined as something above and other than the whims of those in power, (2) the people of Israel had rights that their government was to protect, and (3) those who held any power in government were to use their positions for good and not for evil.

Israel and Judah fell because of the sin and idolatry that were rampant in their cultures. The kings of Israel and Judah should have followed the Lord and stood against the moral and spiritual failings that were taking place; but instead, with very few exceptions, the kings were the leaders in these failings. This proves again the truth of the idea that as the leaders go, so goes the nation.

A Ruler's Limitations

The concept of the divine right of kings developed in Europe in the late Middle Ages. This doctrine held that the powers of a king were absolute and that his decisions were not to be challenged. Since God had put this person in his position as king, the theory held, no one should question the actions or authority of the monarch.

As we have indicated, the Bible does teach that God raises up leaders. However, the Bible does not teach that a ruler has absolute power or is infallible. On many occasions the

Bible describes the failings of those who ruled. The Scriptures mince no words in describing the failures of Saul, David, Solomon, Ahab, Manasseh, and other kings of Israel.

Proverbs 27:24 says, "For riches are not forever, nor does a crown endure to all generations." The testimony of Scripture endorses this truth. Solomon, the author of most of the book of Proverbs, was the second king of the house of David. This family held the throne only because the first dynasty, that of Saul, ended after one generation. God raised up David to be the new king. After Solomon's death, his son lost control over most of Israel

Throne Room in the Fontainebleau Palace, France

when his harsh policies drove the Northern Kingdom into rebellion. Over a period of about two hundred years, the Northern Kingdom saw much political instability and several different royal families. The ruler of a nation might appear to be invincible, but his life will end one day and he can have no guarantees that his descendants or his hand-picked successors will always rule. The lesson of history is that nations experience many changes of government over the years. Indeed, a crown does not endure to all generations.

Thus Psalm 146:3 warns, "Do not trust in princes, in mortal man, in whom there is no salvation." Rulers are fallible. Bad rulers are not to be trusted, and even good rulers can disappoint people from time to time. Rulers are also mortal and will not always be around. We should not look to rulers for our salvation. For that precious gift we must look only to God.

Throne Room of the Forbidden City, Beijing, China

The Worth of the Individual

One principle which runs through both the Old and New Testaments and which has influenced our law and government is the worth of the individual. God made humans in His image, a fact which gives persons immense worth (see Psalm 139:13-16). Persons are so worthwhile, in fact, that Jesus became one of us and died for us on the cross (John 3:16).

This principle has not been followed in every society and culture. Many times people have been seen as little more than objects to be used by a leader for his power, pleasure, or convenience. Those of the ruling or upper classes have often seen themselves as being worth more than those of the lower or slave classes; and many in the lower classes have agreed with this appraisal. But the true value of the individual as taught in the Bible has influenced American government from the days of the colonies. The rights to life, liberty, and the pursuit of happiness were said to be unalienable, something that could not be denied a

Former Slaves in Washington, D.C., 1916

person because of the innate identity and worth that God bestows on people.

Although this principle has long been voiced in our country, it has sometimes not been applied well. For instance, in the early days of our nation, which held that all men are created equal, only free white males who owned property could vote in elections. The right to vote has had to be extended over time to include all males, then blacks, and then women, as American society recognized and applied more completely the Biblical principle of the value of all individuals. The civil rights movement of the 1950s and 1960s was based on the idea that the innate value of the individual human being regardless of his race should be protected by all levels of government in the United States. Still, even though this principle has not always been consistently applied, it has been a motivating force for good in American society whenever Americans have been willing to lay aside their prejudices and follow God's intention for all people, who are made in His image.

From the Bible we get the principle of individual responsibility in government. Also from the Bible we see that government should be devoted to doing good and not to satisfying the desires of those who hold power. We also learn that rulers are fallible and limited and thus we should not look to human beings as our ultimate authority. The Bible's emphasis on the worth of the individual underlies the principles and practices of American society and government. These important ideas from the Bible provide strength to our American system of government.

Righteousness exalts a nation,
but sin is a disgrace to any people.
Proverbs 14:34

Reading

- "Can We Be Good Without God?" by Chuck Colson (*WHTT*, p. 107)

Lesson 4—The Bible on Leadership

All persons possessing any portion of power ought to be strongly and awfully impressed with an idea that they act in trust, and that they are to account for their conduct in that trust to the one great Master, Author, and Founder of society.

—Edmund Burke

Those who hold positions of leadership carry a great responsibility. In many passages of Scripture, God teaches the importance of leaders being godly people.

The Character of a Leader

After God had brought the children of Israel out of Egypt, but before He had given them the Law from Mount Sinai, Moses' father-in-law suggested a system by which the lesser disputes among the Israelites could be handled by people other than Moses. This

Moses

would relieve Moses of some of the burdens of leadership that he felt. It also would enable him to concentrate on being the people's representative before God, teaching the Law to the people, and focusing on the more difficult cases (Exodus 18:17-27). Moses was to choose judges who were "able men who fear God, men of truth, those who hate dishonest gain" (Exodus 18:21). These characteristics were essential so that the men selected would put God first, judge fairly, and not be influenced by bribes. The men appointed to these positions needed to possess these characteristics so that their decisions would be respected by the people.

In this incident God set the pattern for leadership that honors Him. God's main qualification for a leader is not his intelligence, eloquence, or appearance, but his character. A leader must above all else be trustworthy and must possess a godly character. The specifics of his responsibilities are not as important as his being the kind of person who can handle a position of leadership with justice. If a leader has the right kind of character, he will deal with the situations that confront him in the best way possible. A leader does not know what decisions will be thrust upon him as he fulfills the role of a leader. Many times, for instance, the key issues in a presidential campaign bear little resemblance to the crises that the winner of that election eventually faces in office. This is why the character of a leader is so important.

Relying on God and His Word

In the book of Deuteronomy, Moses taught the people what they needed to remember after he was gone. In the last part of chapter 17, he told them what should happen when in later days the people clamored for a king—which is exactly what they did (see 1 Samuel 8).

Moses said that they should never place a foreigner over them and that the king should not multiply for himself horses, wives, or wealth. This kind of greed would corrupt a leader and turn him away from following God. The king was to write for himself a copy of the Law and was to read from it every day. This exercise would force him to become familiar with the Law, and it would humble him and remind him of his dependence on God (Deuteronomy 17:14-20). Consider how different the history of Israel could have been if her kings had followed these directions and ruled according to God's wisdom instead of their own.

God's message through Samuel after the disobedience of Saul gives us another memorable characteristic of God's leader. Samuel said that the Lord had sought out "a man after His own heart" to be ruler over Israel instead of Saul (1 Samuel 13:14). From that time forward, David has been known as a man after God's own heart. We know that David was far from perfect, but he was devoted to worshiping God and was contrite when confronted with his sins. Because of the influence they hold and the example they set, all leaders need to be persons after God's own heart.

Proverbs About the King

As he compiled his collection of proverbs, Solomon had a special interest in the characteristics that a king should possess and the failings that he should avoid. Since the book of Proverbs is presented as the wisdom that a father is passing on to his son, the wisdom that is included about a king had special significance for the heir to the throne of Israel. The glory of kings, Solomon said, was to search out a matter (Proverbs 25:2). In other words, a king was to seek wisdom and understanding in every situation. Here are some of the proverbs that address those who are in positions of leadership.

King Solomon

"By me [that is, wisdom] kings reign, and rulers decree justice. By me princes rule, and nobles, all who judge rightly" (Proverbs 8:15-16). In keeping with the central theme of wisdom in the book of Proverbs, personified wisdom here says that she is so important that she is the key to how kings rule.

"A divine decision is in the lips of the king; his mouth should not err in judgment" (Proverbs 16:10). A ruler bears a weighty responsibility. Because he is put into his position of leadership by God, he speaks with the authority of God when he hands down a decision. Since this is true, one who is in a position of authority should strive not to speak in error. Millions of people can be affected by the judgment of a ruler, but even an audience of one deserves truth from the king.

"It is an abomination for kings to commit wicked acts, for a throne is established on righteousness" (Proverbs 16:12). A position of governmental authority is a position of trust. God has entrusted that person with responsibility, and many people are dependent on him to do what is right and to set a good example. It is a sad betrayal of that trust when one in authority acts wickedly. The only way for the rule either of one man or of a dynasty to be established firmly is by a commitment to righteousness.

"Excellent speech is not fitting for a fool, much less are lying lips to a prince" (Proverbs 17:7). This proverbs is a comparison by contrast. One would not expect a moral fool to have much good to say. Even more inappropriate are lying lips that belong to a prince. We should expect truthfulness from a prince. It is inappropriate for a prince to be someone whose word cannot be trusted.

"A king who sits on the throne of justice disperses all evil with his eyes. . . . Loyalty and truth preserve the king, and he upholds his throne by righteousness" (Proverbs 20:8, 28). Here are four traits that help a king to have a secure and successful reign: justice, loyalty, truth, and righteousness. The Hebrew word for loyalty is *chesedh*, sometimes translated mercy. It is the closest equivalent in the Old Testament to the idea of agape love in the New Testament.

"Take away the wicked before the king, and his throne will be established in righteousness. . . . If a ruler pays attention to falsehood, all his ministers become wicked" (Proverbs 25:5, 29:12). These verses speak of the power and influence of a king's advisors. If the king makes sure that those with whom he surrounds himself are good people, then his reign will be one of righteousness. At the same time, if a ruler is given to doing what is wrong, he creates a culture of wrong that affects his entire administration. We have seen government leaders whose effectiveness was weakened by the wrong kind of aides, and we have seen leaders who set a tone of evil that negatively affected all those around them.

"A leader who is a great oppressor lacks understanding, but he who hates unjust gain will prolong his days" (Proverbs 28:16). A common failure of those in power is to use that power to crush all who differ with them. This might appear to be the way to insure greater control over a realm, but it is actually a foolish policy that weakens a leader's rule. The ruler who uses his office to help others instead of to line his own pockets will have a more effective and longer-lasting tenure in office.

"It is not for kings, O Lemuel, it is not for kings to drink wine, or for rulers to desire strong drink. For they will drink and forget what is decreed, and pervert the rights of all the afflicted" (Proverbs 31:4-5). A ruler must not have personal weaknesses that will compromise his ability to lead with justice and consistency. An alcoholic in a position of leadership and responsibility, for instance, will be unstable and will leave himself open to being manipulated by others.

A Rebuke to the Shepherds of Israel

Ezekiel 34 offers a stinging rebuke to those described in the passage as the shepherds of Israel; that is, those in positions of leadership (kings, elders, priests, and others) who should have done a better job of teaching and exemplifying God's way. This negative example is another way that the Bible teaches us how leaders should be and what they should do (Ezekiel 34 is included in *We Hold These Truths*).

The shepherds of Israel should have been feeding the flock, but instead they had been feeding themselves (Ezekiel 34:1-2). They had taken the best of everything for themselves and had ignored the needs of those over whom God had placed them (verses 3-4). The shepherds had abused the sheep in their care, and the sheep had been scattered for lack of effective leadership (verses 5-6). As a result, the sheep (that is, the people) of Israel had become victims of attackers (verses 7-8).

The Lord declared Himself to be against the shepherds and said that He would remove them from positions of oversight over His flock (verses 9-10). God Himself would seek out and care for His sheep. He would provide for them, and He would bring the failed shepherds to judgment (verses 11-22). Then the Lord would raise up a descendant of David to be the shepherd of the sheep and would provide security for the sheep (verses 23-31).

Shepherd in Israel, c. 1928

It is not wise to cause God to be against you. Whoever gets into a conflict with God will always lose. The shepherds of Israel had failed the sheep that had been placed in their care, and thus they had failed God. God notices when His innocent sheep suffer, and He will not let the guilty go unpunished. Government leaders today hold positions in which they can do good in the name of the Lord. When they fail to serve the people and instead serve themselves, they betray the people but they also betray God; and God will not let their failures go unpunished. When government fails to act as it should, it is not just a political or policy failure; it is a betrayal of the stewardship that God has placed in the hands of one group of people to serve others, especially those who do not have the power and influence to help themselves.

Leadership in the Church

The teachings on leadership in the New Testament deal mostly with leaders in the church; however, the principles that are taught on this subject can be well applied to governmental leadership, too.

Jesus taught His disciples that the world's model of leadership would not work in the church. In the world, rulers lord it over their people and great men throw their weight around. In the church, by contrast, greatness comes by serving; and those who want to be first must be last of all. This was the model of leadership that Jesus Himself set (Mark 10:41-45). Leaders in government might claim to be the servants of the people, but many times their actions say otherwise. We need elected officials who see themselves first as servants, not as masters.

In two separate passages, Paul gives instructions about the characteristics which elders (or pastors or bishops—the terms all refer to the same position) should possess (1 Timothy 3:1-7 and Titus 1:5-9). The key attribute in both passages is that elders must be blameless or above reproach. This does not mean that they have to be sinless, but it does mean that there must not be an outstanding negative characteristic that is associated with them in the minds of the people. Each list also gives other characteristics that an elder must possess. These traits explain what Paul means by being above reproach: not quick tempered, not given to much wine, not belligerent, not driven by

Nineteenth Century Illustration of Paul Writing a Letter from Prison

greed, and so forth. In addition, each list tells the importance of the leader's family life. He must be devoted to his wife and must have children who are faithful and respectful. As Paul noted, "If a man does not know how to manage his own household, how will he take care of the church of God?" (1 Timothy 3:5). The same question could be asked about a potential leader in government. If he has not governed his own family well, how can we expect him to govern a city or a nation well?

Peter also instructs church elders on how they should lead: not because they feel forced to do so but because they want to; not to see what they can get out of leadership but because they want to serve; and not lording it over the flock but being an example to the flock (1 Peter 5:1-4). The "Do as I say, not as I do" style of leadership does not work in either a family, a

Pharisees

church, or a society. This was one of the many failings of the scribes and Pharisees that Jesus pointed out in Matthew 23 (see verses 1-2). This chapter of Matthew, like Ezekiel 34, is a good lesson on how people in leadership positions are not to be.

Paul instructed Timothy not to let his youthfulness be a hindrance to his effectiveness as an evangelist. Instead, the young man was to set the believers an example "in speech, conduct, love, faith, and purity" (1 Timothy 4:12). How desperately we need leaders who will set a good example in these ways! A leader should be an example; he should not simply make excuses for his behavior.

The characteristics of spiritual leadership are traits which all Christians should seek to possess. However, there is one important distinction to be made with regard to leaders. Every Christian should possess these characteristics, but a leader must possess them.

Everyone has the responsibility to live well for God. Those who fill positions of public trust have the responsibility to serve others in the name of the One who is the Creator of government. Anyone who aspires to a position of leadership should understand the great opportunity and the great responsibility that such a position offers. God expects leaders not to use their positions to serve themselves but to influence others for good.

The king's heart is like channels of water
in the hand of the Lord;
He turns it wherever He wishes.
Proverbs 21:1

Reading

- Ezekiel 34 (*WHTT*, p. 4)

Lesson 5—Government in the Bible

History is in a manner a sacred thing, so far as it contains truth; for where truth is, the supreme Father of it may also be said to be, at least, in as much as concerns truth.
—Miguel de Cervantes, Don Quixote

From Genesis to Revelation, the narrative of the Bible tells us about several examples of government in many different times and places. The first reference to a community is in Genesis 4:17, where Cain is described as building a city. Nothing is said about the form of government the city had, but the earliest examples of government we know from history are city-states, in which a king ruled a city and its immediate environs as a small domain. Genesis 10:5 describes the separation of "nations" by language, a development that occurred after the Lord confused the language of those at the tower of Babel (Genesis 11:1-9); but again nothing is said about the governing of those nations.

Kings, Elders, and Judges

Archaeological evidence indicates that when the Lord called Abram to leave his country and family (Genesis 12:1-3), Chaldea and Egypt had fairly complex governmental systems in place, complete with monarchs and extensive bureaucracies. The Pharaoh or king of Egypt is first mentioned in Genesis 12:15. A short time later, an alliance of local kings made war against another alliance of local kings because of the domination that one of the kings exerted over others (Genesis 14:1-10). Early on, then, local monarchies were the pattern of government in the ancient world.

Mount Sinai

Two elements of government emerged in Israel before God at Mount Sinai declared Himself to be the Leader of Israel. First, the practice of having elders in a community or nation is mentioned in Genesis 50:7, both in the family of Israel and in Egypt. God told Moses to gather the elders of Israel and tell them that He had appeared to Moses (Exodus 3:16). Numerous references to elders occur in the Bible after this point. We should not think of these elders as an elected body of representatives. Instead, they were individuals who were recognized by the people as being men of wisdom and good judgment. Often these men were fairly wealthy. In their role as elders they gave advice, settled disputes that were brought to them, and guided the community when decisions were called for.

Second, Moses' father-in-law Jethro suggested a system of inferior judges to decide lesser disputes so that Moses would not become weary from having to handle every dispute that arose among the Israelites. Apparently the judges themselves determined which cases they thought they could handle and which ones needed to be brought to Moses (Exodus 18:13-27). This can be seen as an early example of inferior courts and a supreme court, although no provision was given for appealing a lower judge's decision to Moses.

Moses and Jethro

God as King of Israel

Ancient nations believed that they were under the oversight and protection of their own national gods. Kings claimed to be the servants (and in some cases the sons) of the gods. God's rule over Israel, however, was exceptional in that He Himself would be Israel's king.

God gave Israel their constitution of government. When God called Israel to Himself to be His people, God initiated the covenant relationship by which He committed Himself to be the God of Israel and by which the people of Israel were to live (Exodus 19:1-6). No committee of Israelites drafted the covenant agreement. The people did have to agree to abide by it (Exodus 19:8), and they could have decided to reject it; but the initiative for it and the content of it were completely from God. Moreover, God gave to Israel all of the laws which the nation was to observe as a result of this covenant. He created the system of justice by which disputes were settled (Deuteronomy 16:18-20, 21:5), and He declared the punishments that were to be administered to those who violated the laws (see, for example, Exodus 21:12-22:15).

God also chose the leaders for Israel. Moses was the first human leader over all of Israel, and he was put into that position by God (Exodus 3:10). When some of the people rebelled against Moses' leadership, God saw their actions as rebellion against Him (Numbers 14, 16). Before Moses died, God appointed Joshua to be the next leader of Israel, the one who would lead the people into the Promised Land (Deuteronomy 31:23).

God guided the nation through its conquest of Canaan (Judges 1:1-2). From time to time, God raised up judges to lead armies that delivered Israel from foreign oppressors (Judges 2:16). One judge, Deborah, is described as being so well-respected that she settled legal disputes between Israelites (Judges 4:4-5). Eventually God raised up Samuel to lead Israel (1 Samuel 13:19-21). God's leadership of Israel is the true example of a theocracy—government by God.

The Israelites Demand a King

When the people demanded that Samuel give them a king, the Lord said that they were actually rejecting Him as king over them (1 Samuel 8:7). The people wanted a predictable government and security from constant attacks by the Philistines and by other foreign enemies. They did not think that God's system of raising up judges just when they were needed was good enough. The people wanted a king—in other words, a dynasty—to rule them so that they would be like the nations around them (1 Samuel 8:5, 20). The real problem was not with the system God had been using. The judges whom God raised up generally followed the Lord, and they usually defeated their enemies. The problem was that the people were not willing to submit themselves to God and to His way of providing leadership.

> *Leaders who claim to rule in the name of God but who actually lead by their own initiative are dangerous to the well-being of the people. Such a ruler sees anyone who differs with him as differing with God, so he acts as if he has no choice but to wipe out any and all opponents as part of his service to God.*

The irony is that, by asking for a king, Israel gave up the stability that God's direct leadership provided. They made themselves prey to all of the instabilities that come with human kings. Samuel warned them what would happen when a king began to rule them. Samuel told the people that the ruler would take their sons to serve as soldiers in his battles. Power and wealth would flow away from the people and to the king. They would eventually cry out to the Lord because of their folly, but the Lord would not answer (1 Samuel 8:10-18). Having a king would indeed bring changes to Israel, but stability was not one of them.

Israel experienced much domestic and international instability because of its rulers. Saul's tempestuous tenure gave way to the house of David, whose military exploits frequently took the sons of Israel to their deaths. David's son, Solomon, created a bureaucracy that involved placing deputies over all of Israel. This system supplanted the traditional tribal divisions (1 Kings 4:7-19). The people were forced to support Solomon's lavish lifestyle (1 Kings 4:22-28). Then Jeroboam rebelled against the rule of Solomon's son, Rehoboam, and set up the separate Northern Kingdom. The Northern Kingdom saw constant idolatry, several royal assassinations, and a succession of dynasties. Even the house of David in the Southern Kingdom was not always faithful to God, and it experienced its share of palace intrigues as well. God allowed Israel to have what it wanted—a king—but He also let them experience all of the problems that came with this form of human government.

Israel from the Captivities to the Roman Invasion

The monarchies of the Northern and Southern Kingdoms (Israel and Judah) were removed from power when those kingdoms were taken captive by Assyria and Babylon in 722 BC and 606-586 BC, respectively. The area that God had given to Israel was ruled as a province by foreign powers for centuries: first Assyria, then Babylon, and then Persia. The story of the Old Testament ends with Persia in control of Palestine.

During the period between the Old and New Testaments, Greece under Alexander the Great conquered Persia and assumed control of Palestine. When Alexander died, his kingdom was divided among four of his generals. Of these, Ptolemy ruled Egypt and Seleucid ruled Babylonia and Syria. Israel became a buffer state between these two dynasties, being ruled first by the Ptolemaic line and then by the Seleucids.

In 168 BC, Jews in Palestine rebelled against the oppressive pagan rule of the Seleucid king Antiochus IV Epiphanes. Thus began the Maccabean Rebellion, led by the priest Mattathias and his sons, the most prominent of whom was Judas, called Maccabeus (the Hammer). Judas and his brothers succeeded in throwing off Seleucid rule. Judas was killed in 161 BC, but

Israel

the family continued to rule the area for about a century. In 143 BC, Judas' brother Simon assumed the position of a king. Simon's son, John Hyrcanus, succeeded him on the throne. The period after John Hyrcanus saw political in-fighting within the family and less effective rule by the dynasty. Seizing the opportunity, the Roman general Pompey invaded Palestine in 63 BC and claimed the land for Rome.

The Sanhedrin and the Government of Israel in the First Century AD

The most prominent governing body in the New Testament's description of first-century Israel was the Sanhedrin or ruling council, made up of seventy members. Also called the Great Sanhedrin, this body met in Jerusalem. Lesser sanhedrins or councils met in other towns. According to Jewish tradition, the Sanhedrin had its origin in the seventy elders whom God told Moses to appoint in Numbers 11:16-17 to assist Moses in his work of leadership. A later tradition held that Ezra reorganized the council following the Jews' return from exile in Babylon.

It is important to remember two facts concerning the nature of the Sanhedrin's work and authority. First, the Jews were not concerned about separation of powers in government. The Sanhedrin filled legislative, judicial, and (to some degree) executive roles for Israel. Second, the Jews would not have understood a separation between religion and government. To them, their religion guided their government and their government was part of their religion.

The Sanhedrin

In the first century, the members of the Sanhedrin came from prominent families. These men roughly corresponded to traditional elders. Another key presence on the council were the high priest (who apparently presided over meetings) and those who had formerly served as high priest. According to the Law of Moses, the high priest was to be a descendant of Aaron; but in Jesus' day the high priesthood was a political appointment made by the Roman government without regard for provisions in the Law. Thus several men could have been former high priests, all wielding political influence at the same time. Annas had been high priest before Jesus began His ministry, and he saw five sons and a son-in-law hold the high priesthood after him (see John 18:13-14 and Acts 4:6). The influence of Annas is demonstrated by the fact that, when Jesus was arrested, He was taken first to appear before Annas, and only then was He taken before the current ruling high priest, Caiaphas. The high priest usually came from a politically powerful family, typically one of the families represented in the Sanhedrin. The Sanhedrin also included several scribes, who were recognized as experts in the Law.

The nature of cases heard by the Sanhedrin indicates their role in Jewish society and religion. They heard the charge of blasphemy against Jesus (Matthew 26:57-66), considered whether Peter and John had taught false doctrine (Acts 4), and conducted an inquiry into Paul's alleged violations of the Law (Acts 22-24). These were major charges that went to the very heart of the identity of Israel and of the Law, which the Sanhedrin claimed to uphold.

Ancient Jewish writings tell of the detailed procedures that the Sanhedrin followed. The men sat in a semicircle. One clerk recorded the votes for acquittal while another recorded those voting for condemnation. In a capital case, arguments for acquittal were always presented first. If a member of the council spoke for acquittal, he could not change his position; but if he spoke for condemnation, he could later reverse his stand. The benefit of the doubt always lay with the accused. Voting began with the youngest member and proceeded to the oldest, to avoid younger members being unduly influenced by their elders.

Actual governmental power in first century Israel was a complicated, multi-layered maze. All local authority was subservient to the power of the Roman Empire. Antipater, who was from Idumea (the area formerly known as Edom), was appointed procurator of Judea by Julius Caesar in 47 BC. Antipater's son, Herod, also was involved in overseeing the region and was given the title "king of the Jews" by the Roman Senate in 40 BC. Thus Herod ruled as a king, but it was always as a petty, local king under the authority of Rome. Herod's will provided for his empire to be divided among three sons, Archelaus (Judea), Herod Antipas (Galilee), and Philip (the territories to the northeast of Galilee). Archelaus

---

In the Biblical record, believers sometimes served in pagan governments. Joseph rose to be second only to Pharaoh in authority in Egypt (Genesis 41:40-44). Later, Moses grew up as the grandson of the Pharaoh and thus was considered part of the royal family (Exodus 2:10). Daniel, Shadrach, Meshach, and Abed-nego were chosen "for serving in the king's court" in Babylon (Daniel 1:4). After the period set aside for their training, they "entered the king's personal service" (Daniel 1:19). Daniel was an important advisor to the Babylonian king. Nehemiah was "the cupbearer to the king" of Persia (Nehemiah 1:11). This was officially a role of personal service, but it was an important one. The cupbearer was charged with the responsibility of making sure that the king's food was not poisoned. Because this was such a position of trust, the cupbearer was often a close adviser to the king. Esther became queen of Persia (Esther 2:17), and in that role she played a vital part in saving the lives of her fellow Jews. Her cousin Mordecai eventually became the king's vizier or prime minister (Esther 10:3).

In the New Testament, Roman centurions are sometimes described as men of faith (see Matthew 8:5-13 and 27:54, and the description of Cornelius in Acts 10). Sergius Paulus, a proconsul on the island of Cyprus, became a believer (Acts 13:4-12). Paul sent greetings to the Christians in Rome from "Erastus, the city treasurer" of Corinth (Romans 16:23). An inscription has been found among the ruins of ancient Corinth which says that one Erastus, the "aedile" (a position which included the responsibilities of city treasurer) laid the pavement of a road at his own expense. We have no way of knowing for sure, but it could be that the Erastus of this inscription was the brother in Christ whom Paul mentioned in the book of Romans.

Ruins of Ancient Corinth

was a terrible ruler, and Rome responded to Jewish protests about him by removing him from office and making Judea a Roman province, overseen directly by a governor. Pontius Pilate was governor of Judea for about ten years (26 to 36 AD). The actions of the Sanhedrin were subject to limitations placed on it by Rome. For example, the Jews could not carry out a death sentence without Rome's approval; thus the execution of Jesus was determined by the Sanhedrin but had to be carried out by the authority of Rome.

The Church and the Government

The early church came into conflict with governmental authorities almost from the start. The apostles' hearings before the Sanhedrin were noted earlier. On Paul's missionary journeys, the apostle was most often opposed by Jews (see, for example, Acts 17:5 and 13) and sometimes by pagans (Acts 19:23-28). Pagan government officials are usually described in Acts as having little interest in or concern about what the Christians were doing (see Acts 17:6-9, 18:12-17, 19:35-41). Officials in Philippi were even deferential to Paul and Silas since they were Roman citizens (Acts 16:35-39).

Paul Speaking to a Crowd

Paul used his Roman citizenship in Philippi and Jerusalem to defend himself from abusive treatment (Acts 16:35-39, 22:25-29). In the United States today, everyone who is born in this country is automatically a citizen; but not everyone born in the Roman Empire was a Roman citizen. Citizenship was a special privilege granted only to certain people under certain conditions and was not common in the provinces governed by Rome. Paul was born a Roman citizen (Acts 22:28), which meant that his father had been a Roman citizen before him. Citizenship was unusual for a provincial Jew, but Paul's father might have purchased his citizenship or he might have received it for meritorious service to the empire. Paul's citizenship did not mean he had the right to vote (the Empire did not have elections), but it did guarantee him due legal process and a fair public trial, exemption from certain forms of punishment (including beatings and crucifixion), and the right to appeal to Caesar to be tried for any charges made against him.

The descriptions of government given in the Bible are accurate reflections of governmental practices of the times. For instance, the Persian empire was divided into satrapies, overseen by satraps (Esther 8:9, Daniel 6:7). In Acts, the officials with whom Paul had contact had a variety of titles depending on their locality, such as chief magistrates in Philippi (Acts 16:35-36), proconsul in Achaia (Acts 18:12), and town clerk in Ephesus (Acts 19:35). Archaeologists have confirmed that Luke accurately recorded the different titles used in the various cities.

The Sanhedrin (especially the Sadducees) bitterly opposed Paul (Acts 23:1-10). Rather than appear before the Council again, Paul used his Roman citizenship before governor Festus to appeal to Caesar to hear his case (Acts 25:6-12). Neither Festus nor King Agrippa (Herod's great-grandson) could understand what Paul had done wrong (Acts 26:30-32).

During Paul's ministry, Roman officials did not actively oppose the spread of the Way. By the end of the first century, the situation had changed. The Christian movement was successful enough and different enough to arouse official suspicion and opposition in Rome and in several other places in the Empire. Nero made Christians the scapegoat for the great fire that destroyed much of the city of Rome in 64 AD, and he began active persecution of the church. According to tradition, Peter and Paul both lost their lives during this persecution under Nero. The emperor Domitian initiated another round of persecution in the 90s AD.

The story of the Bible shows how God guides, works with, and sometimes intervenes against the works of men, including the work of human government. In Old Testament Israel, God established the government He wanted them to follow. They rebelled against His rule and created their own system, but God continued to accomplish His purposes through them. In the life of Jesus and in the story of the early church, we see the way of God standing in opposition to the powers of human government. Although those powers seemed victorious in the short term, God promises that His way will be victorious in the end.

And you will even be brought before governors and kings for My sake,
as a testimony to them and to the Gentiles.
Matthew 10:18

Ruins of Ancient Rome

2 The Idea of Government

This unit focuses on the history of government. We consider what governments have generally done, the pattern of ancient and medieval monarchies, democracy in ancient Athens, the republic of ancient Rome, British backgrounds to our American system, and the influence of Enlightenment thinking.

Lessons in This Unit

Lesson 6—What Government Is and What Government Does
Lesson 7—Ancient and Medieval Monarchies
Lesson 8—Athenian Democracy and the Roman Republic
Lesson 9—British Backgrounds to American Government
Lesson 10—Background of the Enlightenment

Activity Idea

Do all people have the right to be free? In his "City on a Hill" sermon, John Winthrop said, "God almighty in His most holy and wise providence, hath so disposed of the condition of mankind, as in all times some must be rich, some poor, some high and eminent in power and dignity; others mean and in submission." On the other hand, one of the motivations stated by President George W. Bush for the war on terror is what he called the God-given right of every person to enjoy personal and political freedom. Is this freedom a Biblical right or is it drawn from Enlightenment thinking? Is it best for some people to be subservient to others? Are some peoples, or some portions of peoples, always destined to be subjugated to others? Write two pages on this topic.

If you are using the optional *Quiz and Exam Book,* answer the questions for each lesson after you have completed the lesson and read any assigned readings in *We Hold These Truths.* After you have completed Lesson 10, take the quiz for Unit 2.

Lesson 6—What Government Is and What Government Does

That to secure these rights, Governments are instituted among Men, deriving their just powers from the consent of the governed . . . .

—Declaration of Independence

What Government Is

A *state* is an organized body of people living within a defined territory and having the power to make and enforce laws. The United Kingdom is an example of a modern state. Northern Ireland and Wales, on the other hand, even though they have limited powers of local control, are parts of the United Kingdom and are not independent states. In previous times, the Cherokee Indian Nation had some characteristics of a state, but those powers were taken away from them by the United States government. Modern-day Israel is a state. Palestinian Arabs have been pressing to become a sovereign state that is recognized by other nations, but thus far only some steps toward that end have been taken.

U.S. Treasury Department Building

A *government* is the institutions and laws, along with the people who make up the institutions and who enforce the laws, which have authority for direction and control of a state. Government is the agent through which the state exerts its will. Congress, the Department of the Treasury, and the United States law code are aspects of the government of the United States. Within the United States, each of the fifty states has a government.

The critical question in determining the source of governmental power is to determine who has *sovereignty* or supreme authority in a state and thus in that state's government. Sovereignty can reside in one person, such as a dictator or a monarch. In the United States, we believe that the people are sovereign; that is, we believe that the people have the ultimate authority for our government. One way to understand where sovereignty lies is to ask this question: Does the government function by consent of the people, or do the people function by the consent of the government? Even with all of our laws and regulations, ultimately in the United States the people tell the government what to do, not vice versa.

The sovereignty of a state's government can be expressed in one of several *forms of government*.

- A *dictatorship* is a government led by one person whose word is final.

- Sovereignty might be held by an *oligarchy*, which is a small group of people. The Executive Committee of the Communist Party was a small group that held

30

sovereignty in the former Soviet Union. A small group of military officers might have supreme authority in a country if they take control of the government.

- A *monarchy* is a government led by a king or queen who usually holds that position by recognized hereditary rights. A *constitutional monarchy* is a government which has a monarch, but the law or constitution that permits the monarch has sovereignty over the monarch. The United Kingdom is a constitutional monarchy. It has a monarch, but the law gives the real authority of government to Parliament, which permits the institution of the monarchy. Throughout most of history, most governments have been monarchies. Today, however, few countries in the world are governed by a monarch who holds absolute power.

- The most common form of government in the world today is the *republic*. A republic (1) gives sovereignty to those who are able to vote, (2) has a chief of state who is not a monarch (usually a president), and (3) governs through elected representatives. Republics can be divided into *presidential* and *parliamentary* governments. In a presidential republic, voters choose the president directly (or, in the case of the United States, through the electoral college). In this form of government the president is both chief of state and chief executive. He is not part of the elected national assembly and may or may not be of the same party as the majority party in the national assembly. In a parliamentary government, on the other hand, the chief executive is a member of the national assembly or parliament. When a party wins a majority of seats in an election for the assembly, the party leader becomes prime minister and chief executive of the government. Sometimes the prime minister is chosen by a coalition of several different political parties that together form a majority in the parliament. Other members of the majority party in parliament become ministers or heads of the executive departments of government.

- In the strict, classical definition, a *democracy* is a government of all of the people (or at least all of the voters), all of whom take part in passing laws and in performing other aspects of government. The New England town meeting is an example of democracy. The residents of a town gather on a specified date to consider passing, repealing, or amending its laws; and the vote taken at the meeting determines the outcome. The cantons of Switzerland practice a high degree of democracy. Citizens vote in many referendums on whether to enact, amend, or repeal laws. The cantons have elected officials, but they usually do not serve for long periods of time. No country today is a pure democracy. Many countries in the world claim to be democracies when in fact they are republics. The word democracy is generally used today to mean "government by the people" and is usually applied to countries where people vote to elect representatives to their national assembly. The United States is sometimes called a democratic republic. The form of our government is republican, but its representatives are chosen in elections which have a high degree of democracy. All adults eighteen or older who have not lost their right to vote can participate in elections in the United States.

Of course, things are not always what they seem or what is claimed regarding government. Communist China calls itself a "People's Republic," but the people have little say in who serves in their government or what the government does. China has elections,

Three key terms used to describe the operation of government are power, influence, and authority. They are not the same thing and often are not held by the same people. Authority is an official position. Power is the ability to get things done. Influence is an informal role which someone uses to have an impact on what government does. For instance, a newspaper editor, a lobbyist, a special interest group, or an advisor might have influence on government officials, even though none of them hold an official elected position. On the other hand, in many small towns the mayor has a position of authority—that is, he or she has to sign a document for something to happen—but the mayor might not have much power to make things happen. Real, practical power in such a situation might reside with the city council or with the chief of police. It is a fascinating and often revealing study to determine where power, influence, and authority reside in a given government.

but only one candidate is listed for each office. Mexico also has elections, but for many years the candidates of one party almost always won both the presidency and a majority of the national assembly. Until recently, other political parties in Mexico had simply not been able to compete with the power of the main party. Some governments that are called republics have elections rigged by the group in power so that their candidates always win. In some times and places within the United States, political bosses dictated who ran for office, who got elected, and what those elected officials did. Thus, the strict definitions of republic and democracy do not always accurately describe the real-life practices within a given state.

What Government Does

God said that the purpose of government is to encourage and protect good and to penalize and prevent evil (Romans 13:3-4). God's Word defines what good and evil are from God's point of view, but governments declare certain activities to be good and acceptable and forbid certain other activities as unacceptable for the people they govern. An old saying is that "You can't legislate morality." This saying means that government should not try to regulate personal behavior by passing laws. According to this view, government will be frustrated if it tries to outlaw certain activities that people want to do (such as selling alcoholic beverages and participating in gambling).

In fact, however, all legislation is a statement of morality. The passing of a law declares that certain behavior (such as setting up a business, organizing a religious body, or homeschooling) is acceptable and thus good, or that other activities (such as cockfighting, burglary, or embezzlement) are not acceptable and thus bad. Communist governments have traditionally taken the stand that organizing a private business is bad. Some state governments in the U.S. have declared that gambling casinos are acceptable and only need to be regulated. These states see casinos as an acceptable form of entertainment and source of tax revenue. What governments declare to be good or bad does not supplant what Scripture says. The declarations of government merely reveal to what extent the government is in agreement with the Word of God.

The basic functions of government include maintaining domestic order (matters within the state) and conducting foreign relations (relations with other states). A government may do whatever its source of sovereignty says it may do. In the United States, the people have set forth the functions of its national government in the Constitution. The functions of state governments are set forth in the various state constitutions.

In domestic affairs, governments declare what people are free to do and what they are forbidden to do. This gives order to society. Government also influences business activity in many ways: through its monetary policy, regulations on business and labor, the enactment of taxes, and many other policies. Governments pass laws that help or protect certain interests or groups, such as business, the environment, the poor and disabled, workers, and the wealthy.

One domestic function that some governments carry out is religious. In a country with an official state religion, that religion receives tax revenues and clergy from that group perform religious functions at official government events. Having an official religion does not necessarily mean that other religious groups are outlawed—although in some Islamic countries it is illegal to practice Christianity—but other groups usually do not have the same privileges and freedoms that the state religion does. These other groups might have to register with the government and give regular reports on their activities. The establishment of a religion is intended to encourage or promote the state religion, but what has often happened is that the official religion becomes simply a part of the culture with little personal meaning for the people. In the Scandinavian countries, for instance, most people are Lutheran and get married in a Lutheran church because the official state religion in those countries is or was Lutheranism; but only a tiny percentage of the population actually attends services and actively practices their faith.

Solna Church, Sweden

In the area of foreign affairs, the government of a country establishes official relations with the governments of other countries. Two governments might agree to help each other if one of them is attacked by a third country. A government might conclude a trade treaty with another country that sets forth guidelines on how businesses in each of the countries can sell their goods in the other country. A government might decide to impose a tariff or tax on products that are imported from another country, either to raise revenue or to limit competition with domestic industry or to penalize a foreign country for its policies (such as human rights violations or aggression toward another country). A government might encourage cultural exchanges with other countries, such as allowing an exhibit of archaeological artifacts to enter and tour the country. Sometimes relations with other countries become strained and can even result in war.

Limited Government

The United States has a tradition of limited government. This means that the national and state governments are only permitted to carry out a defined, limited list of powers. The powers that were not assigned to the national government by the Constitution were reserved by the Tenth Amendment to the states or to the people. This is our tradition, but since the New Deal of the 1930s and the Great Society programs of the 1960s, an increasing number of powers have been exercised by the national government. Many of these had previously been performed by the states. If such new programs are not struck down by the U.S. Supreme Court as unconstitutional, they become part of what the national (often called Federal) government does, regardless of whether they actually violate the Constitution or not.

The trend in the U.S. has been for people to look to the Federal government for programs, protection, and funding. Even a large part of many state government budgets is actually made up of grants from the Federal government for specific programs (public health care is one example). Many people have tended to look to government, especially to the Federal government, for the funding of various programs in which they have an interest. This trend has increased the size of the Federal government and the involvement of the Federal government in our lives. Sadly, the concept of limited government is becoming a thing of the past. This trend will continue unless a major change in the thinking of the public takes place.

What *Should* Government Do?

The real-life, everyday operation of government is a complex matter. Government is involved in such areas as the economy, immigration, and health care—subjects that we will consider more fully later in this curriculum. But should government be involved in these areas, and if so to what extent? Simple definitions and black-and-white alternatives do not address the realities of the world as it is. For instance:

- What happens when state governments do not protect the rights of their citizens that are guaranteed in the U.S. Constitution to all Americans?

- How do we balance the public need for preserving natural areas with the public need for energy production?

- What is the proper amount of government regulation of business in a free economy?

- Sometimes government tries to protect us from ourselves. Laws that require the use of seat belts and motorcycle helmets, for instance, are intended to force people to be responsible. Such laws help to reduce medical expenses that might be borne by others. Is this a legitimate exercise of government power?

- How can and should the rights of minorities be protected from the sometimes erroneous will of the majority?

- What would be the short-term and long-term effect of scaling back or eliminating certain government programs?

These questions are difficult, but as citizens of the United States we have to address them within the context of the form of government that we have. Doing so will help us have a stronger government and a stronger nation.

For it [the government] is a minister of God to you for good.
But if you do what is evil, be afraid;
for it does not bear the sword for nothing;
for it is a minister of God, an avenger who brings wrath
on the one who practices evil.
Romans 13:4

Lesson 7—Ancient and Medieval Monarchies

L'état c'est moi. (The state, it is I.)
—Attributed to Louis XIV of France, 1651

For most of human history, governments have been headed by kings. This has been true around the world in almost every culture and ethnic group. In this lesson we will look at patterns that have characterized many monarchies in history. We will also pay special attention to the kings and queens of Britain as an illustration of how monarchy has worked, since British traditions most directly influenced our American system. We will see that, although we usually think of kings as absolute rulers who answer to no one, even kings have been subject to the power and influence of others within their realms.

The Origin of Monarchies

Throughout history, individuals or heads of families have assumed rule over other people. This has taken place in a variety of ways. Sometimes a man acquired great wealth and was deferred to by those near him as their leader. In other situations, one individual might have inspired resistance against an invading horde. When the horde was defeated, the victors recognized this individual as their king. At times, a wealthy person has been recognized as a king by buying the services of lesser lords. These lords agreed to fight for the king in exchange for the king guaranteeing the security of the lesser lords' households and property. Sometimes an individual has seized power at the point of a sword or gun and forced allegiance to himself from others. During the Middle Ages, a pattern followed by several Germanic tribes was for their leaders to meet and choose one of their number to be their king.

Mural of Germanic Rulers, Dresden, Germany

Kings faced the same issues that confront any government: the desire for peace and prosperity at home and the need to defend against potential foreign invasion. At home, most kings have been primarily concerned with the well-being of their own family and the lords on whom they were most directly dependent. Rarely has a king taken any action to help the common people in his realm. Kings have usually been defenders of the traditional order which has placed them at the top of the social pyramid.

In foreign relations, kings have formed alliances with and fought wars against other kings. A king's power has often been determined by how much land he controlled. This meant that a king had to lead armies to conquer other lands if he was to achieve greatness as the world defines it. Kings have used many pretexts to go to war. At times a king has justified aggression against other lands by saying it was necessary to acquire additional food supplies, natural resources, or living area for his own people. His people would naturally see themselves as superior to other people, and so they believed that they were justified in taking lands held by others. Perhaps one king perceived an insult from another monarch and felt a need to attack the offending monarch's realm in order to defend his own honor. Aggression against other lands, tribes, or nations has also been justified as being the will of the god in whom the king and his people believed.

Influences on the Monarch

Kings have usually had many influences on their thinking and actions. Most kings have gathered around themselves councils of advisors. These councils were made up of people whom the king considered wise or influential and whom the king trusted to give him advice about the policies he should pursue. The king's hope was that these advisors were honest, just, and loyal. Sometimes, however, the advisors schemed about building their own power or pursued other ulterior motives. Some kings were heavily dependent on their councils, while others ignored the council altogether.

As mentioned above, the success of a king's reign depended on the loyalty of the people under his rule. If the lords and barons trusted the king, they gave him financial assistance and military aid. If they did not trust him, they withheld their support in order to get what

Pope Gregory, c. 540-604

they wanted. This encouraged kings not to rule arrogantly but to seek policies that would be agreeable both to him and to the lords.

A major influence on many kings in Europe during the Middle Ages was the Roman Catholic pope. The pope was primarily interested in making sure that kings supported his own agenda for wealth and power. Since the pope had control of the great wealth that belonged to the Catholic Church, he could supply financial assistance to kings who earned his approval. If a king wanted to go to war, the pope could influence other kings to provide soldiers. Most importantly, the pope was seen as Christ's representative on earth. When all else failed, the pope could use the threat of excommunication against a king who did not do what the pope wanted. If the pope thus denied a king the right to participate in communion, the king believed that he was cut off from God's grace and therefore risked the disapproval of his subjects.

Threats to a King's Power

Even an absolute monarch sometimes had to deal with challenges to his authority. Bad kings almost always engendered opposition; and even a good king could have opponents who were jealous, or evil, or who thought they could do a better job. Rivals for the throne might emerge from within the royal family itself or from another family. The lords of the realm working together could exert the greatest counterbalance to a king's power. When the influence of wealthy lords became organized, it eventually took the form of representative bodies like the British Parliament.

A king always had to guard against attacks by traitorous advisors within his circle or pretenders to the throne from without. If a dynasty gave rise to an incompetent ruler, strong lords would often want to wrest the monarchy out of his hands. A king's heir was usually his oldest son. However, if a king did not have an heir, competition could erupt among the lords over who would be the next king and the leader of a new dynasty.

Thus we see that the government of an absolute monarch could be subject to a great deal of political pressure and uncertainty. Often the king's power did not go unquestioned. Even an absolute monarch faced on-going challenges that kept things interesting for him and his adherents.

The English Experience

We can see many of the dynamics we have just described in the history of England. If we changed the names and dates, similar stories could be told about kings in many parts of the world.

Julius Caesar led a Roman army in an invasion of England a few decades before Christ and declared the island and its Celtic people to be subject to Rome. Centuries later, when Roman power had weakened considerably, Anglo-Saxon invaders from Europe gained control of England and pushed the Celtic people living there into what is now Wales, Scotland, and Ireland. The Anglo-Saxons organized themselves into seven kingdoms, including Wessex (West Saxons), Sussex (South Saxons), and Kent (southeastern England). The leaders of these kingdoms often became rivals of each other. In 829 AD, however, Egbert of Wessex was recognized by rulers of the other Saxon regions as king of all Anglo-land (England).

The Saxons, in turn, had to defend their land from Danish and Viking invaders. These Scandinavians from the North (Norsemen) also invaded Europe. Some of them settled in what is now northern France, and the region became known as Normandy (North-men-land). In 1066 AD, William of Normandy asserted his claim to the throne of England by invading the island and defeating the Saxon King Harold at the Battle of Hastings. The Normans imposed their form of government on England, but much of the Saxon language and culture remained.

When the Norman King Henry I of England died in 1135, Stephen of France tried to usurp the English throne from Henry's daughter, Matilda. Rival factions that supported Stephen and Matilda fought a civil war in England until 1153, when Matilda's son, Henry II, gained the backing of enough barons to be recognized as king. When Stephen died the next year, the rule of Henry II was secure. This began the dynasty of the Plantagenet family. A later Plantagenet king, John, was an arrogant ruler and poor military leader. In 1215, the English barons forced John to sign the Great Charter (Magna Carta)

Magna Carta

that guaranteed certain rights to the barons. True to form, John broke his word the following year; but he died shortly thereafter.

While John's son, Henry III, was on the throne, his sister married a French emigre, Simon de Montfort. Simon proved to be an ambitious and unfaithful brother-in-law when he led the barons against Henry's rule. Henry agreed to some limits on royal power in a document called the Provisions of Oxford, but he repudiated those limitations a few years later. When this happened, de Montfort in 1265 called for a Council to be formed of spokesmen from English towns and shires

> *No complete record of the Provisions of Oxford exists, but apparently they called for regular meetings of an elected council of nobles as well as the election of local officials.*

(two burgesses from each borough and four knights from each shire or county) that would meet alongside the barons. This meeting came to be called a parliament (from the French word *parle*, meaning to talk). It was the first step toward the modern British Parliament. Notice that its purpose was to oppose the king.

> *The Magna Carta and the Provisions of Oxford were attempts to establish what came to be called the rule of law. If the actions of government depended only on the whims of the king, and if the strength of the government depended on the personality and skills of the king or on the unity of the barons, the country would be subject to continuous instability. However, if laws could be established that stated what kings, barons, and all the people could and could not do, this would put the government on a more stable footing, regardless of who the kings and barons were. It would give all of the people standards outside of themselves to live up to. A government of laws and not of men is a principle that continues to be followed in America today.*

In 1295 King Edward I called for a parliament of barons, officials of the Roman Catholic Church, and town and shire representatives. This move was an attempt to consolidate his power and unify his realm. This meeting has become known as the Model Parliament

King Richard III

because it set the pattern for an assembly with two groups—lords and commons—that came together to meet with, advise, and sometimes oppose the king. The membership and meetings of Parliament became more regularized as time went on.

The political relationship between a king and Parliament was sometimes adversarial and sometimes conciliatory. The kings wanted revenue to support their lifestyle and to carry on foreign wars. The nobles would only agree to pay these taxes if they were given a voice in government. Thus each side gave a little to the other side in order to get more of what it wanted.

Two families within the Plantagenet house, the Lancasters and the Yorks, became rivals for the throne. The Lancasters won out for a time, but later the Yorks gained control and ruled the country. The last York king, Richard III, was defeated in battle by Henry Tudor, who had challenged Richard's rule. It was this Henry who began the Tudor dynasty, which included Henry VIII, his son Edward VI, his Catholic daughter Mary, and his Protestant daughter Elizabeth I.

Elizabeth I never married and had no heir. Her Catholic cousin, Mary Queen of Scots (not the same person as Henry's daughter Mary), was in line after Elizabeth to inherit the throne of the country, even though England had become officially Protestant under Henry VIII.

> *Before the Norman invasion, the Anglo-Saxon king in each region met with a council of nobles and church leaders that was called a witenagemot. Few records exist of these councils' duties and powers, although they probably met at least in part to give their endorsement to a new king. There is not a direct line from these Anglo-Saxon councils to later Parliaments, but they are another example of how kings had councils of nobles with which they had to deal.*

Queen Elizabeth I

To prevent Mary from being able to assume the throne, Elizabeth had her imprisoned; and she was later executed. When Elizabeth died, the English throne fell to the Protestant son of Mary Queen of Scots, James, who had already been ruling as king of Scotland. This was James I, who came to the English throne in 1603 as the first Stuart king. During James' reign the British planted their first successful colonies in North America. We will pick up the story at this point in Lesson 9.

> *He who loves purity of heart*
> *and whose speech is gracious,*
> *the king is his friend.*
> *Proverbs 22:11*

Reading

- Magna Carta (excerpt) (*WHTT*, p. 37)

- "On the Divine Right of Kings" (excerpt) by James I of England (*WHTT*, p. 41)

Lesson 8—Athenian Democracy and the Roman Republic

The condition upon which God hath given liberty to man is eternal vigilance.
—John Philpot Curran (1790)

Before we proceed with the story of developments that led to the formation of governments by British colonists in North America, we consider in this lesson two atypical forms of government in the ancient world: democracy in Athens and the republic of Rome. Each of these forms of government lasted for many years, and the basic structure of each form of government was fairly constant, but changes took place in each government over the course of time. As a result, some details in accounts you read about them might vary, depending on what period is being described.

The Athenian and Roman governments are sometimes portrayed as the ideal of what democracy and representative government should be, but we will note their failings as well as their strengths. Both governments help us to know what our government today can and should be.

Democracy in Athens

The people who lived on the rugged Greek peninsula in ancient times divided themselves into several city-states. One of these was Athens and its environs. A coalition of Athenians and other Greeks defeated the invading Persian army in 490 BC at Marathon.

Ruins of Athens

The victory gave the people of Athens a great pride in themselves and their abilities. It was around this time that the city developed the form of government called democracy (from the Greek words *demos* meaning people and *kratein* meaning to rule or judge).

The main feature of Athenian democracy was the Assembly, which met every seven to ten days. All free male citizens of Athens could participate. This meant that out of a population estimated to be about 300,000, some 45,000 men were eligible to take part. Usually around 5,000 men actually came to any given meeting of the Assembly. Participants in the Assembly discussed proposals that were put forward by the Council of 500. This encouraged the development of speaking skills, since a persuasive argument could win over a large number of people (it also required strong lungs!). Voting took place by a show of hands or other straightforward means, and a simple majority was required to put a proposal into effect.

The Council of 500 was composed of fifty men from each of the ten districts into which Athens and its surrounding area were divided. A candidate for the Council had to be at least thirty years old. From the candidates put forward in each district, fifty were chosen by lot to serve for one year. No one could serve two years in a row, and a person could serve only twice in his lifetime. The Council prepared an agenda for each meeting of the Assembly. The Council members from each district formed a subcommittee that was responsible for chairing the Assembly for a tenth of the year. Some members of the subcommittee had to be in the Council chambers at all times in case of an emergency.

City officials were chosen by lot for a term of one year. The Board of Ten Generals was also chosen by lot at first, but later the group was elected. This Board became the real authority in Athenian government. Pericles, who served for many years in the mid-400s BC, became the most important figure in Athenian life and politics as a member of the Board. He led in the development of extensive public works that increased the citizens' pride in their city. Pericles saw to it that those on the Council of 500 received pay, which enabled Athenians from all walks to life to serve.

Pericles Addressing a Crowd

The democratic spirit extended into other areas of Athenian life. For instance, trials were conducted before juries of from two hundred to as many as five hundred men. The parties in a trial spoke for themselves and were not represented by attorneys.

In general, individual rights in Athens were made subservient to the public good. For instance, the name of the person who proposed a law was attached to that proposal. If at a later time a court determined that the law violated Athenian principles, the proponent had to pay a huge fine which could bankrupt him. This was intended to prevent frivolous laws that might be enacted by proponents who made base appeals to the crowd. If a citizen were required to participate in the Assembly for whatever reason (such as it being his district's turn to chair a meeting) and he did not attend, a slave was dispatched to find that person and smear his clothes with red paint (from which we get the idea of smearing someone's reputation—the original smear tactic!). This showed everyone who had failed to do his civic duty. Another tradition that exalted the public will over the rights and freedom of the individual was called ostracism. On a given day, people were allowed to write the name of the person they disliked most on a piece of pottery (*ostraca*). If a person were named on a majority of these ballots, he was exiled from the city for ten years. Sometimes good men got on the wrong side of the majority and were ostracized. This practice tended to enforce conformity to the perceived public will.

The Greek word idiotes *was used for someone who kept to himself and did not participate in civil and political life. It is the origin of our word idiot.*

Athens was devastated by a plague in 430 BC, and then it lost the 27-year Peloponnesian War to its bitter rival Sparta in 404 BC. The city's power was greatly weakened by these blows. Its democratic government continued for a while and even spread to other cities, but democracy was eventually replaced by the rule of a single leader over all of Greece. This centralized form of government began in Greece with Philip of Macedon in 337 BC, who united most of Greece under his authority. Philip's son was Alexander the Great.

Democracy worked as well as it did in Athens for several reasons.

- The Athenian people believed that they possessed greater ability and worth than people of other city-states. This gave them pride in their city and their attainments, which was a strong motive for participation in government.

- Most Athenians made sure that they stayed informed on issues that would come before the Assembly.

- The practice of selection by lot was an attempt to keep power from being held by the same few people or small group for a long period of time.

- The Athenian ideal called the golden mean helped their practice of democracy. The golden mean was the belief that what accomplished the greatest common good, not what defined personal interest, was what people should pursue. By contrast, what we call democracy today is characterized by the competition of various interest groups, all of which want what is best for themselves, regardless of how their priorities might affect the entire community.

However, Athenian democracy had its limitations and failings.

- Women and slaves, who made up a large part of the population, were not allowed to participate.

- Citizenship was strictly limited. Under a law passed in the time of Pericles, a citizen was defined as someone whose parents were both citizens. Having one parent as a citizen was not good enough (even though special dispensation was extended at times to such people, including Pericles' own son).

- The high opinion Athenians held of themselves was used to justify imperialistic domination of other peoples. Athenians, they thought, deserved freedom and democracy; but others did not. This philosophy will not maintain a free society based on equality.

- The Athenians gave special deference to those with wealth and influence. The merit of ideas was not judged impartially. Pericles could appeal to the crowd effectively because of his wealth and his policies of lavish government spending.

- The will of the majority could go unchecked, regardless of whether that will was actually good. One strength of modern democracies is the protection of the rights of the minority.

- Pericles did not train successors to carry on after his death; so the skills of leadership were lacking in the long term.

- Finally, Athenian life was pagan, blatantly immoral, and dependent on slave labor. These wrongs negatively affected the good of the Athenian democratic system.

The Roman Republic

Tribes from central Europe probably invaded the Italian peninsula centuries before Christ. Around 750 BC, some of these people founded the city-state of Rome in the region called Latium. They came to be called the Latins. Another group of invaders, the Etruscans, took control of the area around 600 BC. About a century later, the Latins who lived on the seven hills along the Tiber River threw off Etruscan rule and became the most powerful people of the area. In reaction to the authoritarian Etruscans kings, the Latins (or Romans) established a form of government they called the republic (from the Latin words *res* and *publia* meaning the affairs of the people). The Roman Republic lasted for almost five hundred years.

The wealthy landowners in Rome and its environs were called patricians. The ruling body of the Republic was the Senate, composed of about three hundred representatives of patrician families. These senators were chosen for life. Every year, the Senate chose two consuls, who served as military leaders and chief executives of the state. The consuls had equal powers, and each had a veto (Latin for "I forbid") over the actions of the other. After his year of service, a consul became a member of the Senate, which usually meant that consuls tried to go along with the Senate on most matters.

Roman Senators

In a time of national crisis, the Senate could name a dictator for up to six months. Other high officials of government included quaestors (financial officers) and praetors (judges who later came to fill military roles). The office of censor was created to classify citizens by wealth and tax status, a job previously carried out by the consuls. The censor eventually acquired great power, including the authority to dismiss members from the Senate. All of these positions were filled by patricians.

The other main social class was called the plebeians. Plebeians were farmers, artisans, small merchants, traders, and other working people. Plebeians were citizens, but they could not be elected to the Senate or chosen to serve as a consul. Roman law forbade a plebeian from marrying a patrician. Plebeians elected representatives who served in a body called the Assembly, but the Assembly had little real power. No action by the Assembly could take effect without the approval of the Senate. Slaves were numerous in Rome, but they had no legal standing or rights.

Rome was involved in almost constant warfare during the Republic. An Assembly of Centuries was formed to represent the army. This body began to elect the consuls. The army was all-patrician at first, but the need for fighting men led to plebeians being called into service. The patricians tried to hold on to their power; but because the patricians needed the plebeians to fight their wars, raise their food, and carry on their profitable trade, the patricians gave in to the plebeians' demand for a greater share in government.

The plebeian Assembly came to be called the Assembly of Tribes. This body chose ten tribunes each year to be the spokesmen for the plebeian class. The power of the plebeians grew over time. In 451 BC, the Assembly of Tribes brought about the formulation and publication of the Twelve Tables of Roman Law. Power still lay with the patricians; but the Tables of Law helped insure that the law would be applied fairly, even to the plebeians. Tribunes eventually received the veto power; and the Assembly of Tribes obtained the right to pass laws without Senate approval. In 367 BC, a plebeian was elected consul. Eventually, plebeians were allowed to marry patricians; and some plebeians were elected to the Senate.

Senators and wealthy families became more preoccupied with protecting their power and wealth than with doing what was best for the Republic as a whole. Serious conflicts arose in Rome in the two centuries before Christ between warring factions and powerful leaders. Political assassination became commonplace. A series of conflicts between ambitious generals resulted in one general, Sulla, gaining the upper hand. In 82 BC, Sulla was declared dictator and immediately abolished the six-month limit on his office. After Sulla, generals continued to compete for control of Rome until Julius Caesar defied an order by the Senate to disband his army and defeated a force led by his competitor, Pompey. In 44 BC, the Senate appointed Caesar dictator for life. A group of senators who feared and opposed Caesar's power assassinated him on March 15, 44 BC. Following a period of civil war, the forces led by Caesar's adopted son Octavian won out. In 27 BC the Senate, its members weary of conflict and turmoil, declared Octavian to be Augustus ("Exalted One") and hoped that his rule would establish calm. The age of the Republic was over, and the age of the Roman Empire began.

The Roman Senate was not created to insure popular control of government. Instead, its purpose was to protect the interests of the wealthy and to make sure that the patrician class maintained control of government. The self-interest of senators only became more intense over the years. The government and the civil life of the Roman Republic was based on class distinctions, which is ruinous to a society. Roman government had no plan for handling changes in society or for smooth continuity of leadership (the latter was a failing of the Empire also). It also placed no effective limit on the power that one person could obtain. Like Athenian democracy, the Roman Republic fell when challenged by the authoritarian influence of a single leader.

No plan of government can guarantee that a society will have peace and prosperity. Athenian democracy and the Roman Republic had some good aspects that remind us that our form of government can accomplish good. They were not perfect governments, however; and they did not stop the doing of evil that eventually destroyed their own foundations of government. We must have discernment to recognize and support what is good and to avoid what is evil both in governments and in the hearts of men.

When the righteous increase, the people rejoice,
but when a wicked man rules, people groan.
Proverbs 29:2

Reading

- Twelve Tables of Roman Law (excerpt) (*WHTT*, p. 36)

Lesson 9—British Backgrounds to American Government

I conclude then this point touching the power of kings, with this axiom of divinity, that as to dispute what God may do, is blasphemy . . . so is it sedition in subjects, to dispute what a king may do in the height of his power. But just kings will ever be willing to declare what they will do, if they will not incur the curse of God. I will not be content that my power be disputed upon; but I shall ever be willing to make the reason appear of all my doings, and rule my actions according to my laws.

—King James I of England

Developments in English government during the 1600s had a major impact on government in America. During this century, Englishmen began several colonies in North America. The American government that was created in the eighteenth century was to a great degree a reaction to what occurred in England in the seventeenth century.

King James I

The Setting in 1603

When James I became king of England in 1603, explorers and merchants were beginning to develop the country's overseas empire with the official endorsement and assistance of government. The king's wealth grew as trade and tax revenue increased. As trade grew, the merchant or middle class grew. This changed the traditional social structure that had only known royalty, nobility, and commoners. The middle class wanted a greater voice in government, especially since taxes on their profits contributed an increasing share of the royal budget.

It has been estimated that in the 1630s England only had about 2,000 paid public officials, and about half of these were aides and personal servants of the royal family. Most of the government functions that affected most of the people were carried out at the county or shire level. The county bureaucracy oversaw such activities as collecting taxes, conducting trials, and training the local militia (England had no standing army). Many in the county bureaucracy were unpaid volunteers. In general, the county governments and the common people operated in their little world; and the king operated in his. The main overlap involved the taxes that were collected to support the king's lifestyle and foreign wars.

England was officially Protestant, specifically Anglican (Church of England, begun during the reign of Henry VIII in 1534). The Church of England had broken away from the

Roman Catholic Church, but government and church officials did not want people to break away from the Anglican Church.

The March of the Monarchs

James I ruled by what he called the divine right of kings. He believed that God had given him his throne and his power and that it was not only wrong but blasphemous to question a king's actions and authority. Nevertheless, James felt constrained to respect and obey the laws of the realm. In addition, James had to deal with Parliament to obtain the revenues he wanted, and the members of Parliament were not always willing to accept James' ideas as divinely directed. However, Parliament was subject to the king's call and dismissal, so their separate powers served as a check on each other.

James' son and successor, Charles I, kept an even tighter rein on his power than his father had. Since Charles did not want to deal with Parliament, he simply did not call it into session. This angered the lords who believed that they were a rightful part of government. The lords did not want to bow to the king's arbitrary decisions. The political standoff between crown and Parliament was made worse by religious differences. Charles I was a high Anglican bordering on Catholicism, and he looked to Catholic monarchs in Ireland and Spain for support for his power and actions. Most members of Parliament, however, were Puritans: Anglicans who opposed both Catholic and high Anglican practices. In 1642, civil war erupted between supporters of the king and those who favored Parliament. Both the king and Parliament levied taxes on their supporters to finance the war.

The Puritan Parliamentarians won. Charles I was captured, tried, convicted of crimes against the state, and in 1649 was executed with the approval of the Lord Protector of the Puritan English Commonwealth, Oliver Cromwell. Cromwell, who believed that he was on a

Oliver Cromwell

mission from God, abolished the monarchy (so much for the divine right of kings), the House of Lords, and the traditional form of the Church of England. His government also abused civil liberties and denied religious freedom. The Puritan expression of the Christian faith became the state religion.

When the English people had had enough of Cromwell and his son (a much less able ruler), a newly elected Parliament re-opened the doors of traditional Anglican churches and called Charles II (son of the executed king) home from Europe in 1660 to assume the throne. Charles II agreed to grant more religious freedoms, and he worked more harmoniously with Parliament than his father had done. However, Charles II leaned toward Catholicism, a fact which concerned the Anglican majority in Parliament. While he had been in exile in Europe, Charles II had made secret agreements with Catholic monarchs in which they promised him financial support to regain the throne and he promised to restore the Catholic Church as the state religion of England and to become Catholic himself. In 1685 on his deathbed, Charles II was received into the Roman Catholic Church. Charles' successor, his brother James II, was even more openly sympathetic to Catholicism. When James' Catholic wife gave birth to a son and heir to the throne who was given infant baptism as a Catholic, Anglican political leaders were convinced that they had to act.

The leaders of Parliament approached William of Orange in the Netherlands and asked him and his wife, Mary (Protestant sister of Charles II), to become king and queen of England. William led a small force into England in 1688, whereupon James II fled to Catholic France. The next year, Parliament drew up documents detailing James' wrongs and declaring William and Mary to be the legitimate monarchs of England. James II went to Catholic Ireland to gather supporters in an attempt to regain the throne, but William's army defeated James' force at the Battle of the Boyne in 1690. Parliament passed a law stating that the monarch of England had to be Anglican, thus insuring that the crown would safely remain in Anglican hands. In addition, the powers of Parliament, even with the continued presence of a monarchy, were greatly increased. Now the Parliament did not sit at the king's pleasure, but instead the king reigned at Parliament's pleasure.

With the death of Queen Anne without an heir in 1714, the throne reverted to George I of Hanover in Germany, a great-grandson of James I. The new ruler was able enough, but he spoke no English and knew little about Britain. Nevertheless, George I and his successors worked hard to adapt to Britain; and they oversaw an aggressive expansion of its empire. In Parliament, supporters of the king came to be called Tories and opponents were known as Whigs; but not even the king's harshest critics proposed doing away with the monarchy. The crown and Parliament began to govern together instead of against each other. In 1721, Member of Parliament Robert Walpole began to oversee the operation of the king's government and served in effect as the first Prime Minister.

In less than fifty years (1642-1689), England witnessed major political upheavals that included a civil war; the execution of a king; the abolition, restoration, and replacement of the monarchy; and a major shift in power from the king to Parliament. During this time, colonies were being established in America. Colonists and the colonial governments had to be careful about expressing loyalty to the English government, since the government to which they expressed allegiance might be gone in less time than it took to get a message across the Atlantic. Over this period, Americans saw the instability of royalty, the harmful role that religion played in political conflicts, and how everyday people were caught in the middle of factional disputes; and they wanted none of it in their new land. This history helped to shape the ideals of government that Americans pursued.

For many years the British crown did not pay much attention to colonial government, but in the mid-1700s the crown moved to exert more control over its American colonies. This move prompted a reaction among many colonists in America who chafed under British rule and who wanted to control their own destiny.

As the heavens for height and the earth for depth,
so the heart of kings is unsearchable.
Proverbs 25:3

Reading

- English Bill of Rights (excerpt) (*WHTT*, p. 42)

Lesson 10—Background of the Enlightenment

It is not without reason, that [man] seeks out, and is willing to join in society with others, who are already united, or have a mind to unite, for the mutual preservation of their lives, liberties and estates, which I call by the general name, property.

—John Locke

While American colonists reacted to the upheavals in the English government, the ideas that provided the positive foundation for American government were being formed as a product of the philosophical movement known as the Enlightenment. It is helpful to have some understanding of what the Enlightenment was and how it helped to mold the thinking of the men who shaped our American system.

Enlightenment Thinking

The Enlightenment was a movement that exalted human reason as the best basis for understanding life and the world, in reaction to the common reliance on faith and tradition. The period of the Enlightenment is generally seen as beginning with the publication of Isaac Newton's *Mathematical Principles* in 1687 and ending with the French Revolution in 1789. This Age of Reason was an extension of the Renaissance and the Scientific Revolution, both of which immediately preceded it. The term Enlightenment suggests that its adherents saw themselves as being enlightened on what is true, in contrast to previous generations that (in the Enlightenment view) were not enlightened.

In the Middle Ages, most intellectuals, political leaders, and everyday people accepted many long-held ideas as truth. The earth was seen as the center of the universe. The scientific understanding of the ancient Greek philosopher Aristotle was accepted as final truth. In religion, the pope was accepted by most Europeans as the head of the church. In government, kings were seen as the proper rulers of nations.

Some thinkers, however, began to question these long-unquestioned assumptions by appealing to reason and to scientific investigation. Copernicus and Galileo put forth the revolutionary idea, based on their calculations and observations, that the earth revolved around the sun. Scientific investigation began raising questions about Aristotelian ideas on the nature of the world. Martin Luther challenged the authority and practices of the pope. In the area of government, writers started questioning whether kings really had a divine and unquestioned right to rule. It was not in keeping with reason, they said, that one man and his descendants should automatically be the best people to rule a country. Plenty of evidence emerged in seventeenth-century England to show that royal families did not always produce good leaders.

Like most schools of philosophy, the Enlightenment had both good and bad points. It is good not to accept blindly what has long been thought to be the truth. Traditions are not always right. It does not honor God simply to accept religious teachings and traditions without consulting Scripture and knowing His truth for oneself. Many Enlightenment thinkers saw this greater use of man's reason as a way to honor God and to have a firmer grasp on the wonders of His creation.

On the other hand, the man-centered thinking of the Enlightenment sometimes caused people to push God out of the picture altogether. It was not rational, said some, to think that an unseen God controlled the universe and guided our lives. Erroneous Catholic traditions and the history of religious wars were used as evidence for the position that religious faith was a shaky foundation on which to build a life or a society. Better to trust in the solid findings of science, they said, that in the religious opinions of fallible men.

What secular Enlightenment thinkers failed to see was that scientific understanding was subject to error and change also. A better foundation than either religious tradition or scientific tradition is the unchanging and unshakable Word of God. Human reason is good, but it is not ultimate. The mind of God is ultimate, and it is to His understanding of truth that all mankind must ultimately bow.

Locke's *Two Treatises of Government*

Many Enlightenment writers, including the English philosopher John Locke, put forth their ideas about government and society. In 1690, Locke published *Two Treatises of Government*. Appearing when it did, Locke's work was an attempt to explain and justify what was called the Glorious or Bloodless Revolution that brought William and Mary to the throne of England. Locke's work became an important basis for later political thinking and for the events that took place in the American colonies in the mid-1700s.

Locke tried to dig back to the very foundations of human society. He said that man in his natural state is sovereign and good. Men decide to associate with each other in what he called a social contract to preserve their God-given rights, freedoms, and possessions (what he called life, liberty, and property). This association is necessary and logical because some people emerge from time to time who threaten those gifts. When people live and associate in this pursuit of individual happiness, it leads to the common good. Thus a limited government, with checks and balances on its powers, produces the most freedom and the greatest fulfillment of our rights. When a government threatens these rights and these goals, Locke wrote, it is reasonable and necessary for people to change their government, as the English did when Parliament invited William and Mary to be their monarchs.

John Locke

This philosophy of government was based on important assumptions that were different from the ideas that had long been held by many people. First, Locke believed that liberty and rights were gifts from God, not from the king. Second, he held that the people are sovereign. The state only functions with the consent and approval of the people; the people do not function with the state's approval. Third, he believed that government exists for the protection of the people and their property, whereas the traditional view held that the purpose of the people and the government was to protect the life, liberty, and property of the king. To Locke this approach was more rational and enlightened than the traditional thinking about monarchical government. As we will see in the next unit, Locke's ideas had a profound influence on the government that was created for the new American nation in 1776.

Basic Questions

A basic question related to government involves the belief one holds about the nature of man. Do you believe that man is basically good and that he just needs to be set free and left alone, or do you believe that man is basically evil and that he needs to be controlled? The best answer to this is found in Ecclesiastes 7:29, "Behold, I have found only this, that God made men upright, but they have sought out many devices." Man is capable of doing great good, but he is also capable of committing terrible evil. Any human oversight or control over another person (whether by secular government, church leaders, or parents) should be exercised to defeat the evil of which people are capable and to bring out the God-given potential for good in every person.

Other significant questions regarding man must be addressed when we consider the issue of government. What are "self-evident truths," as the Declaration of Independence puts it? King James I had one idea about such truths while John Locke had another. Do all people have a God-given right to be free politically? If one person has a right to be free, do not all people have this right? What is the best way to bring about personal and political freedom? Do women, minorities, and the poor (those who do not own property) have the same rights as property-owning males? How people answer these and other questions about the nature of man and society influences the kind of government that is created and what government does in relation to and on behalf of the people.

> *A French philosopher whose writing influenced James Madison and other American founding fathers was Baron de Montesquieu, who published* The Spirit of the Laws *in 1748. Montesquieu described three kinds of government: monarchies, which are based on honor; republics, which are based on virtue; and despotisms, which are founded on fear. He said that the functions of government can and should be divided into three branches: executive, legislative, and judicial. Montesquieu recognized three classes of society: the monarchy, the aristocracy, and the commoners (he purposefully did not include the clergy as a separate class). He favored hereditary aristocracy but opposed slavery. Montesquieu also propounded the unusual idea that climate is a major influence on man and society; that is, he held that society in a cold climate like that found in northern Europe is different from a society located in the warm climate of the Mediterranean. His ideal climate, not surprisingly, was that of France. Madison and the other founders accepted some of Montesquieu's ideas and rejected others.*

> *There was the true Light which, coming into the world,*
> *enlightens every man.*
> *John 1:9*

Reading

- *Two Treatises of Government* (excerpt) by John Locke (*WHTT*, p. 44)

3 The United States— An Exercise in Government-Building

It is important to understand how the American system of government developed. We should not think that our republic flowed naturally from the British monarchy and grew out of the American Revolution without significant controversy. The Declaration of Independence was a bold and risky move. The Articles of Confederation were a first step toward American self-government, but they were not a perfect step. The process of writing our Constitution involved brilliant minds making shrewd political compromises. The ultimate form that our national government would take was not clear even after the Constitution had been completed. What was clear, however, was the Founders' recognition of and dependence on God. This unit ends with a survey of the Preamble of the U.S. Constitution, which begins our detailed analysis of this document that extends through Unit 9.

Lessons in This Unit

Lesson 11—Assuming a "Separate and Equal Station"
Lesson 12—America as a Confederation
Lesson 13—Writing and Ratifying the Constitution
Lesson 14—America's Foundation of Faith
Lesson 15—The Preamble of the Constitution

Activity Idea

Write two pages on what you believe are the strengths of the American Constitution and our system of government.

If you are using the optional *Quiz and Exam Book*, answer the questions for each lesson after you have completed the lesson and read any assigned readings in *We Hold These Truths*. After you have completed Lesson 15, take the quiz for Unit 3.

Lesson 11—Assuming a "Separate and Equal Station"

We have not raised armies with ambitious designs of separating from Great Britain and establishing independent states.
— "Declaration of the Causes and Necessity of Taking Up Arms,"
adopted by the Second Continental Congress, July 6, 1775

The hardy settlers who came to these shores in 1607, 1620, and the years that followed could hardly have imagined that they were laying the first stones of a foundation for a new nation. Even as late as 1775, as indicated by the quotation above, most political leaders of the colonies wanted only to defend their rights as Englishmen and were not pursuing the status of an independent country.

In the century and a half between the first English settlements and the birth of the new nation, the situation and the thinking of the colonists changed drastically. The leadership of a few men finally seized the moment and, guided by the providential hand of God, brought about the creation of a new nation in a form and manner that were previously unknown in world history.

American Colonists Gathering at the Town Hall

Colonial Government

The British colonies in North America were founded for various purposes. Some provided religious freedom for people in England and Europe whose religious beliefs did not coincide with the beliefs of those in power. Other colonies were begun primarily as profit-making enterprises, in keeping with the economic philosophy of the times which held that overseas colonies were essential to building national wealth. William Penn had a vision for an entirely new kind of community, one that featured toleration and mutual respect for all men based on God's principles as he understood them.

The settlers in each colony saw themselves as British citizens, subjects of the king. In many respects their ties to England were stronger than their ties to the other American colonies. Each colony had a governor, who was the direct representative of the king. The governor usually surrounded himself with a small council of advisors. Each colony had an elected assembly, chosen by property-owning males, that gave input to the governor and that recommended laws; but all decisions had to be approved by the king.

The reality of life in the colonies, as well as missteps by the British government, led to a growing division between the American colonies and the central government in London. The colonies were building dynamic economies of their own, and colonists developed a way of life that was different from that known by most people in England. Political leaders in the colonies increasingly wanted to be free from being controlled by the government in England, but the king and Parliament increasingly wanted to exert greater control over colonial life and business. Since the governors represented the king and the colonial assemblies represented the colonists, the governors and assemblies were often in conflict with each other. The colonists thought that the British victory in the French and Indian War (1754-1763), for which the colonists themselves were largely responsible, would lead to greater freedoms and a greater self-destiny. The English king, however, responded to the war with more taxes and a more oppressive presence in the colonies. Colonial leaders believed that their rights as Englishmen were being denied.

Steps Toward a National Government

Over time, the colonies took a few tenuous steps toward combining themselves into a confederation with a united purpose. The New England Confederation was formed in 1643 among the Massachusetts Bay, Plymouth, Connecticut, and New Haven colonies for the purpose of defending themselves against Indian attacks. When that danger died out, so did the confederation. It ceased to function by 1684.

In 1754, because of the threat posed by France to the British colonies, the British government ordered representatives from several colonies to meet in Albany to discuss greater unity among themselves. Britain's purpose was to insure that the colonies would fight together under the king's leadership in any war. The Albany Congress accomplished little; but a committee there, headed by Benjamin Franklin, proposed a Plan of Union which was adopted by the delegates. The proposal called for a chief executive appointed by the crown and a body of representatives chosen by the colonial legislatures. The proposed government would be able to raise taxes, oversee defense of the colonies, and govern trade and settlement in the area west of the Appalachian mountains. The colonial assemblies thought it gave too much power to the king, and the king thought it gave too much power to the colonies. The king rejected it, and the colonial governments either rejected it or ignored it.

The British Parliament passaged the Stamp Act in February 1765 (which was to go into effect the following November). After the Stamp Act was approved by Parliament, the Massachusetts House of Representatives called on the other colonial assemblies to send delegates to a meeting in New York to consider making appeals to the king and Parliament for relief from the mounting burden of new taxes. Twenty-seven delegates from nine colonies met in October and protested what they saw as unjust taxation since they had no representation in Parliament, although they accepted Parliament's power to oversee colonial trade. Because of opposition in the colonies, the Stamp Act was never effectively enforced and was repealed the following year. Parliament insisted that it had the right to lay taxes on the colonies, but events gave colonial leaders a growing sense of their own power.

In response to colonial protests over Parliament's granting the East India Company a monopoly on the tea market in the colonies (highlighted by the Boston Tea Party in December of 1773), Parliament passed the Coercive Acts of 1774, which restricted trade in and out of Boston and tightened control over other aspects of colonial life. The colonies responded by calling the first Continental Congress to meet in Philadelphia in September of 1774. When the delegates chosen by twelve colonial legislatures met (Georgia declined to participate), they passed resolutions against the Coercive Acts and in favor of boycotting British goods. Before the delegates departed, they resolved to hold another such Congress in May of 1775.

Meeting of the Second Continental Congress

By the time that the Second Continental Congress met (with all thirteen colonies represented), fighting had taken place between British troops and American colonists in the Massachusetts towns of Lexington and Concord. The Congress functioned as a revolutionary national government, even though neither the British king nor the colonies had authorized it to do so. The assembly named George Washington to lead an army that as yet had not been formed. Congress pleaded with the king to end his hostile actions, and the delegates insisted on the right of the colonists to take up arms to defend their rights as British citizens. The Continental Congress met off and on over the next several months.

A growing sentiment among colonial political leaders, as well as the general population in the colonies, was for breaking with Great Britain and becoming an independent nation. In June of 1776, Richard Henry Lee of Virginia proposed a resolution in Congress stating that "these united colonies are, and of right ought to be, free and independent states." The resolution was debated, and a committee was named to write a declaration of independence. Most of the writing was done by Thomas Jefferson of Virginia. His draft was debated and edited by Congress. On July 2, 1776, Lee's resolution was adopted by Congress; and two days later the Declaration of Independence was approved by the delegates.

The Declaration of Independence

The Declaration of Independence is the product of Enlightenment ideas driven by political realities. John Locke's thinking from 1690 had a profound influence on Jefferson and the other delegates. It had become "necessary," Jefferson said, for English subjects in the American colonies to create a new nation. This identity was what the laws of Nature and Nature's God "entitled" them to have.

Jefferson said that certain truths were self-evident; that is, the members of the Continental Congress assumed them to be true. All men are created equal. They have rights that should not be taken away by any government. The purpose of government is to secure these rights, and government is to get its power from the consent of the governed. When a government fails to secure these rights, the people have a right to alter or abolish the government and to create a new government that will secure them. This should not be done lightly, the Declaration noted; but the actions of the British king threatened the American people with the shadow of despotism. Thus they decided that it was their right and duty to reject the king's rule over them.

The bulk of the Declaration is a long list of wrongs and abuses that the king had committed. He had denied them their right to republican government and had interfered in their proper and legitimate trade, society, freedom, and security. In addition, Parliament had attempted to exert "an unwarrantable jurisdiction" over the colonies. The Declaration stated that the colonies were now free and independent states, united in their stand and free from any political connection to the British Crown.

The Declaration reflected two significant changes in the thinking of the colonists. First, they now saw themselves as Americans and no longer as British. Second, they began seeing themselves as a united country and not as thirteen autonomous entities. The form of their government would be worked out over the next several years, but the Declaration provided the basic principles that would serve as the foundation for that government:

- all men are created equal;

- individuals have rights, including the right to life, liberty, and the pursuit of happiness;

- the purpose of government is to protect these rights;

- government derives its power from the consent of the governed;

- God made men, He made them equal, and He endowed them with rights;

- God entitles a people to be a nation; all people answer to God for the rectitude of their intentions and actions; and it is right to appeal to God officially as a nation.

It was for freedom that Christ set us free;
therefore keep standing firm
and do not be subject again to a yoke of slavery.
Galatians 5:1

Reading

- Declaration of Independence (*WHTT*, p. 7)

Signing the Declaration of Independence

Lesson 12—America as a Confederation

The best government is that which governs least.
—John L. O'Sullivan, 1837

From 1776 until 1789, the United States of America operated as a confederation or league of independent, sovereign states. The events of this period powerfully influenced the shape of the new national government that was created by the Constitution.

New State Governments

With the Declaration of Independence, the thirteen colonial governments ceased to exist. The former colonies became independent states, so new governments had to be created. All of the states developed written constitutions, and most of them did so by convening a new institution: the constitutional convention. Convention members were elected by the voters, and the finished work of the convention was submitted to the voters for their approval.

The new state constitutions reflected the thinking of the times. They generally included a bill or list of individual rights (such as freedom of speech, freedom of religion, guarantees against unreasonable search and seizure, etc.) that were considered inviolable and worthy of the state's protection. In reaction to problems that had been encountered with colonial governors appointed by the king, state governors were given few powers. Most governing authority in each state rested with the popularly elected assembly. The courts that were established were assured independence from domination by either the legislature or the governor.

Under these new state constitutions, only adult white males who owned a certain amount of property or who had enough money to pay taxes were allowed to vote. Elected representatives also had to own property. This property requirement reflected the belief that only those who owned property had enough of an interest in society and government to vote and to serve in government responsibly.

In Massachusetts, future President John Adams, who had been a member of the Continental Congress, was elected by his home town as a delegate to the state constitutional convention. Appointed to the committee that was to draft a constitution, the committee gave him the responsibility of developing a document almost single-handedly. The resulting document, which the convention altered in some ways, was adopted by the voters in 1780 and is still in use. Since it predates the American Constitution by several years, the state constitution of Massachusetts is the world's oldest founding document of government that is still in use.

The Articles of Confederation

The delegates to the Second Continental Congress began discussing a formal plan of union in June of 1776. It was not until November of 1777, however, that they finalized the Articles of Confederation and submitted them to the states. Congress operated as best it could while the state legislatures considered the Articles. The process of approval dragged on until the thirteenth and final state, Maryland, ratified the Articles in February of 1781. This officially put the Articles into effect.

Some observers have criticized Congress for accomplishing little during this period, but that was exactly the purpose of the Articles. The main goal of the Articles was to create as limited a central government as possible. The Articles declared, "Each state retains its sovereignty, freedom, and independence, and every power, jurisdiction, and right, which is not by this Confederation expressly delegated to the United States, in Congress assembled." The purpose of the league of friendship formed by the states was to provide for "their common defense, the security of their liberties, and their mutual and general welfare," needs that were especially acute in the context of the war against Great Britain.

Delegates to the national (now called the Confederation) Congress were to be elected each year as each state legislature saw fit. A state could have from two to seven representatives, but each state would have only one vote in Congress. The states provided financial support for their own delegates. The states were to contribute to a national treasury in proportion to the value of land in each state. Congress could not tax the people directly. Congress, not the individual states, had the power to carry on relations with other countries and to conduct war. Relations among the states were to be governed by Congress.

The Articles provided for no national executive. One member of Congress would be elected as presiding officer or president every year, and a committee of one representative from each state would oversee operations when Congress was in recess. Any major issue required the approval of nine of the thirteen states, and any changes to the Articles required the approval of all thirteen state legislatures before it could go into effect. No provision was made for a national court system.

Under the Articles of Confederation, the United States successfully prosecuted the war for independence and concluded a peace treaty with Great Britain that recognized the Mississippi River as the country's western border and the Great Lakes as its northern border. A series of laws, culminating in the Northwest Ordinance of 1787, set the pattern for organizing territories and admitting new states into the Union on an equal footing with the original thirteen. The national government also managed to keep thirteen skeptical, independent, war-weary, and economically uncertain sovereignties together as a nation.

Failings of the Articles

Congress under the Articles of Confederation tried to balance the desire for limited government with the need for effective government. The Articles definitely provided for a limited government. The effectiveness of the government, however, came to be seriously questioned. During the war, Congress had been unable consistently to provide George Washington with the men and material he requested and needed. The Continental dollar paper currency that Congress had authorized was worthless. Unable to raise significant revenue directly, Congress accumulated debt to pay for the War for Independence—debt that was owed to soldiers, wealthy individual creditors, and foreign countries. The states, which had debts themselves, were reluctant to pay taxes to the central government and often ignored Congressional requests for revenue.

The national economy during the 1780s alternated between boom and bust. America lost significant trade revenue when Great Britain closed the West Indies to American goods. On the other hand, the U.S. developed trade with the Netherlands, Sweden, and other foreign nations. Unstable state and national currencies brought much uncertainty and hardship on the citizenry. Some states began to clash over boundaries and fought small wars with Indian tribes. The provisions in the Articles that required nine votes to pass significant laws and the agreement of all thirteen states to amend the Articles created a political paralysis that prevented almost all meaningful change.

It appeared that the rights of "life, liberty, and the pursuit of happiness" for which the Revolution was fought were being threatened. Political wrangling within the states led to uncertainties as to the direction state governments would take. Few questioned the principles of freedom and limited government, but an increasing number doubted that freedom could continue if a strong leader or faction were to emerge and take control of government on either the state or national level. In the winter of 1786, struggling farmers in western Massachusetts rebelled against what they felt was unfair treatment by creditors and the high taxes imposed

Shays' Rebellion

by the state to try to pay its debts. When the state legislature did not provide any relief, Daniel Shays, a Revolutionary veteran, led a band of armed men that forced courts to close in several towns and that seized a military arsenal in Springfield. The state militia (note: not a Federal force) quickly dispersed the group, but the threat of anarchy was felt deeply by leaders in many of the states. Now Americans were taking up arms against each other.

Many feared foreign threats as well. Great Britain continued to man outposts along the Great Lakes and maintained a strong presence in Canada. Spain owned Florida and controlled Louisiana and occasionally showed interest in extending its influence into what would later become Alabama, Mississippi, and Tennessee. Both Britain and Spain occasionally stirred up Indian tribes against the new American nation by emphasizing what the European nations saw as the threat that the United States posed to the Native Americans. It was not at all clear that the United States could successfully defend its borders or the territory it now claimed.

In 1786, before Shays' Rebellion took place, representatives from five states met in Annapolis, Maryland to discuss problems dealing with sea trade and interstate commerce. The Annapolis Convention accomplished little, but the group went on record as favoring the revision of the Articles of Confederation, as the resolution put it, "to render the constitution of the Federal government adequate to the exigencies of the Union." Early in 1787, Congress issued a call for a convention "for the sole and express purpose of revising the Articles of Confederation." The convention was to meet in May of 1787 in Philadelphia.

The former colonies had united as states to a sufficient degree to win the war for independence. The question remained, however, whether the states would unify sufficiently to win the peace. Most Americans feared a strong central government and wanted the preponderance of political power to remain at the state and local level. A few key leaders could see, however, that the existing system might result in the very thing they most feared: anarchy followed by tyranny. The freedom that Americans had sacrificed and died for appeared to be threatened, and the continuance of republican government in America was by no means assured.

> *Behold, how good and how pleasant it is*
> *for brothers to dwell together in unity!*
> *Psalm 133:1*

Reading

- Articles of Confederation (*WHTT*, p. 11)

- "Thoughts on Government" by John Adams (*WHTT*, p. 50)

Massachusetts Farm

Lesson 13—Writing and Ratifying the Constitution

Doctr. FRANKLIN looking towards the Presidents Chair, at the back of which a rising sun happened to be painted, observed to a few members near him, that Painters had found it difficult to distinguish in their art a rising from a setting sun. I have, said he, often and often in the course of the Session, and the vicisitudes of my hopes and fears as to its issue, looked at that behind the President without being able to tell whether it was rising or setting: But now at length I have the happiness to know that it is a rising and not a setting Sun.

—*James Madison*, Debates in the Federal Convention of 1787, *notes on the last day of the convention, September 17, 1787*

The gathering of men that crafted our Federal Constitution was a remarkable assemblage of talent, accomplishment, and political leadership. Thomas Jefferson once referred to them as "an assembly of demigods." In all, the twelve state legislatures (Rhode Island did not participate) chose 73 men to be delegates, but only 55 attended some part of the deliberations. At the close of their efforts, 39 signed the finished Constitution. Most of the delegates were wealthy lawyers, planters, merchants, and the like; and many were well-educated. Seven had served as state governors, eight had signed the Declaration of Independence eleven years earlier, and twenty-one had fought in the war for independence. Their average age was forty-two.

The work of crafting a revision to the Articles of Confederation did not go easily. When the convention opened on May 14, 1787, not enough states were represented for the convention to begin its work. That had to wait until May 25. The delegates agreed to keep their deliberations secret, which meant that they worked in closed rooms through the hot Philadelphia summer. The men even had conflicts over their basic purpose. They agreed that the Articles of Confederation needed revision, but some wanted as few revisions as possible while others desired to scrap the Articles and write an entirely new document. The decision to go forth with a new document pleased most of the delegates but not all of them. At one point, two of the three delegates from New York went home in frustration.

President James Madison

Because the delegates to the Convention agreed to work in secret, no record was kept of the proceedings except shorthand notes by James Madison, who transcribed his notes in the evenings. Except for scattered comments by delegates in letters and other writings, Madison's notes are our only record of what happened in the Convention. To promote unity in the new nation and to protect the reputations of the participants, Madison prevented the publication of his notes until the death of the last delegate, which turned out to be Madison himself in 1836.

The third, Alexander Hamilton, had to go home also even though he approved of the plan. Hamilton later returned and signed the finished Constitution.

A Series of Compromises

Benjamin Franklin

The delegates to the Convention had not accomplished what they had in their lives by being passive and silent. The group included many strong personalities, and as a result the debates were often lively and sometimes heated. James Madison was a brilliant, scholarly, and eager thirty-six-year-old. Benjamin Franklin was eighty-one and contributed little except his wisdom and widely-respected presence. George Mason of Virginia was suspicious of all governmental power. Elbridge Gerry of Massachusetts found fault with just about every idea that was put forth. Mason and Gerry refused to sign the Constitution when deliberations were finished. War hero George Washington was chairman. His presence gave legitimacy to the proceedings, but he participated little in the discussions. Two leading minds of the Revolution were not present. John Adams was serving as the new nation's minister to Great Britain, and Thomas Jefferson was in the same role in France.

Because of their sharply differing points of view, the delegates crafted a series of compromises to get things accomplished. Usually compromises are agreements that leave all the parties feeling as though the end product is less than what any of them wanted. This was true with some of the compromises the convention made. A better way for those who have differences to come to an agreement is by collaborating on a solution that is better than what any one party wanted. With collaboration, everyone feels as though they got more than what any one of them could have accomplished by himself. The completed Constitution turned out to be a good collaboration, even though several delegates and a significant portion of state leaders and the general population had serious reservations about the document.

Strength of the Central Government

Just how strong should the central government be? Most Americans agreed that it ought to be strong enough to do what it needed to do, but not so strong that it threatened the rights and freedoms of the states and of individuals. Where that precise balance lay was the subject of debate. Many Americans feared a strong central government because of their experience as colonies of Great Britain. They wanted most political power to remain with the states. Others, however, focused on the weaknesses of the Confederation system (as outlined in the last lesson) and argued for stronger powers for the central government. Both sides wanted an effective system of government that avoided tyranny and domination by a few, but they differed on the best way to accomplish this goal. The outcome of the convention addressed the issue in several ways.

Delegated Powers. First, the Constitution gave only specific, enumerated, delegated powers to the national government. The Constitution was not an open invitation for the Federal government to take over and do whatever Congress or the president wanted. The

Federal government was not to go beyond its enumerated powers, and the states retained the powers not expressly given to the Federal government.

A key word in understanding American government is *federal*, the word that describes a system of government with divided sovereignty but unity of purpose. The national

government is sovereign in some areas of governmental activity and state governments are sovereign in other areas, but the two levels work together in a unified system.

Separation of Powers. Second, within the operation of the Federal government, the Constitution called for a separation of powers among the three branches of government (legislative, executive, and judicial) and for checks and balances among the branches to keep one branch from dominating the government. One example of the separation of powers is that the president is commander in chief of the armed forces but only Congress has the power to declare war. The separation of powers has often been described in this way: the legislature makes laws, the executive carries out laws, and the judiciary applies and interprets laws. (This ideal distinction has not always been maintained. For instance, executive orders by the president, administrative rules by government agencies, and rulings by the Supreme Court are not laws passed by Congress but all carry the force of law in practice.)

Checks and Balances. The system of checks and balances that the branches have on each other is illustrated by the following examples: the president executes treaties and makes appointments, but the Senate has to approve them; Congress passes laws, but the president can veto those laws—but then Congress can override the veto; the Supreme Court interprets laws, but its members are nominated by the president and must be approved by the Senate; the president is chosen by popular vote through the electoral college and Federal judges can hold office for life, but Congress has the power to impeach and remove from office the president, the vice president, Federal judges, and all civil officers of the United States government.

The result of the convention's deliberations was a national government that was stronger than what it had been under the Articles of Confederation, but not so strong that state governments withered into insignificance or that individuals feared for their personal and political liberties.

The Composition of Congress

The larger states had the most people and the biggest economies, and they wanted to have the most power in the new government. Smaller states feared that they would become irrelevant if the larger states had the preponderance of power. Smaller states generally preferred the system under the Articles that gave each state one vote.

The proposal put forth by the Virginia delegation called for representation in the lower house of Congress to be chosen by population, with an upper house chosen by the lower house from nominees submitted by state legislatures. In response, the New Jersey delegates wanted to retain equal representation for the states in a unicameral (one-house) legislature.

The compromise that resolved this difference was suggested by Roger Sherman of Connecticut. He proposed that the House of Representatives be based on population (which pleased the large states) while the Senate should be made up of two senators from each state, to be chosen by the state legislatures. The senators would vote as individuals, but each state would have the same power in the Senate (which pleased the smaller states).

The arrangement made for the Senate reflected the importance that state governments had at the time. The state legislatures had named representatives to the Continental Congress, to Congress under the Articles, and to the Constitutional Convention; and now they would directly name the members of one of the two bodies of Congress. This provision was also an attempt to win the support of state government leaders for the new Constitution, even though the state legislatures would not vote on the document. Many state political leaders served in both the state legislatures and in the state ratifying conventions.

The Presidency

The proposal for a national executive also caused sharp debate. The idea of a national executive who would have any significant power was a major departure from state practices and from the experience under the Articles where there was no popularly elected executive. Some delegates feared the power that might accrue to a single person, while others thought that an executive would help bring about a more effective government and better relations with other countries.

The compromise regarding the office of president involved strictly enumerating and limiting his powers, allowing his veto to be overridden by Congress, and making him subject to impeachment and removal from office. A few delegates wanted a nationally elected president, but the majority of delegates were not ready for that. James Wilson of Pennsylvania proposed a system of presidential electors, that has come to be called the electoral college, to select the president. Electors would be chosen in the manner that each state legislature decided. The purpose of the electoral college was for a few leading men to choose the president. However, over time state legislatures decided to choose electors by popular vote, and the electors almost always voted for the candidate endorsed by their political party. Thus the electoral college became a semi-democratic method for choosing the chief executive.

Compromises on Slavery

Opinions of the delegates differed on slavery, though not as sharply as opinions would differ seventy-five years later. Northern states had abolished slavery, while the states from Maryland south had retained it. Although some northern delegates considered slavery a moral evil, it was generally agreed that slavery was an issue for the states, not the national government, to deal with. This perspective also deftly allowed the Constitutional Convention and Congress to avoid dealing with a potentially explosive subject.

Slave state delegates wanted slaves to be counted as part of the population that determined representation in the House, even though no state gave slaves the right to vote for those representatives. Northerners thought that this position was

Slaves Working in a Cotton Field

hypocritical, and they insisted that slaves also be counted in the census figures that would determine direct taxes Congress could impose on the states. (A direct tax was revenue that Congress would requisition from the states based on population. Since slaves helped produce a state's wealth, Northerners thought that slaves should be counted to determine what a state owed to the Federal government.) Slave state delegates resisted this idea, hoping that they could thus lessen the burden of Federal taxes on their states. The compromise reached in the convention called for three-fifths or sixty percent of the slave population to be counted for both representation and taxation.

Another issue involving slavery was the continued importation of slaves. Slave state delegates wanted to be able to continue importing slaves, while other delegates wanted to stop the inhuman practice on a national basis (some state governments had already outlawed importing slaves). The compromise reached called for the slave trade to end no sooner than 1808 (when it was in fact outlawed), twenty years after the expected adoption of the Constitution. Congress reserved the right to tax all slaves that were imported until the slave trade ended.

The compromises that the delegates reached on the issue of slavery are examples of how compromise does not really satisfy the parties involved. Supporters of slavery thought that the provisions in the Constitution went too far, while opponents of slavery thought the final document did not go far enough. Sensitivity over the issue is reflected in the fact that the word slavery is not used in the Constitution. The document merely refers to free persons and other persons. The term slavery was not used in the Constitution until the passage of the Thirteenth Amendment in 1865, which banned slavery.

Ratification

The framers of the Constitution decided that approval by conventions in nine of the thirteen states would be sufficient for the new government to take effect. This decision addressed two significant issues. First, approval did not have to be unanimous, which eliminated a weakness of the Articles of Confederation. Second, the ratification vote would take place in conventions, not state legislatures. The delegates feared that the legislatures might resist what they saw as a relinquishment of their power, so the Constitution called for conventions chosen directly by the people. The framers hoped that a majority of voters would see the need for the Constitution and support its adoption.

The convention submitted its work to the states on September 28, 1787. Approval by enough states was not a foregone conclusion. Those favoring adoption,

A popular story says that, when the convention adjourned and Benjamin Franklin walked out into the street, a woman asked him what kind of government they had devised. "A republic, madam, if you can keep it," was supposedly his reply. Many people in that day feared the danger of tyranny by a single leader or a small group.

called nationalists or Federalists, were better organized and communicated their vision of government well. Their outstanding effort was a series of newspaper articles published in New York and circulated to other states. The eighty-five articles, all signed "Publius" (or Public Man), were actually written variously by James Madison, Alexander Hamilton, and John Jay. The thoughtful and literate articles presented the authors' appeal for a strong national government and tried to calm the fears of those suspicious of the proposed Constitution. These articles were eventually collected and published as *The Federalist* or *The Federalist Papers*. Opponents generally were called Antifederalists. In speeches, articles, and state conventions, they warned of what they saw as the dangers of the proposed change. Sam Adams of Massachusetts and Patrick Henry of Virginia are the best-known opponents of ratification.

The ratification process moved slowly, extending on into the summer of 1788. The conventions of only three states (Delaware, New Jersey, and Georgia) ratified the Constitution unanimously. The ninth state convention, that of New Hampshire, gave its approval by a 57-46 vote on June 21, 1788. However, the New York and Virginia conventions still had not taken a vote; and their approval was seen as vital to the Constitution's success. The Virginia convention approved 87-79 later in June, and New York assented 30-27 in July.

The process for creating the new government began, elections were held, and the first Congress met in March of 1789. However, another month passed before a quorum of members of Congress arrived in New York, the first national capital. With Congressional approval of the electoral college, George Washington was sworn in as the first President. Then North Carolina approved the Constitution 194-77 in November of 1789, and finally defiant Rhode Island (dubbed "Rogue" Island by its critics) gave its approval in the closest ratification vote of any state, 34-32, in late May of 1790. Despite strong opposition and several close convention votes, the Constitution went into effect without serious further opposition.

George Washington's Presidential Inauguration

A Lasting Document

The Constitution was a product of its times. It was the result of the Enlightenment view that reasonable men could peacefully form a government that operated responsibly and that respected the rights of individuals. It was not a truly democratic document because the framers mistrusted democracy (what many called mob rule). The Constitution accepted the practice of slavery and did not provide for women and non-whites in the political process.

Yet the Constitution has lasted well beyond its own time and has guided our country admirably for over two hundred years. It has served as the model for constitutions in many other countries. The Constitution has been successful for a number of reasons. First, the framers tried to look past their own personal and contemporary interests to create a document that could continue to work even in changing circumstances. Second, they tried to make the will of the people (as best they understood it) paramount and to limit what government could do. Third, the Constitution is based on ideals of fairness and equality under the law and does not single out one group or class as privileged. Fourth, it has the flexibility that has allowed it to be amended when needed.

Perhaps most importantly, though, the American people have not wanted to change their basic form of government. Small movements for secession arose in New England during the War of 1812 and again during the Mexican War, but little came of them. The country did suffer a major division with the secession of southern states in 1860-61 and the resultant Civil War. The horror of that period has all but completely eliminated revolution and rebellion as viable options in the American political system. Our differences have been many and sometimes deep, and our failings have been serious; but most people most of the time have been willing to play by the rules set forth in the United States Constitution.

"Come now, and let us reason together," says the Lord.
Isaiah 1:18a

Reading

- *The Federalist* Number 2 by John Jay (*WHTT*, p. 56)

- Speech by Patrick Henry Opposing Ratification of the Constitution (*WHTT*, p. 60)

The Constitution

Lesson 14—America's Foundation of Faith

We hold these truths to be self-evident, that all men are created equal, that they are endowed by their Creator with certain unalienable Rights, that among these are Life, Liberty and the pursuit of Happiness. . . . [W]ith a firm reliance on the Protection of Divine Providence, we mutually pledge to each other our Lives, our Fortunes, and our sacred Honor.

—Declaration of Independence

We The People of the State of New York, grateful to Almighty God for our Freedom, in order to secure its blessings, do establish this Constitution.

—New York State Constitution

We, the People of the State of California, grateful to Almighty God for our freedom, in order to secure and perpetuate its blessings, do establish this Constitution.

—California State Constitution

We, the people of the Commonwealth of Kentucky, grateful to Almighty God for the civil, political and religious liberties we enjoy, and invoking the continuance of these blessings, do ordain and establish this Constitution.

—Kentucky State Constitution

To perpetuate the principles of free government, insure justice to all, preserve peace, promote the interest and happiness of the citizen and of the family, and transmit to posterity the enjoyment of liberty, we the people of Georgia, relying upon the protection and guidance of Almighty God, do ordain and establish this Constitution.

—Georgia State Constitution

The United States was founded on belief in God and in His continuing work in the world. The Founding Fathers believed in God. They wanted and expected the acknowledgment and worship of God to be a vital part of American life. As we discussed earlier in this curriculum, the Bible was an important building block for the American system of law and government.

At the same time, the United States was founded as a country that did not have an official, established national religion. Every citizen was free to worship (or not to worship) as his conscience saw fit. Freedom of religion and the guarantee that Congress would not establish an official religion were included in the First Amendment to the Constitution.

In understanding the role that religion played in the founding of our country, we need to understand the balance that was present at its founding. Religion, especially the Christian religion, was an essential element in the founding of the colonies. The men who later led the national government recognized God in their lives and in the life of the nation. Yet these same men, in keeping with Enlightenment thought, consciously chose not to make the United States an officially Anglican, or Catholic, or Congregational, or Calvinistic nation. They saw the problems that established religions had caused in Europe. Part of the American experiment was a reliance on God from the heart and not a reliance on the establishment of an official religion.

Religion in the Colonies

The spread of Christianity was a motivation for the founding of several of the colonies in America. The charter issued by James I for the Jamestown colony, founded in 1607, said:

> We, greatly commending and graciously accepting of their desires to the furtherance of so noble a work [the desire of the men previously named to found a colony] which may, by the providence of Almighty God, hereafter tend to the glory of His Divine Majesty in propagating of Christian religion to such people as yet live in darkness. . . .

The Mayflower Compact, the founding document of the Plymouth colony signed in 1620, read in part:

> In the name of God, Amen. We, whose names are underwritten, . . . having undertaken for the glory of God, and advancement of the Christian faith, and the honor of our king and country, a voyage to plant the first colony in the northern parts of Virginia; do by these presents, solemnly and mutually in the presence of God and one another, covenant and combine ourselves together into a civil body politic, for our better ordering and preservation, and furtherance of the ends aforesaid. . . .

We referred in the Introduction to the Massachusetts Bay colony and the mission of its leader, Governor John Winthrop, for it to be a city on a hill. The Fundamental Orders of Connecticut of 1639 said:

> For as much as it hath pleased Almighty God by the wise disposition of his divine providence so to order and dispose of things; and well knowing where a people are gathered together the word of God requires that to maintain the peace and union of such people there should be an orderly and decent government established according to God, to maintain and preserve the liberty and purity of the Gospel of our Lord Jesus which we now profess, as also, the discipline of the churches. . . .

One of the reasons that Maryland, Pennsylvania, and Georgia were founded was to provide religious freedom for Europeans who had been persecuted for their faith. Certainly the desire to make a profit was one motivation for the founding of colonies in America, even on the part of some who also expressed faith in God; but even so, the religious motive was clearly present. In fact, most of the colonies had official established churches.

Religion in the Founding Documents

The Declaration of Independence, which announced the creation of our country, makes several references to God: "Nature's God"; "all men are created equal" [note: Man did not evolve. Equality is the result of God's having created us]; "they are endowed by their Creator with certain unalienable rights"; and the reference to Divine Providence quoted at the beginning of this lesson. The existence of God and the significance of His creating man were important elements in the rationale for the origin of our country.

The Articles of Confederation refer to "the Great Governor of the world." Twice it notes a date by using the phrase "in the year of our Lord." The Northwest Ordinance of 1787, which established the pattern for territories becoming states, said, "Religion, morality and knowledge being necessary to good government and the happiness of mankind, schools and the means of education shall be forever encouraged." Thus, the Ordinance not only endorsed religion; but it also endorsed the teaching of religion and morality in schools.

Religious Activities in the New Nation

The young nation followed two principles in matters of religion: (1) religious freedom, and (2) an official, stated recognition of and dependence on God. The founding generation saw no conflict in holding to both of these principles.

The first meeting of the Continental Congress in 1774 opened with a prayer, and the tradition of chaplain-led prayer in Congress continued into the government under the Constitution. Congress authorized chaplains to serve the Continental Army. Many times during the war for independence, Congress called for days of prayer to be observed by the people of the country. Several of the new states continued to have an established church for a number of years after the Revolution.

Immediately after passing the First Amendment in 1789, Congress called for a day of thanksgiving to God. President Thomas Jefferson attended church services that were held in the House of Representatives chamber. President James Madison later attended services in the House chamber, and the conducting of church services there continued until after the Civil War.

New England Village

Religious Beliefs of the Founders

Many of the Founding Fathers openly avowed their faith. We will mention just a few. George Washington was an active Episcopalian and made numerous references to God in his speeches. He confessed his dependence on prayer during the Revolutionary War. Washington took the oath of office for the presidency by holding his hand on a Bible, and on his own initiative he added the phrase "so help me God" when he completed the oath prescribed in the Constitution.

John Adams had an active and vibrant faith that guided his entire life. He once wrote in a letter:

> What has preserved this race of Adamses in all their ramifications in such numbers, health, peace, comfort, and mediocrity [meaning evenness]? I believe it is religion, without which they would have been rakes, fops, sots, gamblers, starved with hunger, or frozen with cold, scalped by Indians, etc., etc. etc., been melted away and disappeared. . . .

John Jay, who wrote some of the Federalist essays and who served, among other positions, as the first chief justice of the Supreme Court, was a staunch Episcopalian. He served for a time late in his life as president of the American Bible Society. In *The Federalist* Number 2, Jay wrote:

> Providence has in a particular manner blessed [our country] with a variety of soils and productions, and watered it with innumerable streams, for the delight and accommodation of its inhabitants.

and

> Providence has been pleased to give this one connected country to one united people—a people descended from the same ancestors, speaking the same language, professing the same religion, attached to the same principles of government, very similar in their manners and customs. . . .

However . . .

We must recognize, however, that the practices and beliefs of the colonists and Founding Fathers were not completely supportive of the Christianity that conservative Christians practice today. The Plymouth and Massachusetts Bay colonies wanted religious freedom only in a sense. They wanted freedom from rule by the Anglican Church, but the colonial leaders wanted tight control over the religious practices of the colonists on the basis of what the leaders themselves thought right. A conflict over teaching and practice in the Massachusetts Bay colony led to Roger Williams founding Rhode Island on the basis of more complete religious liberty.

Not all of the Founding Fathers had an orthodox Christian faith. Benjamin Franklin, who at times had positive things to say about God, was a skeptic concerning Christianity and led a sometimes immoral lifestyle. Thomas Jefferson, in classic Enlightenment style, literally cut passages that had to do with miraculous events out of a copy of the Gospels. His strong support of the French Revolution, without condemning the atheistic stance of its leaders, brought him much criticism during his political career. It is generally agreed today that Jefferson fathered a child by one of his slaves. Thomas Paine, whose writings helped to stir the fires of revolution, believed in God but

Baptist Meeting House
Providence, Rhode Island

was a harsh critic of the practice of Christianity. George Washington was an Episcopalian, but he was also a Mason; and many Christians today see the Masonic movement as a cult or religious heresy.

Why does the Constitution not mention God when the Declaration of Independence and the Articles of Confederation had both mentioned Him? Various answers have been offered to that question. Supposedly Alexander Hamilton, perhaps in a humorous vein, said, "We forgot." Some have suggested that America's reliance on God had been clearly established by then, even with no mention of God in the Constitution. Others suggest that the omission was a deliberate attempt to step away from the inclusion of any religious presence or references whatsoever in the new government. However, the fact that the Constitution does not mention God does not mean that no government activity can mention Him. The precedent of reliance on God had been clearly set, and the practices of the new government showed that official expressions of faith in God were seen as compatible with the non-establishment of religion.

Few people in Revolutionary America were declared atheists (few today are either, for that matter). Some Americans (though not the large number as portrayed in typical textbooks) had adopted the religion of Deism, which held that God had created the world but was not directly involved in its ongoing processes. The vast majority of Americans and American political leaders believed in God; and by far most people considered themselves Christians. They did not want or expect the national government to declare an established religion or church, but neither did they see an expression of religious faith by the national government as tantamount to establishing a religion.

Freedom to Believe

Most people today would not endorse every position of the Founding Fathers on every issue. For instance, many of them accepted slavery, and few of them thought that women should be able to vote. However, on some matters they were more right than the majority of our generation. Their perception of the proper and important role of religion in public life is one of these issues.

In the early years of our nation, the government of the United States openly avowed faith in and dependence on God. The movement away from that practice in modern times has weakened our nation morally and spiritually. We can pray that Americans will reawaken to the reality of God and the difference He makes in our individual and national lives. We will be a stronger nation if this happens.

If I shut up the heavens so that there is no rain,
or if I command the locust to devour the land,
or if I send pestilence among My people,
and My people who are called by My name
humble themselves and pray and seek My face
and turn from their wicked ways,
then I will hear from heaven,
will forgive their sin and will heal their land.
2 Chronicles 7:13-14

Reading

- "The Religious Roots of Freedom" by M. Stanton Evans (*WHTT*, p. 113)

Lesson 15—The Preamble of the Constitution

In expounding the Constitution of the United States, every word must have its due force and appropriate meaning; for it is evident from the whole instrument, that no word was unnecessarily used, or needlessly added.
—Chief Justice Roger B. Taney in Holmes v. Jennison *(1840)*

The framers of the Constitution included a paragraph at the first of the document that set forth its origin and purpose. The Preamble not only gave the rationale for the Constitution but also sought to win the hearts of the people. In this lesson we will examine the phrases of the Preamble to understand the original intention of the framers as to the scope and meaning of the Constitution. The inspiring Preamble sentence is worth memorizing.

We the people of the United States, in order to form a more perfect union, establish justice, insure domestic tranquility, provide for the common defense, promote the general welfare, and secure the blessings of liberty to ourselves and our posterity, do ordain and establish this Constitution for the United States of America.

We the People of the United States

The first phrase tells us the source of the American government: the people. Of course, it was the delegates to the Constitutional Convention who framed the document; but they wanted the Constitution to be the best expression they could devise of the will of the people. The Constitution gave expression to a relatively new idea: government by consent of the governed. The American government was not handed down by a king but granted to elected representatives by the people. The Federal government and the Union come from the people, not the states. It is true that the people acted as states in ratifying the Constitution, but the document is presented as the will of the people.

Shipyard Workers in Texas, 1943

The written Constitution is an example of the covenant or contract idea. The people of America entered into a covenant with each other and with those who serve in government. The powers of government were not arbitrarily declared by a king or a council, but instead they were stated clearly and given expressed limits for all to see.

The short phrase "We the people" encompasses a large meaning. Even at the birth of the nation, the people came from a wide assortment of ethnic backgrounds. Most were English, but many were Scots-Irish (and they would never let you think of them as English!). Some were Swedish, Dutch, or German. All of those who were involved in writing the Constitution were immigrants or descendants of immigrants. Differences among people are often seen as a hindrance and an irritation, but God tells us that we should see differences as a blessing and a strength (see Romans 14:1-15:13 and 1 Corinthians 12:1-31).

Because of man's sins of jealousy, hatred, and discrimination, unity is not always easy to accomplish. We find ways to separate from and to be suspicious of others. One manifestation of this in our country (and in other countries) has been sectionalism. Even in the early days of the nation, people in the different sections of the country had different priorities and viewed those from other sections with disdain. Another attitude that has kept us from having complete unity has been racism. It took a long time for black Americans to be brought into the American dream. To a great degree, Native Americans never have been invited to the table. These truths tell us that we still have a way to go in fulfilling the noble ideal of "We the people."

Native American Chiefs in front of the U.S. Capitol, 1927

In Order to Form a More Perfect Union

There follows in the Preamble a series of purpose clauses, telling why the people had created this Constitution. The first reason was to form a more perfect union. The Articles of Confederation had declared that the Union was perpetual. Of course, people could break the Union apart if they wished; but the intention of the founders was that it be permanent. However, the Union faced serious problems coming out of the Revolutionary War because of the inadequate form of its national government. The framers saw this moment as the opportunity to establish a better and longer-lasting republic.

It is a compliment to the wisdom and vision of the founders that the Constitution has lasted as long as it has. When the country began, it consisted of thirteen states along the Atlantic coast with vast territories to the west. Most of the population lived in a narrow band of settlements along the coast. Some of the framers had a dim dream of the nation stretching to fill the continent, but it was by no means certain that such would happen. It did happen, however; and the Union formed in 1776 and made more perfect by the Constitution has continued. In recent times the citizens of this vast Union have been brought closer together by improved travel and electronic communication. We have been able to connect coast to coast because we are a Union, and our ability to connect coast to coast has helped us to be a closer Union.

Establish Justice

The Constitution called for a Federal system of courts and national law, which had not been provided for under the Articles of Confederation. A civil society requires the protection of individuals and their rights and the prosecution of wrongdoers. A system of justice implies the recognition that justice exists, that absolute standards of right and wrong should be applied, and that fair punishments should be meted out. Perhaps a system of justice is most appreciated when we see what happens where one does not exist. In such cases an individual citizen is helpless against the power of those who have money or who exert influence in the courts.

Insure Domestic Tranquility

Just as a system of justice is needed for a civil society, domestic order is also a necessity. Shays' Rebellion was the manifestation of what many feared would happen without a stronger national authority. Indeed, after the adoption of the Constitution other small rebellions occurred; but they were quickly quelled.

U.S. Troops in Iraq, 2006

Provide for the Common Defense

Another basic and essential function of government is the defense of the homeland. The newly won freedom of the United States had to be defended. Military activities under the Articles had not been as effective or efficient as many had wanted. The defense of the country depended in large part on state militias and on the states responding to requests for funds by Congress. General Washington often did not know who was under his command, how many troops he had, or when they might leave and go home. States often ignored requests by Congress for funds, and this uncertainty coupled with the resultant dependence on foreign loans spurred the framers to pursue a different course.

Military spending is now one of the largest expenditures of the Federal government; and military preparedness is a constant issue before Congress, the president, and the people. World War II was the last time that Congress declared war; but Korea, Vietnam, Operation Desert Storm, the war on terrorism, and other smaller actions have made "the common defense" a major function of government nonetheless.

Of course, defending the country's interests through diplomacy is preferable to engaging in war. For many years the United States was relatively isolated from the rest of the world and survived quite well. We live in an age, however, where our vital national interests involve areas and issues beyond our shores. It is also an age when hard-to-identify enemies can wage an undeclared war on us, even using domestic American airliners to attack our people and our national sovereignty. The common defense involves much more than simply training and maintaining the armed forces.

Promote the General Welfare

This is a broad phrase that says the Federal government is to be involved in promoting the general well-being of the country. This has been used to justify the Federal government's efforts to insure the safety of foods and drugs on the American market, the safety of places where Americans work, the safety of cars sold in America and those who travel in them, and other programs.

We should note that the phrase refers to the general welfare and not to the welfare of specific groups. Trying to identify and provide assistance for specific groups opens the government up to an endless stream of demands from all sorts of groups to help their individual welfare, regardless of what such assistance might mean for the population as a whole.

And Secure the Blessings of Liberty to Ourselves and Our Posterity

Liberty offers benefits to those who have it. The blessings of liberty were what the Revolution was fought to obtain. The framers perceived that the unrest and uncertainty in the country under the Articles threatened liberty's blessings. The founders believed in the power of liberty as opposed to coercion to accomplish good for mankind.

These blessings of liberty were desired not only for that generation but for their posterity, for generations to come. Just looking out for themselves was too short a view. What we do will be different if we are concerned about those who will come later, even after we are gone, as opposed to merely looking after our own personal, immediate interests. The framers had this longer view in mind.

This concern for posterity has been applied in at least two issues that are crucial for us today. First, the state's interest in posterity has been used by some to argue that abortion should be limited or banned altogether. If abortion is permitted, we will have less posterity to whom we can pass along the blessings of liberty. The Supreme Court considered this "posterity" argument in *Roe v. Wade*, but decided that the compelling interest of posterity

was limited to the point of a fetus' viability (ability to live outside of the womb). Thus the Court decided that a younger fetus was not protected as part of our posterity. The *Roe v. Wade* decision is extremely flawed and has resulted in millions of abortions, including those performed on viable fetuses. Moreover, the definition of viability has changed since the 1973 decision. We will discuss the abortion issue in more detail later in this curriculum.

A second application of the state's interest in posterity involves environmental policy. If our natural resources are not protected now, our posterity will not have them to use and enjoy. If our forests are not protected, they will likely be consumed by short-sighted developers concerned only about immediate profits. If our air and water are not protected, our posterity will live in an unhealthy environment. We have seen enough smog and other pollutants in our own country and in other parts of the world to know that a lack of regulation causes a genuine problem.

Climbing Mt. Rainier in Washington, 1906

At the same time, each generation should be able to use our natural resources safely and responsibly. Just because a special-interest group says, for example, that an Alaskan oil pipeline is harmful to the environment does not make it true. The development of careful yet practical environmental policy is a difficult task that the government has in accomplishing the goal of securing the blessings of liberty to our posterity.

Do Ordain and Establish This Constitution for the United States of America

To ordain is to create or to invest officially. The Constitutional Convention created the document and set it in place as the foundational law of the land, subject to ratification by the people of the states through their conventions. The document created a national government and outlined that government's relations to the states.

In the next unit we begin discussing the components of this remarkable document: what the words mean, what the framers intended, how the Federal government has applied the provisions of the Constitution, and how the Federal government works today. As we study the Constitution, remember that you and your family are part of "We the people." This is your government. You have a responsibility and an obligation to help our government be the best it can be "for ourselves and our posterity."

They will come and will declare His righteousness
to a people who will be born, that He has performed it.
Psalm 22:31

Greeting Soldiers from the Pennsylvania National Guard, 2006

Part 2

The American
Constitution

4 Article I— Congress (Part 1)

The Constitution begins by establishing Congress. The methods for choosing members of Congress have changed over the years. Congress has developed its own rules and traditions by which it operates. It is helpful to understand who the members of Congress are, what Congress does, and how it does it. The committee system and political party alignments are crucial to an understanding of how Congress works—and sometimes why it doesn't work.

Lessons in This Unit

Lesson 16—Election to the House of Representatives
Lesson 17—Choosing the Senate
Lesson 18—The Operations of Congress
Lesson 19—Who They Are and What They Do
Lesson 20—Committee and Political Party Organization

Activity Idea

Here is an opportunity for you to think about something you don't like about how our government operates and to express yourself on it in a positive way. Is it the role that money plays in American politics? The petty political wrangling that paralyzes meaningful action? The power that incumbents enjoy? Write a two- to three-page speech in which you outline the problem, tell how things ought to be, and suggest a practical way in which things can change. Imagine that you are to give this speech before a civic club, homeschool debate society, or some other organization.

If you are using the optional *Quiz and Exam Book*, answer the questions for each lesson after you have completed the lesson and read any assigned readings in *We Hold These Truths*. After you have completed Lesson 20, take the quiz for Unit 4.

Lesson 16—Election to the House of Representatives

You can not possibly have a broader basis for any government than that which includes all the people, with all their rights in their hands, and with an equal power to maintain their rights.

—William Lloyd Garrison (1889)

(As you study the various parts of the Constitution over the next several units, read in *We Hold These Truths* the section of the Constitution being discussed in a lesson before you read the lesson itself. Read Sections 1 and 2 of Article I before you study this lesson.)

Article I, the first substantive section of the Constitution after the Preamble, is the longest section of the document. The framers expected Congress, as the part of government closest to and most representative of the people, to be the most important and most powerful part of the new national government. As a result, they felt that the duties, expectations, and limitations of Congress had to be outlined in great detail.

The Bicameral Congress

The Constitution vests the legislative or law-making power of the national government in Congress, which is made up of two bodies, the House of Representatives and the Senate. A legislative branch that is made up of two bodies or houses is called bicameral, from the Latin meaning two chambers.

Congress has two houses for several reasons. The first is tradition. The British Parliament and most colonial governments set the precedent by having two houses. Second, the House and Senate reflect the political realities of the early national period. The two bodies gave representation both to the people and to the states. Third, bicameralism enables the two bodies to act as a check on each other in the consideration of legislation. It is less likely that both houses will be swayed to impulsive action in the heat of the moment the way a single legislative body might be.

Only Pennsylvania and Georgia had unicameral (one-body) legislatures before the Constitution was adopted. Both instituted the two-house approach by 1790. Today Nebraska is the only state that has one legislative house.

The House of Representatives

The more numerous of the two houses of Congress is the House of Representatives. Its members are also called Congressmen. In the original Constitution, the House was the only element of the national government that was elected directly by the people. Everyone who qualified to vote for the most numerous branch of a state's legislature can vote for members of the House. This distinction was significant in the early days of the country, when voting rights were somewhat limited; but today almost everyone who is eighteen or older can vote in the United States. Voters are called electors in the Constitution.

To be elected as a member of the House, a person must be at least 25 years old and have been a citizen for seven years. The age provision is fairly young and probably reflects the relative youthfulness of the delegates to the Constitutional Convention. In actual practice, Congressmen in their twenties have been rare. A Representative does not have to have been born in the United States. He or she can be a naturalized citizen.

A Congressman must also be a resident of the state from which he or she is elected. At first, some states elected Congressmen on an at-large basis; that is, all the Representatives were elected by all the voters in the state. Other states divided their population into districts and elected Representatives by those districts. In 1842, Congress required that all states elect Congressmen by districts and gave state legislatures the responsibility for drawing district boundaries. The Constitution does not require a Representative to live in the district he or she represents. However, it would be difficult to convince voters that someone who does not live in their district really understands their situation and their problems.

Number of Members of the United States House of Representatives by State

Apportionment

Seats in the House of Representatives are assigned or apportioned on the basis of population. States with relatively more people have more Representatives. Originally, states were to have no more than one representative for every thirty thousand people. The Constitution set out the number of representatives for the thirteen original states and provided for a census to take place every ten years to determine any changes in representation. The first census took place in 1790, and a census has been taken every ten years since then. Changes on the basis of a census take effect in the Congressional elections two years later (for example, results from the 2000 census were reflected in Congressional elections beginning in 2002).

As the population of the country grew and new states were added, the number of Representatives in the House increased. The first Congress had 65 members. The first census increased that number to 106. By 1912, the House had grown to 435 members; and effective action with such a large group was becoming difficult. Congress was faced with the dilemma of either adding even more seats after the 1920 census or reapportioning the existing 435 seats, which would have meant that some Representatives from states growing more slowly would have lost their seats. Faced with the need for political courage, Congress took no action after the 1920 census. Finally, in 1929 (just before the 1930 census), Congress passed the Reapportionment Act. This law stated that the permanent size of the House would be 435 members and that those seats would be apportioned to the states as fairly as possible following each census.

> *When Alaska and Hawaii became states in 1959, each new state received one House seat. This temporarily increased the membership of the House to 437, but the regular 435 seats were reapportioned among the fifty states following the 1960 census for the 1962 election.*

> *States set their own qualifications for voting. Most states have a requirement that a person be a resident of the state for a period of time, sometimes as little as thirty days. Voters usually have to register a few weeks before the election, but in some cases voters can register on election day. Voter registration requirements are attempts to prevent people from voting several times in different places. Convicted felons are generally not allowed to vote. Some states used to have requirements that a person own a certain amount of property, pay a certain amount in taxes during a year, pay a poll or voting tax, or be able to read in order to qualify to vote. These requirements were defended as reserving the vote to those who were responsible citizens. In actual practice, the poll tax and literacy test were used to deny black people the right to vote. These practices are now outlawed.*

Ballot Boxes, 1927

The 2000 census showed a U.S. population of 281,421,906 on April 1, 2000. This means that, ideally, each Congressman represented 646,946 people. However, each state is guaranteed one Representative, and the populations of the states do not divide out that evenly. Wyoming, the least populous state with a 2000 census of 493,782, had one Congressman. Delaware had 783,600 people, but it also had only one Representative. California had the most Congressmen with 53, meaning that the average district population there was 639,088. Michigan's Congressmen each represented an average of 662,563 people. Georgia's district average was 629,727.

The legislature of each state is where the real political battles occur over drawing congressional districts. Both Democratic and Republican parties in the states want to win majorities in the legislatures in census years, since the legislatures elected in those years oversee the redrawing of district lines for that state's Congressional seats. Reapportionment for seats in the state legislature happens at the same time. By law, Congressional districts must be contiguous (that means they cannot be separated into two or more areas that are not geographically connected); and they must have as even a population distribution as possible within the state. In theory, district lines would simply be drawn as fairly and equitably as possible; but politics is not always fair and equitable.

The majority party in the legislature wants to protect the Congressional and legislative seats held by its party. Thus, they might draw district lines in such a way that voters who might vote against their party are divided into several districts; or they might put as many friendly voters into the same district as possible. Consider the map of Tennessee's Congressional districts, drawn by a Democrat-controlled legislature. Districts 1, 2, and 3 are considered safe Republican seats. To make the Fourth District more strongly Democratic, the legislature made the Third District a narrow band that stretches all the way from the Georgia border to the Kentucky border. The Fifth District includes Democrat-controlled Nashville and its largely rural (and Democratic) suburbs around it. The county to the south of Nashville, Williamson, has many Republican voters. By connecting suburban Williamson County to southern West Tennessee by means of a narrow strip, Nashville was kept safely Democratic. The Ninth District is urban Memphis, a traditionally Democratic seat, while the suburbs around Memphis are more Republican. Drawing the lines as they did, the legislature kept Republican voters out of the Ninth District and divided them between the Seventh and Eighth Districts, thus giving Democrats a better chance of winning in those districts.

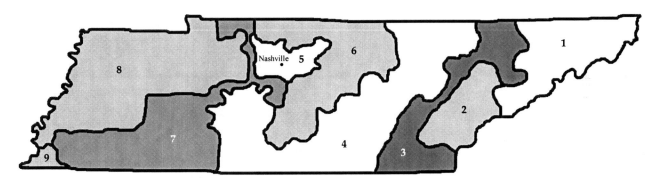

Tennessee's Congressional Districts

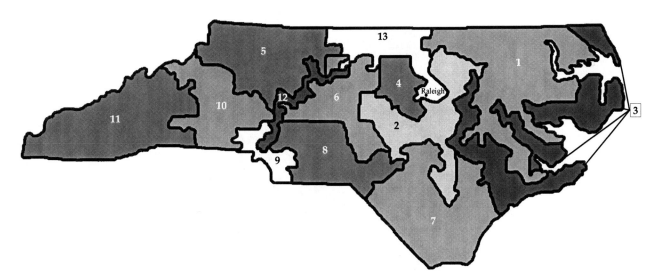

North Carolina's Congressional Districts

In North Carolina, the Twelfth District snakes through the middle of the state to connect several urban, university-based, ethnically-mixed areas into a single district that will likely vote Democratic. This is an example of gerrymandering, or giving a Congressional district an odd shape for political purposes. The term is named for Massachusetts politician Elbridge Gerry. In 1812, with Republican Gerry as governor, the Republican Massachusetts legislature drew an oddly-shaped state senatorial district that looked like a snake or serpent on the map. A political cartoonist added a head, wings, and claws to make it look like a dragon or salamander and called it a "Gerrymander."

Groups of voters or representatives of the opposition party routinely challenge redistricting plans in court, but courts are generally reluctant to become embroiled in the political activities of legislatures unless an obvious violation of voting rights is involved. Even North Carolina's Twelfth District has survived court challenges.

When a vacancy occurs in a House seat through death or resignation, the governor of that state calls a special election for the voters in that district to choose a new Congressman.

> *If the original standard of one Congressman for every thirty thousand people were still followed, the House would now have over 9,300 members!*

Now therefore, apportion this land for an inheritance
to the nine tribes and the half-tribe of Manasseh.
Joshua 13:7

Reading

- *Wesberry v. Sanders* (excerpt) (WHTT, p. 73)

Gerrymander Cartoon

Lesson 17—Choosing the Senate

Although the Senate is much given to admiring in its members a superiority less obvious or quite invisible to outsiders, one Senator seldom proclaims his own inferiority to another, and still more seldom likes to be told of it.

Henry Adams, The Education of Henry Adams *(1907)*

(Read Section 3 of Article I and the Seventeenth Amendment of the U.S. Constitution.)

The United States Senate has sometimes been called the greatest deliberative body in the world. It is considered the upper or more prestigious house of Congress since it has fewer members than the House and since Senators serve for six years instead of two. It also is supposedly insulated from the whims of public opinion since Senators serve for six years and since only one-third of the Senate is chosen every two years. Although Senators represent individual states, they often speak as though they represent national interests and not just the interests of one state.

A person must be a little older to serve in the Senate than what is required to serve in the House. A Senator must be at least thirty years old and a citizen for nine years, as well as being a resident of the state he or she represents. Each state has two Senators, which gives less populous states the same power in the Senate as more populous states. Senators from less populous states have often been leaders in the Senate and have sometimes used their positions in that body to gain national prominence.

A Continuing Body

The Senate was established to be a continuing body, with only one-third of its members up for re-election every two years, as opposed to the House, where all 435 seats are contested every two years. This provides for greater continuity in the Senate than in the House.

When a Senate seat becomes vacant through death or resignation, the state governor appoints someone to fill the seat until the next Congressional election (except in Alaska, Massachusetts, and Oregon, where the governor no longer has this power). This appointed Senator is recognized as a full member of the Senate, but he or she is the most junior member of the body and has little power. Often the governor gives the appointment to a long-time public servant as a reward for his or her service. Usually the governor appoints someone from his or her own political party, even if the previous Senator had been from another party. It has occasionally happened that a governor has appointed himself to fill a Senate seat.

At the next Congressional election, candidates run to fill the remaining two or four years of the term. If the appointed Senator wants to run in the next election, he or she has at least some of the power and prestige of an incumbent. A state occasionally elects two Senators at the same time, if one Senator's six-year term is ending and the remainder of the other Senator's term is being filled in the same election. When a partial term is completed, the next campaign for that Senate seat is for the full six-year term.

Popular Election of Senators

In the original Constitution, Senators were chosen by state legislatures. This provision gave state governments a direct role in the formation of the national government and supposedly provided for more reasoned deliberation in the selection of Senators than if they had been chosen by popular vote. It also provided an inducement for state political leaders to support the ratification of the Constitution. As we have seen in this curriculum, state legislatures played an important role in the early national government.

However, during the nineteenth century support grew for the direct election of U.S. Senators by popular vote. Many people saw the direct election of Senators as a change that would be in keeping with the trend toward democracy. Moreover, state legislatures did not always handle well the responsibility of naming Senators. The continuation of state political battles, rather than the selection of the best person to be a U.S. Senator, sometimes became the main dynamic in a legislature. Occasionally, political wrangling in state legislatures caused Senate seats to remain unfilled for as long as two years (in Delaware around the turn of the twentieth century, a vacancy lasted four years).

One item in the Populist Movement agenda of the late nineteenth and early twentieth century was the direct election of Senators. The Populists maintained that the selection of Senators by state legislatures kept the process out of the hands of the people and left it in the hands of politicians, lobbyists, and special interest groups. State legislatures often proved themselves to be the protectors not of people's rights but of their own turf and privileges. Direct election of Senators, it was argued, would make the upper house of Congress more responsive to the people and less responsive to the intrigues of politicians.

In the years leading up to 1912, twenty-nine states adopted a form of popular election of Senators by holding primaries or referendums, the results of which were binding on state legislators. The Seventeenth Amendment to the U.S. Constitution, which provided for the direct election of Senators, was proposed many times but consistently defeated in the Senate. In 1912, however, the number of directly-elected Senators had increased to the point that the amendment was finally approved and sent to the states. The amendment was ratified in 1913 and took effect in the 1914 election.

It would be difficult to decide whether, on the whole, better Senators were chosen before or after the change. Good men as well as embarrassing men have been elected under each process. It is a certainty, however, that the direct election of Senators has lessened the influence of state legislatures in the national government.

Advice and Consent Role

According to Article II, Section 2 of the Constitution, the Senate has a special check-and-balance role with regard to certain actions of the president. The Senate must ratify by a two-thirds majority treaties that the president makes with other countries; otherwise the treaties do not apply to the United States. In addition, the Senate must give a simple majority approval to important appointments that the president makes: ambassadors, Federal judges, Supreme Court justices, heads of the executive departments (Cabinet members), and certain other appointments. This is called the advice and consent role of the Senate, after the phrase used in the Constitution.

The most controversial treaty consideration by the Senate involved the Treaty of Versailles that ended World War I. Democratic President Woodrow Wilson saw to it that the treaty included the creation of a League of Nations, a forerunner of the United Nations, as an attempt to prevent such a terrible war from ever happening again. The Republican majority in the Senate, however, wanted to withdraw from involvement in world affairs and did not want the United States to be committed to taking part in a world organization. The Treaty of Versailles was defeated in the Senate, the United States never joined the League of Nations (which proved to be incapable of preventing World War II), and the United States concluded separate peace treaties with the nations against whom it had fought in World War I.

Generally the Senate approves those whom the president nominates, unless a nominee proves to be involved in a scandal or unless so many members of the Senate oppose a nominee for political reasons that approval is impossible. One issue that aroused a fair amount of controversy in the early years of the nation was whether the president could remove from office someone whom he had nominated and the Senate had confirmed. This issue arose during the presidency of Andrew Jackson, who fired a cabinet member that the Senate had approved. Jackson said that he had the right to get rid of those who served under him, while Jackson's political opponents said that the Senate's power to confirm also gave it the power to determine whether someone stayed on the job. The same issue was at the heart of the conflict between President Andrew Johnson and Congress

Ballot Boxes in the Senate, 1929

over the Tenure of Office Act following the Civil War. In 1926, the Supreme Court in *Myers v. U.S.* declared the Tenure of Office Act to be unconstitutional and said that the president's right of removal was not subject to the Senate's approval.

The Constitution does give the president the power to make appointments during a recess of Congress (Article II, Section 2, Paragraph 3). These appointments can be made any time that Congress is in recess, even if that recess is only for a few days or weeks. The appointed person may serve until the end of the next session of Congress. During that time, the president can choose to submit that person's nomination to the Senate to hold the position permanently. This provision had more practical importance when Congress was not in session for long periods of time. Fifteen Supreme Court justices began their tenure as recess appointments. Recess appointments are politically risky for the president. They allow him to fill a post with someone he wants who might have a hard time winning confirmation by the Senate, but they tend to anger the opposition party in the Senate who might try to make confirmation more difficult.

Upon hearing this, they entered into the temple
about daybreak and began to teach.
Now when the high priest and his associates came,
they called the Council together,
even all the Senate of the sons of Israel,
and sent orders to the prison house for them to be brought.
Acts 5:21

Lesson 18—The Operations of Congress

A decent and manly examination of the acts of government should be not only toler-ated, but encouraged.

—William Henry Harrison (1841)

(Read Sections 4, 5, and 6 of Article I and the Twentieth and Twenty-Seventh Amendments of the U.S. Constitution.)

The first three sections of Article I establish the Congress and tell who may be elected to each house. Each chamber is to organize itself, but only limited guidelines for this are given in the Constitution. We will discuss in later lessons how the House and Senate are organized as well as matters related to the process of impeachment.

Section 4: Elections and Sessions of Congress

The Constitution left the carrying out of elections in the hands of the states. The states already had a framework for conducting elections that could be expanded to include the choosing of Federal representatives; and the Congressmen and Senators were, after all, representatives from the states. The Constitution did give Congress the right to legislate on elections except on the subject of the place where Senators were chosen (namely, the state legislatures).

Congress was to meet at least once every year, with the sessions to begin on the first Monday in December. In the early years of the country, this led to a year or more passing after some elections before elected officials took office. Senators and Representatives who were elected in the fall of 1866, for instance, did not actually take office until December of 1867 (not all states held elections at the same time; some states conducted their elections in the odd-numbered years). This passage of time was acceptable when travel and communication were slow and when state elections took place at different times.

U.S. Capitol, c. 1871

Over time, however, travel and communication became faster and state elections came to be held at the same time of year. The Twentieth Amendment, ratified in 1933, brought both the inauguration of the president and the convening of Congress up to date. Instead of the president waiting until March 4 after his election to take office, the inauguration was moved up to January 20. The new Congress now convenes on January 3 following the election, instead of waiting over a year after the election.

Each Congress has two sessions, one for each of the two years in which it meets. The first session of the first Congress convened in 1789; the second session of the first Congress met in 1790. The first session of the 110th Congress began on January 4, 2007; the second session of the 110th Congress convened on January 3, 2008.

A session is adjourned when Congressional leaders decide that no further work can be accomplished. In the early days of the country, Congress met for only a few months out of the year and almost always was in recess during the hot days of summer in swampy, un-air-conditioned Washington. Today, Congress meets for almost the entire year but takes long breaks from time to time. In election years members of Congress try to be finished (or at least to be able to take a recess) in time for the fall campaign. Meetings of Congress that occur after an election and before the new Congress begins are called lame-duck sessions, since some of the members will be retiring or have been defeated in the elections.

The Constitution allows for the president to adjourn Congress and to call it into special session in extraordinary circumstances (Article II, Section 3). Since Congress is now almost always in session, special sessions are rare. No president has ever adjourned Congress. Presidents have sometimes called the Senate into special session to consider pending treaties or appointments.

Section 5: Proceedings

Each house of Congress is given the right to judge the fitness of its own members. The House does not sit in judgment on the Senate, nor vice versa, nor do the president or the Supreme Court have the right to question who sits in Congress. The positive side of this rule is that neither the House nor the Senate

U.S. House of Representatives Chamber

have to bow to the wishes of any other branch of government on who its members are. The negative side is that the members of each body are extremely reluctant to question the fitness of fellow Congressmen or Senators. If the members of one party go after a member of another party and call for his expulsion, the same process might come down on one of their own at some later time. Only with a two-thirds majority can a body expel one of its members. In other words, there must be clear and convincing evidence of the need to expel a member.

Each house must have a majority of members present to conduct business. This is called a quorum, the number needed to take official action. The quorum requirement prevents a small group from meeting to do something that the majority would not want to do. However, the minority has rights too. It can compel members to come to the chamber for business to be conducted. This is known as a quorum call. The right to call a quorum enables the minority to compel at least the possibility of taking action that it sees as necessary, if the majority is trying to avoid doing so.

Neither house may adjourn for more than three days during a session without the consent of the other. This keeps one body from paralyzing the work of Congress by simply refusing to meet. In actual practice, the leaders of both houses work together to determine the length of the sessions, when Congress will recess for vacations, and when the House and Senate will adjourn to end a session. The House and Senate may not decide to meet in a location other than where both have agreed to meet. This again prevents one body from meeting secretly or pulling away to disrupt business. These provisions have prevented the shenanigans that sometimes occur in the legislatures of other countries.

> *If you have ever watched the proceedings of Congress on C-SPAN or visited the Capitol while Congress was in session, you will have noticed that much time is spent with few members actually present on the floor of the House and Senate. Members can make speeches from the floor that will go on the public record, but the other members don't have to listen to them.*

Each house is to keep a journal of its proceedings and must publish the journal on a regular basis. This is the origin of the *Congressional Record*, which helps the American people keep up with the work of Congress and the speeches and debates in Congress. However, the *Congressional Record* has now ballooned to such an extent that the average citizen can hardly keep up with what Congress does. The House and the Senate allow members to revise their speeches before they appear in the *Record* and to include material in the *Record* that has never been spoken on the floor of either chamber. Members can simply insert into the *Record* what they want to have published under their names.

Section 6 (Part One): Salary

Members of Congress receive a salary and the payment of expenses from the United States Treasury. Under the Articles of Confederation, the states paid their own representatives in Congress. At first, members of Congress received $6.00 per day while Congress was in session. In 1815, the pay was increased to $1,500 per year. As of 2006, the salary for a member of Congress was $158,100 per year. The majority leader and minority leader in each house was paid $175,600, while the Speaker of the House received $203,000. A cost of living adjustment is made each year unless Congress votes not to accept it. These are good salaries, but salary is not by any means the entire picture of the financial benefits that accrue to a member of Congress.

Each member of Congress receives an allotment of about $1 million per year to hire staff workers, pay for office expenses in Washington and in their home district or state, and pay for other expenses related to their roles. Included in the expense account is the mail or franking privilege, which allows Congressional mail to be sent at government expense. In addition to regular correspondence and responses to constituent requests, the franking privilege allows for what are called informative mailings from members of Congress to addresses in their districts. These mailings inform residents (i.e., voters) about what a Senator or Congressman has accomplished. You might especially notice these as election time draws near; it's one of the perks of an incumbent. In all fairness, we should note that purely political campaign mailings must be paid for by campaign contributions.

Congress employs thousands of staff personnel. Members of the House have a total of over seven thousand staff members, while Senators hire over four thousand. Another twelve hundred workers are staff for the standing House committees, and about seven hundred more people work for the standing Senate committees. The political leaders (Speaker, majority and minority leaders, and so forth) in the House and Senate have even more staff available to them. These staff members do not include security and maintenance personnel, Library of Congress employees, and others whose work directly relates to Congress.

In addition, members of Congress receive health insurance coverage and participate in the Federal Employees Retirement System. If someone serves in Congress for at least five years, he or she is eligible to receive a pension. Members can receive a pension beginning at age 50 if they have twenty years of service, or at any age after twenty-five years of service, or after the age of 62 regardless of his length of service. The pension is based on years of service and the highest three years of salary. The starting pension cannot be more than 80% of the retiree's final salary. In 2004, 413 retired members of Congress were receiving government pensions based at least in part on service in Congress (some had held other positions in the Federal government as well). These pensions averaged about $3,900 per month each.

House Speaker Gillett and Vice President Coolidge Exercising in the House Gym, 1923

Members of Congress may earn up to fifteen percent of their salary from outside sources, such as speaking fees and legal fees; and they have no limit on what they can make from book royalties. Senators and Congressmen also enjoy many unofficial financial benefits from contributors, lobbyists, and special interest groups that want to influence how he or she votes. Congress has passed laws that eliminate blatant bribery, but the laws also carefully allow certain benefits (such as a company or contributor paying for a vacation as long as it is disclosed). Some former members of Congress work for Washington lobbying or consulting groups after their tenure in Congress and do quite well financially.

The 27th Amendment to the Constitution, first proposed in 1789 and finally ratified in 1992, says that a pay raise passed by Congress (a "law varying the compensation for the services of the Senators and Representatives") cannot go into effect until a Congressional election has taken place. The amendment was an attempt to prevent a sitting Congress from giving itself a pay increase. The automatic cost of living increases that Congress receives every year (enacted by Congress a few years ago) have been challenged in Federal court as a violation of this amendment, but Federal courts have held that such adjustments are not new salary laws and therefore do not violate the amendment. Of course, it should be noted that Congress sets the salaries for Federal judges; and pensions for retired Federal judges are based on the pensions for retired members of Congress.

Section 6 (Part Two): Immunity and Limitations

History tells of many times when kings had their political opponents arrested and executed. The framers wanted to protect members of Congress from this kind of political intimidation. As a result, Senators and Representatives cannot be arrested while attending a session of Congress or while going to or returning from such sessions, except if the charge is treason, felony, or breach of the peace. In addition, they cannot be made to face any criminal charges for anything they say in any speech or debate in Congress. This results in some outrageous statements, accusations, and outright lies being expressed on the floor of Congress with complete impunity.

A Senator or Representative while in office may not hold an appointed government position that was created or the pay for which was increased while he or she was in office. This prevents a member of Congress from helping to create a position or increasing the pay of a position and then filling that position. Likewise, no civil servant may serve as a Congressman or Senator. In the British Parliamentary system of government, ministers in the Cabinet are members of Parliament; but in the United States the branches of government are kept more separate.

It is not unusual, however, for a former member of Congress to be appointed by the president to a post in the executive branch. Bill Brock, for instance, was a Republican U.S. Congressman and Senator in the 1960s and 1970s. He later served as Secretary of Labor and then as U.S. Trade Representative in the Reagan Administration. Democratic Senator Jim Sasser was named Ambassador to China by President Clinton after Sasser was defeated for re-election.

> *For many years, Congress exempted itself from some of the laws that it passed. For instance, members of Congress were not part of the Social Security system until 1984. They participated in the Civil Service Retirement System, which was started fifteen years before Social Security began. In addition, members of Congress were not subject to civil rights laws in the hiring of their office staff. When Republicans regained control of Congress in 1994 after forty years of one or both houses having Democratic majorities, the first law passed by the new Congress in 1995 made Congress subject to the same laws that it enacts for the American people.*

Daniel Webster

These rules about what members of Congress may and may not do have been more carefully defined in recent years. In the past, the regulations were not so sharply drawn. Daniel Webster, for instance, while serving in Congress, argued cases before the Supreme Court as a private attorney. In addition, he also was for several years retained with pay as an attorney for the Bank of the United States. His role with the Bank came as the result of his support for the Bank and his national prominence. His income from the Bank (not to mention several favorable loans he received from the Bank) no doubt influenced his continued support of the Bank in Congress. Neither of these roles that Webster held actually violated the terms of this section of the Constitution, but the possibility for conflict of interest in such a situation is obvious.

He who profits illicitly troubles his own house,
but he who hates bribes will live.
Proverbs 15:27

Lesson 19—Who They Are and What They Do

Government is too big and too important to be left to the politicians.
—Chester Bowles (Twentieth century American diplomat & economist)

Members of Congress are not a cross-section of the American public in terms of race, gender, and wealth. Of course, the Constitution does not say that they have to be. Leaders are often the exception to the norm. By and large, Senators and Representatives are people who can afford long and expensive campaigns and who have accomplished a great deal in the legal, business, and political fields.

Statistics About the Members

The average Congressman is about 55 years old. The average Senator is about 60. Both of these averages are many years older than the minimum age requirements in the Constitution. This average age has increased in recent years, which perhaps is an indication that members of Congress are serving longer in office and that candidates are older when first elected to serve.

Of the 435 Representatives in the 109th Congress (which began in 2005), 65 were women; and of the 100 Senators, 14 were women. These numbers were the highest in history. About two-thirds of the women were Democrats, one-third Republican.

The 535 members of the House and Senate included 55 African-Americans, 25 Hispanics, five Asian-Americans, one Native American and one Asian-Indian. Just over half of the members of Congress listed their religious preference as Protestant Christian. About a third were Roman Catholic. There were 35 Jews and 15 Mormons in the 109th Congress. About half of the members of Congress were lawyers. One-third of the Senators listed their profession as businessman. In a recent Congress, about seventy Representatives and thirty Senators were millionaires, some of them multi-millionaires. It is highly unusual for a salaried or wage-earning man or woman to be elected to Congress. They usually don't have the time or money to conduct a campaign that can last for as long as a year. In a contested House race, the incumbent might spend $2 million and the challenger $1 million. The cost of Senate campaigns often runs into the multiple millions of dollars.

Most members have held elective office prior to being chosen to serve in Congress. Many Senators used to be Representatives, many Representatives used to be in state legislatures, and so forth.

Redecorating the U.S. Senate Chamber, 1925

Incumbency and Length of Service

Congress usually sees little turnover in its membership. The rule of thumb is that incumbents, those who are already in office and are seeking re-election, almost always win. Over the years, about 90% or more of incumbents have been re-elected. In 1996, for example, 361 of 384 House incumbents won re-election, and 19 of 21 Senators were re-elected.

Most House districts and Senate seats are considered safe for one party or the other. In a safe seat, the incumbent often has no or only token opposition because the opposition party does not want to waste its resources on what it sees as a hopeless cause. Even when an incumbent retires from a safe seat, someone from his or her party usually wins the next election. The drama that unfolds on election night concerning which party will control Congress usually centers on a relatively few races. A change in the party that holds a House or Senate seat often occurs (1) when a Congressman or Senator retires, creating what is called an open seat, (2) if a controversy has weakened the popularity of an incumbent, (3) if one political party targets a seat for defeat, or (4) if a presidential candidate enjoys a landslide victory and carries his party's Congressional candidates along on his coattails.

In the 106th Congress (1999-2001), only 41 or about ten percent of Representatives were freshmen (in their first term). Over half (236) had served between two and nine years, 104 had served between ten and nineteen years, 46 had served over twenty years, and seven

---

Term Limits

One issue that has received a fair amount of discussion is whether members of Congress should have term limits, a maximum number of terms or years that they can serve. The offices of President and state governors have term limits; but of course, it is the legislative bodies (not the executives) who propose term limits, usually in the form of constitutional amendments. Legislators are not likely to vote themselves out of a job.

The arguments in favor of term limits include the fact that incumbents have a great advantage over challengers in elections in terms of name recognition and in terms of what they can do and what they can promise to do for voters. This helps to make a real contest between an incumbent and a challenger quite rare. In addition, incumbents can become more concerned about taking care of themselves and their power than about doing what is best for the people. Long-term service seems to be a far cry from the citizen-representative ideal of everyday people serving only a few years, doing what they believe is genuinely best for the populace as a whole, and not building a personal power base for themselves.

Against the idea of term limits is the argument that voters should have enough sense and enough freedom to elect whom they want. If they want to re-elect the same person campaign after campaign, they should be able to do so. Previously holding an office should not be a disqualification for holding that office. In addition, representatives with long tenure have the seniority within the system to be given important positions and to get things done. All else being equal, an elected official who has been in office for a long time in the current system can do more for his home state or home district than a freshman can.

Perhaps the most convincing argument against imposing term limits is that we already have term limits. They are called elections. Every term of every elected office has a limit to it, and the person who holds that office has to run again or retire from it. The best solution to problems in the system is for the populace to stay informed and involved and to support good candidates.

had served for over thirty years. In the Senate, eight had served less than two years, 39 had been in the Senate between two and nine years, 33 had held their seats for ten to nineteen years, fourteen had served from 20 to 29 years, and six had served for over thirty years.

What Representatives and Senators Do

Senators and Congressmen represent their constituents in Congress and in the operation of the Federal government. This involves speaking and voting in official sessions, but it also means being an advocate in the Federal bureaucracy when a constituent has a need or a problem.

The most obvious work that a Senator or Congressman does involves considering and voting on legislation that comes before them on the chamber floor, but that is by far not all that they do. Much of their time is spent in committee work: attending hearings and considering research for bills that are before their committees. They also have informal discussions with their staff and with other members of their chamber (especially those of the same party) as they consider the merits of legislation and suggest changes. Members of Congress want to make sure that their districts are included when expenditures are planned in the Federal budget, so they or their staff will take time to talk with sponsors of legislation or members of the appropriations committees. They also meet with lobbyists who want to influence how he or she votes on a particular piece of legislation.

Members of the U.S. House of Representatives, c. 1920

Contact with their constituents is an important part of the work of a Senator or Representative. The offices of Representatives and Senators receive thousands of letters, phone calls, and emails every week from the folks back home. Some give praise while others offer criticism or ask questions. Often a constituent will seek help from his Congressman or Senator about a problem involving a Federal agency. Perhaps a Social Security payment has not been received, or someone needs help with an application for a loan from the Small Business Administration, for example. Congressional offices can provide passes to the visitor galleries if a constituent is planning a visit to Washington. Many times this correspondence is handled by the staff. The percentage of people who care enough about issues to write their representatives is very small; and these genuine, individualized letters do have an impact (probably even more than e-mail).

> It is good to know who your Senators and Congressman are. Make a note of their names, party affiliation, phone numbers, mailing addresses, and websites.

Always in the back of a member's mind is the next election. Members of Congress have to be involved in fund-raising; making calls and sending letters to stay in touch with party workers back home; developing publicity for newspapers, mailouts, and their websites; and meeting with visiting groups. A considerable amount of time can be spent in traveling between the home state and Washington.

Members sometimes go on international trips (called junkets) to meet with foreign political leaders, visit troops stationed at overseas bases, or engage in fact-finding work regarding trade, immigration, or other topics. These trips are regulated

Senate Page Boys at School, c. 1920

as to length and cost, but Congressmen can extend their trip at their own expense. If several members travel together, it is called a congressional delegation trip. Some travel by members can be paid for by private companies. For example, if a company wants to build a factory in another country, it can pay for a trip by the relevant committee chairmen in Congress to get their support if any regulations or treaties will be needed.

A good name is to be more desired than great wealth,
favor is better than silver and gold.
Proverbs 22:1

Reading

- "On a Visit to the Senate When He Was Twelve" from *The Education of Henry Adams* by Henry Adams (*WHTT*, p. 99)

Washington Monument

A visit to Washington, D.C. is a wonderful experience. Historic sites and historic monuments are everywhere, and you can learn a great deal about the operation of your Federal government. In addition to being able to get passes to visit the galleries of the House and Senate, you might be able to attend a committee hearing. It is best to contact the Representative's office several weeks in advance. Members want to be available to constituents who visit Washington, so you might even be able to arrange a brief visit with your Senator or Congressman.

Lesson 20—Committee and Political Party Organization

Anyone who is unfamiliar with what Congress actually does and how it does it, with all its duties and all its occupations, with all its devices of management and resources of power, is very far from a knowledge of the constitutional system under which we live.
— *Woodrow Wilson,* Congressional Government *(1885)*

Two realities, neither of which are mentioned in the Constitution, have a profound influence on the way Congress operates. These realities are political parties and the Congressional committee system.

The House chooses its Speaker or chairman along with its other officers. The vice president of the United States is the president or chairman of the Senate, and the Senate chooses a president pro tempore and other officers. Nothing in the Constitution suggests that these positions of leadership are to be political prizes, but that is what they quickly became and what they remain today. In fact, many of the Founding Fathers feared the influence of what they called factions, or groups that align themselves together to promote a certain candidate or agenda. Today we call those factions political parties.

The Party Spirit

Party alignment developed in the earliest days of the government. Representatives and Senators who favored a strong central government tended to combine themselves around leaders such as John Adams and Alexander Hamilton and were called Federalists. Those who favored strictly limiting the power of the central government and

Political Cartoon Showing a Democratic Donkey and a Republican Elephant

who promoted the power of the states gathered around Thomas Jefferson and came to be known as Republicans. The Federalists began to lose power after Thomas Jefferson became President in 1801, and the party eventually faded away. As the idea of democracy became more acceptable, the Republicans came to be called Democratic Republicans and finally, by the time of Andrew Jackson, Democrats. For a time it was the only major party, but factions within the party still allowed for plenty of political competition.

Opponents of Jackson came together as the Whig party in the 1830s. The Democrats generally favored protection of slavery in the states and wanted to have the freedom to expand slavery into the territories, while the Whigs were against the expansion of slavery outside of the states where it already existed. In the 1850s the Whig Party fell apart and a new party, the Republicans, was formed that took a harder stance against the expansion of slavery. From just before the Civil War until today, the two major political parties in the United States have been the Republicans and the Democrats. Minor parties have occasionally emerged, and several exist today, including the Constitution Party, Green Party, and Libertarian Party; but they have not as yet been able to challenge the power of the two main parties.

The Speaker of the House

In 2007 Nancy Pelosi became the first female to serve as Speaker of the House.

The Speaker is the most powerful member of the House. Since the Representatives generally vote along party lines, the majority party in the House is able to name the Speaker. The Speaker presides and maintains order during House sessions, but on a practical basis the Speaker often does not use his or her time this way. This role is frequently filled by a temporary chairman who is also chosen by the House. Most of the Speaker's important work is done behind the scenes. The Speaker decides which committees consider bills that are proposed, and he or she has a major influence on which bills come to the floor for a vote.

The Speaker can vote on all matters that come before the House, but to participate in debate he must appoint a temporary chairman to take his place. The Constitution makes no other provision for organization in the House.

President of the Senate

The vice president of the United States is the president of the Senate. In his absence, the president pro tempore (from the Latin meaning *for a time*) presides. Since the vice president is not a member of the Senate, he cannot vote except to break a tie.

In practical terms, the vice president rarely presides over meetings of the Senate. John Adams regularly served as chairman of meetings in the first Senate while he was Vice President, but today the vice president has many more pressing (and many more politically valuable) obligations to perform. The routine sessions of the Senate, like those in the House, are usually not that electrifying or pivotal. The vice president will preside if a close vote is expected or in other extraordinary circumstances.

The Role of Parties in Congress

Party alignment has come to be the way the House and Senate are organized and how legislation is considered. The Speaker is the leading member of the majority party in the House. In addition, each party has a leader (called the majority leader and the minority leader) and assistant leaders (called majority and minority whips) in both the House and in the Senate. These leaders determine what bills will come to the floor for consideration, and then they try to influence the members of their respective parties to vote in a particular way when those bills come up.

The party's plans are discussed at a meeting of the party's members in a given chamber, which is called a caucus (House Democratic Caucus, Senate Republican Caucus, and so forth).

To encourage members to vote the party line, party leaders might appeal to party principles (or to the dire consequences of the opposition's success), or they might offer to see about funding a program for a Congressman's district, or they could agree to appoint a Senator or Representative to a particular committee in exchange for his vote. If a member decides not to vote the way that the majority of his party votes, he or she might be overlooked when funding for programs is planned or when a committee position becomes vacant.

The Committee System

Much of the work of the Senate and the House takes place in committees. Committees study bills that are introduced, conduct investigations that might lead to new legislation, and hear testimony from Administration officials and other experts regarding matters of interest. Each standing or permanent committee and its subcommittees has a subject area on which it works, such as trade, immigration, crime, or homeland security. Sometimes a bill might be examined by more than one committee.

Standing Committees of the Senate	**Standing Committees of the House of Representatives**

Agriculture, Nutrition, and Forestry
Appropriations
Armed Services
Banking, Housing, and Urban Affairs
Budget
Commerce, Science, and Transportation
Energy and Natural Resources
Environment and Public Works
Finance
Foreign Relations
Health, Education, Labor, and Pensions
Homeland Security and Government Affairs
Judiciary
Rules and Administration
Small Business and Entrepreneurship
Veterans Affairs
 	
**Special, Select,
and Other Senate Committees**
 	
Indian Affairs
Select Committee on Ethics
Select Committee on Intelligence
Select Committee on Aging
	Agriculture
	Appropriations
	Armed Services
	Budget
	Education and the Workforce
	Energy and Commerce
	Financial Services
	Government Reform
	Homeland Security
	House Administration
	International Relations
	Judiciary
	Resources
	    (Natural Resources and Environment)
	Rules
	Science
	Small Business
	Standards of Official Conduct
	Transportation and Infrastructure
	Veterans Affairs
	Ways and Means
	Permanent Select Committee on
	    Intelligence

Joint Committees (with members from both the House and Senate)	
Joint Committee on Printing Joint Committee on Taxation	Joint Committee on the Library of Congress Joint Economic Committee

Members of Congress want to be appointed to committees that have special relevance to their home districts and states. Many Midwestern Congressmen, for instance, want to serve on the Agricultural Committees. Representatives from Florida, Texas, and California might want to be named to committees that deal with immigration policy.

A few committees are considered the most prestigious. The Armed Services Committees in both houses work on military policy. The Senate Judiciary Committee, among other tasks, considers nominations for Federal judgeships. The House Ways and Means Committee handles revenue and spending legislation and serves as a steering committee for much of the legislation that comes before the House. The role of chairman of a committee usually goes to the member of the majority party who has served the longest on that committee.

House Judiciary Subcommittee Hearing, 1974

The committee system is one way in which the majority party exercises great power in the House and Senate. The majority party chooses all of the committee chairmen and a majority of committee members. Obviously, legislation that the majority party supports will be what is actively considered. Each committee also has what is called a ranking member, who is the committee's longest-serving member from the minority party.

In the next unit we will see how bills that are introduced in Congress make their way through a set process in order to become law. We will also see the role that committees and political parties play in passing and defeating proposed legislation.

And there occurred a great uproar;
and some of the scribes of the Pharisaic party stood up
and began to argue heatedly, saying,
"We find nothing wrong with this man;
suppose a spirit or an angel has spoken to him?"
Acts 23:9

Reading

- "The House of Representatives" from *Congressional Government* by Woodrow Wilson (*WHTT*, p. 101)

5 Article I— Congress (Part 2)

The first two lessons in this unit tell how a bill that is introduced in Congress becomes law. The next two lessons tell what Congress can do and what limitations Congress and state governments have. Finally, we look at the process of impeachment.

Lessons in This Unit

Lesson 21—How a Bill Becomes Law (Part 1)
Lesson 22—How a Bill Becomes Law (Part 2)
Lesson 23—The Powers of Congress
Lesson 24—Limitations on Congress and the States
Lesson 25—When Powers Collide: The Process of Impeachment

Activity Ideas

Devise a bill that you would like to see Congress pass. Make a list of the benefits and possible objections, and determine what you would have to do and whom you would have to influence to get it passed. What public relations campaign might you try to carry out with the public to get their support? Who might support your bill, and who might oppose it?

Watch the movie *Mr. Smith Goes to Washington* starring Jimmy Stewart.

If you are using the optional *Quiz and Exam Book*, answer the questions for each lesson after you have completed the lesson and read any assigned readings in *We Hold These Truths*. After you have completed Lesson 25, take the quiz for Unit 5 and the first exam, which covers Units 1-5.

Lesson 21—How a Bill Becomes Law (Part 1)

All government,—indeed, every human benefit and enjoyment, every virtue and every prudent act,—is founded on compromise and barter.
> *—Edmund Burke, "Speech on the Conciliation of America," 1775*

(Read Section 7 of Article I of the U.S. Constitution.)

Article I, Section 7 offers the barest outline of how a bill before Congress can become law. The rules that Congress has established for itself in filling out this Constitutional provision have added more steps to the process. This lesson and the next one discuss this procedure that Congress and the president follow. The way that laws are enacted in Congress is largely the same as that followed in state legislatures.

Introducing a Bill

Any member of Congress may introduce legislation. Moreover, a member of Congress must introduce a bill for Congress to consider it. The president might want a bill to be introduced in Congress, and popular sentiment about an issue might be riding high; but a member of the House or Senate has to introduce a bill in Congress before any idea can become law.

The bill that is introduced might be written by the member himself, one of his or her staff, someone in the president's administration, or a combination of such people. A bill can originate in either chamber, except that the Constitution requires revenue bills to originate in the House (the body closest to the direct will of the people). In the House, a member merely hands his or her bill to the clerk or puts it into a box called the hopper. In the Senate, a Senator must be recognized by the chairman to announce the introduction of a bill.

Each bill is assigned a number (for example, HR100 or S100, the letters standing for House of Representatives and Senate), labeled with the sponsor's name, and sent to the Government Printing Office for copies to be made. A bill can be sponsored by more than one member. Proposed legislation may be in one of four forms, each of which must follow a particular style that has been established by the rules of Congress.

- A bill, the most common form, calls for the enactment of regulations or the spending of money on a work. The bill might create a program for a limited, specified time; or it might propose a permanent change in Federal law. The proposed legislation can be either a public bill or a private bill. Public bills apply to the entire country, while a private bill relates to one specific area, group, or person. A private bill might be a commitment to pay a disputed invoice for work done or a law regarding funds for a national park along the Gulf Coast.

- A joint resolution is similar to a bill. It can be introduced in either house, and it will often include a preamble explaining the purpose of the proposed legislation. These documents are designated as H.J. Res. or S.J. Res.

- A concurrent resolution affects the operation of or states the opinion of both houses of Congress. This legislation is not sent to the president for his signature since it merely expresses the will of Congress. These proposals are designated H. Con. Res. or S. Con. Res.

- A simple resolution (H. Res. or S. Res.) involves the operation of or opinion of one house of Congress. It is not sent to the other chamber for its approval, nor is it sent to the president for his signature.

Authorization and Appropriation Bills

Congress often considers two different kinds of legislation for the same subject. An authorization bill legally establishes (or continues) a program, agency, or department. This authorization can be for one year or for a longer period. The authorization bill will usually include a maximum amount of money the new program will be permitted to spend.

However, a separate appropriation law is needed to appropriate or earmark money for the program to begin. The appropriation bill will often provide less money than the authorization bill requested. It is possible for a program to be authorized by Congress but then have no money appropriated for it. Authorization bills are prepared by the various committees of Congress, while appropriation bills are prepared by the House and Senate appropriations committees that oversee the entire Federal budget.

This process of involving two bills and two committees on the same matter increases the complexity of an already complex Federal system. Moreover, it is possible for a Senator or Congressman to have it both ways. He can tell one group that he voted for (to authorize) a particular program, but then he can tell another group that he voted against funding (appropriating money for) that same program.

Your Tax Dollars at Work

Congress must pass a law for the government to be able to spend money (Article I, Section 9, Paragraph 7). These funding laws can take three different forms.

(1) A *mandatory* program is one that is so well established that Congress sees itself as having no option but to continue it. Social Security payments and funds to subsidize housing for the poor are two examples of what Congress calls mandatory spending. These mandatory expenditures are sometimes called entitlement programs because Congress has said that citizens who qualify are entitled to receive this money. About half of the Federal budget is considered mandatory spending because (1) members like to make sure that their pet projects are always funded and (2) members do not like to vote on expensive and controversial projects. Renewed consideration of a project can bring about the possibility that it will be voted down.

(2) *Discretionary* programs are those about which Congress feels it has a choice. This kind of funding pays for a program that has a specific ending date. Money to help hurricane victims is a discretionary program that would need a new law to be passed for it to continue.

(3) Congress often gets into heated debates about the Federal budget. When this happens, sometimes Congress does not pass the laws that are needed to continue paying for some government operations before the end of the fiscal year. The Federal fiscal year runs

from October 1 of one year to September 30 of the following calendar year. If a new budget is not passed in time, Congress will often pass a *continuing resolution*, which usually continues spending at the level of the previous fiscal year.

Consideration by Committee

When a bill or resolution is introduced, it is assigned by the House Speaker or by the Senate's presiding officer to a committee for its consideration. Committees have time to examine only a relatively few pieces of legislation in each session of Congress. The chairman of a committee has a great deal of power in deciding what bills the committee will study. By far most bills that are introduced are never considered, and they die in committee. A Congressman or Senator might introduce the same bill over and over again, every time a new Congress convenes.

As a committee studies a bill, it might call for testimony from technical experts, members of the Administration, or citizens who have an interest in the legislation. The committee might engage in debate among its members or hear reports from committee staff persons about their research. Sometimes committees suggest changes to the bill's content.

Committees can also engage in investigations on topics that are not related to specific pieces of legislation but that are subjects which committee members want to study. When the president nominates someone for a Cabinet position, the appropriate Senate committee will conduct hearings into the nominee's qualifications. Special committees are formed to look into especially controversial or serious topics.

After a committee conducts hearings on a bill, it often holds what is called a markup session, in which the members go over every aspect of the bill and mark it up with proposed changes. These proposals then become part of the committee's recommendation if it votes to send the bill to the full chamber.

If the committee considering a bill decides to take action on it, the committee will vote. If it passes, it is said to be voted out or reported out to the entire House or Senate. If the bill is defeated in committee, it is usually dead. On rare occasions a committee will decide to let a bill or a nomination be considered by the entire chamber even though a majority of committee members opposed it.

What happens when a bill makes it out of committee and reaches the floor of Congress is described in the next lesson.

Lobbying

An informal but important influence on the workings of the Federal government are lobbyists. Representatives of groups that seek to influence laws and policies are called lobbyists because the traditional site of their conversations with lawmakers is not in the chamber itself but in the lobby outside of the chamber. The term "special interest group" is also used to describe a group which seeks to influence Congress.

All lobbyists must register with the government, and they must abide by strict rules regarding what they can say and do and what favors they can bestow on government officials. Outright payments to members are against the law. About 35,000 lobbyists, representing hundreds of groups, work in Washington. These groups spend a total of over one billion dollars each year trying to influence government laws and policies. We usually associate lobbyists with the work of Congress, but lobbyists can also try to influence the president or other officials in the executive branch of government.

Lobbyists represent a wide variety of interests: labor unions, individual corporations (for instance, companies that build military equipment), industry groups (such as the lumber industry, tobacco companies, drug manufacturers, insurance companies, automakers, etc.), public interest causes such as environmental protection and child safety, and even foreign governments that want favorable trade relations or perhaps military supplies. Lobbyists might be people who are experts in their fields, or they might be former Congressmen or former employees of government agencies who know members of Congress and are familiar with how to get things done in Washington.

A lobbyist will meet with a member of Congress (or, perhaps more often, a member's staff) and provide information about how a proposed bill might affect a particular group or interest. Drug company lobbyists, for instance, would explain how importing drugs from Canada could hurt their profits. A tobacco representative might encourage a law to limit liability payments that tobacco companies have to make as a result of lawsuits. Automakers will want to give input on how proposed safety requirements for cars will cost them more money. Groups that have a political agenda might try to make a nominee to the Supreme Court appear dangerous or unreliable with regard to protecting personal freedoms. Lobbyists give special attention to members of Congressional committees that consider legislation relevant to their causes. In addition, special interest groups might try to influence executive departments to develop new regulations or to back off strict enforcement of existing regulations.

More indirect means of exerting pressure include advertising campaigns aimed at the general population, in the hope that voters will encourage their Senators and Representatives to vote a certain way. Public interest groups and industry organizations sometimes send press releases to newspapers and broadcasters, hoping that the media will carry a story favorable to their point of view.

Lobbyists can provide good information about their causes that members of Congress should consider. Their efforts are part of the free exchange of ideas in an open society. However, their money and organizational power can sometimes exert an improper influence on government policy. When this happens, the process gets out of hand. Activities that take place behind the scenes are sometimes illegal. In 2005 a Republican Congressman from California resigned his seat after admitting that he took over two million dollars in payoffs, mostly from defense contractors, in return for using his influence to steer contracts their way. The same year, a lobbyist associated with Republican causes was arrested after a long criminal investigation that looked into alleged illegal activities.

Left out in the cold far too often in the legislative process are the average citizens who do not have the time or money to engage in organized lobbying but who pay for government programs through taxes or higher costs for goods and services that come as a result of increased regulations. Some groups, such as People for the American Way and Common Cause, claim to speak for the average American; but such groups usually have an ideological agenda of their own. Truly non-partisan groups are rare and usually wield little influence.

Make my joy complete by being of the same mind,
maintaining the same love,
united in spirit, intent on one purpose.
Philippians 2:2

Lesson 22—How a Bill Becomes Law (Part 2)

Man's capacity for justice makes democracy possible, but man's inclination to injustice makes democracy necessary.

—*Reinhold Niebuhr (theologian), 1944*

In the 107th Congress, which met in the years 2001 and 2002, almost 9,000 bills and 178 joint resolutions were introduced. The majority of both kinds of legislation were initiated in the House. In a typical session, only a few hundred bills are voted on; and only a portion of those become law. And, no, the members of Congress do not read all of the bills—not even all of the ones they vote on.

The previous lesson described how a bill is introduced and assigned to a committee. This lesson surveys the process that Congress follows for a bill that is reported out of committee to the floor of the House or Senate.

Making It to the Floor

A bill approved by a committee is placed on the House or Senate calendar and scheduled for consideration by the full chamber. It is possible for a bill to be reported out and still not be considered on the floor, if the political leaders decide not to pursue it or if Congress simply runs out of time. On the floor, members debate what they see as the merits and the dangers of the bill. They can also propose amendments.

If a bill passes one house, it is sent to the other chamber where the entire process begins again. The relevant committee in the other chamber might already have considered a similar or identical bill to speed up the process. If a bill passes both houses in identical form, it is sent to the president. If the second chamber makes any amendments to the bill, it is referred to a conference committee made up of members of both houses. The conference committee comes up with a form that it recommends to both houses, and both houses vote on the conference committee version. If it passes in both houses, it is sent to the president.

Filibuster

The House has adopted strict rules governing floor debates on legislation because of the number of members it has. The time that each member is permitted to speak is limited to a relatively few minutes. In the Senate, however, the rules of debate are more relaxed; and Senators may speak for longer periods. One technique that Senators sometimes use to block a vote is called a filibuster, a term which comes from a Dutch word meaning pirate. Filibusters were once allowed in the House as well, but its increasing membership made its elimination there essential.

In a filibuster, one or more Senators who oppose a bill gain control of the floor and talk—and talk, and talk. They do not necessarily have to talk about the legislation. They can talk about the weather, read recipes, recite historical documents, and say anything they wish. Their goal is to delay and disrupt the work of the Senate to such an extent that supporters of the bill give up and either agree to amendments or abandon it altogether so that the Senate can move on to other business. The majority sometimes tries to wear down the filibusterer by holding day and night sessions to make him talk continuously for several hours straight. As long as a filibusterer holds the floor, he can continue for as long as he is physically able. The longest non-stop filibuster by a single Senator was for just over 24 hours by Strom Thurmond of South Carolina in 1957 in opposition to a civil rights bill. A group of Southern Senators conducted a filibuster to oppose another civil rights bill in 1964.

Senator Strom Thurmond, 1951

Even a filibuster, however, has a limit. In 1917, President Woodrow Wilson asked for a law permitting the U.S. government to arm merchant marine vessels against attacks by German submarines. The measure passed the House by an overwhelming majority and was favored by a large majority of the Senate; however, a small group of Senators was able to filibuster against it, and they eventually killed the bill. Wilson fumed, "[The] Senate of the United States is the only legislative body in the world which can not act when its majority is ready for action. A little group of willful men, representing no opinion but their own, have rendered the great government of the United States helpless and contemptible."

The President proposed a rule change that would allow a vote to end debate. This rule is called cloture; and the rule that was established says that if two-thirds of the Senate votes to end debate, it must end. The new rule was used two years later to end a filibuster against the Treaty of Versailles following World War I. Cloture was also called to end the filibuster against the civil rights bill in 1964. In 1975, the majority needed to bring cloture was reduced to three-fifths, or sixty of the one hundred Senators.

An actual filibuster rarely takes place. Today, all that has to happen is that forty-one Senators merely indicate that they will support a filibuster (or, alternatively, not vote for cloture). Filibustering generates negative publicity, but the threat of it is still a potent weapon for a minority of the Senate to use.

The House and Senate can give a voice vote on a bill and the presiding officer simply decides whether the bill is accepted or defeated. A rarely-used option is for the members to divide physically and go to different sides of the chamber to be counted. Twenty percent of the members can request a roll call; and this is how most voting is done, especially on major legislation. Since 1973, the House has used an electronic voting system to record votes. Members have a set period of time (usually several minutes) to record their votes. The Senate does not use an electronic system. It generally gives members a fifteen-minute period (which the presiding officer can extend at his discretion) in which Senators can come by the desk of the Senate clerk to tell him or her how they are voting. The clerk then announces the votes of each Senator orally. During these voting periods, members mill around the Senate floor talking to each other. Sometimes members are called to the floor from their offices or committee meetings to cast votes.

Playing the Game

Legislation before Congress can have all sorts of interesting side angles. For instance, members can propose amendments to a bill that have nothing to do with the main purpose of the bill, in the hope that they can get a pet project approved as part of a popular or needed piece of legislation. For example, an amendment to fund improvements to bridges in one member's district or state can be attached to a bill that provides money for the Department of Defense. A research grant for a university department can be made part of a law that deals with hurricane relief. These are called earmarks or pork barrel amendments because they add on fat dipped from the barrel of Federal funds (i.e., taxpayer money). Congress usually approves the bill even with the extraneous amendments because (1) the major purpose of the legislation is seen as necessary and worth the extra cost and (2) next time, someone who opposed this project might want funding for something else in his or her district.

Pork Barrel Cartoon

Members of Congress sometimes trade votes to help each other get what they want for their individual districts. For instance, a Congressman from a seacoast area might work out a deal in which he will vote for increasing farm price supports if a Congressman from an agricultural state agrees to support continued funding for a naval base in the coastal Representative's district. It's a matter of "I'll scratch your back if you'll scratch mine," and in this way majorities are built to pass legislation.

Some laws enacted by Congress are called unfunded mandates. This means that Congress creates new requirements for states and localities to follow but does not provide the funding needed to meet those requirements. For instance, Congress might pass a law saying that schools must improve literacy levels by a certain percentage by a certain date in order to continue receiving Federal funds for other programs, but the law provides no money for schools to hire additional reading teachers. How the mandate is to be met is left up to state departments of education and local school districts to figure out and pay for.

The President's Options

When a bill has passed Congress and goes to the president, he has three options:

(1) He can sign the bill, at which time it becomes law.

(2) He can veto the bill and send it back to Congress with his objections. If two-thirds of both houses approve the bill, the action is called overriding the veto; and the bill becomes law without the president's signature. A two-thirds majority is not easy to achieve. One party rarely has a two-thirds majority in both houses, and few bills obtain that level of bipartisan support. As a result, presidential vetoes are usually not overridden.

(3) He can do nothing. If Congress remains in session for ten more days (not counting Sundays), the bill becomes law without the president's signature. This is called a pocket

veto, by which the president expresses his disapproval of the bill but admits that the bill would probably pass Congress over his veto. If Congress adjourns before ten days have elapsed, the bill does not become law. This prevents foolish, last-minute bills passed by Congress from becoming law.

> *When Congress proposes an amendment to the Constitution, it does not go to the president for his signature. Instead, the joint resolution goes to the Archivist of the United States who submits it to the states for them to consider for ratification.*

As you can see, a bill has to follow a complicated procedure to become law. It faces many hurdles and roadblocks. While this process can prevent unwise legislation from becoming law, it can also keep good proposals from being enacted.

When there are many words, transgression is unavoidable,
but he who restrains his lips is wise.
Proverbs 10:19

Reading

- "It's Time to End the Filibuster Rule" by Ray Notgrass (*WHTT*, p. 120)

President Lyndon Johnson Signing the Medicare Bill, 1965

Lesson 23—The Powers of Congress

Let the end be legitimate, let it be within the scope of the constitution, and all means which are appropriate, which are plainly adapted to that end, which are not prohibited, but consist with the letter and spirit of the constitution, are constitutional.
　　　　　　　　　　　　　—*John Marshall*, McCulloch v. Maryland *(1819)*

(Read Section 8 of Article I of the U.S. Constitution.)

The areas of governmental activity in which Congress is empowered to act are outlined in the Constitution. The intention of the framers was that these powers be enumerated (listed) and that they be limited to that list. This is stated specifically in the Tenth Amendment: "The powers not delegated to the United States by the Constitution, nor prohibited by it to the States, are reserved to the States respectively, or to the people." If Congress did not specifically have a power given to it in the Constitution, it was not to legislate in that area.

In other words, the Constitution tells what Congress may do and what the states may not do. Any other powers are reserved to the states and to the people, not to Congress. However, Congress has generally found ways to do what it wants to do; and usually the only thing that gets in the way of Congressional action is the Supreme Court overturning a law as unconstitutional.

Financial Matters

Section 8 of Article I lists the powers of Congress. All of these are fairly specific, except the last clause, which we shall discuss below. In our treatment of these enumerated powers we will define terms that may be relatively unfamiliar to us today.

The Constitution gives Congress the power to *impose and collect taxes, duties, imposts, and excises*. A tax is a payment to the government for a given reason (a sales tax paid when purchasing an item, for instance) or on a given value owned by a citizen (a tax on the value of property that a person owns is one example). Duties and imposts are taxes paid on items being imported into the country. They must be paid by the business bringing the goods into the country. As the Supreme Court stated in *Flint v. Stone Tracy Co.* (1910), "Excise taxes are those laid upon the manufacture, sale or consumption of commodities within the country, upon licenses to pursue certain occupations, and upon corporate privileges." Excise taxes are imposed on such activities as the buying of tobacco or the manufacture of alcoholic beverages. These taxes are also associated with optional or luxury items such as jewelry, expensive boats, and the like. The government figures that if you want to use tobacco, for instance, you will be willing to pay higher taxes to do so. Excise taxes do not usually arouse as much opposition as regular sales taxes or income taxes.

Duties, imposts, and excises are to be uniform throughout the country. Congress may not impose higher duties on imports or higher excise taxes in one part of the country than in another. This prevents Congress from punishing or favoring one port or one state over another. It also enables states and cities to develop their economies without undue advantage or disadvantage from the Federal government.

Congress also has the authority and the responsibility to *pay the debts of the government, provide for the defense of the nation, and promote the general welfare.* This is what the Federal government may do with the revenue it takes in.

Borrowing Money

The Federal government has the authority to borrow money to pay for its operations. One common situation for borrowing money is for military expenses. When the United States becomes involved in war, the military needs equipment and supplies immediately. The government borrows the money to pay for these supplies and hopes to pay it back over several years after the military threat has passed. Non-military borrowing takes place to pay for other programs. The government hopes that these expenditures will stimulate the economy and produce enough revenue to pay back the loans.

World War I Poster

Whenever the United States government pays out in expenditures more than it takes in through revenues, it must borrow money to meet those obligations. The most common ways that the government borrows money today are (1) through U.S. Savings Bonds and Treasury notes, by which Americans loan money to the government, and (2) through loans from banks and foreign investors. Of course, borrowed money has to be paid back, usually with interest; so the short-term gain of having more money to spend brings with it the long-term pain of having to pay back more than was borrowed. When the Federal government spends more than it takes in through revenues in a given year, this is called an annual budget deficit. The accumulation of deficits that have occurred over the years is called the national debt.

For fiscal 2006 the Federal budget was about $2.77 trillion. The budget deficit was almost $400 billion that year, which the government borrowed and added to its debt. In November of 2005 the national debt was just over $8 trillion. We will discuss taxes, budgets, and deficits in greater detail in a later lesson.

Commerce and Other National Concerns

Congress *regulates trade or commerce* with foreign nations, among the states, and with Indian tribes. It would not be good for individual states to make their own trade agreements with other countries or for states to get into trade wars between themselves. Trade with Native American tribes has turned out to be a tiny part of the American economy.

Congress has the authority to legislate in several areas where consistent and uniform laws are needed throughout the country: overseeing naturalization (citizenship requirements for immigrants), establishing bankruptcy laws (states could have conflict if some were easier places in which to file for bankruptcy), coining money and regulating its value, establishing uniform weights and measures, punishing counterfeiters, maintaining post offices and building roads to enable mail delivery, and making patent and copyright laws for inventors and authors. Congress is also authorized to create courts that are inferior to the Supreme Court. The courts that Congress has established are Federal district courts, courts of appeal, and a few specialized courts (such as those related to maritime issues). These will be discussed in more detail in Unit 8.

Military Affairs

The armed forces have been essential to America's continued freedom. However, many times in history military leaders have threatened the peace of their own country and even become dictators. The founders of our country learned from the experience of history and made the military subject to civilian control. Moreover, they divided the oversight of the military between the legislative and executive branches to further ensure that the military would not become a threat to domestic or world peace.

Congress is empowered to oversee matters related to the armed forces and to naval issues. It has the authority to declare war. Congress can pass laws related to piracy and regarding felonies that involve American shipping. It can grant letters of marque and reprisal. These letters are documents issued by a government to a private citizen, authorizing him to seize the goods of a foreign party or nation that has attacked or seized property belonging to the United States or to a U.S. citizen. Marque means border, referring here to a national border. A person to whom a letter of marque and reprisal is issued is called a privateer. Without this official authority from a government, a person engaged in such reprisals could be considered a pirate under international law. A letter of marque and reprisal usually includes limitations on what a privateer can do or how much he can seize, lest his reprisal go beyond the original damages. Congress is also authorized to pass laws related to persons, ships, or goods of enemy nations that are seized by American forces.

Members of the 101st Airborne Division in Iraq, 2006

Congress can raise and pay for an army and a navy and make rules regarding what these military forces can do. No appropriation for the military is to last for more than two years. The framers did not want to fund a standing army that could be a threat to either domestic or international peace. As a result, military appropriations must be approved by Congress every year or two.

Congress can also call up state militias (now called the National Guard) to carry out Federal laws, suppress rebellions, and turn back foreign invaders. Presidents Eisenhower and Kennedy federalized state National Guard units to enforce civil rights laws in the 1950s and 1960s. Congress must authorize payment for militia units thus Federalized. In the early years of the country, states oversaw the appointment of militia officers and the training of the militias. Through the Civil War, officer commissions in state units were often awarded to men of prominent families or to political supporters of state officials without regard to military training or ability. Today the National Guard is considered a part of the Army and follows Army regulations. The Guard can be called upon to perform either state responsibilities, such as helping with natural disasters, or Federal responsibilities, including overseas assignments.

Oversight of the District of Columbia

Congress governs the District of Columbia, which is the seat of the Federal government. The location of the ten square mile district was chosen to be between Virginia and Maryland as part of the deal to get Virginia to support the Constitution. George Washington selected the actual site, which is near his home of Mount Vernon. Virginia took back its portion in 1847. At first, Federal City was a small area within the District (as were Georgetown and other localities), but now Washington and the District share the same boundaries.

Mount Vernon

The local government that Congress has allowed in the District has taken various forms throughout the years (elected city council, territorial government, and appointed overseers). In 1973 Congress granted the district the right to elect a mayor and city council for the first time in about one hundred years. Residents of the District do not have representation in Congress, but District voters have three electoral votes in presidential elections.

The "Necessary and Proper" Clause

The last paragraph of Section 8 has been called the "Necessary and Proper" clause or the Elastic clause, because it gives Congress broad and undefined authority to make all laws which are "necessary and proper" for carrying out the powers of the Federal government that had just been enumerated. Many times what has been necessary and proper has not been a matter of controversy. For instance, nothing is said in the Constitution about an air force; but the realities of twentieth century warfare made an air force a necessary and proper part of the American military. The U.S. Air Force began as part of the Army and became a separate branch of service after World War II.

On the other hand, the Elastic clause has also been used to justify a steady expansion of the areas in which Congress has chosen to legislate. A major role for the Supreme Court has become making decisions on whether laws passed by Congress are actually within the bounds of its Constitutional authority. Even if this clause had not been in the Constitution, some battles would probably have developed over Congressional authority.

In *The Federalist* Number 41, James Madison said that the powers of the Federal government enumerated in the Constitution were the "necessary means of attaining a necessary end," that end being a viable national government. Usually in human affairs, he said, "the choice must always be made, if not of the lesser evil, at least of the GREATER, not the PERFECT, good; and that in every political institution, a power to advance the public happiness involves a discretion which may be misapplied and abused."

This thinking guided the framers. Since they were aware of how one man or a small group might abuse government powers, they sought to limit the powers of government in order to give the people as much freedom over their lives and as much control of the government as possible. They saw government as something good and necessary but not as the source of all blessings for every citizen.

A just balance and scales belong to the Lord;
all the weights of the bag are His concern.
Proverbs 16:11

Lesson 24—Limitations
on Congress and the States

The number of individuals employed under the Constitution of the United States will be much smaller than the number employed under the particular States. . . . The powers delegated by the proposed Constitution to the Federal government are few and defined. Those which are to remain in the State governments are numerous and indefinite.
—*James Madison*, The Federalist *Number 45 (1788)*

(Read Sections 9 and 10 of Article I of the U.S. Constitution.)

It was not enough that the powers of Congress be enumerated in the Constitution. The framers wanted Congress to be expressly excluded from certain key areas. They also felt the need to address certain issues regarding the powers of the states.

Section 9: What Congress May Not Do

Ban the Slave Trade Before 1808. The delicately-phrased opening paragraph of Section 9 forbade Congress from banning the importation of slaves before 1808. However, Congress could impose an import duty on each person, not to exceed ten dollars per person. This clause was part of the compromise regarding how slavery was to be handled in the new nation.

Suspend Writs of Habeas Corpus. The right to have a writ of habeas corpus was not to be denied except in cases of rebellion or invasion, when such suspension would be deemed necessary. *Habeas corpus* is a Latin phrase meaning "You have the body." The writ is a statement by an arresting authority explaining why a person is being held in custody. This ban was to keep the Federal government from jailing political opponents without giving them a reason. During the Civil War, Abraham Lincoln had some opponents of the Union cause put in jail without issuing them writs of habeas corpus. He did so in the name of maintaining order during the rebellion of the Confederate states.

Pass a Bill of Attainder or Ex Post Facto Law. Congress may not pass a bill of attainder. This is a law which declares that someone is guilty of a crime, usually treason, without giving that person the right to a trial. Congress is also forbidden from passing an ex post facto law. This is a law that declares an act to be a crime after the deed has been committed. For example, if someone floats aloft in a balloon, Congress cannot then pass a law declaring balloon flights illegal and have that balloonist arrested. The law would only apply to future balloon flights. If an act was not against the law when it was done, only those who violate the law after it is passed can be prosecuted under the law. These provisions against bills of attainder and ex post facto laws are a defense of individual rights.

Impose a Direct Tax. Congress could not impose a direct tax on people except on the basis of the census. Direct taxes are also mentioned in Article 1, Section 2, Paragraph 3. There are two kinds of taxes, direct and indirect. Direct taxes are taxes on a person simply for being alive. Indirect taxes are taxes on activities that can be avoided if one so chooses, such as import duties or sales taxes. One can avoid paying indirect taxes by not engaging in those taxable events. A business can avoid the impact of indirect taxes by passing the cost of the taxes on to others. For example, an importer can charge a retailer enough to cover the cost of import duties. The retailer then charges customers enough to cover his costs. You cannot avoid a direct tax because it is on you as a person.

At first, the Federal government could obtain revenue by import duties, by charging fees for certain Federal activities, and by placing head (or capitation) taxes on the states based on population. States were to collect the taxes as they saw fit. This was done most simply by each state placing a head tax on the people. In this way, everybody bore the cost of government equally. The Sixteenth Amendment did away with the limitation on direct taxes. It allowed the Federal government to tax income directly, without regard to apportionment among the states or to the census. Now, if you have income that falls within Federal tax guidelines, you have to pay taxes on it.

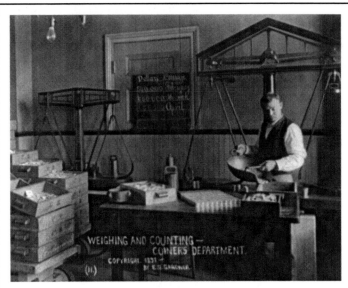

Coiner's Department at the U.S. Mint in New Orleans, Louisiana, 1897

The Constitution does not say that the Federal government can print paper money. It says that Congress can coin money and that the states cannot coin money or print paper money. The purpose of these provisions was to create a sound national currency. The right of Congress to coin money has been interpreted to include the right to print paper money.

Other Limitations. Congress may not lay duties on items exported from a state. Export duties are seen as a discouragement to business. Congress may not regulate trade in any way that favors or penalizes one state or port over another.

All spending of money from the Federal treasury has to take place with the authority of specific appropriations passed by Congress. This prevents the president, the military, members of Congress, or anyone else from obtaining money from the public's treasury in an underhanded way.

Congress cannot grant titles of nobility; and no person holding an office of public trust may accept any gift, title, office, or money from a foreign ruler or state. Having seen the problems associated with such practices in Great Britain and other European countries, the founders wanted the United States to have no titled nobility. They also wanted those in government not to become beholden to foreign powers.

Section 10: What States May Not Do

In the last part of Article I, the Constitution places certain limits on the powers of the states. The founders wanted to avoid competition and chaos among the states and between the states and the Federal government. They had seen enough conflict and chaos under the Articles of Confederation.

States may not impose their own import duties. They may not make anything but gold and silver coin to be legal tender for the payment of debts, a provision that discouraged the printing of state currencies. States have to respect the rights of citizens in the same way that Congress does (namely, no bills of attainder or ex post facto laws, no laws impairing the obligation of contracts, and no titles of nobility).

A state may not make a treaty with a foreign country, nor may it engage in war, except that, if a state is invaded or threatened, the militia can be mobilized until the national government is able to respond.

A Delicate Balance

The Constitution gives Congress the power to regulate commerce, maintain the military, establish national standards and a national coinage, and act as a single government in dealing with foreign countries. At the same time, the Federal government had to respect individual rights and was limited in how it could raise and spend revenues.

States, meanwhile, were limited in what they could do with regard to areas over which the Federal government had sovereignty, in their treatment of individuals, in matters regarding exports and imports, and in dealings with foreign nations.

The framers could not foresee all of the questions that would develop regarding these areas of sovereignty, but they provided a good outline of limited government and divided sovereignty. For the framers, this was not an idle or theoretical exercise. A great deal was at stake in what the new Constitution proposed. As James Madison put it in *The Federalist* Number 44:

C-SPAN (Cable-Satellite Public Affairs Network) is a non-profit, advertising-free broadcasting company paid for by a small fee charged to cable and satellite subscribers. C-SPAN receives no government funding and strives to be non-partisan. The network began in 1979 with telecasts of the U.S. House of Representatives. C-SPAN2 debuted in 1986 and provides coverage of Senate sessions (the Senate had resisted allowing television cameras in the chamber until then). C-SPAN3 began in 2001 and broadcasts other public affairs programming and archived programs from the first two C-SPAN channels. C-SPAN Radio took to the airwaves in 1997 as a local station in Washington, D.C., and simulcasts many C-SPAN programs. The C-SPAN channels provide coverage of Congressional committee hearings; speeches by political figures; talk and interview shows; various educational programs; and special events such as the annual State of the Union address, dedication of national monuments, and coverage of national political conventions. C-SPAN coverage of major news events is provided without commentary or analysis by reporters. BOOK-TV (on C-SPAN2 on weekends) offers presentations by and interviews with authors of new books. The C-SPAN website (www.c-span.org) provides streaming video and audio of its broadcasts.

We have now reviewed, in detail, all the articles composing the sum or quantity of power delegated by the proposed Constitution to the Federal government, and are brought to this undeniable conclusion, that no part of the power is unnecessary or improper for accomplishing the necessary objects of the Union. The question, therefore, whether this amount of power shall be granted or not, resolves itself into another question, whether or not a government commensurate to the exigencies of the Union shall be established; or, in other words, whether the Union itself shall be preserved.

Library of Congress

The Library of Congress (LOC) was one of the first agencies created by the Federal government. It began with a $5,000 appropriation in 1800 to purchase "such books as may be necessary for the use of Congress—and for putting up a suitable apartment for containing them therein. . . ." The Library was first housed in the Capitol building, but that structure was destroyed along with the books when the British burned Washington in 1814.

Library of Congress Thomas Jefferson Building

After the fire, former President Thomas Jefferson offered to sell Congress his extensive personal library as a replacement. His collection included a wide range of books, which began the tradition of the LOC gathering books on all types of subjects. Jefferson's offer was accepted in 1815, and Congress paid $23,950 for the former President's collection of over 6,000 books.

Library of Congress Main Reading Room

The Librarian of Congress for most of the last half of the nineteenth century, Ainsworth Rand Spofford, set the LOC on the course of making it the major institution that it is today. By his urging, Congress passed a copyright law in 1870 that required applicants for official copyright to send two copies of their work to the LOC. This caused an avalanche of publications, music, maps, and photographs to descend on the Library; and it led to Spofford's request for a new, separate building for the collection.

Congress authorized construction in 1886, and the LOC finally moved out of the Capitol building and into its beautiful new home across the street in 1897.

Today the LOC holds over 130 million items (including 29 million books and other publications, 58 million manuscripts, and 12 million photographs) on 530 miles of shelves. It continues primarily to be the research headquarters for Congress, but it also effectively serves the nation as a whole. The LOC maintains a website (www.loc.gov) that provides information about the Library and the activities of Congress as well as pictures and articles on many topics in American history.

Library of Congress John Adams Building

[The Pharisees sent their disciples,
along with the Herodians, to Jesus and asked Him,]
"Tell us then, what do You think? Is it lawful to give a poll-tax to Caesar, or not?"...
Then He said to them, "Then render to Caesar the things that are Caesar's;
and to God the things that are God's."
Matthew 22:15-21

Reading

- *McCulloch v. Maryland* (excerpt) (WHTT, p. 67)

Library of Congress Main Reading Room

Lesson 25—When Powers Collide: The Process of Impeachment

Government is a trust, and the officers of the government are trustees; and both the trust and the trustees are created for the benefit of the people.

—Henry Clay (1829)

Impeachment is the ultimate check that Congress has against members of the executive and judicial branches of the Federal government. Political figures often criticize each other; and most modern presidents have had critics who have mumbled, "He ought to be impeached." The impeachment process, however, goes beyond political criticism to address the issue of whether the official in question is fit to remain in office.

The term impeachment is often misunderstood. Many people think that to be impeached is to be found guilty, but it actually means to be accused of wrongdoing. This is why the Constitution speaks of "Impeachment for, and Conviction of." Impeachment and conviction are two separate steps.

Historical Background

Impeachment in the English system of government dates back to the Middle Ages, when Parliament used it to challenge the fitness of royal officials to continue in office. A member of the House of Commons could make an accusation against an official; and if the full

Trial of Warren Hastings

House upheld the charge, the House of Lords would conduct an impeachment trial. As the Constitutional Convention met in Philadelphia in 1787, Warren Hastings, governor of India, was the subject of an impeachment trial in the House of Lords (he was eventually acquitted). Reflecting British practice, colonial laws and state constitutions included provisions for the impeachment and trial of public officials.

The delegates to the Convention agreed that the Constitution needed to provide for impeachment, but they disagreed over how to phrase the cause for removal and what the venue for an impeachment trial should be. After much debate, Article II, Section 4 was written to say, "The President, Vice President and all Civil Officers of the United States shall be removed from Office on Impeachment for, and Conviction of, Treason, Bribery, or other high Crimes and Misdemeanors."

Mirroring the English system, the Constitution provides that the House of Representatives can bring, by a simple majority vote, articles of impeachment (which are like a charge or indictment in a court) against an official. When this is done, the Senate sits as the jury in an impeachment trial (Article I, Section 2, Paragraph 5; and Section 3, Paragraphs 6 and 7). A two-thirds majority of the Senate (currently 67 votes) is required for conviction. When the president is being tried, the Chief Justice of the Supreme Court presides over the trial.

The meaning of the phrase "high crimes and misdemeanors" is the subject of continuing debate. Some have said it refers to any offenses that would be subject to indictment in a court of law. Others say that it means wrongs that are related to the office which the accused person holds, actions which are a violation of the public trust and a misuse of the powers of the office.

The penalty for being found guilty in an impeachment trial cannot extend further than removal from office and disqualification from holding any office of trust in the United States government. However, the defendant might also have to stand trial in and face the punishments of regular courts for wrongs he has done.

Non-Presidential Impeachments

The impeachment process is so serious and severe that, despite almost constant political bickering throughout the history of Congress, actual impeachment proceedings have begun only 62 times in the House. Over two-thirds of these have not gone beyond the investigation stage in that chamber. Seventeen Federal officials have been impeached by the House. Two were presidents, one was a Senator, one a Cabinet member, twelve were Federal judges, and one was an associate justice of the Supreme Court.

In 1797, Senator William Blount of Tennessee became involved in a plot to attack and take over Spanish Florida with the assistance of British and Indian forces. His actions reflected the widespread concern on the western frontier over possible Spanish designs on the area between the Appalachian Mountains and the Mississippi River. When the plot became known, Blount resigned and the House voted to impeach him. In the impeachment trial, the jurisdiction of the Senate was questioned since Blount had already resigned; and the case was dropped in 1799. No other member of Congress has ever been impeached, and Congress has since limited its actions against its own members to censure and expulsion.

Federal judge John Pickering was impeached and removed from office in 1804. Pickering suffered from mental problems and probably did not need to remain on the bench. However, he was a Federalist; and the impeachment was pursued by a Republican Congress. The next year, the Senate impeached associate Supreme Court justice Samuel Chase. Chase was a signer of the Declaration of Independence and had been a Federalist activist. He often let his political views come through in what he said in court. Chase was acquitted, but the message was sent that judges needed to stay out of politics.

In two other impeachment trials that took place before that of President Andrew Johnson in 1868, one Federal judge was convicted and one was acquitted. In impeachment proceedings against Federal judges since Johnson's trial, five have been convicted and removed from office (the last in 1989), two resigned before a trial could be held, and two were found not guilty.

In 1876, President Grant's Secretary of War, William Belknap, was accused of using his office for personal gain by accepting bribes from those to whom he awarded lucrative contracts for trading with Indian tribes. Minutes before the House voted to impeach him, the secretary resigned. The House still voted unanimously to impeach Belknap and the Senate held a trial, but the votes fell short of the majority needed to convict. Many Senators were generally convinced of his guilt, but they believed that they no longer had jurisdiction in the case because Belknap had resigned. Since the penalty in an impeachment trial may only extend to removal from office and disqualification from any other Federal post, impeachment proceedings against an official who has resigned are largely pointless.

Trial of President Andrew Johnson

Presidential Impeachments

House impeachment proceedings against a president have reached a significant level three times in our nation's history. In each case, the majority party in Congress was different from the president's political party.

In 1868, the Republican-led House accused Democrat Andrew Johnson of violating the Tenure of Office Act. This law had been passed as a direct challenge to Johnson's authority. Johnson was also impeached on other charges of committing more vague wrongs, including criticizing Congress. The trial was the result of a long-standing conflict between Johnson and the majority in Congress in the difficult period following the Civil War. The Senate fell one vote short of the two-thirds majority needed to convict Johnson and remove him from office.

In 1998, the Republican-controlled House of Representatives passed two articles of impeachment against Democrat Bill Clinton, charging him with obstruction of justice and perjury in connection with Clinton's handling of an investigation against him regarding an affair with a White House intern. The Republican-led Senate conducted an impeachment trial in 1999, but Clinton was not convicted on either charge.

On another occasion, impeachment proceedings in the House led to the only resignation by a president. In 1974, Congressional investigations into the Watergate scandal indicated that President Richard Nixon had agreed to and participated in a cover-up of evidence about the Watergate break-in. The evidence showed that personnel from the White House and from the President's 1972 re-election committee had been involved in the crime. The investigation also revealed a pattern in the Nixon Administration of using government power (such as that wielded by the FBI and the Internal Revenue Service) against political opponents. During the investigation, the

President Bill Clinton

Nixon Administration resisted turning over documents to the House investigation, claiming executive privilege.

The House Judiciary Committee voted to send articles of impeachment to the full House, charging Nixon with obstruction of justice, refusing to cooperate with the committee, and abuse of executive power. At that point, Nixon resigned rather than endure a debate on the charges in the House and a likely Senate impeachment trial. Nixon was a Republican, and both houses of Congress were led by Democrats. A month after Nixon resigned, President Gerald Ford granted Nixon a pre-emptive pardon to avoid any future trials on any wrongs he had committed.

President Richard Nixon

Conclusion

In *The Federalist* Number 65, Alexander Hamilton commented on the difficulties of conducting an impeachment procedure:

> A well-constituted court for the trial of impeachments is an object not more to be desired than difficult to be obtained in a government wholly elective. The subjects of its jurisdiction are those offenses which proceed from the misconduct of public men, or, in other words, from the abuse or violation of some public trust. They are of a nature which may with peculiar propriety be denominated POLITICAL, as they relate chiefly to injuries done immediately to the society itself. The prosecution of them, for this reason, will seldom fail to agitate the passions of the whole community, and to divide it into parties more or less friendly or inimical to the accused. In many cases it will connect itself with the pre-existing factions, and will enlist all their animosities, partialities, influence, and interest on one side or on the other; and in such cases there will always be the greatest danger that the decision will be regulated more by the comparative strength of parties, than by the real demonstrations of innocence or guilt.

Impeachment is a power of Congress that is often discussed but has seldom been used. This has probably contributed to the stability of the American system. Nevertheless, the threat of impeachment stands as a warning to government officials that they will be held accountable for their conduct in office.

Brethren, even if anyone is caught in any trespass,
you who are spiritual, restore such a one
in a spirit of gentleness; each one looking to yourself,
so that you too will not be tempted.
Galatians 6:1

6

Article II— The Executive

The president of the United States is chief executive of our national government, commander in chief of our military forces, highest representative of our country in relations with other countries, and leader of his political party. This unit outlines the president's responsibilities and how he carries them out.

Lessons in This Unit

Activity Idea

From what you know about the men who have filled the office of president, how have they reflected America and how have they been different? What stories about the backgrounds of presidents inspire you? Write two to three pages about how our presidents have embodied American ideals and how they have sometimes failed those ideals.

If you are using the optional *Quiz and Exam Book,* answer the questions for each lesson after you have completed the lesson and read any assigned readings in *We Hold These Truths.* After you have completed Lesson 30, take the quiz for Unit 6.

Lesson 26—Choosing the President

I pray Heaven to bestow the best of blessing on this house and all that shall hereafter inhabit it. May none but honest and wise men ever rule under this roof.
          —*John Adams (upon moving into the new White House, 1800)*

(Read Article II and the Twelfth Amendment of the U.S. Constitution.)

The office of president of the United States has been called the most important and the most powerful job in the world. He is commander in chief of the strongest military force in the world, the leader of the free world, and our nation's highest representative to other nations. Within the United States itself, he oversees the huge bureaucracy of the Federal government. He is the main proponent of new legislation for Congress to consider. In an unofficial capacity, he is also the leader of his political party. The president and the vice president are the only officials elected by the entire country. In many ways the president embodies and symbolizes our Federal government.

Who Gets Elected

The president and vice president are elected for a term of four years. The president must be a natural born citizen, be at least 35 years old, and have resided within the United States for at least fourteen years. The same requirements apply to the vice president, since he might have to serve as president at any time. This means that no naturalized citizen can be president. The framers created this requirement and the residency requirement to eliminate the possibility of foreign influence within the United States government. The danger of foreign intrigue against the government was a matter of genuine concern in the new nation. Foreign service and military service do not count against the fourteen year residency requirement. William Howard Taft had been governor of the territory of the Philippines before becoming President. Dwight Eisenhower had been Supreme Commander of the Allied forces in Europe during World War II and was later the head of NATO forces in Europe before returning to the United States to run for president.

George W. Bush was elected as the forty-third President (Grover Cleveland served two non-consecutive terms and is always counted twice, as the twenty-second and twenty-fourth President). The average age of a president at the time of taking office is 55, twenty years older than the Constitutional minimum. Theodore Roosevelt was not quite 43 when he became President after the death of William McKinley, which made him the youngest person ever to become President. John Kennedy was 43 years and eight months old when he was inaugurated, which made him the youngest person to win a presidential election. Bill Clinton was 46 years and five months old, and Ulysses S. Grant was 46

Abraham Lincoln was the tallest President at 6 feet 4 inches in height; James Madison was the shortest at 5'4". Since the early 20th century, the taller candidate of the two major parties has almost always won the Presidential race. The 2004 contest between 6'4" John Kerry and George W. Bush (just a shade under 6 feet) was a rare exception. Apparently the American people want the President to look presidential.

years and ten months old, when they were elected to their first terms. On the other hand, Ronald Reagan was almost 70 when he took office. William Henry Harrison was 68, James Buchanan was 65, and George H. W. Bush was 64.

The average age of vice presidents when they have taken office is 54. Alben Barkley was the oldest Vice President. He was 71 when he was sworn into office in 1949. By contrast, John C. Breckenridge was barely 36 when he became Vice President in 1857. Richard Nixon had just turned 40 when he took the vice presidential oath in 1953. Dan Quayle was almost 42 in January 1989. Seven vice presidents have died in office, and two have resigned.

The states from which the presidents have come are somewhat difficult to identify, since many presidents were born in one state but grew up elsewhere and may have been living in still another place when they were elected. All the states, of course, want to claim as many presidents as possible. Eight presidents were born in Virginia, including seven of the first twelve, which indicates Virginia's importance in the early years of the country. Eight presidents were born in Ohio; in addition, William Henry

Sculptors Carving the Face of George Washington on Mount Rushmore, c. 1932

Harrison (born in Virginia) was living in Ohio when he was elected. Seven of these Buckeye presidents were among the twelve presidents between U.S. Grant and Warren G. Harding inclusive (1868-1963). This shows the political importance of Ohio in the sixty years following the Civil War. Four presidents were born in New York, and three others were living there when they were elected.

Military and political experience have carried considerable weight on presidential resumes. Seven have been army generals, and many others have been lower-ranking officers in various branches of the armed forces. About half of all presidents have served in the military. Fourteen presidents were state governors at some time before becoming president, and thirteen have been U.S. Senators. Fourteen have been vice president, and nine of them became president upon the death or resignation of their predecessor. However, only four sitting vice presidents have been elected to move directly into the presidency (John Adams, Thomas Jefferson, Martin Van Buren, and then 152 years later George H. W. Bush in 1988).

Between 1953 and 2008, all of the Presidents were either Republicans or Southerners (or both), with the exception of John Kennedy. Eisenhower, Nixon, Ford, Reagan, and the two Bushes were Republicans. Lyndon Johnson, Jimmy Carter, and Bill Clinton were Southern Democrats. The two Bushes count Texas as their home state, so they were Republicans and Southerners. This indicates the importance of carrying the South in winning a Presidential election.

The religious leanings of the presidents have also not always been easy to identify. Many presidents have claimed to be religious but have not been closely associated with any particular denomination. Thomas Jefferson and Abraham Lincoln, for example, believed in God but did not have active membership in a church. Eleven presidents are described as Episcopalian. This is a percentage far higher than the percentage Episcopalian membership has been of the American public at large. Seven presidents have been Presbyterians, five Methodists, five Baptists, five Congregationalist/Unitarians, three Disciples of Christ/Christian Church, two Quakers, and one Roman Catholic. Two men who were religiously active before they became president were James Garfield, who was an elder and part-time preacher in the Christian Church, and Jimmy Carter, a Baptist who regularly taught a Sunday School class and who engaged in evangelistic mission trips.

Two sets of fathers and sons have been President: John Adams and John Quincy Adams, and George H. W. Bush and George W. Bush. William Henry Harrison was the grandfather of Benjamin Harrison. Theodore Roosevelt and Franklin Roosevelt were fifth cousins (the same level of kin that Franklin was to his wife Eleanor). Many Presidents have been distantly related to other Presidents. Families in many places have a long history of serving in government. Some examples are the Byrd family in Virginia and West Virginia, the Bayh family in Indiana, the Ford family in Tennessee, and the Talmadge family in Georgia.

George H. W. Bush

George W. Bush

The Electoral College

The framers of the Constitution spent a great deal of time debating how the president should be chosen and what his responsibilities should be. One idea was for Congress to choose him, but it was thought that this would upset the system of checks and balances and lead to backroom deal-making. Other ideas included selection by the state legislatures and by a special panel of distinguished individuals. Direct popular election was considered but was not seen as a viable option. The founders were not ready for that level of democracy.

The plan that emerged from the convention's deliberations was called the electoral college. Each state was to have a number of electors equal to that state's total number of senators and representatives. The electors were to be chosen in a manner that each state legislature decided. Most were chosen by popular vote, but a few state legislatures chose the electors in the first years under the Constitution. The electors were to meet in each state, and each elector was to cast two votes. The results were then to be sent to Congress. There the vice president (as president of the Senate) was to announce the results on a given day. The person who received the votes of a majority

Electors meet in their respective state capitals on the Monday after the second Wednesday in December following a presidential election. Their votes are then sent to the sitting Vice President, who announces the results to a joint session of Congress on January 6. This means that the Vice President has sometimes announced either his own victory or his own defeat in the election.

of electors would be named president, and the person with the second highest total would be vice president. If there was a tie, the House of Representatives would choose between them with each state having one vote. If no one had a majority, the House would choose from the top five of those receiving electoral votes. If there was a tie for second place, the Senate would choose the vice president. At least some of the framers assumed that this entire process would have to be followed fairly often.

The Senate has chosen the Vice President only once. In 1836, Martin Van Buren's running mate was Richard Johnson of Kentucky. Johnson had some unusual views and was unpopular with many people because he had had two common-law wives (in succession) who had been slaves. Some electors, including some from Kentucky, refused to vote for him, so he fell short of having a majority of electoral votes. However, Van Buren used his influence to have the Senate choose Johnson in early 1837.

Changes in the System

This original plan turned out to be idealistic and cumbersome. First, the founders did not envision the role that political parties almost immediately came to play. The framers hoped that electors would vote for the best men in the country, without regard for political loyalties. This did not happen.

Second, the plan ran aground in the heated presidential contest of 1800. Republican Thomas Jefferson defeated the Federalist John Adams in the voting; but in the electoral college loyal Republican electors each cast one vote for Jefferson and one for Aaron Burr of New York, who had been put forth as the Republicans' vice presidential choice. This created a tie between two men of the same party; and Aaron Burr, always looking for a way to promote himself, refused to step aside. What complicated matters even more was that the House that would make the final choice in early 1801 was still controlled by Federalists, who hated Thomas Jefferson. The newly elected Congress that would have a Republican majority would not be formed until December of 1801. Federalist Alexander Hamilton (also of New York) disliked Jefferson but distrusted Burr even more, so he used his influence to help Jefferson be elected by the House.

As a result of this fiasco, the Republican Congress passed, and in 1804 the states ratified, the Twelfth Amendment, which created the system we still follow today. Under this plan, electors vote separately for president and vice president. The person who receives a majority for each office is elected. If no one has a majority for president, the House (voting by states) chooses the president from among the three who received the most electoral votes. If no vice presidential candidate has a majority, the Senate chooses the vice president from the two highest vote-getters.

When a person votes in a presidential election, he or she actually votes for the electors who have committed themselves to voting for a party's Presidential and Vice Presidential nominees. Some states list the electors on the ballot, while others simply say "the electors committed to voting for" one candidate or the other. The political party organizations in each state choose who the electors are. Many times being chosen as an elector is an honor given to someone for years of faithful service to the party or a recognition given to a retired office-holder. The parties want people as electors who will keep their word and not cast a surprise ballot when the time comes.

Testing the System

The Twelfth Amendment plan was tested in 1824. The lone national party was the Republicans, but it was splintered among several candidates. Andrew Jackson received the most electoral votes (as well as the most popular votes) for president but not a majority. John Quincy Adams had the second highest. William Crawford placed third, but he had suffered a stroke and was not seriously considered by the House. Speaker of the House Henry Clay had been another candidate, but he had placed fourth and was out of the running. Apparently Clay (who was a bitter rival to Jackson) had a secret meeting with Adams and then used his influence to have Adams elected in the House. Adams then named Clay to be his Secretary of State, a position that was seen in that day as a stepping stone to the presidency. Jackson and his supporters angrily charged Adams and Clay with having made a "corrupt bargain." Jackson immediately began another race for the White House, which he won in 1828.

The only other times that the electoral college results have been in question were in 1876 and 2000. In both cases, the popular vote counts were questioned from some states (four states—including Florida—in 1876, and Florida alone in 2000). Congress established a commission to decide the matter in 1876. In 2000, after weeks of court battles, the Supreme Court decided that the Florida electoral laws in place at the time of the election should be followed, which gave George W. Bush the victory over Al Gore Jr.

Questions About the System

The current system is actually fifty state elections (fifty-one counting the District of Columbia) all held at the same time. If the president and vice president were elected strictly by the national popular vote, a new Federal law might be required to standardize voting requirements in all states. States with a shorter residency requirement, for instance, might be seen as having an unfair advantage over states with longer residency requirements. As it is, states are free to establish their individual requirements within the restrictions set by the Constitution and by laws passed by Congress (no poll tax or literacy requirements, for example).

All states except Maine and Nebraska have a winner-take-all arrangement for their electors. The candidate who wins the popular vote in a state, even if it is just by one vote, receives all of that state's electoral votes. In Maine and Nebraska, the statewide winner receives two electoral votes; but the other electoral votes are decided by vote totals in the Congressional districts. Most states also require a pledge that the winning electors will actually vote for the candidates of the party they represent. It has happened a few times that electors vote for someone else, but it has never affected the outcome of an election.

The Presidency is seen as the culmination of a politician's career. However, two Presidents have served in Congress after leaving the White House. John Quincy Adams represented Massachusetts in the House of Representatives for seventeen years after being defeated in the 1828 Presidential race. During his career in the House, Adams helped to start the Smithsonian Institution and was a constant critic of slavery. Andrew Johnson was chosen by the Tennessee legislature to be a U.S. Senator after his term as President ended in 1869. Johnson served only a few months before he died of a stroke.

The electoral college has been criticized ever since it began. Because the votes are counted by states, it is possible for a candidate to lose the national popular vote but win the electoral vote. This happened in 1876, 1888, and in 2000. Critics charge that this result defeats the will of the majority of American voters. In addition, in close races, the presence of third parties has frequently caused a candidate to receive only a plurality of the popular vote even though he wins in the electoral college. Several presidents have been elected with less than 50% of the popular vote: James K. Polk in 1844, Zachary Taylor in 1848, James Buchanan in 1856, Abraham Lincoln in 1860, James Garfield in 1880, Grover Cleveland in 1884 and 1892, Woodrow Wilson in 1912 and

1916, Harry Truman in 1948, John Kennedy in 1960, Richard Nixon in 1968, and Bill Clinton in 1992 and 1996.

Supporters of the electoral college say that the system maintains the importance of all the states. If the election were decided strictly by popular vote, candidates might concentrate even more than they do now on only the most populous states. Advocates of the electoral college say that the system can also provide a clear winner even if a candidate receives only a plurality of the popular votes. This prevents further complications to electing a president, such as having Congress decide or holding a runoff election between the top two vote-getters some weeks after the current election day. Another advantage to the electoral college system, some observers say, is that it maintains the two-party system. If we had a truly popularly-elected president, many smaller parties might form to try to influence who would be elected.

Delegates Wearing Jimmy Carter Smile Masks at the Democratic National Convention, 1976

Presidential Campaigns

The electoral college is the way that presidents are elected according to the Constitution, but in practical terms presidential campaigns are conducted to appeal to all of the voters in a process that has developed apart from what the Constitution says.

Candidates announce that they are running for their party's nomination well over a year before the general election. Party nominees are determined by a complex process that includes several state primaries held in the early part of an election year. These primaries (and, in some states, caucuses or meetings of party members) select delegates for the national conventions who are pledged to support particular candidates. Candidates maintain a hectic schedule of campaigning and fund-raising. As primaries are held, some candidates emerge as front-runners while others drop out of the race. Usually the nominees of the Democratic and Republican parties are determined well before the national conventions are held in the summer. The presidential campaign dominates the news through the fall until the election is held in November. The voting by the electoral college in December is usually an anti-climax to the general election.

> *The cost of elections has become ridiculously high. The total spending in the 2004 Presidential race by candidates, political parties, and special interest groups was about 1.2 billion dollars. The expenses for campaigns for Congress were an additional 2.7 billion dollars that year. Candidates for Federal offices spent about 144 million dollars of their own money.*

The king gives stability to the land by justice,
but a man who takes bribes overthrows it.
Proverbs 29:4

Lesson 27—Succession, Salary, and the Oath of Office

Anyone who thinks that the vice-president can take a position independent of the president of his administration simply has no knowledge of politics or government. You are his choice in a political marriage, and he expects your absolute loyalty.
—Hubert Humphrey (Vice President 1965-1969)

(Read the Twenty-Second and Twenty-Fifth Amendments of the U.S. Constitution.)

The Constitution in Article II, Section 1 provides for what is to happen if the president dies or is no longer able to carry out the responsibilities of his office, but questions arose beginning in 1841 as to the precise meaning of these steps. Later laws and a Constitutional amendment clarified the arrangement and made further provisions for presidential succession.

It is not an eventuality we want to think about, but about every twenty years between 1841 and 1963 a president died in office (1841, 1865, 1881, 1901, 1923, 1945, and 1963). In 1974, the President resigned from office. The Federal government obviously needs an orderly process of transition when the office of president becomes vacant.

President John Tyler

Presidential Succession

The basic provision of the Constitution says that if the office of president becomes vacant or if the president is unable to carry out his duties, the role is to be filled by the vice president. In addition, Congress was empowered to create an order of succession if both the presidency and vice presidency should be vacant.

This situation did not arise until 1841, when William Henry Harrison died one month after taking office. Vice President John Tyler took the oath of office and became President—or did he? Some observers, especially Tyler's critics (and there were many) said that he was only Acting President. The Constitution says that if the president is unable to "discharge the powers and duties" of the office, "the same shall devolve on the Vice President." The question was whether the vice president actually became president or only carried out the president's duties. Tyler believed that he became President, and this has been the accepted understanding ever since.

At different times Congress has passed laws that extended the presidential line of succession beyond the vice president. The first, in 1792, named the President Pro Tempore of the Senate and the Speaker of the House as the next two in line. A new law in 1886, following presidential assassinations in 1865 and 1881, dropped the Congressional leaders and put the Cabinet members in line in the order in which their departments were created, starting with the Secretary of State. A section of the Twentieth Amendment, ratified in 1933, provided for what would happen if the president or vice president were not able to assume office when they were supposed to. In 1947, following Franklin Roosevelt's death, the line of succession was changed again, with the Speaker of the House and the President Pro Tempore being put back at the top of the list after the vice president and before the Cabinet members.

Still, no provision was made for filling the office of vice president if it became empty or in the case of a living president being unable to serve. Following the assassination of John Kennedy in 1963, the United States had no vice president for fourteen months during a critical time in the Cold War with the Soviet Union. In 1965, Congress proposed the Twenty-Fifth Amendment to the Constitution, which was ratified by the states in early 1967. The amendment contains several provisions:

(1) It specifically states that in the case of a vacancy in the office of president, the vice president shall become president.

(2) When the office of vice president is vacant, the president shall nominate a successor who must be approved by a majority vote of both houses of Congress.

(3) If the president notifies the Speaker of the House and the President Pro Tempore of the Senate that he is unable to carry out the duties of the office (for instance, if the president requires anesthesia for surgery and expects to have a long recovery afterward), the vice president becomes acting president. The president can then notify the same officials when he is again able to carry out his duties.

However, if the vice president and a majority of the Cabinet heads disagree and believe that the president is still not able to carry out his duties, they can communicate to the Speaker and the President Pro Tempore that the president is not able to perform his duties. Congress must then consider the issue. If each house votes with a two-thirds majority within 21 days that the president is unable to discharge his duties, the vice president continues as acting president; otherwise, the president resumes his duties. This might happen if the president became insane or if he were injured and were unable to communicate with the leaders of Congress himself.

The provisions of this amendment regarding a vacancy in the vice presidency have been applied twice. When Spiro Agnew resigned as Vice President in 1973, President Richard Nixon nominated House Minority Leader Gerald Ford to take his place. Then when Nixon resigned in 1974, Ford assumed the presidency and nominated former New York Governor Nelson Rockefeller to be Vice President.

Order of Presidential Succession

Vice President
Speaker of the House
President Pro Tempore of the Senate
Secretary of State
Secretary of the Treasury
Secretary of Defense
Attorney General
Secretary of the Interior
Secretary of Agriculture
Secretary of Commerce
Secretary of Labor
Secretary of Health and Human Services
Secretary of Housing and Urban Development
Secretary of Transportation
Secretary of Energy
Secretary of Education
Secretary of Veterans Affairs
Secretary of Homeland Security

John Adams, after holding the office of Vice President for a time, wrote "My country has in its wisdom contrived for me the most insignificant office that ever the invention of man contrived or his imagination conceived." John Nance Garner, Franklin Roosevelt's Vice President for eight years, was alleged to have said that the office wasn't worth a bucket of warm spit. Through most of American history the Vice President has had few official duties except to preside in the Senate (which he rarely does) and be there in case the President dies. Most Vice Presidents toil in obscurity and are soon forgotten.

Usually a party's Presidential nominee chooses the person he wants to fill the second spot on the ticket. The choice is made to try to balance the ticket in some way, such as selecting someone who is a little more conservative or liberal than the Presidential candidate, or someone from another region of the country or from a key state the party wants to win. Surveys indicate that Presidential candidates are more likely to lose votes because of a poor choice for Vice President than they are to win votes on the basis of a good choice.

In more recent years the Vice President has become more involved in the work of the Administration. He attends meetings of the Cabinet and the National Security Council and carries out diplomatic, social, and political assignments for the President and for their political party. If the President trusts him, the Vice President can be a key advisor in the President's inner circle.

Salary

The rest of Article II, Section 1 involves the president's salary and the oath of office. Congress is empowered to set the president's salary. It cannot be increased or decreased during a president's term of office, nor can he receive any other pay while he is in office.

George Washington's salary was set at $25,000. This was not changed until 1873, when it was doubled to $50,000. In 1907 Congress added an annual $25,000 non-taxable expense account. The president's salary increased to $75,000 in 1909 and to $100,000 in 1949. Also in 1949, the expense allowance increased to $90,000. In 1969 Congress raised the president's salary to $200,000, with an additional $100,000 for travel and $50,000 for expenses. In 2001 the salary increased to $400,000.

In reality, the expenses for presidential activities mount up far beyond his own account. As a result, Federal agencies pick up the tab for some events that involve the president. The Department of Defense, for example, will cover the cost of having a military band play at White House functions.

Congress has made no provision for an annual cost of living increase in the president's salary, as it has for its own salaries. However, the president does get a nice, big house to live in rent free; access to the Camp David retreat; a large staff; and many other tangible and intangible benefits. But nobody seeks the office of president for the salary.

Retired presidents did not receive a pension until 1958, when Congress granted retired presidents a pension of $25,000 per year, plus an office and a

The Constitution originally set no limit on the number of terms to which a President could be elected. George Washington established the informal precedent of serving a maximum of two terms. This tradition was honored until Franklin Roosevelt was elected four times in the 1930s and 1940s. Following Roosevelt's death, the Republican Congress passed and in 1951 the states ratified the Twenty-Second Amendment, which stipulated that a person may be elected to the Presidency no more than twice. If the Vice President or some other person holds the office for more than two years, that person can only be elected once.

staff. Congress has since increased the pension several times. Former presidents now receive a pension that is the same as the annual salary of a Cabinet secretary, which was $180,100 in 2005. They and their families also receive Secret Service protection for a period of years.

Beginning with Bill Clinton, ex-presidents (or their surviving widows or widowers) will receive funds for an office and staff for four and one-half years after they leave office. With book deals, speaking fees, and other activities, as well as their own personal wealth in most cases, former presidents generally don't have to worry about making ends meet.

In 2006 the vice president's salary was $208,100, fixed by law to be the same as that of the Speaker of the House and the Chief Justice of the United States Supreme Court. He also received an additional $10,000 expense allowance.

The Oath of Office

The oath that the president recites upon taking office is provided in the last paragraph of Section 1 of the Constitution. When George Washington took the oath for the first time in 1789, he voluntarily added the phrase "so help me God." Every president since then has added the phrase when he was sworn into office. The president is traditionally sworn in by the Chief Justice of the Supreme Court, but in emergencies others have administered the oath.

The Constitution does not give an oath that the vice president is to take. Here is the oath that Congress created:

> I do solemnly swear that I will support and defend the Constitution of the United States against all enemies, foreign and domestic, that I will bear true faith and allegiance to the same: that I take this obligation freely, without any mental reservation or purpose of evasion, and I will well and faithfully discharge the duties of the office on which I am about to enter. So help me God.

The Inauguration of President Herbert Hoover

Through 1933, the vice president was sworn into office in the Senate chamber. Now both oaths are administered in the same ceremony, with the vice president being sworn in just before the president. The oath can be administered by the retiring vice president, an associate justice of the Supreme Court, or another official.

The president-elect used to give his inaugural address before taking the oath. Now he is sworn in before giving his address (William Henry Harrison took the oath during his very long inaugural speech). The vice president does not give a speech at the inauguration.

Samuel said to all the people,
"Do you see him whom the LORD has chosen?
Surely there is no one like him among all the people."
So all the people shouted and said, "Long live the king!"
1 Samuel 10:24

Lesson 28—Commander in Chief

Freedom itself was attacked this morning by a faceless coward.
Freedom will be defended.
—President George W. Bush, September 11, 2001

The military forces of the United States are under the command of the president. He commissions military officers and is commander in chief of the military and of the National Guard when it is called into the service of the country.

The Importance of Civilian Control

It is significant that U.S. forces are under the oversight of civilians. The president is a civilian. The Cabinet member who heads the Department of Defense is a civilian. Under the Secretary of Defense are the civilian Secretaries of the Army, Navy, and Air Force (the Marines Corps is part of the Navy). The Coast Guard is overseen by the Secretary of Homeland Security, another civilian Cabinet member.

The founders did not want a powerful standing army answerable only to itself that might compete with the civilian government for control of the country. Civilian oversight of the military also helps the government know how the military's actions have an impact on the nation as a whole.

Ordering Troops into Action

Congress has the power to declare war, but the operation of armed forces in the field is under the oversight of the president. The U.S. Congress has declared war only five times: 1812 (against Great Britain), 1846 (against Mexico), 1898 (against Spain), and 1917 and 1941 (both times against Germany and her allies). In actual practice, however, presidents have ordered troops to take the field dozens of times (some say up to 200 times, depending on how one defines military action) without a formal declaration of war. These mobilizations have ranged from the attacks on the Barbary Pirates along the coast of northern Africa ordered by Thomas Jefferson, to Operation Iraqi Freedom commanded by George W. Bush. Not even the extensive military operations of the Civil War were based on a Congressional declaration of war. A president's use of troops to rescue American citizens or to protect American embassies usually goes unquestioned. What is more complicated is the use of American forces to attack an unfriendly nation.

The reluctance of Congress to declare war stems from several reasons. A formal declaration puts the entire nation on a wartime footing and affects almost every aspect of national life. It is perceived as a much more serious step than simply committing troops into a particular area. What puts the lie to this line of thinking are conflicts such as the Vietnam War. It was undeclared, but it still eventually consumed the entire country. A declaration of war also plays more seriously on the world stage. Diplomats have convinced themselves that undeclared wars are not as much of a threat to world peace as declared wars are.

The kinds of situations in which a president has ordered troops into action have been varied. In 1983 President Ronald Reagan sent about 7,000 American troops to the tiny Caribbean country of Grenada. In the chaotic political situation there, Marxists had seized power and aligned themselves with Cuba and the Soviet Union. This was perceived as a threat to the U.S. and to the peace of the Western Hemisphere. The American troops rescued about 600 American medical students who were studying there and helped Grenadan nationals to bring down the Marxist government.

In 1989 President George H. W. Bush sent troops into Panama to arrest dictator Manuel Noriega because of his corrupt practices, including his involvement in selling illegal drugs. Again, the U.S. perceived the situation to be a threat to the stability of the region and the hemisphere. Noriega eventually was convicted in a trial held in the United States and was sentenced to prison.

In 1980 President Jimmy Carter ordered troops to engage in a rescue attempt of American hostages being held in the occupied American embassy in Tehran, Iran. The rescue was not accomplished because of mechanical failures and other problems with the aircraft being used. In 1998 President Bill Clinton ordered the bombing of a chemical factory in the Sudan that had been linked to terrorist leader Osama bin Laden.

Congressional Resolutions

Rather than declaring war, Congress has chosen in recent years to authorize the president to deploy troops by means of joint resolutions. In the early 1960s, the United States was providing military and naval support to the army of South Vietnam against the aggression of Communist North Vietnam and Communist insurgents within the South who were called the Viet Cong. Apparently North Vietnam fired on a U.S. ship that was in international

President Lyndon Johnson Greeting U.S. Troops in Vietnam, 1966

waters in the Gulf of Tonkin off of North Vietnam. In response, President Lyndon Johnson asked for and Congress passed the Tonkin Gulf Resolution in August of 1964. This resolution authorized the President to use military force to support South Vietnam and other countries with whom the U.S. had treaty obligations. This brief resolution was the legal basis for the entire military buildup in Southeast Asia and the long and costly Vietnam War. The Tonkin Gulf Resolution was revoked by Congress in 1971.

A similar resolution was passed by Congress in 1990 to authorize the President's use of force against Iraq because of its takeover of Kuwait. This Congressional resolution was in response to United Nations resolutions condemning Iraq's actions. At the time, President George H. W. Bush said that the UN resolutions were justification enough for taking military action, but he wanted Congressional support as well for what he planned to do.

In 2003 President George W. Bush asked Congress for its support for action he planned to take against Iraq to enforce UN resolutions and to lessen the threat of terrorism against the United States and the rest of the world. Congress passed a resolution supporting military action against Iraq.

War Powers Act

In 1973 Congress attempted to limit the power of the president to deploy troops by passing the War Powers Act. This was in response to the military buildup in Vietnam that had taken place under Presidents Johnson and Nixon on the basis of the Tonkin Gulf Resolution. Among other things, the War Powers Act says that the president must inform the leaders of Congress within 48 hours of any military action he orders. In addition, he must withdraw troops within 60 days (although a 30-day extension is possible) unless Congress specifically approves of the action he has taken.

The War Powers Act has been widely criticized as an unconstitutional limitation by Congress on the president's authority as commander in chief, but it has never been ruled unconstitutional by the Supreme Court. Defenders of it say that, without it, the president can in effect declare war instead of Congress, and that the law merely codifies the responsibility of Congress to authorize the use of troops in combat situations.

United Nations Commitments

A major factor that leads to U.S. military involvement are resolutions by the United Nations Security Council that call for force to be used in certain situations. This is how American troops became involved in Korea in 1950. President Truman committed troops in response to a call by the United Nations for help in stopping Communist forces that had invaded South Korea. This commitment of troops was part of the world-wide effort to stop Communist aggression wherever it occurred because it was a threat to freedom and democracy.

Many years later, Iraq's refusal to cooperate with international weapons inspectors after the 1991 Gulf War led to UN resolutions approving the use of all necessary measures against the Iraqi government. These resolutions were the basis for the invasion of Iraq in 2003 by forces from the United States and other countries.

Treaties and Executive Agreements

Formal agreements between two countries or among several countries are called treaties. The president and his representatives are authorized to pursue treaties with other governments, but these treaties must be ratified by a two-thirds vote of the Senate to take effect. A treaty might be on one of any number of subjects. It could be an agreement to limit certain kinds of nuclear weapons, or a commitment by each country to come to each other's aid in case one is attacked. It might be a trade treaty in which the countries involved promise to send and receive stated amounts of goods from each other.

The president can also sign an executive agreement with the head of another country. This agreement commits the U.S. to a certain course of action, but it does not require Senate approval. President Franklin Roosevelt, for instance, agreed in 1940 to give Great Britain fifty older naval destroyers in exchange for the U.S. receiving long-term leases for military bases around the world that were under British control. This agreement strengthened the defenses of both countries in ways that both needed. Executive agreements are made by every president. They are sometimes submitted to Congress for a majority vote, especially when an appropriation of money is needed to implement one.

The President as Head of State

We can be thankful that the president's relations with other countries do not always involve war. Besides being commander in chief, the president is also head of state or chief of state for the United States. This means that he is in charge of carrying on diplomatic relations with other countries. These relations involve formal recognition of the governments of other countries, appointing ambassadors and other officials (with the consent of the Senate) to represent the United States in those countries, and receiving ambassadors and other representatives from foreign countries. America's diplomatic and trade relations with other countries will be explored in more detail in later lessons.

President George W. Bush with Israeli Prime Minister Ehud Omert and Palestinian President Mahmoud Abbas, 2007

The president is our nation's official representative with other countries. In most cases, this contact is friendly and is intended to develop or maintain good relations with the countries involved. How the president conducts these relationships can help or hinder American trade and security. In some cases, however, the vital interests of the United States are threatened by the actions of other countries. In these situations, the president's role as commander in chief leads him to have to defend American lives, soil, and interests by using the military strength of the U.S.

And He will judge between the nations,
and will render decisions for many peoples;
and they will hammer their swords into plowshares
and their spears into pruning hooks.
Nation will not lift up sword against nation,
and never again will they learn war.
Isaiah 2:4

Reading

- Tonkin Gulf Resolution (*WHTT*, p. 77)

- Joint Resolution to Authorize the Use of United States Armed Forces Against Iraq (*WHTT*, p. 78)

Lesson 29—The President as Chief Executive

*A government that is big enough to give you all you want
is big enough to take it all away.*

—*Barry Goldwater, 1964*
(20th century Republican senator, 1964 Republican presidential nominee)

The president is responsible for seeing that the laws passed by Congress are carried out. This involves managing the huge Federal bureaucracy, which has the task of executing Federal laws and implementing Federal regulations. The executive branch of government includes the Cabinet departments and numerous independent agencies and commissions.

> *A bureaucracy literally means government by desks or clerks. When the government takes on more and more tasks, it hires more and more people to do them. The larger the bureaucracy, the greater the possibility that requests will be misplaced and that accountability will decrease.*

The Growing Bureaucracy

The trend for many years has been for the number of Federal employees to increase, and it is not likely that this trend will change. According to the Office of Personnel Management, in July 2005 the total number of Federal civilian employees was 2,725,117, almost all of them full-time. Of this number, over 2.66 million worked in the executive branch. This does not count uniformed military personnel or workers in intelligence and security agencies such as the Central Intelligence Agency and the Defense Intelligence Agency. When these categories are added in, the total Federal government payroll comes to about four million people. Obviously the president does not personally hire all of these people or sign their paychecks.

The president is responsible for appointing a few thousand of the highest level officials (Cabinet members, chairmen of agencies, etc.), subject to confirmation by the Senate. Personal advisors to the president are hired at his discretion. Most lower level Federal workers are civil service employees, which means that they cannot be fired just because the president might want to replace them with his friends and political supporters. The White House chef, telephone representatives in the Social Security Department, National

President Calvin Coolidge with Members of His Cabinet, 1924

Park rangers, and experts with the U.S. Army Corps of Engineers are examples of civil service workers who are hired to carry out specific responsibilities for the government.

National Park Ranger at Pearl Harbor, Hawaii, 2006

The Federal bureaucracy has developed a life of its own that does not depend on who is president or what party controls Congress. Congress has passed and presidents have signed into law many programs that are intended to help in specific situations (for example, public education and workplace safety) or particular groups (such as the poor, minorities, or the owners of small businesses). Once these programs are in place, it is extremely difficult to end them. Politicians often promise to create or increase government programs in the hope that those who might benefit from the programs will vote for them. Campaigning to end a program runs the risk of alienating voters.

For many years Republicans campaigned to cut the size of the Federal bureaucracy, but once they gained power they were reluctant to eliminate jobs. In his 1980 campaign, Ronald Reagan talked about eliminating the U.S. Department of Education, which had been created the year before under Democrat Jimmy Carter. However, after he was elected, Reagan did not take any meaningful steps to eliminate the department. Democrats have generally proposed more new Federal spending, while Republicans have generally taken a "Me too, just less of it" stance. Both parties campaign on what they say they want government to do for people instead of promising to leave people alone. At the same time, much of the populace has come to depend on and expect government programs to help them. These are major reasons why the Federal budget has ballooned to the size that it has.

In addition, Congress has frequently assigned to the bureaucracy the responsibility for developing rules and regulations to accomplish the purposes of the laws it passes. For example, when Congress created the Occupational Safety and Health Administration (OSHA), the law itself did not stipulate what place on the wall a fire extinguisher had to be mounted in a workplace. That regulation was developed by the OSHA bureaucracy, and it has the force of law. If an employer violates the regulation, OSHA can order the company to pay a fine until the regulation is met. The same is true with regulations formulated by the Environmental Protection Agency and many other Federal offices. This gives the bureaucracy a great deal of power, and Congress is usually unwilling to limit that power and take the responsibility for formulating regulations itself.

The bureaucracy has a life of its own also because of civil service laws protecting Federal employees. Before 1883, government workers were subject to dismissal by the president whenever he wished. When a president from a different party took office, he regularly cleaned house and appointed his political supporters to fill government jobs. This was called the spoils system, from the saying, "To the victor (in a battle) goes the spoils." The appointees did not have to be able; they just had to be politically loyal. In 1883, Congress passed the Pendleton Civil Service Act, which protected several thousand Federal employees from political dismissal. This was a step toward creating a professional bureaucracy, in which workers were hired for their ability to do a job well, not for their political loyalties. Later legislation expanded the number of Federal workers protected by civil service regulations. At the same time, laws have also limited the political activity in which Federal employees may engage. These laws are a double-edged sword. They protect people from being fired just because a president wants his supporters to get Federal jobs, but they also make it very difficult for a Federal worker to be fired for incompetence.

The White House Bureaucracy

The Federal bureaucracy includes fifteen Cabinet departments and all of the offices, bureaus, and administrations within them; independent agencies and regulatory commissions; and independent government corporations. We will look in more detail at this overall bureaucracy in the next unit.

The President's Desk in the Executive Offices Near the White House, c. 1920

In this lesson we will look at the White House bureaucracy. The president's personal and official staff numbers about 4,000 persons. The president is responsible for them all, but day-to-day oversight is handled by the White House Chief of Staff, who has a significant staff himself to carry out his work. The White House staff includes the press secretary (the president's public spokesman), legal staff, a number of personal advisors, and several councils and offices (with their staffs) that deal with specific issues for the president. These bodies were established at various times, mostly by laws passed by Congress. The White House staff extends the vision of the president and enables much more to be done than one man could do. Some of these White House councils and offices are described below.

- The Council of Economic Advisors is a three-member panel appointed by the president and confirmed by the Senate that prepares reports on the economy, reviews the impact on the economy of activities by the government and private businesses, and makes recommendations to the president about economic policy.

- The National Security Council is a group that includes the vice president, some Cabinet officers, and other selected officials. This body advises the president on foreign relations and other matters of national security.

- The Office of Management and Budget is responsible for preparing the annual Federal budget and for seeing that it is properly executed in the agencies of the executive branch. It makes recommendations on how the Federal bureaucracy can be made more efficient and effective.

- The Domestic Policy Council advises the president with regard to such issues as health, housing, transportation, welfare, and labor.

- The Homeland Security Council focuses on immigration issues and policies regarding new immigrants and how to handle immigrants living in the U.S.

- The Council on Environmental Quality coordinates environmental policies and helps to prepare new proposals for Federal action regarding the environment.

- The National Economic Council coordinates policies related to national and world economic issues.

- The Office of National AIDS Policy advises the president regarding Federal policies on AIDS research.

- The Office of National Drug Control Policy establishes goals, priorities, and policies to reduce the manufacture, sale, and use of illegal drugs as well as drug-related crime.

- The Office of Science and Technology Policy advises the president with regard to the impact of science and technology on domestic and international affairs. For example, it reports on the importance of information technology in the field of medicine and the significance of the space program in developing scientific knowledge.

- The Office of the U.S. Trade Representative develops and coordinates U.S. trade policies with other countries, including the negotiating of trade agreements. The Trade Representative is a Cabinet-level position.

- The Foreign Intelligence Advisory Board is a group of people from outside of the government who advises the president on the quality of strategic intelligence the U.S. government is gathering about other countries.

- The USA Freedom Corps encourages volunteer service in the U.S. and oversees the work of the Peace Corps in other countries.

- The White House Military Office assists the president in carrying out his role as commander in chief. This office is especially involved in maintaining clear communication between the president and the operations that are under the oversight of the Department of Defense.

- The Office of Administration oversees the operations of the White House and provides technical support (such as research assistance) to other White House offices.

- The Office of Faith-Based and Community Initiatives was created by President George W. Bush to help religious groups and community-based groups compete equitably for Federal money in trying to serve the needs of Americans.

Executive Orders

A tool that presidents use to implement their agenda without having to wait for Congress to pass a law is the executive order. Since the president is head of the executive branch, he can issue guidelines and regulations that those under him must follow. Many times these executive orders set a pattern for the rest of society. For instance, for many years, states observed various days as Thanksgiving. Franklin Roosevelt issued an executive order declaring the last Thursday in November as the Thanksgiving holiday for Federal workers (it was later changed to the fourth Thursday). States and cities fell in line with this order, even though they did not have to. In another and more significant move, President Harry Truman ordered the military to end racial segregation in the composition of its units. This was one step in the long process of bringing racial equality to our country.

Although abortion is legal in the United States, the president can decide how the bureaucracy spends money to support it overseas. Republicans Ronald Reagan and George H. W. Bush issued executive orders forbidding Federal money going to private groups that sponsored abortions or distributed abortion information in other countries. They also banned abortions in military hospitals. When Bill Clinton became President, he issued new executive orders reversing those policies and making such activities legal. Then when George W. Bush became President, he reinstituted the previous bans.

President Harry Truman, 1950

Presidential Agendas and Leadership Styles

The Constitution says that the president must take care to see that Federal laws are faithfully executed. However, every president has his own agenda of programs he wants to emphasize. A presidential candidate emphasizes certain issues. If he is elected, he believes that he has a mandate to pursue those issues. In doing this, he can direct the Attorney General to pursue enforcement of some laws and lessen enforcement of other laws. A president might make enforcement of civil rights laws a high priority and overlook enforcement of immigration laws, for instance. He might order an investigation of labor union activities but not strictly enforce workplace safety regulations.

A president also sometimes decides on a course that is not what most people expect him to do. For example, Republicans have not been known for their concern for environmental issues; but it was during Republican Nixon's term that the Environmental Protection Agency was created (by a vote of the Democratic-controlled Congress). In another example, Democrats have long favored increasing the number and scope of Federal programs. However, Democrat Bill Clinton (with a Republican majority in Congress) oversaw the most significant reform of welfare in a generation. Clinton also initiated the National Performance Review, which attempted to streamline the operation of the Federal bureaucracy by simplifying standards and procedures. A president often finds that the priorities he has to pursue while in office are different from the campaign agenda on which he ran for the office.

Individual presidents also have different management styles that characterize their administrations. Franklin Roosevelt tended to carry out his own ideas on foreign policy, which made his Secretary of State, Cordell Hull, a less important player. By contrast, Richard Nixon depended heavily on his Secretary of State, Henry Kissinger. Jimmy Carter tended to be a detail person, taking time to micro-manage the operation of the White House staff. He also wanted American foreign policy to encourage the protection of human rights in other countries. Richard Nixon was more pragmatic in his foreign policy, showing a willingness to overlook human rights issues if a government was willing to help the United States in opposing Communism. Ronald Reagan tended to pursue major ideas and let his Cabinet and staff deal with details. George W. Bush governed by consensus, working with his Cabinet and staff to determine the best policies to pursue.

President Ronald Reagan (right) with
Secretary of Defense Caspar Weinberger, 1983

Then Nebuchadnezzar the king sent word to assemble
the satraps, the prefects and the governors,
the counselors, the treasurers, the judges,
the magistrates and all the rulers of the provinces
to come to the dedication of the image
that Nebuchadnezzar the king had set up.
Daniel 3:2

Lesson 30 — The President's Relations with Congress

The Presidency's single most important political relationship is that with Congress.
—Chester Bowles

The presidency and Congress are different branches of government, but they have an important relationship to each other. Let us review the aspects of this relationship:

- When no one wins a majority in the electoral college (which has happened twice in American history), the president is selected by the House of Representatives.

- The vice president is the presiding officer of the Senate.

- Congress passes laws, and the president sees that the laws are carried out and enforced.

- The executive branch draws up the Federal budget, Congress passes it, and the president oversees the spending of the money.

- The president informs Congress of the state of the Union and recommends legislation that he thinks Congress should enact.

- Congress declares war, while the president is commander in chief of the military forces.

- The president can veto legislation passed by Congress, and Congress must pass a vetoed bill by a two-thirds majority for it to be enacted over the veto.

- The Senate must approve treaties that the president makes with other countries and nominations that the president makes to fill positions such as Federal judges, ambassadors, and Cabinet members.

- The president can call a special session of Congress, and he has the authority to dismiss Congress (though the latter has never been done).

- Congress sets the salary for the president and other officials of the executive branch.

- The president and vice president are elected by national vote, while Senators and Representatives are elected by states and districts.

- Congressional committees can and often do investigate actions of the president and other executive officials.

- The House has the power to impeach the president and the Senate has the power to hold an impeachment trial.

In this lesson we will further examine the complex and sometimes difficult relationship between Congress and the president.

Initiative for Legislation

The primary initiative for offering suggestions for new laws lies with the president, but this has not always been the case. In the early days of the republic, Congress was understood to have the more powerful role in the Federal government; and members of Congress proposed the most significant pieces of legislation that the House and Senate considered. Most early presidents saw their main job to be merely carrying out what Congress passed.

A few presidents were exceptions to the rule. Andrew Jackson was the most activist president before

> *When a President nominates someone for a Federal judgeship or some other Federal position, he will try to be sure that the Senators and Representatives of his party in the nominee's home state support the nomination. Traditionally, the Senate has confirmed nominees when the Senators from the nominee's home state support him.*

the Civil War in terms of pushing his own legislative agenda. Presidents after the Civil War sometimes had specific ideas they promoted, such as a cut in tariffs. Theodore Roosevelt in the early 20th century began to change the image of the presidency. Roosevelt was a reformer who wanted to use his position to accomplish good. He initiated many reforms, such as greater conservation of natural resources and better food inspection laws. He also used the

President Woodrow Wilson, c. 1913

prestige of the presidency to bring labor and management together when a union strike threatened the economy.

Woodrow Wilson was also a progressive who wanted to see Congress pass specific reforms. This tradition of presidential action continued with Franklin Roosevelt in the 1930s as he urged the Federal government to respond vigorously to the Great Depression. Now presidential candidates run for office by promoting the various proposals they want to see Congress pass.

The State of the Union

The Constitution requires the president to give to Congress information on the state of the Union and to recommend to Congress legislation that he deems important. Since 1790, presidents have given an annual State of the Union address to Congress. These used to be given in December when the Congressional session began. They were called the president's annual message, and for many years they were delivered by someone other than the president. Thomas Jefferson was a poor public speaker, and he had his first address read by his personal secretary, Meriwether Lewis. Woodrow Wilson was the first modern president to give his

President Jimmy Carter Surrounded by Members of Congress at the 1980 State of the Union Address

State of the Union speech in person. Now that Congress convenes in January, the president gives his State of the Union speech a few days after the start of the Congressional session to a joint session of Congress, with the Cabinet, the Supreme Court, and a selected audience present, and to a nationwide television and radio audience.

In the speech, the president touches on what his administration has accomplished; but in most cases the speech is dominated by the president's legislative proposals. A few moments of State of the Union speeches are memorable. It was during the 1823 speech that President James Monroe declared the idea that European nations should no longer consider the Western Hemisphere as open to colonization and that the United States claimed a primary interest in the affairs of the region. This became known as the Monroe Doctrine, and it has guided American foreign policy to a significant degree to this day. In 1848, President James K. Polk confirmed in his annual message that gold had been discovered in California. This set off a gold rush the next year, as "Forty-Niners" headed for California to try to make their fortune.

> For each State of the Union address, one Cabinet member is selected not to attend the speech, just in case a national emergency occurs during the speech that would require a member of the executive branch to make an immediate decision. During the speech, members of Congress often applaud and cheer the President's points. The justices on the Supreme Court, however, do not join in the applause and cheering.

Pressing His Case

The president's relations with Congress involve much more than just delivering a speech once per year. Even if Congress is led by the president's party, Congress does not want to be just a rubber stamp for whatever the president wants. Individual members have their own initiatives that they want to pursue, members often want to modify what the president has requested, and members of the opposition party will sharply criticize the president's proposals and put forward alternative ideas of their own. This means that the president must continue to make his case to Congress and to the American people. He can do this through making speeches to influence public opinion, issuing statements to the press, and using his influence with individual members of Congress.

It is a significant event for the president to invite one or more members of Congress to meet with him personally. At such meetings he can remind the members of their party principles and of the importance he places on his legislative agenda. Often an assistant to the president will telephone members of Congress to try to get their support for a measure. The president may offer to fund a program for a member's district or state in the annual budget in exchange for the member's vote. Alternatively, the president can make it clear that a vote against his agenda will likely mean that the member's district will not receive the funding that the member might like to have.

Sometimes the members of the president's own party will not support the president's agenda. Senators and Congressmen have their own constituencies that they represent, and the voters in those districts may not support the president's program. For example, civil

President and Mrs. Clinton Debarking from Air Force One, 1993

rights legislation that was proposed by Democratic Presidents John Kennedy and Lyndon Johnson in the 1960s was fiercely opposed by most Democratic Senators and Representatives from the South. These members of Congress did not believe that such changes were best for the country; and they did not want to lose the support of voters back home, most of whom opposed greater equality for black people.

One of President Bill Clinton's early initiatives was his desire to make a radical change in the nation's health care system and place more of it under Federal control. First Lady Hillary Clinton chaired a commission to draw up a proposal to submit to Congress. However, the ideas that Clinton proposed were too radical even for many Democrats to support. The idea died in Congress, even though the Democrats had majorities in both the House and the Senate. Partly as a result of Clinton's overreaching on his health care agenda, in the 1994 Congressional elections the Republicans gained majorities in both houses for the first time in forty years.

Gridlock

When the president is of one party and the other party has majorities in Congress, it is easy for the two sides to become hardened in their opposition to each other. This situation is called gridlock, a term used to describe a traffic jam in a big city. In the 1980s, after several years with a

> *The President's party tends to lose seats in Congress in off-year elections, when there is not a Presidential race. After the President has been in office for two years, some people want to see a change.*

Republican president and a Democrat-controlled Congress, some people came to like the idea of Congress being controlled by one party and the presidency by the other. They felt safer that Congress would not act to infringe on their freedoms or to pass new taxes!

> *For several years in the late twentieth century, Presidents asked Congress to pass a law that would give the President a line-item veto. This would enable him to veto certain sections of a law passed by Congress without his having to veto the entire bill. It was thought that a line-item veto could be a check on pork barrel spending but still allow needed legislation to remain intact. The Republican Congress enacted a line-item veto that was to take effect January 1, 1997. President Clinton employed the line-item veto, but it was almost immediately challenged in court. In June of 1998, the U.S. Supreme Court struck down the line-item veto as unconstitutional. The Court held that the Constitution gave the President the right to veto legislation, not parts of legislation. A line-item veto, the Court said, was tantamount to letting the President craft legislation instead of Congress doing so.*

However, when Congress and the president get into ugly squabbles, both sides lose. In 1995, the Republican-led Congress came to a standoff with Democrat Bill Clinton over the budget he proposed. Congress refused to enact it, and the President refused to change it. In the fall of that year, many non-essential aspects of the Federal government (such as national parks and many offices in the bureaucracy) were shut down for a few days. Neither side gained much respect from the American public in the showdown. The Republicans in Congress probably lost more respect than the President did.

Congress has generally stood behind the president in foreign affairs, especially during wartime, even if the president's party does not control Congress. A divided government can make our military effort look weak and uncertain. However, this is not always the case. Opposition by Democrats in Congress to Lyndon Johnson's Vietnam War policies was a key factor in Johnson's decision not to run for re-election in 1968. Today the atmosphere in Washington has become so partisan that even during the war against terrorism, President George W. Bush's critics spoke openly about their opposition to the war, despite their initial support for him immediately after the September 11, 2001 terrorist attacks.

> One power of the President that could be considered a judicial role is his right to grant a pardon or reprieve to anyone convicted in Federal court, although he cannot issue a pardon to someone convicted in an impeachment trial. A pardon sets aside the conviction; and a reprieve changes the person's sentence, such as from the death penalty to life imprisonment or to time served. It is common for a President to issue such pardons a few days before he leaves office. Many times the pardons are given to his political friends who have run afoul of the law. It is a personal favor he can extend to his supporters, and Congress cannot do anything about it. Members of the opposition party in Congress might wonder if a President has received bribes as an inducement to issue the pardons, but usually nothing ever comes of such charges.

The relationship between the president and Congress has a major influence over what the Federal government does. When the relationship is good, laws can be passed even if different parties control the executive and legislative branches. When the relationship is poor, little is accomplished, even if the same party controls both branches. While both sides claim to be acting in the best interests of the American people, it is often the American people who are caught in the middle when a political tug-of-war takes place in Washington.

Like a roaring lion and a rushing bear
is a wicked ruler over a poor people.
Proverbs 28:15

Reading

- 2004 State of the Union Address by George W. Bush (*WHTT*, p. 84)

7 The Modern Bureaucracy

This unit takes you on a journey through the Federal bureaucracy, which is primarily part of the executive branch of government that is under the president. We will survey each of the Cabinet departments and introduce several of the independent agencies that carry out the laws passed by Congress.

Lessons in This Unit

Lesson 31—Departments of State, Treasury, and Defense
Lesson 32—Departments of Justice, Interior, and Agriculture
Lesson 33—Departments of Commerce, Labor, HUD, and Transportation
Lesson 34—Departments of HHS, Energy, Education, Veterans' Affairs,
                     and Homeland Security
Lesson 35—Independent Agencies

Activity Idea

Which functions of the bureaucracy seem appropriate, and which seem redundant, unnecessary, or unconstitutional? Write a letter to the editor of a newspaper (about 300 words) and make a clear case for your position.

If you are using the optional *Quiz and Exam Book*, answer the questions for each lesson after you have completed the lesson and read any assigned readings in *We Hold These Truths*. After you have completed Lesson 35, take the quiz for Unit 7.

Lesson 31—Departments of State, Treasury, and Defense

To be prepared for war is one of the most effectual means of preserving peace.
—George Washington (1790)

In this unit we will survey the Federal bureaucracy to give an idea of the many areas of American life in which the Federal government operates. We will look at the departments of the executive branch (the Cabinet departments), in the order in which they were created, to convey the changing and broadening emphasis of what the Federal government does. The final lesson will look at the independent agencies of the Federal government which do not come under an executive department.

Secretary of War Dwight Davis, 1925

The Constitution says that the president can require written opinions from the heads of the executive departments regarding any aspect of the duties of their offices. This means that the president is over and is responsible for the actions of the executive departments. However, the relationship between the chief executive and the members of his Cabinet goes far beyond an occasional request for a written opinion. The Cabinet officials are expected to promote and carry out the vision of the president in their various areas of service. Most presidents have met with their Cabinet at least on a weekly basis for an exchange of ideas and information.

The Department of State

The State Department was the first executive department to be created, and the Secretary of State is considered to be the highest ranking Cabinet member. The Continental Congress established a Department of Foreign Affairs in 1781. Under the Constitution, the name was changed to the Department of State in 1789. Thomas Jefferson was the first Secretary of State, serving under George Washington.

The purpose of the State Department is to oversee America's relations with other countries and to use American influence for peace around the world. The Secretary of State is the president's chief advisor and chief spokesman with regard to foreign policy. The Department oversees the work of U.S. ambassadors, consuls, and other diplomats in foreign countries. In addition, the State Department is responsible for negotiating treaties with other nations.

The Secretary of State is assisted by a Deputy Secretary of State, formerly called the

> *In the early years of the country, the Secretary of State was seen as the chief stepping stone to the presidency. Six men who served in the position went on to become president by the 1840s, and several men who aspired to be president also filled the post.*

The Cabinet also includes officials that the president wants to be part of the meetings and whose work he believes is important enough for them to be included. The vice president is part of the Cabinet meetings, as are these other Cabinet-level officials: the White House Chief of Staff and Deputy Chief of Staff, the administrator of the Environmental Protection Agency, the director of the Office of Management and Budget, the head of the National Drug Control Policy, the U.S. Trade Representative, the U.S. ambassador to the United Nations, the Director of the Central Intelligence Agency, the White House counsel (the president's attorney), the president's National Security Advisor, and the Director of National Intelligence.

Under Secretary of State. Beneath them are various offices headed by Under or Assistant Secretaries for specific issues, such as Political Affairs or Arms Control, or for specific regions of the world; for example, African Affairs, Near Eastern Affairs, and Western Hemisphere Affairs. All Cabinet departments are organized with Under or Assistant Secretaries overseeing various sub-departments. The U.S. ambassador to the United Nations is considered to be part of the State Department's organization. Several other offices are also part of the State Department, including the United States Information Agency, which disseminates information (some say propaganda) about the United States to other countries.

Cordell Hull, Secretary of State under Franklin Roosevelt, was instrumental in establishing the United Nations in 1945. For his work, Hull received the Nobel Peace Prize.

The State Department promotes the work of peace in trouble spots around the world, oversees security agreements that the United States has with other countries (such as NATO, the North Atlantic Treaty Organization), and initiates economic assistance from the United States to other countries. Following World War II, Secretary of State George Marshall, a former Army general, encouraged American public and private investment in the rebuilding of Europe. This effort came to be known as the Marshall Plan and was a key to rebuilding Europe after the war. During the Cold War between the United States and the Soviet Union, the State Department conducted negotiations that resulted in the limitation and eventual reduction of nuclear weapons held by both countries. Nixon's Secretary of State, Henry Kissinger, conducted what was called shuttle diplomacy in the Middle East, going back and forth between the leaders of Israel and of Arab countries that did not recognize Israel, in an attempt to ease tensions in the region.

Secretary of State Cyrus Vance (left) with Soviet Foreign Minister Andrei Gromyko, 1977

Today the primary work of the Secretary of State and the State Department involves encouraging other countries to participate in the war on terrorism and promoting democracy around the world, especially in places such as Iraq and Cuba.

Perhaps the most common way that the average American citizen has contact with the State Department is through the issuance of passports and visas to American travelers and through the department's advisories of places in the world where travel by Americans might not be safe.

The Department of the Treasury

Just as the State Department guides American involvement in world affairs, the Treasury Department oversees the economic life of the nation. The department was founded in 1789. Alexander Hamilton was the first Treasury Secretary.

The work of the Treasury Department includes collecting and disbursing revenue, but its responsibilities are much more diverse than that. The Bureau of Engraving and Printing handles the production and distribution of our nation's paper currency. It also prints Treasury investment securities (Treasury notes). The Bureau printed U.S. postage stamps for over a century until that part of its work was discontinued in 2005. The U.S. Mint produces the coins that we use. The Comptroller of the Currency maintains oversight of the nation's banking system. The Treasurer of the United States (not the same person as the Secretary of the Treasury) oversees the paying out of funds as set forth in the Federal budget. The Bureau of the Public Debt (how sad that we need an entire bureau devoted to the public debt!) borrows money that the Federal government needs and also issues Treasury securities, which are a major part of our public debt. The Treasury Department also maintains the country's holdings of gold bullion at Fort Knox, Kentucky.

*Secretary of the Treasury
Andrew Mellon, 1929*

The largest office within the Treasury Department is the Internal Revenue Service (IRS), which collects taxes within the United States. The IRS checks the accuracy of tax returns sent in by American citizens and enforces tax laws passed by Congress and tax regulations formulated by the IRS itself. This is no small task. The IRS Code runs to thousands of pages and is filled with complicated provisions, exceptions, and formulae that make the filing of taxes a burden for many Americans. At times IRS agents can be oppressive in their treatment of private citizens. The dreaded IRS audit can cause great hardship and worry for an individual or family. Wealthier taxpayers hire accountants and lawyers who help them chart their course through the maze of tax laws and who find loopholes in the tax code that enable them legally to avoid paying taxes they would otherwise owe on their income.

The Treasury Department formulates government policies with regard to the economy and issues reports on economic conditions and trends. The Department is also involved with guiding the country's involvement in the world economy.

Several functions that were traditionally carried out by the Treasury Department have been transferred to other executive departments. The U.S. Customs and Border Protection Bureau, the Coast Guard, and the Secret Service have become part of the Department of Homeland Security. The Bureau of Alcohol, Tobacco, Firearms, and Explosives is now part of the Department of Justice.

Department of Defense

The third original executive department created during Washington's first term was the Department of War. Then in 1798, the Department

> Today's military operation is large, but it was even larger during World War II when the United States had over 16 million men and women in uniform at some point during the conflict.

of the Navy was formed. Between 1947 and 1949, the nation's military structure underwent several changes that resulted in the War and Navy Departments becoming part of the all-encompassing Department of Defense (DOD). The headquarters of the DOD is one of the most recognizable buildings in the world: the Pentagon in Arlington, Virginia, just across the Potomac River from the District of Columbia.

Secretary of the Treasury Henry Fowler (left) and Secretary of Defense Robert McNamara Meeting at the Pentagon, 1966

The mission of the Defense Department includes protecting our country and our vital interests from attack and providing a military response when we are attacked. The Department of Defense is the nation's largest employer. About 1.4 million men and women are on active duty, and another 650,000 civilian employees support their service. In addition, another 1.2 million Americans serve in the National Guard or Reserves. Uniformed personnel or other DOD workers are in over 140 countries.

The military draft is the process through which men between certain ages are required to register with the Selective Service System and are liable to be called to active duty in the United States Army (the other branches of service have always been volunteer). A draft was instituted during the Civil War and was widely unpopular. It was reinstituted during World War I and discontinued following that conflict. The first peacetime draft began in 1940 as the country began preparing for possible involvement in World War II. Drafting men continued to be the government's policy after World War II ended. During the Korean War, the time of service for draftees was set at two years. The draft continued through the 1950s, when perhaps the most famous draftee, Elvis Presley, was ordered into the Army. Selective Service supplied many men for the Army during the Vietnam conflict, but it became a controversial policy as the war effort became unpopular. A yearly

A U.S. Marine in North Korea, 1951

draft lottery based on birthdates of men turning 18 was instituted by President Nixon. Only those whose birthdays were drawn early in the lottery were likely to be drafted. This allowed most men—those who were not chosen in the lottery—to be relieved of concern about being drafted. Exemptions called deferments for those in college and for other reasons were common. The draft was ended in 1973. Young men are still required to register with Selective Service when they turn 18, in case their service is needed in a time of national emergency; but the Army is now an all-volunteer force.

The budget of the Department of Defense for fiscal 2006 was $419 billion. During the 1960s, the Defense budget consumed over half of the total Federal budget, whereas today the Defense outlay is only about 16% of total Federal expenditures. Defense spending has grown, but Federal spending in other areas has far outstripped increases in the military budget.

The Joint Chiefs of Staff (JCS) are the highest ranking members of the U.S. military. The Army, Navy, Air Force, and Marines each have one representative in the group. The military officers who are Chairman and Vice Chairman of the JCS can come from any of the branches, although the Chairman has traditionally come from the Army. The Joint Chiefs advise the president, the Secretary of Defense, and the National Security Council. The Chairman coordinates military operations and oversees the National Military Command Center (or "war room").

All U.S. military forces are organized into nine Unified Combatant Commands (UCC). The UCCs oversee actions in five geographic areas of the world plus the work of the specific task commands of Transportation, Joint Forces, Special Operations, and Strategic Commands.

The Constitution does not use the term Cabinet to refer to the heads of the executive departments. During his presidency, George Washington began meeting with the heads of the departments for their advice. The group came to be called the Cabinet, the French word for a small room, suggesting the place where these private meetings took place. President Andrew Jackson spent more time with and was more influenced by a group of political friends and advisors than his department heads. This group came to be called the kitchen cabinet, a wry term which suggested the informal nature of their meetings.

The horse is prepared for the day of battle,
but victory belongs to the Lord.
Proverbs 21:31

Chairman of the Joint Chiefs of Staff Navy Admiral Mike Mullen, 2008

Lesson 32—Departments of Justice, Interior, and Agriculture

I think our governments will remain virtuous for many centuries; as long as they are chiefly agricultural.

—Thomas Jefferson (c. 1787)

The Department of Justice

The office of U.S. Attorney General was created by Congress in 1789. The law stipulated that the role was to be filled by someone "learned in the law." He was to be the attorney representing the Federal government in cases that came before the Supreme Court, and he was to advise the president and the heads of the executive departments on matters of the law.

The work of the Attorney General quickly grew to the point that several assistants were added to the staff. Private attorneys were hired to prosecute individual cases in Federal courts. The legal workload for the Attorney General's office increased dramatically following the Civil War. As a result, in 1870 Congress established the Department of Justice (DOJ) to be headed by the Attorney General. This department conducts the legal business of the United States government. It enforces Federal law and prosecutes cases in Federal court. Today most of the legal work is done by attorneys who work in the department as opposed to private attorneys hired on a case-by-case basis.

The 1870 law also established the position of Solicitor General within the DOJ. The Solicitor General and his assistants are the government's representatives before the U.S. Supreme Court. His office is involved in about two-thirds of the cases that come before the Supreme Court (some cases involve two individuals or a suit by an individual against a state). The Solicitor General decides which cases the government should appeal to the Supreme Court if the judgment of the Federal appeals court goes against the government. He can also file an amicus curiae (Latin for "friend of the court") brief in a Supreme Court case if the government is not a party but has a special interest in how the case turns out.

As the nature and extent of Federal law has grown, the work of the DOJ has grown as well. The Attorney General still advises the president and Cabinet heads on legal matters, but the DOJ also supervises Federal prisons, advises the president with regard to requests he receives for paroles and pardons, oversees the work of U.S. district attorneys and U.S. marshals, and conducts programs to educate the public on crime prevention.

The DOJ now includes many offices and bureaus that work with specific matters relating to the execution of justice on the Federal level. Perhaps the best known of these are U.S. Attorneys, who represent the government in Federal district courts, and the Federal Bureau of Investigation (FBI), which investigates threats of terrorism and foreign intrigue against the country as well as alleged violations of Federal criminal law. The U.S. marshals are best known for being the law enforcement officers in the old West, but they still function today. In fact, they are the oldest Federal law enforcement agency. U.S. marshals usually carry out Federal death sentences. Until the 1865 creation of the Secret Service, U.S. marshals pursued counterfeiters.

Among the many other agencies of the DOJ are the Drug Enforcement Administration; the Bureau of Alcohol, Tobacco, Firearms, and Explosives; and the Civil Rights Division, each of which enforces Federal law in those areas. The Tax Division enforces laws dealing with internal revenue. The Department has an Environmental and Natural Resources Division and an Office of Tribal Justice (the latter dealing with laws related to Native Americans and Indian reservations). The Office of Juvenile Justice and Delinquency Prevention deals with juvenile offenders and their victims. The U.S. National Central Bureau works with the international police organization INTERPOL in tracking down criminals who operate on a world-wide scale.

The Federal Bureau of Prisons oversees the operation of Federal prisons and penitentiaries. The U.S. Parole Commission considers requests for parole by those who have been convicted of Federal crimes, and it oversees the conduct of those who have been given parole. As with any large bureaucracy, the DOJ has offices that deal with internal and non-enforcement matters, such as the Community Relations Office, the Office of Information and Privacy, and the Office of Professional Responsibility.

Department of the Interior

On the last day of its existence, March 3, 1849, the 30th Congress created the first new executive department since the Washington Administration. The Department of the Interior was formed as a catch-all agency charged with overseeing a wide range of domestic activities of the Federal government. It was intended as the complement to the State Department, which handled the government's relations with foreign countries.

In the past, the responsibilities of the Interior Department have included the Patent Office, the Census Bureau, the Interstate Commerce Commission, the Bureau of (Veterans') Pensions, the Bureau of Labor, and the Bureau of Education. None of these agencies was large at first, so it made sense for them to be placed in the department responsible for domestic affairs. All of these responsibilities have been transferred to other departments. One can see why Interior has been called "The Department of Everything Else."

Today the Interior Department is charged with protecting the natural environment; developing the country's natural resources; and managing our national parks, monuments, and wildlife refuges. The Department is responsible for just over 500 million acres of land, or about one-fifth of the nation's land area. It also has oversight of the minerals underneath that land area, which means that Interior controls about two-thirds of our oil and gas reserves. It protects over 1,200 endangered or threatened animal species.

Federal agencies issue a total of about 4,500 new regulations every year that have the weight of law. Few regulations are ever removed, so the total number of government rules is almost always growing.

The Bureau of Indian Affairs manages Indian reservations and maintains the Federal government's relations with over 500 tribes. The U.S. Geological Survey produces maps and conducts scientific research in such areas as geology, earthquakes, and water quality. The Fish and Wildlife service works to protect fish, wildlife, and their habitats from contamination and abuse. The Bureau of Reclamation returns to usability land and water that have been damaged by previous poor use. The Interior Department sees that mining operations are conducted with safety for the workers and respect for the land. As a specific example of the Department's work, the Minerals Management Service has helped local governments restore sand to Florida beaches that were damaged by hurricanes. The Department also has responsibility for oversight of many U.S. territories, including Guam,

Pago Pago, American Samoa

American Samoa, and the U.S. Virgin Islands.

One area of controversy in the Department's responsibilities involves how it manages the mineral reserves under its care. Some people want to see the oil reserves used so that the U.S. will be less dependent on foreign oil. This involves leasing to private companies the right to drill wells on public land. Those who oppose such a policy say that drilling for oil will damage the environment and will endanger the habitats of irreplaceable wildlife. These opponents advocate energy conservation and the development of alternative sources of fuel, such as solar and wind power. Different presidents pursue different priorities on this issue, depending on their own personal beliefs and on the special interest groups that support them (namely oil companies or environmentalists).

The issue is not completely in the hands of the Interior Department. Congress can pass legislation requiring action on a particular issue, such as either releasing or protecting the oil reserves under the Arctic National Wildlife Refuge (ANWR) in Alaska.

Department of Agriculture

The Department of Agriculture (USDA) was begun in 1862 as a non-Cabinet level agency of the Federal government. It became an executive department in 1889. It was during this period that the Midwest and Great Plains became the food basket for the United States and the world. The Agriculture Department was formed to oversee the operation of our country's first industry, agriculture. Also in 1862, Congress passed (1) the Homestead Act, which encouraged individuals to establish 160-acre farming homesteads, mostly in Midwestern and Plains states, and (2) the Morrill Act, which encouraged states to establish universities to teach agricultural and mechanical arts.

The USDA inspects and grades foods that are produced in the U.S. and imported into the country. It supervises farm production to help prices be fair and to help farmers get a fair return for their work. The Department provides subsidies for growers of certain crops and sponsors programs to improve farming techniques. It also helps develop markets for U.S. farm products in other countries.

The work of the Agriculture Department, like that of other executive departments, is extensive. The Food and Nutrition Service provides food and dietary education to school children and low-income families. The Forest Service protects American forests and grasslands. The Rural Development Office offers financial assistance and educational programs to rural areas. The Natural Resources Conservation Service (formerly called the Soil Conservation Service) offers help in conserving and improving our natural resources and environment.

The Cooperative Extension Service of the USDA has offices in most U.S. counties. Extension Agents provide information on a variety of subjects, such as food safety and nutrition, sustainable agriculture, and waste management. The 4-H Club program is administered by the Cooperative Extension Service.

USDA regulations are intended to insure that the foods we buy in the market are accurately labeled. The Department, for example, sets standards on what procedures qualify an item to be sold as organic. This prevents a company from using pesticides and chemical fertilizers and then marketing the product as organic. Large agricultural companies want as few regulations as possible, so the USDA must strike a balance between the public's right to know and a food company's right to produce and market its goods.

One area of the Department's work that has aroused controversy is its program of farm subsidies and price supports. Farming is an unusual business in that, if farmers work hard and produce a bigger crop, the price they get can go down because of the greater supply that is on the market. Farmers can suffer from a general depression, wartime interruption of markets, or such factors as drought or insect plagues. Yet, farming is vital to the welfare of the nation. In addition, up to seventy years ago, farmers made up a large bloc of voters.

During the Depression, the Federal government began paying farmers subsidies to limit their production so that prices for farm products would go up. The goal was to help farmers have an adequate income through a combination of higher prices and government subsidies. Farmers now have acreage allotments, which tell how much each farmer is allowed to grow as a fraction of the total national production. If a farmer decides not to remain within his allotment, he will not receive a subsidy.

Department of Agriculture Poster
Encouraging Gardening During World War II

During World War II, increased farm production was required. Congress passed a law that encouraged farmers to produce more by promising that farmers would receive at least a set minimum price for what they produced. If the market price fell below the minimum, the Federal government would make up the difference so that farmers would still receive the minimum price. This minimum price was called parity, which was the price farmers had received in a good previous year, adjusted for inflation.

This all makes for a delicate balancing act involving farmers, the government, and the marketplace. Government planners are deeply involved in agricultural production, and the subsidy and parity programs are a major factor in American agriculture today.

The earth is the Lord's, and all it contains,
the world, and those who dwell in it.
Psalm 24:1

Reading

- "Our Unconstitutional Congress" by Stephen Moore (*WHTT*, p. 122)

Lesson 33—Departments of Commerce, Labor, HUD, and Transportation

[T]he chief business of the American people is business. . . . Of course the accumulation of wealth cannot be justified as the chief end of existence. . . . We make no concealment of the fact that we want wealth, but there are many other things that we want very much more. We want peace and honor, and that charity which is so strong an element of all civilization. The chief ideal of the American people is idealism. I cannot repeat too often that America is a nation of idealists. That is the only motive to which they ever give any strong and lasting reaction.

—Calvin Coolidge (1925)

The recent rapid growth of the Federal bureaucracy is reflected by these facts:

- The creation of the first eight Cabinet-level executive departments took 124 years, from 1789 until 1913.

- After the Commerce and Labor Departments were divided in 1913, another forty years passed until the Department of Health, Education, and Welfare (HEW) was formed in 1953. HEW was divided in 1979 to become the Departments of Health and Human Services and the Department of Education.

- However, just since 1965, six more Cabinet departments have been created. Moreover, most of the independent Federal agencies (which will be discussed in Lesson 35) were also created in the last half of the twentieth century.

Department of Commerce

The Agriculture Department was established in 1889. Only fourteen years later, in 1903, the Department of Commerce and Labor was created. This development reflected the growing importance of industry and other business to the national economy. However, the areas of business and labor were often in conflict. Labor unions were still in their early days, and many businesses refused to recognize unions as legitimate representatives of the workers. Thus in 1913, matters relating to labor were moved to a new Department of Labor, while the existing Cabinet department was renamed the Department of Commerce.

The Commerce Department oversees the president's economic policies. It encourages growth in the national economy and promotes trade by American

Department of Commerce Building, Washington, D.C., c. 1920

companies with other countries. Commerce representatives meet with Congressional committees and individual members of Congress to report on the economy and encourage passage of the president's economic proposals. They also work to prevent other countries from violating trade agreements and thus hindering American business. The Department of Commerce is charged with encouraging the development of American technology to keep our economy competitive in the world market.

A major function of the Commerce Department involves gathering and publishing statistics. For example, the Census Bureau is part of the Commerce Department. This agency conducts the national census that is taken every ten years. In the years between censuses, the bureau issues reports based on studies of the census and keeps up with changes in the population count. On a more routine basis, the Commerce Department gathers and reports data having to do with the activity of the national economy. When you hear statistics on economic growth, housing construction, retail sales, consumer confidence, and other topics related to business and industry, they usually originate in studies done by the Commerce Department.

The Commerce Department includes several bureaus whose work influences American business.

- The National Institute of Standards and Technology establishes accurate weights and measures, as called for in the Constitution, and makes sure that businesses follow these standards (for example, making sure that a can of food said to hold sixteen ounces actually does, and that medical radiology equipment meets safety standards for emissions and for levels of radiation used).

- The National Oceanic and Atmospheric Administration (NOAA) is best known for weather forecasting and disseminating weather data that it gathers from satellites and other sources. NOAA also conducts research in the seas and skies and carries out other functions. The weather can have a major influence on business activity.

- The United States Patent and Trademark Office approves or denies applications for patents of inventions and registers trademarks that businesses use to promote their products (remember that copyrights for creative works are filed with the Library of Congress).

Department of Labor

A Bureau of Labor was created in 1884 as part of the Interior Department. It later became an independent agency of the Federal government, then was combined with Commerce in 1903, and finally became a separate executive department in 1913.

The Labor Department was created to protect the rights of American workers. It oversees working conditions and enforces laws and regulations regarding such matters as workplace safety, non-discrimination in hiring, and payment of the minimum wage. Department agencies provide assistance to military veterans who want to be trained for new careers, protect the rights of women in the workplace, encourage the hiring of disabled workers, and carry out other functions on behalf of laborers.

Another function of the department is the collection and publication of statistics regarding American workers. The Bureau of Labor Statistics publishes monthly reports on the unemployment rate, the average hourly wage, worker productivity, and other matters related to the American labor force.

As with other departments, different administrations follow different policies regarding labor. The Secretary of Labor in a Republican administration might encourage open shops, which are places where a worker does not have to be a member of a union. The Democratic Party has traditionally received the support of labor unions, so Democratic administrations usually want to strengthen the power of unions.

Both industry and labor say they want to help the American economy, but each group will often have its own vision of what that means. Labor will press for higher wages and more benefits. Business management will want to limit these factors in order to increase their profits. American labor generally wants to keep factories operating in this country so that Americans can have jobs, while many businesses are moving production to other countries where they can pay workers less. The Departments of Labor and Commerce sometimes work at cross purposes as they promote the interests of workers and business owners.

Workers in a Parachute Factory, 1942

The Department of Housing and Urban Development

In the 1960s, the Johnson Administration was concerned about the inadequate housing in which many Americans lived. A related problem was the decaying state of many inner city areas. Businesses and families were moving to the suburbs, and many urban apartment houses were becoming dilapidated and crime-infested. President Johnson and the Democratic majority in Congress wanted the Federal government to step into these areas and provide the means for people to have safe, affordable housing and for cities to have more attractive and functional downtown areas. The Department of Housing and Urban Development (HUD) was created by Congress in 1965.

A major part of HUD's mission is to encourage homeownership. This reflects the widespread belief that those who own their homes will be motivated to maintain their property and will have a major investment that will help them financially in later years. Most of HUD's programs are directed toward low and middle income families.

The Federal Housing Administration (FHA) is a program begun in the New Deal and now overseen by HUD. The FHA insures mortgages that private banks make to homeowners. If the homeowner defaults on his payments, the FHA makes sure that the bank does not lose money. FHA loans are somewhat easier to obtain than conventional mortgages. For instance, they don't require as much of a down payment and the mortgage payment can be a larger percentage of a family's income than is the case with standard mortgages. In return, the FHA requires that the house being bought meets certain standards so that it can be sold more easily if the buyer defaults on his loan.

Another way that HUD encourages homeownership is by helping more money be available to use for mortgages. It does this through overseeing and regulating Federally-chartered investment corporations. The Federal National Mortgage Association (FNMA, nicknamed Fannie Mae) pools together FHA mortgage loans and sells these large packages to investors, who expect to make a profit over the long term. The money that investors pay is used to provide other mortgages. Two other similar investment corporations that HUD oversees are the Federal Home Loan Mortgage Corporation (FHLMC, or Freddie Mac) and the Government National Mortgage Association (GNMA, or Ginnie Mae). These corporations make a profit by charging fees to the investors who buy the loan packages.

HUD assists renters by providing subsidies to apartment owners who rent apartments to low-income families. A developer can apply to HUD for a contract to build an apartment complex. He agrees to rent apartments to people at a rate below what he needs to make

Former HUD Secretary Mel Martinez Assisting in the Construction of a House in Washington, D. C.

a profit, and HUD makes up the difference by paying the rest of the rent for the tenants. Family income determines how much rent a tenant actually pays. In some cases, the rent tenants pay is just a few dollars per month. These arrangements and the apartments that are built are supposed to follow Federal guidelines (for instance, the tenants may not use illegal drugs, and the apartments are to be properly maintained by the owner of the complex); but in actual practice the guidelines are sometimes not enforced.

HUD also makes sure that landlords and property sellers do not practice discrimination against potential tenants and buyers. Federal law says that a landlord cannot refuse to rent property to someone on the basis of race. The same is true regarding the selling of real estate. When a racial discrimination complaint is filed, HUD investigates the charge to see if it is true.

Another part of HUD's work is urban renewal or urban development. A city or a property owner in a city can apply for a HUD grant. The recipient will then use the grant money to rebuild or beautify a downtown area, in the hope that businesses will be encouraged to open in the area and that shoppers will be

attracted to come to the stores. A grant might also be used to build an office building to attract professional tenants so that downtown property might become more valuable and attractive. The goal of such investments is for HUD expenditures to help local economies.

Department of Transportation

Transportation is an integral part of American life. The first colonists traveled here by ships, and later settlers traveled further inland by wagons. River traffic extended the reach of the nation to the Mississippi, while railroads later connected the East and West Coasts. The age of the automobile that began in the early twentieth century radically changed American life. Cars influence where people live and work and where they go on vacations. Air traffic has now become a central part of the American transportation system.

The Interstate Highway system was begun in 1956. Ten years later, responding to the perceived need for unified Federal oversight of the nation's transportation system, Congress created the Department of Transportation (DOT). The Transportation Department develops the nation's transportation plans and policies. Various agencies within the Department oversee such areas as maritime and rail transportation, truck and bus transportation, and the development of mass transit systems. The Federal Highway Administration allocates funds for road construction projects, promotes construction site safety, and funds other programs related to our highways.

Transportation agencies with which many people are familiar include the Federal Aviation Administration (FAA), which establishes rules for air traffic. One part of this office is the National Transportation Safety Board, the body that investigates accidents involving airplanes. Another agency is the National Highway Traffic Safety Administration, which establishes rules for safer travel on the road, conducts crash tests on cars, and promotes the use of child restraint systems in cars.

Federal road construction projects are now commonplace, but at one time they were controversial because the Constitution nowhere gives the Federal government the authority to undertake such projects. They came to be accepted as a way to promote the general welfare of the country. Sometimes Congressional jurisdiction of Federal involvement in highways has been imaginative in order to make it legitimate. For instance, the Interstate system was promoted not only for public use but also as a way to help move military equipment and personnel around the country if the need arose.

In another example of legislative creativity, speed limits have always been a matter of state regulation. However, Congress

> An infrastructure is the basis or foundation upon which a system operates. The American transportation infrastructure includes roads, bridges, rail lines, and airports. The Department of Transportation oversees this infrastructure.

has sometimes made Federal funding for construction projects dependent on whether a state set its speed limits at or below what the Congressional law called for. Construction grants would only be given to a state if the state followed Federal speed limit guidelines. Since Federal funds often provide up to 90% of construction costs, no state would risk losing its share of funds by ignoring the Congressional speed limit requirement.

You who ride on white donkeys,
you who sit on rich carpets,
and you who travel on the road—sing!
Judges 5:10

Lesson 34—Departments of HHS, Energy, Education, Veterans' Affairs, and Homeland Security

A government that robs Peter to pay Paul can always depend upon the support of Paul.
— George Bernard Shaw, English dramatist and critic (1944)

Department of Health and Human Services

Congress created the Department of Health, Education, and Welfare in 1953 to replace the Federal Security Agency, which had been formed in 1939. In 1979, Education became a separate executive department; and the remaining functions were reorganized as the Department of Health and Human Services (HHS). The 300 or so programs of HHS have been one of the main reasons why the Federal budget and bureaucracy have grown as they have over the last twenty-five years. These statistics demonstrate the growth:

- In the 1960s, HEW accounted for about 3% of Federal expenditures.

- Today, HHS accounts for about 23% (or almost one-fourth) of Federal outlays.

- HHS alone has over 67,000 employees.

The works of HHS that affect the most people are Medicare, which provides health care for many elderly, and Medicaid, which helps states provide health care for low-income families. About one in four Americans are covered by one of these two programs. Other health-related agencies of HHS include:

- the Food and Drug Administration (FDA), which certifies the healthiness of foods and cosmetics sold in America and approves new prescription drugs;

- the National Institutes of Health, which is currently conducting 38,000 research projects related to health and disease; and

- the Centers for Disease Control and Prevention, which collect statistics on diseases, formulate policies for reducing disease, and issue public health warnings about dangers to the health of the nation.

HHS offers programs to help Indian tribes, the elderly, and the rural and urban poor; the Head Start preschool program; and welfare payments to an estimated five million people (most of whom are children).

The U.S. Public Health Service is an agency of 6,000 health professionals who work in various government offices. The head of the Public Health Service is the Surgeon General, who is nominated by the president and approved by the Senate. It was the Surgeon General's report issued in 1964 on the effects of smoking that sparked the government's efforts to reduce smoking.

Sometimes the Surgeon General can be a spokesperson for the president's health agenda. Dr. C. Everett Koop was President Ronald Reagan's Surgeon General and promoted ideas that many Christians endorsed. On the other hand, President Bill Clinton's first Surgeon General was Dr. Joycelyn Elders, who infuriated conservatives with some of her comments and policies. Dr. Elders served less than two years, and the post remained vacant for almost four years after her departure.

President George W. Bush Meeting with His Cabinet, 2005

Department of Energy

For most of the nation's history, energy resources were abundant and relatively inexpensive. Coal mining was a major industry, water power ran mills and later created electricity by means of hydroelectric dams, and domestic oil production provided most of the country's needs. In the 1970s, much of that changed. The Arab oil embargo of 1973 cut off a significant supply of petroleum to the country. Now the United States is even more dependent on foreign oil than it was in 1973, and restrictions on domestic production have limited the expansion of American oil output. Nuclear-powered energy was growing in Europe but was strongly opposed in the U.S. The days of cheap and easily-obtained energy were gone. It was clear that the country needed an overall energy strategy.

The Department of Energy was created by Congress in 1977. It promotes the president's plan for providing the energy that the country needs for its homes and industries and for the military. The Energy Department supports research in energy technology and encourages conservation. It also tries to make energy production and consumption safer for the environment. The Department of Energy is responsible for resolving issues related to the legacy of nuclear and radioactive materials left over from the Cold War era. It also is involved in protecting energy sources in the face of the threat of terrorism. Research into alternative and renewable sources of energy, such as solar and wind-powered energy, makes up a small portion of the Department's budget. The power of the traditional oil companies has thus far discouraged an all-out effort to find other workable sources of energy.

Department of Education

The Department of Education was created by an act of Congress in October of 1979 and began functioning in 1980. The creation of the Department was an effort by the Democrats to insure the support of the National Education Association, the liberal teachers' union, an effort

that has so far succeeded. The Department pulled together several programs that were scattered among a number of Federal departments. Today, the Department of Education's budget exceeds $70 billion and has significantly extended the reach of the Federal government into a field that was long reserved to the states.

Education now administers over 150 programs, such as the granting of student loans, training for migrant workers, vocational education, and programs for the handicapped. The Department provides grants to states and communities for various programs. It conducts research on education issues and publicizes statistical reports on school performance. The Education Department promotes the educational goals of the administration and works to prohibit discrimination in any form in the nation's schools.

Education Secretary Richard Riley, 1999

Department of Veterans' Affairs

The United States has often called upon its young men and women to defend our nation and our freedom. With that call comes the responsibility to provide financial support to those who serve. The American government has also accepted the responsibility of providing assistance to veterans after they leave military service and to the families of veterans. This is especially urgent for those who become disabled because of their military service.

Government pensions for Union Civil War veterans and assistance for World War I veterans, as well as support for the widows of servicemen, were major political issues in the years following those wars. Over time the Federal government began a few programs that were consolidated in 1930 in the Veterans Administration (the VA). The VA handled programs for veterans until 1989,

> *The VA notes on its website that caring for veterans, spouses, dependents, and survivors can continue for many years. It was not until 1911 that the last dependent of a soldier who fought in the Revolutionary War passed away. In 2006, the VA still provided benefits for five children of Civil War soldiers and over 400 widows and children of Spanish-American War service personnel.*

when the Cabinet-level Department of Veterans' Affairs was formed (keeping the familiar VA abbreviation). Raising the VA to the status of an executive department was a recognition of the commitment that the nation has to its military veterans and of the important social and political impact of veterans and their families.

Probably the best-known VA program is the system of health care facilities across the country. These services are provided to veterans (and sometimes to their dependents) at little or no cost. In 2004 five million persons received care at VA hospitals, clinics, and other facilities. Programs for veterans that were begun after World War II include VA mortgage loans, which make it easier for veterans to buy homes, and the GI Bill, which paid the expenses for discharged service personnel to attend colleges and vocational schools. Millions of veterans have taken advantage of these programs. The VA also offers other benefits to the nation's 24 million veterans.

Department of Homeland Security

One result of the terrorist attacks on the U.S. that occurred on September 11, 2001 was the most widespread reshuffling of the Federal government since the reorganization of the War Department in 1947. Almost immediately after the attacks, President George W. Bush announced the creation of the Office of Homeland Security to coordinate the government's efforts to make the country more safe from attacks in the future. Congress passed a law in early 2003 to create the Department of Homeland Security (DHS), which gave the program Cabinet status.

Homeland Security pulled together 22 agencies that had been in various Cabinet departments into one unified organization. These include the Secret Service and the Customs Service (formerly in the Treasury Department), the Coast Guard (originally a part of the Treasury Department but since 1967 in the Department of Transportation), the Transportation Security Administration (from the Transportation Department), the Immigration and Naturalization Service (from the Justice Department), and the Federal Emergency Management Agency (FEMA, which had been an independent agency).

The Department of Homeland Security analyzes intelligence regarding potential terrorist attacks and issues a threat advisory that indicates the likelihood of such an attack. The levels are Low, Guarded, Elevated, High, and Severe. Most of the time since 9/11, the level has been at least Elevated. In addition, the Department works to make such attacks less likely and formulates plans for how to respond in case of an attack. FEMA leads the Federal government's response to natural disasters such as the devastation from Hurricane Katrina along the Gulf Coast in the fall of 2005.

DHS provides public education about preventing terrorist attacks and makes grants to state and local law enforcement agencies by which those agencies can purchase equipment which can be used for emergency response.

I will say to the Lord, "My refuge and my fortress,
My God, in whom I trust!" . . .
You will not be afraid of the terror by night,
or of the arrow that flies by day.
Psalm 91:2, 5

Lesson 35—Independent Agencies

And as for interstate commerce—what is interstate commerce, anyway?
—"Grandpa Vanderhof," played by Lionel Barrymore,
in the movie, "You Can't Take It With You" (1938)

In addition to the Cabinet departments already described in this unit, the Federal government has created a number of independent agencies to oversee various areas on which Congress has legislated. Most of these agencies are part of the executive branch, but a few report directly to Congress.

These agencies, like the Cabinet departments, were created to address perceived needs. Some provide services to the public, while others regulate certain areas of the economy. A few were designed to coordinate governmental efforts that had become too complex to be left as they were. The Environmental Protection Agency is an example of an agency that was created to meet the need for coordinating efforts.

The agencies under Congressional oversight include the Library of Congress, the Government Printing Office, and the Government Accountability Office. The GAO, formerly called the General Accounting Office, is a watchdog agency created in 1921 to insure that the activities of Federal government offices and personnel stay within the law and within budget guidelines. It is understandable that the GAO needs to be separate from the branch of government that does most of the law enforcement and spending that is carried out by the Federal government.

The heads of most of these agencies are appointed by the president with approval by the Senate. This lesson does not list all of the independent agencies of the Federal government. Those discussed below show the wide range of activities carried on by the agencies.

Interstate Commerce Commission

The first independent agency that Congress created was the Interstate Commerce Commission (ICC), which came into existence in 1887. This seven-member panel was started for the purpose of overseeing the practices of railroads. Midwestern farmers had complained that the rail lines charged them high rates to carry their products and gave secret breaks to companies that did a great deal of business with the railroads. As it turned out, the ICC not only protected consumers but also sometimes protected businesses by allowing them to charge high rates. The commission was relatively slow to ban racial discrimination. It did not outlaw racial segregation on interstate buses and in bus stations until 1962. The ICC oversaw telephone service from 1910 to 1934, when the telephone system was taken over by the Federal Communications Commission.

Interstate commerce became more complex as the twentieth century progressed, with the coming of such developments as truck lines and air transport. In addition, pressure mounted from the public and from transportation companies for deregulation; that is, a lessening of government rules and regulations. The tasks of the ICC were either ended or given to other agencies, and the commission was abolished by an act of Congress in 1995. However, the ICC was the model for several other regulatory agencies that were established during the twentieth century, including the Federal Trade Commission, the Securities and Exchange Commission, and the Federal Communications Commission.

Economy and Business

The Federal Reserve Board of Governors (often called the Fed) oversees the system of Federal Reserve Banks, created in 1913, that serves as the nation's central bank. The Fed influences the nation's economy by varying the amount of money in circulation and by adjusting the interest rates that it charges banks for the money the banks use to make loans. It also regulates private banks and provides other banking services to the government and the public.

Federal Reserve Building, Washington, D.C., 1941

The Federal Deposit Insurance Corporation (FDIC) insures the deposits that people have in banks. It was created in 1933 following the failure of many banks in the Great Depression. Because it bears the risk of bank failures, it has the power to oversee the activities of banks. The FDIC does not receive government funding. It is supported by insurance premiums that financial institutions pay and by investments that it makes in Treasury securities.

The Federal Trade Commission was established in 1914 for the purpose of making trade in America fair, truthful, and safe for consumers. The commission enforces truth in advertising and truth in lending regulations, approves proposed business mergers to prevent monopolies, and works to protect consumers from fraud.

The Securities and Exchange Commission (SEC) was created in 1934 following the Stock Market crash of 1929. The agency makes sure that companies that sell stocks (often called securities) tell the truth about their business and about their profits and losses. The SEC also insures that stocks and bonds are sold in an open and honest manner. The Commodities Futures Trading Commission is a similar body that regulates the buying and selling of commodity futures. A commodity future is the purchase of commodities such as wheat and pigs that are to be delivered at a designated time in the future. Investors make a profit when the selling price at the time of delivery exceeds what they paid.

The Small Business Administration (SBA) provides assistance, information, and loans to the nation's small businesses. It was created in 1953 as a successor to earlier, similar agencies. Two examples of services that the SBA provides are start-up loans for new businesses and recovery loans to businesses that suffer losses from natural disasters.

The SBA has established size standards for various kinds of enterprises that define what a small business is. Generally, a manufacturing company must have less than 1,500 employees, while other small businesses (retail, wholesale, construction, etc.) are defined by the amount of annual sales they have. The 23 million small businesses in the U.S. account for over 99% of American employers and about half of the nation's employees and business output. Small businesses are often flexible enough to provide important innovations in the marketplace in terms of goods and services. The SBA focuses on small businesses because large companies usually have more resources available to them and often benefit directly from legislation that Congress passes.

The Farm Credit Administration (FCA) coordinates and regulates the network of Farm Credit Associations throughout the country. This system provides loans to farmers who want to expand their operations or who need short term loans until they sell their crops. The FCA sets standards for granting loans and makes sure that the local associations operate according to government regulations. Franklin Roosevelt created the FCA by executive order in 1933. A 1971 law is now the basis for the agency.

> *Agency regulations carry the weight of law. When an individual or group wants to appeal a ruling against them by an agency, the agency has established guidelines for what that person or group must do. When these avenues are exhausted, the case can be taken to the D.C. Circuit Court of Appeals and then to the U.S. Supreme Court.*

Regulation

The Federal Communications Commission was created in 1934 and regulates communication by radio, television, telephone (cellular and traditional), telegraph, satellite, and cable. It grants licenses for radio and television stations, makes sure that cable and satellite rates are reasonable, and sets standards for broadcast decency.

The Federal Election Commission was created in 1975 to enforce regulations that Congress passed regarding elections. These rules regulate fundraising and expenditure laws applicable to House, Senate, and presidential elections. The agency also oversees funds distributed to qualifying presidential candidates collected from voluntary contributions people make on their income tax returns. Elections have traditionally been left to state oversight, but the 1975 law was a major step in Federal involvement in elections.

The Environmental Protection Agency was formed in 1970. It develops and enforces guidelines regarding environmental issues, such as air and water pollution, the use of pesticides, and the cleanup of toxic dump sites. The agency awards research grants and provides educational materials that tell Americans what they can do to help us all have a cleaner and safer environment.

The Consumer Products Safety Commission began operation in 1973. It reviews the safety of about 15,000 consumer products sold in the U.S. The commission enforces standards, recalls dangerous products, and informs the public about hazardous products and what they should do in response to such hazards. The public reports about 10,000 product-related injuries and deaths to the commission each year.

The Equal Employment Opportunity Commission was created in 1965 to help enforce regulations forbidding discrimination in the workplace. The major work of the commission has focused on racial discrimination, but the agency also addresses complaints regarding alleged discrimination on the basis of gender, age, disability, religion, and other factors.

The National Labor Relations Board (NLRB) was created in 1935 by the National Labor Relations Act, and the board's mission is to enforce provisions of that law. The NLRB conducts elections by workers at a company (when the workers request it) to determine whether a majority wants to be represented by a labor union. It also investigates and attempts to settle charges of unfair labor practices by employers. The NLRB was a major step in the growth of union rights with regard to how employers treat their workers.

Services

The Social Security Administration administers the Social Security program, which offers retirement, disability, and survivor benefits. The program began as part of Franklin Roosevelt's New Deal. Most American workers pay Social Security taxes on their income, and the amount of benefits they receive in the future is based on how much they pay into the system. This agency registers people to participate in the Social Security program, educates the public on how to derive the most benefits from the system, pays out benefits, and investigates charges of fraud. Social Security has been so popular that it has become one of the untouchable programs. Politicians do not usually propose doing away with Social Security. Benefits have increased over the years, but so have the taxes collected to finance the benefits.

> *New Deal legislation initiated by Franklin Roosevelt created a plethora of agencies, most of which were known by their initials. So many were formed so quickly that observers dubbed it an alphabet soup of offices.*

The National Aeronautics and Space Administration (NASA) was created in 1958 to organize and encourage the country's space exploration program. Before that time, different branches of the military had begun developing their own (sometimes competing) space programs. NASA oversees our country's manned and unmanned space program and carries on research in the aerospace field.

Central Intelligence Agency Headquarters, Langley, Virginia

The Central Intelligence Agency (CIA), created in 1947, coordinates the intelligence-gathering work for the government. This involves finding out information through agents and mechanical means (such as wiretapping and satellite reconnaissance) that the government needs to maintain our security. It reports this information to the president and the National Security Council. The CIA is not allowed to spy on American citizens within the United States.

The National Endowment for the Arts (NEA) and the National Science Foundation provide grants for artistic endeavors and for scientific research, respectively. The NEA has occasionally created controversy because of the nature of the works of art that it has funded.

Government Services

The National Archives and Records Administration maintains historic documents such as the Constitution and the Declaration of Independence (on display at the National Archives building in Washington, D.C.) as well as other records. Its collection includes original manuscripts, motion pictures, sound recordings, still pictures, and computer data. The Archives also holds records that can be helpful for genealogical study and for families that want information about a family member's military service.

Such a large bureaucracy as the Federal government requires some effort to maintain itself. The General Services Administration purchases materials for the government and maintains property, vehicles, and equipment. It also sells surplus equipment. The Office of Personnel Management oversees retirement and health insurance programs, makes sure that employees are treated fairly, and keeps political influence out of the civil service system.

Government Corporations

A few organizations were started by the government but function as semi-private corporations. They have some characteristics of a private business and some aspects of a government agency.

The Tennessee Valley Authority (TVA) was a New Deal program designed to develop the resources of the area in and around the Tennessee River. The TVA is best known for providing relatively inexpensive electricity to poor rural areas of the South, but it is also involved in flood control and in maintaining recreational lakes behind its dams.

The United States Postal Service (USPS) is a public corporation that replaced the Post Office in 1971. It carries out the delivery of mail and maintains thousands of post offices around the country. The Postal Service works with the mail services of other countries to deliver international mail. The Postal Rate Commission, a separate body, sets postage rates based on USPS requests. The Postal Service has competition in the delivery of packages from private companies such as United Parcel Service (UPS) and Federal Express; but except for local courier services, the USPS has a monopoly on delivering regular mail.

The National Railroad Passenger Corporation (commonly called Amtrak) was created by Congress in 1971. It brought together the passenger services of most of the country's private railroads into a unified system. Amtrak is a for-profit corporation, but all of its preferred stock is owned by the government and the members of its board of directors are nominated by the president and confirmed by the Senate. Amtrak has never made a profit and has relied on subsidies from the government to survive. Conrail is a similar company formed by the government in 1976 as a merger of three failing freight rail lines in the Northeast. Freight service is more profitable than passenger service, and Conrail has shown a profit at times.

As we have seen in this unit, the operations of the government are vast and complex. They relate to many areas of life for the American public. While the bureaucracy provides many positive services, one result of growth in the size of government means that more and more people are dependent on the government for more and more services. As long as politicians promise more government programs and the American people want them, it will be difficult to change this trend.

There are three things which are stately in their march,
even four which are stately when they walk:
the lion which is mighty among beasts and does not retreat before any,
the strutting rooster, the male goat also,
and a king when his army is with him.
Proverbs 30:29-31

Reading

- "The Real Cost of Regulation" by John Stossel (*WHTT*, p. 129)

8 Article III— The Judiciary

The third branch of government is the judiciary, or the court system. This unit presents a fictional Federal court case to describe how the court system works. We look at the various Federal courts, and then we focus on the U.S. Supreme Court. The final lesson in the unit is a study of how the Supreme Court's position on questions regarding slavery and race has changed over the years.

Lessons in This Unit

Lesson 36 — A Federal Case
Lesson 37 — The Provisions of Article III
Lesson 38 — District Courts, Specialty Courts, and Courts of Appeal
Lesson 39 — The Supreme Court
Lesson 40 — How the Supreme Court Has Addressed Slavery and Race

Activity Idea

What is the best way for Christians to bring about change in America, in addition to prayer? Do Christians have any realistic hope for influencing the secular culture in which we live? Public schools cannot even consider the concept of Intelligent Design, let alone teach the Scriptures. Why is it that conservatives seem to be able to win elections but are losing the culture war? Is our best hope to withdraw from the political arena and focus on training our own children, or is there a more effective way for Christians to be salt and light in America? Given our government, our courts, our schools, and the media, how should we then live? Write a thoughtful, prayerful two- to three-page essay about these questions.

If you are using the optional *Quiz and Exam Book,* answer the questions for each lesson after you have completed the lesson and read any assigned readings in *We Hold These Truths.* After you have completed Lesson 40, take the quiz for Unit 8.

Lesson 36—A Federal Case

If men were angels, no government would be necessary.
—James Madison, The Federalist *Number 51 (1789)*

The Arrest

At 4:00 a.m. on November 10, six Federal agents broke into the apartment of a surprised Tom McHenry. He looked at them with amazement as he awoke in his bed. The agent in charge told him that he was under arrest and ordered him to get up and get dressed. Meanwhile, other agents began disassembling his computer set-up and going through his drawers and files. A package of specially-made paper often used in counterfeiting was found in McHenry's apartment.

At the same time, two miles away, six more Federal agents crashed into the home of Terry Kavanaugh. Kavanaugh was believed to be the leader of a counterfeiting operation. His computer revealed sophisticated software designed to reproduce U.S. currency.

McHenry and Kavanaugh were arrested and charged with counterfeiting U.S. currency, which is a violation of Federal law. They were taken to the county jail to be fingerprinted and photographed. The two men would be held there until they could appear before a Federal magistrate to answer the charge.

One important function of government is to enforce the law. Federal law enforcement procedures are similar to those of state authorities in many ways, but there are some significant differences. Since we are emphasizing the Federal government in this curriculum, we will discuss a fictional Federal case here and note where state procedure is different. We will also provide some additional comments about state courts in Lesson 50.

Secret Service Personnel in Washington, D.C., 2005

The Background

The arrests of McHenry and Kavanaugh culminated a six-month investigation by Federal authorities that began after counterfeit twenty-dollar bills began showing up in stores in the men's town and in a larger city about sixty miles away. Secret Service agents collected evidence, interviewed store employees, and began observing the two men's actions. The Secret Service believed that McHenry and Kavanaugh were involved in an even larger counterfeiting operation based in Chicago. Agents gathered information about trips the two men had made to Chicago. Neither man had a previous history of criminal activity.

The Federal authorities went before a Federal magistrate to obtain a warrant to tap the men's phone lines and listen to their conversations. They later obtained search and arrest warrants after they became convinced that McHenry and Kavanaugh were actively engaged in producing the phony money. The search warrants were required to list specific items that the authorities wanted to take: computers (including software, documents, and emails), scanners, printers, paper, briefcases, billfolds, and other items relevant to the case.

The Legal Procedure Begins

When they were arrested, each man was told that they had the right to remain silent, that anything they said could be used against them, that they had the right to have an attorney present at any interrogation, and that if they could not afford a lawyer one would be appointed for them. This procedure for informing an arrested person of these rights is the result of a 1966 Supreme Court ruling, *Miranda v. Arizona*. Each man asked for an attorney to be appointed for him.

The two men said nothing to the Federal authorities. Their lawyers advised the men to remain silent and to speak only to their lawyers about the case. The men appeared before a Federal magistrate two days later, and each pleaded not guilty to the charge of counterfeiting. A magistrate is an official who has limited judicial authority. He can issue search warrants, set bonds, and hear initial pleadings from suspects. Most of these initial steps in a Federal case are handled by a magistrate, although a judge is sometimes involved instead. A Federal judge hears the actual case.

The magistrate then had to set the bond that would be required for the men to be released from jail until the trial. Bond or bail is money that is guaranteed to the court. It is a promise that the men will not run away if they are released from jail and that they will appear at future court proceedings. If they do flee, the court can seize the accused person's assets. This is an inducement for the accused person not to run away. The defendant would also face additional charges for his flight. If the accused does not have the money for bond, a bail bond company recognized by the court will guarantee the money for him for a fee (often ten percent of the bond amount that the court sets). If the defendant flees, the bonding company goes after the person's assets to recover its loss. If the defendant is released on bail and does not run away, the amount of bond money never changes hands.

Every accused person has the right to post bond, except in capital cases (where the penalty is the death sentence) for which the evidence is compelling. However, a judge or magistrate has the discretion to set the bond so high that the defendant cannot possibly produce it. In this case, the assistant U.S. attorney present at the bail hearing told the judge that it was possible the men would try to run away or that they might try to inform their contact in Chicago that the counterfeiting ring had been discovered. Their defense lawyers argued that since they had no prior criminal record and were not a threat to public safety, their bond should be set relatively low. Because the arrests were part of an on-going Federal investigation, the judge decided to set bond at $500,000 each. Neither man could post this amount, so they had to remain in jail until the trial.

Grand Jury and Pre-Trial Hearings

The magistrate bound the cases over to the Federal grand jury. A grand jury is a specially-called group of citizens who hears the government's evidence against accused persons and decides whether the evidence is strong enough for a trial to be held. Federal grand juries can consist of between 16 and 23 persons (state justice systems have grand juries also). A grand jury does not decide guilt or innocence, but they can request evidence and order witnesses to appear to answer questions. A grand jury does not have to reach a unanimous decision for a trial to take place. It takes twelve votes on the grand jury to indict the defendant. A Federal grand jury usually lasts for eighteen months. They might meet anywhere from once a month to once a week, depending on the number of cases brought to them by the government.

> *To indict someone is formally to charge him with a crime. An indictment is the document that sets out the charge.*

The cases against Kavanaugh and McHenry were assigned to an assistant U.S. attorney. On the basis of the evidence and the testimony that the government provided, the grand jury voted that a trial was justified. An attorney representing the state government is usually called a district attorney. In some states another term is used. In Illinois, for example, he is the State's Attorney, while in Kentucky he is the Commonwealth Attorney.

The U.S. attorney's office considered how it would prosecute the cases. It was decided to hold two separate trials for the two accused men instead of trying them together. The prosecutor also decided to offer a plea bargain to McHenry. If he would plead guilty, the government would ask for a lesser sentence or perhaps even mere probation in exchange for his testimony against Kavanaugh. The prosecutor believed that convicting Kavanaugh would be more helpful in breaking up the Chicago counterfeiting ring.

The Federal district judge held several pre-trial hearings at which he heard defense motions regarding the trials. The job of a defense attorney is to get his client off the hook, so the lawyer will try anything he can to bring about acquittal (being found not guilty) or dismissal of the charges. The defense attorneys asked for a change of venue or location for the trial. The arrests had received extensive local publicity, and the defendants' attorneys argued that finding enough objective people to make an impartial jury would be difficult if not impossible. The defense attorneys also questioned the search warrants that the agents used, claiming that they were too vague; and they asked that the evidence obtained by them be suppressed and not introduced in court. If they succeeded in this motion, it would make the prosecution's case more difficult. However, the judge denied all of these defense motions and set a date for the trial to begin. Both defendants continued to be held in the county jail.

During the period before the trial, the opposing attorneys gathered evidence and interviewed people whom they might call to testify. The two sides exchanged witness lists and the evidence they obtained. This period is called pre-trial discovery. Attorneys know for the most part how their adversaries plan to make their case and how they themselves will respond even before the trial begins. Dramatic revelations and surprise witnesses during a trial like those portrayed in television courtroom scenes are rare. Depositions are pre-trial interviews given under oath that can be introduced in court. These, however, are mostly used in civil cases. The counterfeiting charge was a criminal procedure (the difference between civil and criminal law will be discussed in an upcoming lesson). A prosecutor is required to inform a defense attorney of any evidence he uncovers that would suggest that the defendant is not guilty. However, a defense attorney does not have to inform the prosecutor if he finds evidence pointing toward the accused person's guilt.

A Federal attorney talked with McHenry's attorney several times to outline their case and to try to convince McHenry to accept their plea bargain offer. Most charges that are brought, in both Federal and state courts, are settled by a plea bargain before being brought to trial. Usually the defendant agrees to plead guilty to a lesser charge rather than risk being convicted by a jury of the original, more serious charge and thus receiving a stiffer sentence. A conviction for counterfeiting can bring a sentence of up to fifteen years in prison. In this case, a month before the trial was set to begin, McHenry agreed to plead guilty and to testify against Kavanaugh.

The Trial

Eight months after he was arrested, Terry Kavanaugh went on trial in Federal district court on charges of counterfeiting U.S. currency. The first step was to select a jury. A group of seventy-five potential jurors, drawn from voting records and driver's license records, had been summoned to form a jury pool, from which a jury of twelve members and two alternates would be chosen. Opposing attorneys in a trial question potential jurors to see if they will be able to hear the case impartially. A potential juror will be excused from serving on a jury if he or she has already decided if the defendant is guilty or innocent, if he knows or is related to the defendant, or if he is ill. An attorney must state a reason why he or she thinks a potential juror must be dismissed, and the judge must agree. A juror cannot be dismissed simply because of his or her race, gender, or religion. Each side has a limited number of peremptory challenges. A peremptory challenge is a decision by an attorney to reject a potential juror for which he does not have to state a reason. However, if he is challenged on this decision, his reason cannot be based on the potential juror's race, gender, or religion. Some defendants hire jury experts, who help them know what sort of people (rich or poor, old or young, those of certain ethnic backgrounds, etc.) might be more likely to vote for their acquittal.

In many states, a pool of jurors is called to be available for a period of one to three months. Juries that are needed during this time are selected from this pool. This prevents officials from having to summon a new pool of potential jurors for every case that comes up. An individual citizen will probably not have to serve on a jury more than once during the time that he or she is called for possible service. Once a person has been summoned for the pool, he cannot be summoned again for a year.

After two days of screening potential jurors, a jury was empaneled to hear the Kavanaugh case. Attorneys for both sides made opening statements, in which they summarized their cases for the jury. Since a defendant is always considered innocent until proven guilty, the government always goes first to make its case against the defendant (traditionally, the prosecuting attorney sits closer to the jury box). The prosecutor called several witnesses, including personal friends of Kavanaugh and store clerks who identified Kavanaugh as the person who gave them counterfeit bills. Federal agents who took part in the arrest raids testified regarding what they found in Kavanaugh's home. McHenry's testimony was especially damaging to Kavanaugh's defense. Kavanaugh's attorney tried to tear down the testimony of the government's witnesses in his cross-examination of the witnesses, and he tried to raise doubts about the facts of the case as the prosecution presented them. The defense attorney called a few witnesses on Kavanaugh's behalf, all of whom denied knowing anything about the defendant's involvement in counterfeiting.

Following four days of testimony, the attorneys gave their closing arguments and the judge issued his charge to the jury. The judge read to the jury the law under which Kavanaugh had been arrested, and he gave them instructions about how they were to consider the evidence and testimony and how they were to conduct their deliberations. A jury must reach a unanimous verdict of guilty beyond a reasonable doubt in order to convict a defendant. After six hours of deliberation, the jury returned a verdict of guilty.

A Federal judge follows established guidelines in sentencing those who are convicted of crimes. In this case, the judge sentenced Kavanaugh to ten years in Federal prison, less than the maximum because it was his first offense. Sentences are routinely shortened because of prison overcrowding and because inmates earn time off for good behavior. Kavanaugh would likely serve no more than five years, and he might serve less time by going on parole for the rest of his sentencing period. Parole officers, who are government employees, check on parolees to make sure they do not engage in further illegal activity. If they do, they have to go back to prison, usually for their full sentences.

The Appeals Process

Convictions are routinely appealed to higher courts. An appeals court reviews the transcripts of cases brought to it, but it does not retry cases. It only considers matters of procedure or (in rare cases) the constitutionality of the law. In Kavanaugh's case, a procedural appeal might be based on the defense attorney's claim that the search warrant was flawed, or that Federal agents interrogated Kavanaugh illegally, or that the trial was not conducted properly. If any of these claims is accepted by an appeals court, it would void the conviction. The appeals court can either uphold the conviction or send the case back to the lower court. If it is sent back, the prosecution has to decide if it wants to retry the case or if the procedure required by the appeals court (such as the suppression of certain evidence) would make a conviction unlikely. A constitutional challenge could be raised if the defense attorney believed that the law by which Kavanaugh was convicted violated the Constitution. On rare occasions, the appeals court will sustain a constitutional challenge to the law.

The losing side in a U.S. Circuit Court of Appeals can appeal to the U.S. Supreme Court. One way to summarize the work of the Supreme Court in hearing appeals is to say that the Court reviews law and procedure. Most of the Court's headline-making criminal cases have to do with whether the actions of the police violated a defendant's rights or whether trial procedures properly protected the defendant's rights. If the Supreme Court agrees to review the Kavanaugh case, arguments will be presented to the Court regarding whether the law as written or the procedure used in the arrest and trial violated Kavanaugh's constitutional rights. The Supreme Court can either (1) uphold the law and the conviction, (2) uphold the law but send the case back for retrial with different procedure, or (3) declare the law to be unconstitutional and void the conviction.

A conviction in a state court can be appealed all the way to that state's highest appellate court. State appellate court decisions can be appealed to a Federal Court of Appeals and then to the U.S. Supreme Court if there is a question regarding the constitutionality of the state law. Courts of appeal review all cases brought before them, but the Supreme Court can decide whether or not it wants to review a case.

No one case in either Federal or state court can illustrate all of the possible ways that a case can develop. This fictional counterfeiting case was intended to describe some of the typical processes that the government follows in enforcing the law. In the next few lessons we will discuss in more detail Federal district and appeals courts and the U.S. Supreme Court.

The first to plead his case seems right,
until another comes and examines him.
Proverbs 18:17

(My thanks to John Maddox, an assistant district attorney for Anderson County, Tennessee, who reviewed the accuracy of this lesson and the portion of Lesson 50 dealing with state courts. Any errors in these lessons are my responsibility, not his.)

Lesson 37—The Provisions of Article III

Scarcely any political question arises in the United States that is not resolved, sooner or later, into a judicial question.

—*Alexis De Tocqueville,* Democracy in America *(1835)*

(Read Article III and the Eleventh Amendment of the U.S. Constitution.)

Legal disputes between persons or groups have occurred throughout history. A society develops a system to determine who is guilty and who is innocent of crime and to determine what is a fair settlement of disputes. Moses' judging of disputes among the people of Israel was one of the first issues he had to face after leading the Israelites out of Egypt (Exodus 18:13-26).

The American legal system is based largely on that of England, which was systematized by King Henry II in the last half of the 1100s and refined during the century that followed. The practice of jury trials began with the custom of calling together men of a town who would swear that someone had committed a crime (the word juror originally meant one who took an oath). Over time, the jury became a group of impartial citizens who heard the testimony for and against an accused person and decided that person's guilt or innocence. The practice of appealing a decision of one court to a higher court also goes back many centuries. When Paul believed that the Jewish charges against him would not be handled well in Palestine, he used a right of Roman citizens and appealed to Caesar to have his case heard in Rome (Acts 25:11).

Men Sitting on a Jury, c. 1919

The American colonies had courts that administered English law, and after independence the states established their own court systems; but no national court system was formed under the Articles of Confederation. Disputes that arose were heard in the courts of the various states, and those courts applied the law as they saw fit. Article IX of the Articles of Confederation provided for a complicated procedure for appealing a case or dispute to Congress, but it was seldom used. The result was confusion and uncertainty with regard to the laws of the country as a whole and their application.

Article III of the Constitution provided for a national legal system. As we consider this part of the Constitution, we will have to define certain legal terms to understand what the Constitution means on this subject.

The Judicial Power (Section 1)

The Constitution vests the judicial power of the United States in the Supreme Court and in other courts that Congress might establish. The Supreme Court is the only Federal court created by the Constitution. All other Federal courts have been created by acts of Congress.

The Federal system as it now functions includes U.S. District Courts, which hear most cases involving Federal law; U.S. Circuit Courts of Appeal, to which a party can appeal to ask for a reconsideration of the district court decision; Federal specialty courts that handle certain kinds of cases; and the U.S. Supreme Court. We will describe the makeup of these various courts in the next two lessons.

Federal judges are nominated by the president and confirmed or rejected by the Senate. No qualifications for any Federal judge are given in the Constitution, but judgeships are generally filled by those who have established a good reputation in the legal profession or who have served as a judge in a lower court. A president might consult with members of Congress or receive input from professional bar associations to get their recommendations for appointees. Judges are supposed to apply the law even-handedly, but generally speaking Republican presidents appoint those who appear to have conservative beliefs and Democrats nominate those whose record reflects a more liberal outlook.

Federal judges are appointed for life, provided that they maintain good behavior; but they are subject to impeachment by Congress. The founders, wanting to insulate Federal judges from the whims of public opinion, believed that judges should not have to stand for election. A judge's desire to please enough voters to be elected or re-elected might outweigh his responsibility to apply the law fairly. The ruling of a judge might not be popular even though it is legally accurate. For example, Federal judges who enforced civil rights laws in the 1960s were often not popular; but in enforcing the law they did the right thing. If a judge had to run for office, the judge might be voted out by a populace that did not want to follow the law.

> *Congress has allowed judges who have served for a long time to enter semi-retirement. These judges are called senior Federal judges. They continue to receive a salary but hear a smaller number of cases each year. This provision has been taken by many judges who want to continue hearing cases but who don't want the rigors of a full-time schedule.*

On the other hand, not having to stand for re-election can lead a judge to apply his own opinions in a case and not follow the law, since he does not have to answer to anyone for his decisions except in the extreme and rare case of being impeached.

Federal judges receive a salary. Only independently wealthy men and women could be Federal judges if they were expected to serve without pay (although many judges are wealthy because of their lucrative law practices before they became judges). Their salary cannot be lowered while they continue to serve. Congress may not punish judges by lowering their salary.

Justices of the Supreme Court of the United States, 1894

In 2006 the Chief Justice of the Supreme Court received a salary of $212,000 (all salary figures in this paragraph are in addition to other benefits, including an office and staff and a retirement pension). Associate justices of the Supreme Court earned $203,000. A judge on a Federal appeals court received $175,100, while a district court judge earned $165,200.

Congress usually approves a modest cost of living increase every year, but overall the salaries of Federal judges have fallen in real value since 1969. Many high profile lawyers earn much more than these amounts in private practice.

Jurisdiction and the Right to a Jury Trial (Section 2)

Federal courts hear cases involving Federal law and equity. Traditionally, the law has been divided into criminal law and civil law. Criminal law involves crimes against the people in general. Murder is perhaps the best known area of criminal law. When a murder occurs, the well-being of the people as a whole is endangered. Besides, the wronged person is not able to pursue the case since he or she is dead. The government (state or Federal) always initiates and prosecutes the case when it involves criminal law, and the accused person is the defendant. The defendant is always assumed to be innocent until proven guilty, and the burden of proof rests on the state (although if the defendant claims to be insane or that he acted in self-defense, the burden of proof for these claims is on the defendant). His guilt must be proven beyond a reasonable doubt by a jury of his peers. The punishment for a crime is spelled out in the law that makes the act a crime. If the defendant is found guilty, punishment might include spending time in prison or on probation, or he might receive the death penalty.

Civil law involves a dispute between two individuals or parties (an alleged breach of contract, for instance). Society is not threatened, but someone has allegedly wronged another person. In civil law, a private party (an individual or corporation) initiates the action and is the plaintiff (the one with the complaint). The person accused is the defendant. The plaintiff must prove his case with a preponderance of evidence. The standard of "beyond a reasonable doubt" does not apply in civil cases. If the defendant is found guilty, he is not sent to prison or executed. His punishment involves paying the plaintiff for losses resulting from his behavior.

Equity deals with a court's determination of fairness (the basic meaning of equity is that which is equitable or fair). A matter of dispute might not involve the breaking of a specific law, but someone might believe that he is not being treated fairly and thus needs to have the recourse of taking the alleged wrongdoer to court. Courts of equity can set punishments and can forbid someone from taking certain actions.

Federal courts hear cases involving Federal law: matters involving the Constitution, laws passed by Congress, and treaties into which the United States has entered. State courts do not hear cases involving Federal law, and Federal courts do not hear cases involving state law (except on appeal). Section 2 of Article III lists the kinds of cases which Federal courts hear:

- Cases involving ambassadors, ministers, and consuls. The framers did not want the representatives of foreign governments harassed by state courts.

- Cases involving admiralty and maritime issues. Admiralty questions involve actions that take place on the high seas or on navigable waters. Maritime cases deal with things that happen on land but are directly related to water, such as a dispute between shippers and receivers at a dock. A state's jurisdiction in such matters would be easily questioned.

- Cases in which the U.S. government is a party. Again, the framers did not want the national government to be subject to state courts.

- Cases involving a dispute between two or more states, between one state and citizens of another state, between citizens of different states, between citizens who might live in the same state but who have a dispute regarding land grants from a different state, or between a state or its citizens and foreign states or citizens. This section was amended by the Eleventh Amendment in 1798. This amendment says that a state cannot be sued in Federal court by a citizen of another state or country. This can happen only if the state agrees to be taken to Federal court. The amendment was the result of the case of *Chisholm v. Georgia* (1793), in which a citizen of South Carolina sued the state of Georgia. Georgia claimed to be a sovereign government, not subject to Federal courts, and thus sent no representatives before the Court. The Supreme Court decided in favor of Chisholm. This was an unpopular decision, so Congress passed and the states ratified the Eleventh Amendment, limiting Federal court jurisdiction over the states.

The Supreme Court has original jurisdiction in cases involving ambassadors, ministers, and consuls. In other words, such a case is heard directly by the Supreme Court and not by a lower Federal court. In all other Federal cases, the Supreme Court has appellate jurisdiction; that is, it can hear a case only if the case is appealed. Congress can make laws regulating and making exceptions to these jurisdictions, but it cannot extend the Supreme Court's area of original jurisdiction. This is what the Court struck down in *Marbury v. Madison* (1803). The Judiciary Act of 1801 had given the Supreme Court an additional original jurisdiction in a matter, and the Court said that Congress could not do that.

All Federal criminal trials (except impeachment trials, which are heard by the Senate) must be decided by juries. A Federal trial must take place in the state in which the alleged crime occurred. Congress can decide where a trial must take place if the alleged crime did not occur within a state.

Treason (Section 3)

Treason is the only crime defined by the Constitution. It is said to consist of making war against the United States or by allying oneself with an enemy of the United States by giving the enemy aid and comfort. Treason involves an American citizen making an overt act against the American government. It does not consist of thoughts or words critical of the American government or giving praise to the enemy. In eighteenth-century England, a person could be convicted of treason on the basis of his thoughts. The framers of the U.S. Constitution wanted to avoid this and to guarantee the right of freedom of speech and thought, even if the person's thoughts and words were directed against his own country.

No one can be convicted of treason unless at least two witnesses testify to the same overt act, or unless the accused person confesses in open court. The requirement of two witnesses was stated in Deuteronomy 17:6 regarding the sin of idolatry and had been part of British law since 1695. One person might be mistaken or have a personal vendetta against another and so lie about him; but if the testimony of two witnesses coincides, that is sufficient for conviction. A confession of treason must take place in open court. A forced confession behind closed doors is not allowed.

Congress was given the authority to impose the punishment for treason. It did not impose the death penalty for treason until 1942. "No attainder of treason" (a verdict of being found guilty of treason) "shall work corruption of blood." In other words, a traitor's family cannot be tainted by punishment or loss of citizenship because of what the traitor did. The government can seize the traitor's property, but when he dies the property must be returned to his family.

The Supreme Court Building, Washington, D.C.

About thirty treason trials have taken place in the United States. Some of these were conducted in state courts for treason against a particular state. Vice President Aaron Burr was tried for treason against the U.S. in 1807 as a result of some mysterious actions of his that apparently involved a desire to create a new country in the Louisiana Territory. Chief Justice John Marshall presided in the case and gave an extremely literal definition of treason. He said there had to be "an actual assembling of men" for the purpose of waging war for a person accused of treason to be found guilty. Burr was found not guilty. John Brown was convicted of treason by the state of Virginia in 1859 for his raid on Harper's Ferry. Several people were put on trial for spying during and after World War II. Julius and Ethel Rosenberg were found guilty of espionage (spying) for the Soviet Union in 1951 and were executed in 1953.

Wash yourselves, make yourselves clean;
remove the evil of your deeds from My sight.
Cease to do evil, learn to do good;
seek justice,
reprove the ruthless,
defend the orphan, plead for the widow.
Isaiah 1:16-17

Reading

- "The Threat from Lawyers Is No Joke" by Walter Olson (*WHTT*, p. 135)

Lesson 38—District Courts, Specialty Courts, and Courts of Appeal

Nothing is settled until it is settled right.

—Louis D. Brandeis,
Supreme Court Justice (1916-1939)

Federal District Courts

The laws that Congress enacts are Federal laws. Trials based on Federal law take place in Federal courts. The lowest level of the Federal legal process are U.S. District Courts.

Congress has divided the fifty states into 89 districts. States with greater population have proportionally more Federal court districts. In addition, a Federal court has been created for the District of Columbia and for each of the U.S. territories of Puerto Rico, the Virgin Islands, Guam, and the Northern Mariana Islands. As a result, there are a total of 94 U.S. District Courts. Many of the districts have more than one judge because of the number of cases that are heard in those districts. There are a total of 678 Federal judgeships on the District Court level. Usually only one judge hears a particular case.

U.S. District Courts

Each Federal judge has to be nominated by the president, considered by the Senate Judiciary Committee, and debated and voted on by the full Senate. Many nominations are fairly routine, but politics can become involved. When Senate Democrats stalled several of President George W. Bush's nominations, those Federal judgeships remained vacant for a long time. This meant that fewer judges were available to hear cases, which resulted in longer delays before the trials could take place.

Specialty Courts

The Federal system also includes a few specialty courts that hear only certain kinds of cases.

- The Court of International Trade, which meets in New York City, considers cases involving customs disputes. These cases address issues surrounding the bringing of goods into the country.

- Federal Bankruptcy Courts hear cases involving Federal bankruptcy laws. Remember that Congress, not the states, enacts bankruptcy laws for the entire country.

- The Court of Federal Claims was created in 1982 to hear charges made against the Federal government. For instance, if a contractor is hired by the government to build a new post office, the government might decide that the work was not done properly and withhold part of the contract price. The contractor might then sue in Federal Claims Court to get all of his money if he believes the government is not treating him fairly.

- The U.S. Tax Court hears cases arising under Internal Revenue Service rulings on the IRS Code. It has nineteen judges, but cases are heard by only one judge with no jury. The Tax Court office is located in Washington, D.C., but sessions are held in various places around the country. Taxpayers are allowed to represent themselves if they wish to do so. Most disputes are settled out of court without a trial actually being conducted before a judge.

Federal Circuit Courts of Appeal

When a case is decided in Federal District Court, it can be appealed to a U.S. Circuit Court of Appeals. An appeal for the trial to be reviewed has to be made on one of two grounds:

(a) The procedure of the District Court is claimed to have been faulty. Perhaps false or illegally obtained evidence was used to convict the person, or the Federal judge might have been lax in his duties, or the defense attorney was poorly prepared to defend his client, or some other reason might be given why the convicted person did not get a fair trial.

(b) The law by which the person was convicted is claimed to be faulty. Laws that required racial segregation, for instance, were appealed as being in violation of the U.S. Constitution's guarantee of equal protection under the law. The New York law that required a prayer to be said each day in public schools was challenged as an unconstitutional establishment of religion, thus violating the First Amendment.

In other words, in District Court the defendant is on trial. In the Appeals Court, the trial or the law itself is on trial. Most District Court cases must be appealed to a Court of Appeals, while a few can be appealed directly to the Supreme Court.

The Circuit Courts of Appeal were created in 1891 to relieve the Supreme Court of hearing all appeals made from district courts. Congress divided the United States into circuits, and the judges of the Appeals Courts travel on circuits to meet in various places within those regions. Additional regions were created more recently, so that now there are eleven regular appellate districts or circuits. In addition, the District of Columbia Court of Appeals hears Federal cases arising in the District. This means that much of their work involves considering laws passed by Congress. Serving as a justice on the D.C. Court of Appeals is often a stepping stone to the U.S. Supreme Court, since the justices on the D.C. Court hear highly publicized cases and can be well known by the president and by Senators.

The U.S. Emergency Court of Appeals was established in 1942 to hear cases involving price control rules associated with World War II. Its first Chief Justice was Fred Vinson, who later became Chief Justice of the U.S. Supreme Court. During its early years, the court's decisions were almost always in favor of the government. The court was finally abolished in 1961.

A thirteenth court, the U.S. Court of Appeals for the Federal Circuit, was formed in 1982. It absorbed the work of the Customs and Patent Appeals Court and the Claims Appeals Court. The Federal Circuit Court has nationwide jurisdiction in certain kinds of cases: international trade, patents, and claims against the government (usually a dispute regarding a government contractor's work or payment). The Federal Circuit Court also hears appeals from some rulings made by agencies of the executive branch when they are enforcing agency rules that have the effect of law.

Two other appeals courts are the Court of Appeals for the Armed Forces, which is made up of civilian judges who hear court-martial cases, and the Court of Appeals for Veterans' Claims. This latter court was created as a service to veterans to allow judgments in their cases to be made more quickly than what usually happens in the regular appeals system.

Judges for the U.S. Court of Appeals for the Armed Forces
Answering Questions About the Military Judicial Process, 2005

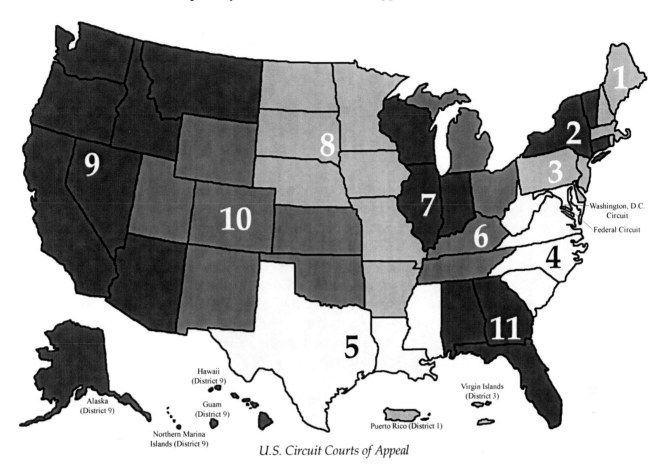

U.S. Circuit Courts of Appeal

The U.S. Circuit Courts of Appeal have varying numbers of justices, from six in the First Circuit (New England) to 28 in the Ninth Circuit (California and other western states). As of 2006, a total of 178 Appeals Court justices and an additional 102 senior (part-time) judges were serving on the bench. Usually a three-judge panel will hear an appeal, although in some cases up to nine judges will consider a case. When an appeal is made, attorneys for the two sides file written briefs explaining their positions and citing previous cases that support their views. When the case is heard, attorneys for the two sides make oral arguments before the judges. The judges then consider the case and submit a written decision sometime later. The decision might uphold the lower court's verdict, or the Appeals Court might send the case back to the lower court and order a new trial. Appeals Courts do not have juries; and, again, they do not determine guilt or innocence.

Thousands of cases are appealed every year to the Supreme Court. That highest judicial body in the land is the subject of the next lesson.

The exercise of justice is joy for the righteous,
but is terror to the workers of iniquity.
Proverbs 21:15

Lesson 39—The Supreme Court

Presidents come and go, but the Supreme Court goes on forever.
—William Howard Taft, U.S. President
and later Chief Justice of the U.S. Supreme Court

The nine members of the United States Supreme Court are arguably the most powerful group of persons in our government. Neither Congress nor the president can reverse any decision they make. Their judgment cannot be appealed to any other court. A decision by the Supreme Court can wipe laws off the books that have been enforced for generations. The only way that a Supreme Court decision can be reversed is either by a later Supreme Court decision or by the difficult process of ratifying a Constitutional amendment. Our entire society can be permanently and seriously affected by what a five-person majority of these unelected judges thinks about an issue. A Supreme Court justice can never be forced to retire unless he or she is impeached of high crimes and misdemeanors, convicted, and removed from office—a scenario that has never happened.

*Supreme Court Justice
Thurgood Marshall, 1976*

Thurgood Marshall was an African American attorney who successfully argued landmark civil rights cases before the Supreme Court. Later, he became the first black Supreme Court justice.

The Justices

The Supreme Court began in 1789 with six members. It eventually grew to ten by 1863. Three years later, Congress, wanting to prevent Andrew Johnson from nominating someone, passed a law that said the next three vacancies would not be filled. Two vacancies reduced the Court to eight members. A new law passed in 1869 (after Johnson's presidency ended) set the membership of the Court at nine, where it has remained ever since.

One hundred and ten persons have served on the Supreme Court, including seventeen who have held the position of Chief Justice. For all of American history, the average tenure for a justice has been about fifteen years and a vacancy has occurred approximately every two years. However, since 1970 the average tenure of justices has increased. In this most recent period, the average length of service on the Court has been about twenty-five years. This means that vacancies occur less frequently. Jimmy Carter is the only President to have served at least one full term who was not able to nominate anyone to the Court. The average age at appointment is 53 years. The current average age of the sitting justices is 68 years.

An appointment to the Supreme Court has not always been the culmination of a long and distinguished career as a judge. Through much of American history, many of the men appointed to the Court have been actively involved in politics. For example, Hugo Black was a U.S. Senator from Alabama when he was appointed. Earl Warren was governor of California. Fred Vinson had been a Congressman from Kentucky and had filled several different posts in the Franklin Roosevelt and Truman administrations. William Howard Taft had been U.S. President. Since Warren Burger's appointment in 1969, however, all justices that have been approved have come to the Supreme Court after holding judgeships in lower courts.

In 1937 President Franklin Roosevelt proposed a plan to add one new justice for every sitting justice over the age of seventy, up to a maximum of six new justices or a total of fifteen on the Court. This was a blatant attempt to remake the Court after it had struck down several New Deal programs. The plan never got anywhere in Congress or with the public, but the Court did begin to uphold New Deal legislation after Roosevelt made his proposal. During his long tenure in the presidency, Roosevelt was able to nominate eight justices.

Supreme Court nominations have not always been the hot political topic that they are today. Presidents have generally been able to have their say about who they wanted to serve on the Court. A nomination made by Abraham Lincoln was approved by the Senate a half hour after it was placed before the body! However, the Senate (and the court of public opinion) have had some influence in the matter of who has served on the Court. Twelve nominees have been voted down by the Senate, and another twenty or so nominees have withdrawn from consideration before the Senate voted on them.

Nominations are a pivotal issue today for several reasons. First, the longer recent tenures mean that a justice might be on the Court for thirty years or more. Second, since the Court has such a pivotal role in determining what government does and how laws are interpreted, political interests want to make sure that their perspectives are at least represented on the Court, if not in the majority. Third, Washington is a strongly partisan place; and both sides want to win in any and every situation or controversy that arises.

The Work of the Court

The Supreme Court has original jurisdiction in only a few kinds of cases. These include cases involving foreign ambassadors, ministers, and consuls; cases in which two states are the parties; or in a dispute between a state and the Federal government. In addition, each justice is assigned to at least one of the thirteen U.S. Circuit Courts of Appeal to hear emergency appeals, such as requests for a stay (or postponement) of execution if someone is facing the death penalty.

Supreme Court justices used to "ride the circuit" to hear cases in Federal courts, in addition to performing their tasks with the high court. Justices complained about having to travel a great deal, a task that became even more difficult as the nation grew in size. Moreover, a justice might have already participated in a case that came before the Supreme Court, so his objectivity in such situations could be questioned. Circuit riding by Supreme Court justices ended in 1891 with the creation of U.S. Circuit Courts of Appeal.

The primary task of the Supreme Court has come to be determining whether the laws of the United States government and the laws of the individual states are within the scope of the Constitution and therefore legitimate. Without some process for determining whether a particular law is within the bounds of the Constitution, the Constitution would be meaningless. As Chief Justice John Marshall wrote in *Marbury v. Madison* (1803), "It is, emphatically, the province and duty of the judicial department, to say what the law is." Marshall was the first Chief Justice to exercise judicial review widely, although this power of the Court was anticipated in *The Federalist* Number 78.

The Court cannot simply decide to declare its position on a topic. It only speaks when a particular case is brought before it that raises a constitutional issue. The Court tries to answer the question, "How does the law apply in this case?" and then generalizes on whether the law is constitutional or not.

The U.S. Supreme Court, 1888

A case is brought before the Court on appeal, usually from a U.S. Circuit Court of Appeals or the highest appellate court in a state, by one of the parties involved in the case. When the justices decide to review a case, the Court issues a writ of certiorari, in which the Court orders a lower court to send the records of a case to the Court for their review. Over 7,000 cases are appealed to the Court each year. Of these, the Court accepts only about 100. The justices hear oral arguments in 80 or 90 of these and render summary judgments without hearing further arguments in the others. When the Court is considering which cases to review, at least four justices must vote to accept a case before the Court will review it.

Procedures and Traditions

A term of the Supreme Court begins on the first Monday in October. It officially runs for a full year, but regular sessions usually end by late June. During a term, the Court alternates a two-week sitting, when they hear oral arguments, with a two-week recess, when the justices study and discuss cases and work on their written opinions.

Public sessions for hearing oral arguments are held Monday through Wednesday, 10 a.m. to 3 p.m. with a hour lunch break. Each case receives one hour, which means that each side has thirty minutes to present oral arguments. The justices can ask questions of the attorneys at any time during their thirty minutes. Before oral arguments are heard, each side submits briefs which summarize their arguments. Other groups or individuals can file amicus curiae (friend

The Supreme Court maintains long-standing traditions. For over a century, the justices have exchanged the "conference handshake" when they are preparing to appear for a public session and when they begin their Friday conferences. Each justice shakes hands with every other justice, indicating that they all share the same purpose even with their differences. As the justices approach the bench to hear oral arguments, the Marshal announces, "The Honorable, the Chief Justice and the Associate Justices of the Supreme Court of the United States. Oyez! Oyez! Oyez! All persons having business before the Honorable, the Supreme Court of the United States, are admonished to draw near and give their attention, for the Court is now sitting. God save the United States and this Honorable Court!" (Oyez is an old English word meaning "hear ye"). White quill pens are placed on the attorneys' tables, as they have been since the earliest days of the Court.

of the court) briefs to support one side or the other, telling why they think a particular ruling is needed. For instance, if the Court is considering a case involving environmental policy, the Environmental Defense Fund or a similar group can file an amicus curiae brief. In important cases numerous amicus curiae briefs will be filed on behalf of each party. An average of about 130 petitions are filed each week.

During the Court's private conferences, usually held on Friday, the justices discuss cases for which they have heard oral arguments. The Chief Justice begins the discussion. Sometimes an informal vote is taken. The voting begins with the most junior member of the Court going first. When the Chief Justice decides that the Court is

> *The Court's traditions add an interesting twist to its consideration of church and state issues. In addition to the prayer, "God save the United States and this Honorable Court!" that opens each public session of the Court, above the justices in the public chamber is a marble frieze depicting great law-givers throughout history. One of those portrayed is Moses holding tablets on which are written the Ten Commandments in Hebrew. Mohammed is also pictured in the frieze, a fact to which Muslims object since Islamic belief holds that it is blasphemy to portray Mohammed.*

ready for an opinion to be written, he will assign the writing of it to one of the justices or he will take the responsibility for it himself. Separate or concurring opinions can also be written, as well as dissenting opinions by those who disagree with the majority. Dissenting opinions can sometimes influence decisions in later cases in which earlier, majority opinions are qualified or even reversed. Draft opinions are circulated among the justices for criticism and refinement before they are finalized and announced.

Justices of the U.S. Supreme Court, 1929

Guiding Principles

Supreme Court justices are not bound to follow any traditions or standards as they consider cases brought before them, except their understanding of the Constitution itself. However, a few key principles have developed that guide the Court's consideration of issues. Probably the most important principle is the concept of *stare decisis*, which is Latin for "Let the decision stand." In other words, the precedent of previous Supreme Court decisions plays an important part in the Court's deliberations. It is rare that a Court overturns a previous and standing decision. Usually quite the opposite happens. As time goes on, succeeding decisions reinforce earlier decisions, so overturning a previous decision becomes even more unlikely. It took about sixty years, for instance, for the Court to overturn the "separate but equal" doctrine of racial segregation that was accepted in *Plessy v. Ferguson* in 1896.

A significant exception to the principle of *stare decisis* was the tenure of Earl Warren as Chief Justice (1953-1969). The Warren Court accomplished a breathtaking revolution in

American law and society. Its decisions ended state-sponsored racial segregation, brought about reapportionment in the U.S. House of Representatives and in state legislatures, granted broader rights to those accused of crimes and placed strict limitations on what police authorities could do, gave a wider interpretation to the First Amendment right of free speech, and placed greater limitations on religious expression in anything approximating a state-sponsored venue. We will look at some of these issues in later lessons. The Warren Court is the prime example that people cite when they say they oppose judicial activism or legislating from the bench.

Justice Sandra Day O'Connor

Another major principle followed by the court is the reluctance to become involved in political issues and legislative actions. Generally, the justices want to defer to Congress and to state legislatures unless a flagrant violation of the Constitution is involved. For instance, in January 2006 the Court in *Ayotte v. Planned Parenthood of Northern New England* struck down only one part of New Hampshire's parental notification law regarding a minor obtaining an abortion. Justice Sandra Day O'Connor wrote,

> Generally speaking, when confronting a constitutional flaw in a statute, we try to limit the solution to the problem. We prefer, for example, to enjoin only the unconstitutional applications of a statute while leaving other applications in force.

A third principle that is followed by the modern Court is the protection of personal liberty and individual conscience. This has been part of the basis of the Court's decisions outlawing school prayer and other religious activity in public facilities. The Court has inferred an individual's right to privacy from the Constitution (although the Constitution does not use that term), and this has influenced decisions that have established or maintained the right to an abortion.

In earlier eras the Court protected the rights of states to legislate for their people as they saw fit. It also limited the actions of Congress, as when several New Deal programs were struck down as unconstitutional. In more recent times, the

> *A highly readable book that gives a balanced study of the Court since 1969 is* First Among Equals: The Supreme Court in American Life *(published in 2002) by Kenneth Starr. Starr was the special prosecutor in the Whitewater investigation that eventually led to the impeachment and trial of Bill Clinton.*

Court has supported broader Federal powers and tended to limit state power. As we will see in the next lesson, the Court in the 1950s and 1960s struck down state laws that segregated the races.

What the Law Is

The United States is a nation of laws. Our government was founded by the Constitution, and the national and state governments act on the basis of laws passed by legislatures elected by the people. The person or body that is able "to say what the law is," as John Marshall put it, obviously has a powerful role in our government. That role is filled by the Supreme Court.

> *Hear a just cause, O Lord, give heed to my cry;*
> *give ear to my prayer, which is not from deceitful lips.*
> *Let my judgment come forth from Your presence;*
> *let Your eyes look with equity.*
> *Psalm 17:1-2*

Reading

- "The U.S. Supreme Court" from *Democracy in America* by Alexis de Tocqueville (*WHTT*, p. 97)

U.S. Supreme Court Building, Washington, D.C.

Lesson 40—How the Supreme Court Has Addressed Slavery and Race

Under our constitutional system, courts stand against any winds that blow as havens of refuge for those who might otherwise suffer because they are helpless, weak, outnumbered, or because they are nonconforming victims of prejudice and public excitement.
—Supreme Court Justice Hugo Black, Chambers v. Florida *(1940)*

The issues surrounding slavery and the status of blacks in American society have been difficult, costly, and long-running problems in American life. These issues led to the Civil War, which was the culmination of decades of bitter feelings and increasing hostilities. After the Civil War, the treatment of blacks in all parts of the country was a continuing shame. The Civil Rights movement of the 1950s and 1960s challenged many widely-held beliefs and firmly-ingrained practices.

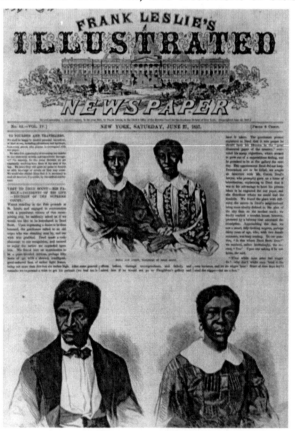

1857 Newspaper Article about Dred Scott and the Supreme Court Decision

The Federal judicial system has played an important part in the status of blacks in American society. At times the judiciary has supported laws and social conventions regarding racial inequality, while at other times the courts have gone against long-standing practices by pointing the way to greater equality. In this lesson we will see that the position of the U.S. Supreme Court on matters of race has changed dramatically over time.

The *Dred Scott* Decision

All thirteen original colonies allowed the enslavement of blacks. When the United States became a nation, northern states abolished slavery while southern states continued the practice. Slavery spread into some but not all new states when they were formed. Some free blacks lived in the United States, but they were usually treated with social prejudice and legal discrimination.

The landmark case of *Dred Scott v. Sandford* reached the Supreme Court in 1857. Scott was a slave who was owned by an Army officer in St. Louis. The officer took Scott into the free state of Illinois and then into the Wisconsin territory (also free of slavery on the basis of the Northwest Ordinance of 1787) before returning to Missouri. After his master died, Scott claimed in Missouri court that he was free since he had lived in free areas of the country. The case was eventually appealed to the U.S. Supreme Court.

Chief Justice Roger Taney delivered the official opinion of the Court, although each justice wrote a separate opinion. In his decision, Taney expressed some views that we find amazing today. Taney first addressed the question of whether the descendants of slaves could even be citizens of the United States. He said they were not citizens. (In this lesson the block quotations from Court decisions are in italics.)

The question before us is, whether the class of persons described in the plea in abatement compose a portion of this people [the citizens of the United States], and are constituent members of this sovereignty? We think they are not, and that they are not included, and were not intended to be included, under the word 'citizens' in the Constitution, and can therefore claim none of the rights and privileges which that instrument provides for and secures to citizens of the United States. On the contrary, they were at that time considered as a subordinate and inferior class of beings, who had been subjugated by the dominant race, and, whether emancipated or not, yet remained subject to their authority, and had no rights or privileges but such as those who held the power and the Government might choose to grant them.

The second question Taney addressed was that of state versus national citizenship. In another surprising bit of reasoning, he said that just because someone was a citizen of a state did not necessarily mean that he was a citizen of the United States.

We must not confound the rights of citizenship which a State may confer within its own limits, and the rights of citizenship as a member of the Union. It does not by any means follow, because he has all the rights and privileges of a citizen of a State, that he must be a citizen of the United States. He may have all of the rights and privileges of the citizen of a State, and yet not be entitled to the rights and privileges of a citizen in any other State. . . .

Chief Justice Roger Taney, c. 1857

Thus, according to Taney, Scott had no standing to bring a suit to the Court because (1) he was not a citizen and (2) he could not become a citizen.

Going beyond that procedural matter, Taney then declared the 1820 Missouri Compromise law to be unconstitutional for two reasons. First, Taney said that the Constitution gave Congress the right to make rules and regulations for the territories of the United States that the country possessed when the Constitution was adopted, but not for territories acquired later. Second, Taney declared the Missouri Compromise to be unconstitutional because it outlawed slavery in the Louisiana Territory north of the southern border of the state of Missouri (except for Missouri itself), and Congress had no right to interfere with an American citizen's right to property.

. . . The right of property in a slave is distinctly and expressly affirmed in the Constitution. The right to traffic in it, like an ordinary article of merchandise and property, was guaranteed to the citizens of the United States, in every State that might desire it, for twenty years. And the Government in express terms is pledged to protect it in all future

time, if the slave escapes from his owner. This is done in plain words—too plain to be misunderstood. And no word can be found in the Constitution which gives Congress a greater power over slave property, or which entitles property of that kind to less protection, than property of any other description.

Aftermath of the Civil War

Then came the Civil War, one consequence of which was the ending of slavery. After the Civil War, the Fourteenth Amendment defined citizenship—both state and national—and gave all Americans the right to equal justice under the law and the right of due process of law on both the state and Federal levels. In practical fact, however, blacks were still considered second-class citizens. States enacted laws that blatantly discriminated against blacks, and the Federal government did little to enforce equality. The Supreme Court ruled in 1873 that the Fourteenth Amendment applied only to actions by the Federal government, not the states. This gave the states a free hand to discriminate against blacks in any way they wished.

The Fifteenth Amendment forbade the denial of the right to vote on the basis of race, color, or previous condition of servitude. The Amendment added that Congress could enforce this right by "appropriate legislation." In 1870 Congress passed the Enforcement Act to insure that the Amendment was applied. Two Kentucky election officials refused to count the vote of a Negro citizen and were indicted under the act. The case, *United States v. Reese,* was appealed to the Supreme Court, which ruled on it in 1876. While the Court recognized the Fifteenth Amendment, it struck down the Enforcement Act as being too vague. States, the Court said, regulate their own elections. Congress can enforce the provisions of the Fifteenth Amendment with appropriate legislation, but the Enforcement Act did not limit its effect to questions regarding the Fifteenth Amendment. "We find [in the law] no words of limitation, or reference even, that can be construed as manifesting any intention to confine its provisions to the terms of the Fifteenth Amendment." In thus encroaching upon the traditional sovereignty of the states to conduct its own elections, the law was not "appropriate legislation" and was therefore unconstitutional. This opened the door for states to continue to discriminate against blacks by preventing their voting in some other way (using literacy tests, payment of a poll tax, or some other device).

In 1875 Congress passed the Civil Rights Act, which outlawed racial discrimination in transportation facilities (primarily railroads), public accommodations (such as inns and theaters), and in the selection of juries. Addressing a group of cases in which the law had been applied, the Court ruled in 1883 that the Fourteenth Amendment and the Civil Rights Act applied only to official actions by state authorities and not to actions taken by individuals against blacks.

> *. . . Until some state law has been passed, or some state action through its officers or agents has been taken, adverse to the rights of citizens sought to be protected by the fourteenth amendment, no legislation of the United States under said amendment, nor any proceeding under such legislation, can be called into activity, for the prohibitions of the amendment are against state laws and acts done under state authority. . . .*

Thus the court said that states could turn a blind eye to racial discrimination practiced by individuals. In so doing, states could achieve the same result that discriminatory state legislation would pursue. The decision went on to say, in effect, that former slaves just needed to get over it and not expect any special treatment.

> *. . . When a man has emerged from slavery, and by the aid of beneficent legislation has shaken off the inseparable concomitants of that state, there must be some stage in the progress of his elevation when he takes the rank of a mere citizen, and ceases to be the special favorite of the laws, and when his rights as a citizen, or a man, are to be protected in the ordinary modes by which other men's rights are protected. There were thousands of free colored people in this country before the abolition of slavery, enjoying all the essential rights of life, liberty, and property the same as white citizens; yet no one, at that time, thought that it was any invasion of their personal status as freemen because they were not admitted to all the privileges enjoyed by white citizens, or because they were subjected to discriminations in the enjoyment of accommodations in inns, public conveyances, and places of amusement. Mere discriminations on account of race or color were not regarded as badges of slavery. . . .*

In 1880 the Court struck down a West Virginia law that barred blacks from serving on juries. In the same year, the Court considered a petition from two blacks who were indicted and convicted by all-white juries in Virginia. Virginia did not have a law against blacks serving on juries, but the custom of the state was not to include blacks on juries. In *Virginia v. Rives*, the Court ruled that merely being convicted by an all-white jury did not mean that the person's civil rights were violated. The burden of proof was on the black man to show before his trial began that the state had taken discriminatory actions against him.

> *If, as in this case, the subordinate officer whose duty it is to select jurors fails to discharge that duty in the true spirit of the law; if he excludes all colored men solely because they are colored; or if the sheriff to whom a venire is given, composed of both white and colored citizens, neglects to summon the colored jurors only because they are colored; or if a clerk whose duty it is to take the twelve names from the box rejects all the colored jurors for the same reason, — it can with no propriety be said the defendant's right is denied by the State and cannot be enforced in the judicial tribunals. The court will correct the wrong, will quash the indictment or the panel, or, if not, the error will be corrected in a superior court. . . .*

After the Civil War, southern states tried to restrict the voting rights of former slaves by various means. Two of those ways were imposing a literacy test and requiring a poll tax to be paid. These laws did keep many blacks from voting; however, these barriers also excluded some whites as well. To lessen the impact of the restrictions on whites, some states passed voting rights laws that included what were called grandfather clauses. The grandfather clause exempted from the literacy or poll tax requirements those men whose fathers or grandfathers were allowed to vote as of 1867. Since few blacks could vote in that year, blacks still had to meet the poll tax or literacy requirements; thus the law continued to prevent blacks from voting but allowed more whites to vote. These discriminatory laws were declared unconstitutional by the U.S. Supreme Court in 1915 in the Guinn v. United States *case because they violated the right to vote that was guaranteed by the Fifteenth Amendment.*

Today, a grandfather clause in a new law is an exemption granted to an existing person or entity from the requirements of the new law. For example, if a new law requires sprinkler systems in all restaurants in a city, it might be made to apply only to new restaurants built after the law is enacted. Restaurants that were already open when the law was passed might be exempted from the requirement. Such restaurants are sometimes said to be "grandfathered" into the new law.

Plessy v. Ferguson

The state of Louisiana enacted a law in 1890 that required railroad companies to provide "equal but separate" accommodations for white and black passengers, by either separate cars or by partitioning the same car. Homer Plessy, who was seven-eighths Caucasian (that is, one great-grandparent was black), took a seat in a rail car designated for whites and was forcibly ejected from the train and charged with breaking the law. John Ferguson was the judge who first heard Plessy's case. The matter was appealed to the U.S. Supreme Court, which issued its ruling in 1896. The Court upheld the law as an appropriate expression of the state's police power and an appropriate recognition of the accepted differences between whites and blacks. The Court ruled that the law did not violate the Fourteenth Amendment guarantee of equality.

> *The object of the [Fourteenth] amendment was undoubtedly to enforce the absolute equality of the two races before the law, but, in the nature of things, it could not have been intended to abolish distinctions based upon color, or to enforce social, as distinguished from political, equality, or a commingling of the two races upon terms unsatisfactory to either. Laws permitting, and even requiring, their separation, in places where they are liable to be brought into contact, do not necessarily imply the inferiority of either race to the other, and have been generally, if not universally, recognized as within the competency of the state legislatures in the exercise of their police power. The most common instance of this is connected with the establishment of separate schools for white and colored children, which have been held to be a valid exercise of the legislative power even by courts of states where the political rights of the colored race have been longest and most earnestly enforced.*

The Court thus legitimized state policies of segregation in every area of life, and there the matter stood legally for over forty years. "Separate but equal" became the standard that states followed.

Twentieth Century Decisions

The reality was, however, that facilities for blacks were indeed separate but were usually unequal. Some members of the African American community and their white supporters did not accept the situation and worked to change law

African American School in Kentucky, 1916

and practice. Their efforts bore fruit first in graduate level education. In 1938, the Supreme Court struck down a Missouri law that called for the state to pay expenses for blacks to attend law school out of state rather than to build a separate law school for blacks within the state.

In 1950, the Court ruled in the case of *Sweatt v. Painter*. Herman Sweatt was an African American who was denied admission to the University of Texas School of Law in 1946 simply because he was black. When he challenged the decision, the state undertook to build a law school for blacks that was to open in 1947. The Court decided the case in 1950. It recognized that the separate facilities were hardly equal.

The University of Texas Law School, from which petitioner was excluded, was staffed by a faculty of sixteen full-time and three part-time professors, some of whom are nationally recognized authorities in their field. Its student body numbered 850. The library contained over 65,000 volumes. Among the other facilities available to the students were a law review, moot court facilities, scholarship funds, and Order of the Coif affiliation. The school's alumni occupy the most distinguished positions in the private practice of the law and in the public life of the State. It may properly be considered one of the nation's ranking law schools.

The law school for Negroes which was to have opened in February, 1947, would have had no independent faculty or library. The teaching was to be carried on by four members of the University of Texas Law School faculty, who were to maintain their offices at the University of Texas while teaching at both institutions. Few of the 10,000 volumes ordered for the library had arrived; nor was there any full-time librarian. The school lacked accreditation.

Since the trial of this case, respondents report the opening of a law school at the Texas State University for Negroes. It is apparently on the road to full accreditation. It has a faculty of five full-time professors; a student body of 23; a library of some 16,500 volumes serviced by a full-time staff; a practice court and legal aid association; and one alumnus who has become a member of the Texas Bar.

Whether the University of Texas Law School is compared with the original or the new law school for Negroes, we cannot find substantial equality in the educational opportunities offered white and Negro law students by the State. In terms of number of the faculty, variety of courses and opportunity for specialization, size of the student body, scope of the library, availability of law review and similar activities, the University of Texas Law School is superior. What is more important, the University of Texas Law School possesses to a far greater degree those qualities which are incapable of objective measurement but which make for greatness in a law school. Such qualities, to name but a few, include reputation of the faculty, experience of the administration, position and influence of the alumni, standing in the community, traditions and prestige. It is difficult to believe that one who had a free choice between these law schools would consider the question close.

The Court ordered that Sweatt be admitted to the UT Law School.

Brown v. Board of Education of Topeka

In the early 1950s the Court accepted several cases involving legally segregated public schools. On May 17, 1954, the Court announced its unanimous decision in four cases, two from Southern states, one from Delaware, and one from Topeka, Kansas.

The decision noted the status of public education in 1868, when the Fourteenth Amendment was adopted.

In the South, the movement toward free common schools, supported by general taxation, had not yet taken hold. Education of white children was largely in the hands of private groups. Education of Negroes was almost nonexistent, and practically all of the race were illiterate. In fact, any education of Negroes was forbidden by law in some states. Today, in contrast, many Negroes have achieved outstanding success in the arts and sciences as well as in the business and professional world. It is true that public school education at the time of the Amendment had advanced further in the North, but the effect of the Amendment on Northern States was generally ignored in the congressional debates. Even in the North, the conditions of public education did not approximate those existing today. The curriculum was usually rudimentary; ungraded schools were common in rural areas; the school term was but three months a year in many states; and compulsory school attendance was virtually unknown. . . .

Today, education is perhaps the most important function of state and local governments. Compulsory school attendance laws and the great expenditures for education both demonstrate our recognition of the importance of education to our democratic society. It is required in the performance of our most basic public responsibilities, even service in the armed forces. It is the very foundation of good citizenship. Today it is a principal instrument in awakening the child to cultural values, in preparing him for later professional training, and in helping him to adjust normally to his environment. In these days, it is doubtful that any child may reasonably be expected to succeed in life if he is denied the opportunity of an education. Such an opportunity, where the state has undertaken to provide it, is a right which must be made available to all on equal terms.

We come then to the question presented: Does segregation of children in public schools solely on the basis of race, even though the physical facilities and other "tangible" factors may be equal, deprive the children of the minority group of equal educational opportunities? We believe that it does.

To separate [black students] from others of similar age and qualifications solely because of their race generates a feeling of inferiority as to their status in the community that may affect their hearts and minds in a way unlikely ever to be undone. The effect of this separation on their educational opportunities was well stated by a finding in the Kansas case by a court which nevertheless felt compelled to rule against the Negro plaintiffs:

"Segregation of white and colored children in public schools has a detrimental effect upon the colored children. The impact is greater when it has the sanction of the law; for the policy of separating the races is usually interpreted as denoting the inferiority of the negro group. A sense of inferiority affects the motivation of a child to learn. Segregation with the sanction of law, therefore, has a tendency to [retard] the educational and mental development of negro children and to deprive them of some of the benefits they would receive in a racial[ly] integrated school system."

Whatever may have been the extent of psychological knowledge at the time of Plessy v. Ferguson, *this finding is amply supported by modern authority. Any language in* Plessy v. Ferguson *contrary to this finding is rejected.*

We conclude that in the field of public education the doctrine of "separate but equal" has no place. Separate educational facilities are inherently unequal. Therefore, we hold that the plaintiffs and others similarly situated for whom the actions have been brought are, by reason of the segregation complained of, deprived of the equal protection of the laws guaranteed by the Fourteenth Amendment.

The Court recognized that the consequences of its decision were complex and far-reaching. However, when some states acted slowly or not at all to implement this decision, the Court a year later declared that the integration of public schools was to proceed "with all deliberate speed." This had little effect in bringing about desegregation of schools. Instead, the ruling was met with what was called massive resistance by state governments. It was well into the 1960s, following the passage of the 1964 Civil Rights Act, that school integration gained significant momentum. Even then, many white citizens protested the change and many white officials delayed implementation every way they could. Suits brought in Federal court by advocates of integration resulted in court-ordered integration, which sometimes involved the busing of children (both black and white) away from their neighborhoods to other schools across town to achieve a racial mix.

School Segregation Protest, St. Louis, Missouri

Extension into Private Transactions

In the 1960s, the Court ruled on discrimination issues involving private businesses. Previous decisions, you will remember, addressed only official state actions. In *Burton v. Wilmington (Delaware) Parking Authority* (1961), the Court said that a restaurant located in part of a publicly-owned parking garage could not deny service to blacks. In *Heart of Atlanta Motel, Inc. v. United States* (1964), the Court said that a motel could not refuse to accept black customers because the motel was involved in interstate commerce, over which Congress had authority to legislate. Then in 1968, the Court upheld a new law by Congress that barred discrimination in the selling of homes.

Affirmative Action

School integration leveled the playing field for blacks and whites, but some said that this was not enough to achieve true integration of American society. The idea was proposed to give preferred treatment to blacks to help them catch up from years of being the object of discrimination. These programs were generally called "Affirmative Action" initiatives. Under these policies, for instance, a certain percentage of government contracts had to go to minority-owned businesses, whether or not they had submitted the lowest bids. Colleges had to admit a certain number of black students, even if their academic qualifications were lower than those of some white students. The Supreme Court has tried to take a middle ground on affirmative action cases. It has not denied the need for blacks to receive a helping hand in achieving equality, but it has tried to limit the impact of such programs on non-blacks.

The University of California Medical School at Davis set a quota for the number of what it called "disadvantaged" students it would admit. A white applicant, Alan Bakke, was denied admission to the school even though his grades and test scores were better than some black students who were admitted. Bakke sued, claiming that he was denied equal protection under the law as provided for in the Fourteenth Amendment. In its 1978 decision, the Court struck down the quota system; and Bakke was admitted. The Court said that race and ethnicity could be factors used to grant or deny admission, but the admission process had to be narrowly drawn in order to harm as few people as possible.

In 2003, the Court handed down two different decisions regarding admissions policies at the University of Michigan. The Law School admissions standards, which included the consideration of race, were found to be narrowly drawn and thus acceptable. The undergraduate admissions policy, however, was not so carefully drawn. It was deemed to have a negative effect on applicants and thus was struck down.

From this study, we see that the position of the Supreme Court can change over time. We can hope and pray that in other areas in which the Court has been wrong, most notably in legalizing abortion, the day will come when these wrongs will be made right as well.

There is neither Jew nor Greek,
there is neither slave nor free man,
there is neither male nor female;
for you are all one in Christ Jesus.
Galatians 3:28

New York City, 1965

Washington, D.C., 1955

Integrated School Classrooms

9 Other Articles and the Amendments

This unit concludes our study of the U.S. Constitution. We examine the remaining articles and consider the amendments that are not discussed in other lessons.

Lessons in This Unit

Activity Idea

An on-going debate involves the question of whether the Constitution is a living or a dead document. The dead document view holds that the meaning of the Constitution must be determined by its original meaning and by the intentions of the framers. Those who say it is a living document believe that the meaning of the Constitution changes as society changes. Part of the speech by Stephen Markman in *We Hold These Truths* addresses this issue. Which do you believe? Is it possible that some elements of both positions are correct? State your position in about two pages.

If you are using the optional *Quiz and Exam Book*, answer the questions for each lesson after you have completed the lesson and read any assigned readings in *We Hold These Truths*. After you have completed Lesson 45, take the quiz for Unit 9.

Lesson 41—Article IV: States and Territories

The true theory of our Constitution is surely the wisest and best, that the States are independent as to everything within themselves, and united as to everything respecting foreign nations.

—*Thomas Jefferson (1800)*

(Read Article IV of the U.S. Constitution.)

The remaining articles of the Constitution deal with various matters including relations among the states, relations between the states and the Federal government, the ratification and amendment processes, and other issues.

Section 1: "Full Faith and Credit"

Each state is to extend "full faith and credit" to the public acts, records, and court proceedings of the other states. Congress was empowered to determine how these matters would be proved among the states and what such recognition meant. The full faith and credit clause means that the states are to recognize and not disallow the laws, records, and court actions of other states. The purpose of this clause was to keep the states from falling into squabbles with each other over legal differences while allowing states to make their own laws.

A few examples will illustrate the point.

(1) A person's will that was legally drawn up in one state must be recognized by another state. If, for example, the state where the will was executed does not require certain language to be used while the state where the person was living when he died does require that language, the second state must still recognize the will as having been properly drawn up.

(2) California requires the possessions of all people entering the state to be subjected to an inspection. The purpose of the inspection is to prevent a disease or blight on fruits and vegetables from entering the state and affecting the state's agriculture industry. Another state cannot tell its citizens that they don't have to stop for the inspection. Other states must recognize California's right to inspection.

(3) Generally speaking, states recognize marriages that are performed in other states. If a couple gets married in Illinois or Texas and then moves to another state, the latter state recognizes the marriage as valid even though it did not happen in that state.

However, this full faith and credit clause is not absolute. For instance, casino gambling is legal in Nevada. This does not mean that a person can set up a gambling casino in Georgia and say, "Well, it's legal in Nevada, so it has to be legal everywhere." Georgia has to recognize Nevada's right to legalize casino gambling, but Georgia does not have to be ruled by Nevada law.

Another exception is in professional licensure. Each state establishes standards by which, for example, an electrician or an attorney may practice in that state. Just because someone is a licensed electrician in one state does not necessarily mean that he can practice in another state. Some states do have reciprocal agreements with other states through which those licensed in one state are recognized by another state. If two states have such an agreement, an electrician licensed in one state might not have to take a test to obtain a license in the other state if he moves to or does business there, although he would still have to obtain a license from the second state.

One issue that has generated considerable controversy is the legitimacy of gay marriage, or marriage between two persons of the same gender. The Massachusetts Supreme Judicial Court has ruled that the state must extend the same rights, privileges, and protections to homosexual marriages that it does to marriages between a man and a woman. Some claim that since one state has recognized gay marriage, other states will be forced to recognize those couples as married if they move to another state.

However, legal practice does not support this view. In the first place, states are not required to recognize the laws of another state if those laws violate a state's strongly held practices and policies. One example is the casino issue mentioned above. Second, states have always defined legal marriages for themselves; and state laws do vary. For instance, one state may allow persons to get married when they are fifteen, while another state sets the minimum age for getting married at seventeen. If two fifteen-year-olds get married in the first state and then move to the second state, their marriage would not be recognized by the second state. States also make laws on what close relations cannot marry (two first cousins, or an uncle and a niece, for instance). These differences cannot be imposed on other states that have different laws. Third, a marriage is not an act of the legislature or a court that states must recognize with "full faith and credit." A marriage is a licensed arrangement that is regulated by the legislature, in some ways like an electrician's license. States must recognize other states' authority to regulate marriage, but not the particular laws of other states.

Still, given our day and age there is no telling how a Federal District judge or a U.S. Appeals Court or the U.S. Supreme Court might rule on the question if it were to come before them, as it probably will. Because of this, a Federal Marriage Amendment was introduced in Congress. The proposed amendment defined marriage as being between a man and a woman. If it is ratified and becomes part of the Constitution, all contradictory state laws would be struck down and no court could overrule it. States might still create arrangements called civil unions, but if the amendment is part of the Constitution states could not permit persons of the same sex to be legally recognized as being married to each other.

Section 2: Privileges and Immunities

Citizens in each state have the rights and privileges granted to citizens "of the several states." This clause has been seen as somewhat ambiguous, but it has generally been interpreted to mean that a state cannot discriminate against citizens of other states in terms of the legal rights and protection afforded to them. "The several states" would seem to mean "states in general" or the country as a whole. For example, states cannot forbid people from other states from traveling through the state. Visitors are to be given the same legal protections that citizens have. Residents of one state can own property and conduct business in another state.

This does not mean that states cannot establish any differences between residents and non-residents. A state can charge non-residents higher fees for hunting and fishing licenses. State universities can charge higher out-of-state tuition to students from other states. These differences are legitimate because state residents pay a portion of the costs of these programs in taxes that non-residents do not. However, the Supreme Court has ruled that the difference has to be reasonable and must be based on the real impact of residents' taxes. For instance, a state may not charge a resident $3.00 for a fishing license and a non-resident $100.00.

The second paragraph of Section 2 requires the extradition of a fugitive back to the state from which he fled when the governor of the state of origin requests it. This clause is intended to prevent conflicts between states and to prevent the harboring of criminals by a state. Courts have ruled on some exceptions to this clause. If the fugitive is also wanted as a criminal in the state to which he fled, the receiving state may hold a trial and even have him serve his sentence before returning him to the state from which he fled. In addition, a governor may refuse to extradite a suspect if he believes the person will not receive fair and humane treatment from the state requesting extradition.

The final clause of this section provided that fugitive slaves did not gain their freedom by escaping to a free state. If the owner wanted the slave back, the slave was to be delivered over to him. The Compromise of 1850 included a new fugitive slave law that compelled even private citizens of free states to help in the capture of runaways. This law was widely resented in the north and often not obeyed. This clause became obsolete with the passage of the Thirteenth Amendment that outlawed slavery.

Section 3: Territories

Congress is empowered to admit new states into the Union, with some restrictions:
(1) no new state may be formed within an existing state; and
(2) no new state may be formed by joining two or more states or portions of states, unless
(3) the state legislatures involved and Congress agree to it.

The Northwest Ordinance of 1787, enacted prior to the ratification of the Constitution, set the pattern for territories becoming states. After Congress establishes a territorial government, when the population reaches 60,000 the territory can apply for statehood by submitting a petition for admission to Congress. Congress then passes an enabling act or organic act that provides for a convention to write a state constitution. The document has to be approved by the voters of the territory, and then Congress passes an act of admission.

Congress can put conditions on a territory's application for coming into the Union. For example, Utah was required to outlaw polygamy before its statehood was approved. Utah's population is predominantly Mormon, and Mormons had accepted polygamy for many years before the territory applied for statehood. In another case, President Taft vetoed the first admission act of Arizona because its constitution provided for the popular recall of judges. The offending passage was removed from the state constitution, Arizona was admitted, and soon thereafter a referendum restored the popular recall of judges to the state constitution.

West Virginia's admission to the Union during the Civil War was an aberration to the usual process and stretched the Constitutional provisions. The counties of northwest Virginia voted overwhelmingly against secession. When Virginia left the Union, a new government was formed in the western area and applied to the Federal government for admission. This new government was recognized by Washington and the state was admitted as West Virginia in 1863. Two more counties voted that year to join the new state. When Virginia rejoined the Union, it rescinded its secession resolution and claimed the two counties. Congress passed a resolution favoring the counties being part of West Virginia. In 1871, the U.S. Supreme Court ruled in favor of the transfer of the counties to West Virginia.

In the late 19th century, the acquisition of a world empire was a goal of many countries in the world. The United States joined in this quest, and as a result of the Spanish American War the U.S. gained the territories of Cuba and the Philippine Islands. Both of these became independent nations during the twentieth century. The push for a territorial empire has passed; but the United States has acquired other territories, mostly Pacific Islands like Guam, American Samoa, and several smaller islands, as well as the U.S. Virgin Islands in the Atlantic.

Patrol Boat in Apra Harbor, Guam

Puerto Rico and the Northern Mariana Islands are considered commonwealth territories of the United States. Territorial governments are generally autonomous, but Congress exercises oversight of them.

Alaska and Hawaii were the last states admitted to the Union, both entering in 1959. No territories are currently on track for admission as states. Puerto Rico holds a referendum every few years to gauge public opinion about applying for statehood, but so far the result has always supported continuing as a commonwealth territory.

Section 4: Federal Guarantees to the States

The United States must guarantee a republican form of government to every state. This means that every state must have a government of elected representatives, limited powers, separate branches of government, and so forth. A republican government was guaranteed by the framers to protect against a person or group seizing control of a state government and instituting a dictatorship or monarchy. This is why the guarantee is tied to the Federal government's responsibility to protect states against foreign invasion and (with the request of a state legislature or governor) against domestic violence. The creation by Lincoln and Johnson of provisional state military governments during and after the Civil War was held by the Supreme Court in 1869 to be a justifiable action in view of the rebellion and as a necessary step toward the re-establishment of regular republican governments in those states.

Each of them will sit under his vine and under his fig tree,
with no one to make them afraid,
for the mouth of the Lord of hosts has spoken.
Micah 4:4

Lesson 42 — Articles V, VI, and VII

The problem to be solved is, not what form of government is perfect, but which of the forms is least imperfect.

—James Madison (1833)

(Read Articles V, VI, and VII of the U.S. Constitution.)

Article V: The Amendment Process

The Founding Fathers knew that the Constitution they were drafting would probably need amending at some point. They also knew that the procedure under the Articles of Confederation had been cumbersome and ineffective. Here they included a process that was not easy but could be accomplished when a large consensus developed as to the need for an amendment.

Congress can submit an amendment to the states when two thirds of both houses approve the amendment. Any majority greater than 50% plus one is called a super majority, and this is what is called for here. The framers were not thinking in terms of political party alignment; but given today's major parties, it is rare for one party to have a two-thirds majority in both houses. This means that the members of the Senate and House must cross party lines to some degree for an amendment to be proposed and approved by Congress.

This is the only way that amendments have ever been proposed. The second method provided for in this Article of the Constitution has never been tried. The legislatures of two thirds of the states can petition Congress to call a convention for the purpose of proposing amendments. This other method has never been used because of the unknowns involved in it. First, the size of the convention and other details about it are left up to Congress. Second, it is not clear whether a convention could propose only amendments suggested by Congress or the states or if it could come up with proposals of its own. These questions about the convention approach have caused politicians to shy away from using it rather than to risk a convention that got out of control (at least, as some people would see it).

Any amendment approved by Congress must be approved by three-fourths of the states. Either the legislatures or special state conventions, whichever Congress stipulates, must approve the amendment. Only the Twenty-First Amendment called for conventions. All of the other amendments have been approved by state legislatures.

The Article provided two limitations on amendments. The clause calling for an end to the slave trade in 1808 and the clause concerning capitation or direct taxes could not be amended before 1808. Also, no state could be denied its equal representation in the Senate without its consent (which, of course, no state would ever give).

Amendments have tended to occur in bunches. The first ten were approved by 1791 and the next two were ratified by 1804. Then no amendments were added until the period following the Civil War, 1865-1870. Another long period without amendments passed until four were ratified between 1913 and 1920. Two more were approved by the states in 1933, one in 1951, three in the 1960s, and one became part of the Constitution in 1971 (the lessons on the amendments will explain this further). It appears to be the case that once an amendment is ratified, the passage of other amendments seems more possible to Congress and the American people.

Failed Amendments

In addition to the amendments that have been ratified by the states (which we will discuss in the next two lessons), a few amendments have been proposed that were not ratified. Some had expiration dates while others could conceivably still be approved even though many years have passed since Congress proposed them.

One amendment proposed with the original Bill of Rights had to do with gradually increasing the number of persons a member of the House would represent. It also said that once the House reached 100 members it could not have fewer, and once it had 200 it could not have fewer. The idea didn't catch on with enough states; and since the House now has over 400 members, it is a moot question.

In 1810, Congress submitted an amendment to the states which said that if an American citizen accepted a title of nobility from a foreign nation or if he accepted a gift from a foreign power without the approval of Congress, that person would cease being an American citizen. It was only ratified by twelve states.

On the eve of the Civil War, in an attempt to head off further secession and what appeared to be an inevitable conflict, Congress passed in early 1861 an amendment which said that no

The U.S. Capitol

amendment could be ratified which gave Congress the power to interfere with the domestic institutions of any state. "Persons held to labor or service" (i.e., slaves) were specifically mentioned. By that time, however, the die of division was cast and only two states ratified the proposal.

An amendment was submitted to the states in 1926 giving Congress the power to regulate the labor of children under eighteen years of age. No expiration date was included, so the amendment is still outstanding. However, Congress and the states already regulate child labor, so the amendment is moot.

The Equal Rights Amendment (or ERA) was passed by Congress and sent to the states in 1972. It said:

Section 1. Equality of rights under the law shall not be denied or abridged by the United States or by any State on account of sex.

Section 2. The Congress shall have the power to enforce, by appropriate legislation, the provisions of this article.

Section 3. This amendment shall take effect two years after the date of ratification.

The proposed amendment was probably the high point of what was called the women's liberation movement—and the high point of opposition to the movement. Proponents saw it as the long-awaited opportunity for women to achieve equality with men in every area of American life. Opponents warned of immeasurable and far-reaching consequences. For instance, they said that churches could lose their tax-exempt status if they refused to allow women to be ministers because of their understanding of Biblical teaching. Congress at first gave it seven years to be ratified, then later extended the time to ten years; but the amendment fell short of the required number of states and died in 1982.

Washington, D.C.

The final failed amendment was one proposed in 1978 that would have given the District of Columbia the status of a state in terms of representation in Congress and the ratification of amendments, as well as in the electoral college (which it already had under the Twenty-Third Amendment). The amendment was passed by a Democrat-controlled Congress during the term of a Democratic President (Jimmy Carter). The District of Columbia typically votes heavily Democratic for president. Not enough states wanted to do that big of a favor for the District and the Democratic Party, so the amendment died after failing to be ratified by enough states within the seven-year time limit Congress established.

Article VI: Various Matters

Debts Valid. The Constitution said that the new government would honor the debts incurred by the nation before the adoption of the Constitution. This was significant since it was common for new governments to renounce the debts of previous governments. The short-term pain was intended to bring about long-term gain because validating the debts gave the nation credibility in the eyes of its creditors and potential investors (and also encouraged their support for the survival of the country).

Supremacy Clause. The Constitution, laws made under it, and all treaties that the nation had entered into or would make in the future are here declared to be the supreme law of the land. State judges were to recognize it as such and were to understand that these documents overrode any state laws. This meant, among other things, that South Carolina was in error when it threatened to nullify a Federal law in 1832. Under the Constitution that each state accepts, states do not have the right to choose which Federal laws it will obey. The clause also meant that future treaties were to be subject to the Constitution and not vice versa. Otherwise, the Constitution could be amended by a treaty.

Oath, No Religious Test. All members of Congress, all officers of the executive branch, all Federal judges, and all members of state executive departments, legislatures, and judiciaries

must take an oath or affirmation that they will uphold the Constitution in carrying out their duties. There must not be any question regarding the loyalty of those who fill government positions at any level. On the other hand, no religious test can ever be required of anyone who fills a Federal position. This means that no Federal employee, elected or appointed, can be forced to agree to any particular religious belief or doctrine. The phrase "So help me God" is customarily added

The Swearing-In of Vice President Al Gore, 1997

to presidential oaths and is almost always added to every oath that is taken by Federal personnel, but this is not seen as accepting a particular religion or doctrine.

Six states have in their constitutions provisions that require office-holders, jurors, and witnesses in court to believe in God and/or to have a belief in a future state of reward and punishment. Some states include the phrase "So help me God" in required oaths. These provisions were put in the state constitutions many years ago to prevent unbelievers from holding government office. The South Carolina state supreme court held in 1997 that the provision in that state's constitution which required an oath in the name of God was unconstitutional. These provisions are not enforced and probably would not hold up under a constitutional challenge before the U.S. Supreme Court.

Article VII: Ratification

As we discussed earlier, the Constitutional Convention decided to put the document into effect when nine states had ratified it. They did not want one or two holdout states to paralyze the national government. The writing of the Constitution was completed in September of 1787. All but two states ratified it by the end of the following summer. North Carolina followed in 1789 and Rhode Island in 1790.

A majority of each of the twelve delegations at the convention supported the document, so the work was completed by "unanimous consent of the states present" (Rhode Island was not present). The date of completion was given as September 17, "in the year of our Lord" 1787.

Whatever I command you, you shall be careful to do;
you shall not add to nor take away from it.
Deuteronomy 12:32

Lesson 43—The First Amendment

It is the ferment of ideas, the clash of disagreeing judgments, the privilege of the individual to develop his own thought and shape his own character which makes progress possible.

— Calvin Coolidge (1925)

(Read the First Amendment to the U.S. Constitution.)

The First Amendment to the U.S. Constitution has been the center of much controversy since the middle of the twentieth century. Before we look at the issues that have arisen regarding First Amendment rights, we need to consider the significance of the Bill of Rights as a whole.

The Need and Desire for a Bill of Rights

Those who hold the reins of power sometimes abuse their fellow citizens because of their position. This is why the Old Testament prophets reminded corrupt leaders of the need to defend the rights of the people. The English nobles who forced King John to sign the Magna Carta in 1215 were defending what they understood to be their historic rights. The English Bill of Rights that was developed in 1689 as part of the Glorious Revolution listed the "true, ancient, and indubitable rights and liberties of the people." The American Revolution of 1776 and the French Revolution of 1789 were expressions of resentment over what people saw as royal indifference to the rights of citizens as human beings.

Some framers of the Constitution, such as James Madison and Alexander Hamilton, were not at first greatly concerned about a Bill of Rights being in the Constitution. They believed that a limited government would not be a threat to personal freedom. On the other hand, Thomas Jefferson and many of those who opposed ratification of the Constitution were strong advocates for a specific list or bill of rights.

During the ratification debates in the states, many Federalists promised to develop and support a Bill of Rights if the Constitution were ratified. State conventions proposed about 350 amendments to be considered, although many of these were duplications. James Madison, a member of the House of Representatives in the first Congress, edited these proposals and put forward twelve amendments for Congress to consider. These twelve were passed by Congress and submitted to the states. Ten were ratified by enough of the states to become part of the Constitution. One dealing with representation in the House was never ratified, and the other was finally ratified in 1993 as the 27th Amendment.

The Bill of Rights limits the power and intrusiveness of the Federal government. These amendments were at first understood only to apply to actions of the Federal government. Later Supreme Court decisions applied the provisions of the Fourteenth Amendment regarding limitations on the actions of state governments to the Bill of Rights. As a result, state governments may not abridge the freedoms and immunities that are guaranteed in the Bill of Rights to all Americans.

Few people will argue with the general principles stated in the Constitution. Controversies and court cases arise, however, when these principles are applied in specific situations:

- "Does this provision in the Constitution mean that I can do THIS or that I cannot do THAT?"

- "May the government engage in THIS action and not be in violation of the Constitution?"

- "Does THIS law violate the Constitution?"

- "Does the Constitution mean THIS?"

Should the provisions of the Constitution be applied narrowly, with as limited a meaning as possible, namely the meaning intended by the framers? Or should the Constitution be interpreted broadly to address issues in American life, society, and government as we face them today? This is the great debate regarding how the Constitution should be understood and applied.

We will discuss the First Amendment provisions regarding religion in later lessons. In this lesson we will focus on the guarantees of freedom of speech found in the amendment.

"Congress shall make no law . . . abridging the freedom of speech, or of the press"

The founding fathers realized the importance of the right of free speech to a free society. They knew how governments throughout history had from time to time curtailed that freedom. No good comes from muzzling critics. The only thing that happens in such a case is that those in power pretend that everyone agrees with them and that anyone who does not agree with them does not deserve to speak—or live. It has often been said that the true test of freedom of speech is determined by how freely those in power allow their opponents to speak. A common tendency is to try to shut down one's opponents in the name of limiting what "ought" to be heard or what people "ought" to hear. When the government starts defining the issue in these terms, censorship has begun.

Freedom of the press indicates the health of a society. When the media are engaged in a healthy debate about the policies

Town Meeting Sponsored by USA Today, *1988*

of the government, truth can be the victor. The print media and the Internet have almost no government controls over them. As a result, one can find almost any idea imaginable in those media. Some are good, while some are ridiculous.

The right of free speech and freedom of the press are not absolute. Certain kinds of expression are not protected by the First Amendment. These include libel and slander (defamatory speech that the person making it knows is false), as well as speech that presents a clear and present danger to national security or public safety (such as a threat to blow up the U.S. Capitol). In the 1919 *Schenck v. United States* decision, Supreme Court Justice Oliver Wendell Holmes Jr. stated that dangerous speech could be regulated by the government.

> The most stringent protection of free speech would not protect a man in falsely shouting fire in a theater and causing panic. . . . The question in every case is whether the words used are used in such circumstances and are of such a nature as to create a clear and present danger that they will bring about the substantive evils that Congress has a right to prevent.

The 1969 case *Brandenburg v. Ohio* refined the "clear and present danger" test to mean speech in which "imminent lawless action" is being encouraged and is likely.

> . . . The constitutional guarantees of free speech and free press do not permit a State to forbid or proscribe advocacy of the use of force or of law violation except where such advocacy is directed to inciting or producing imminent lawless action and is likely to incite or produce such action.

The original purpose of the First Amendment clause related to political speech. Its meaning has been extended to include speech that many find offensive in moral terms. The Court attempted to define obscenity in the 1973 case *Miller v. California*. It said that obscene material was that which (1) the average person, applying community standards, would find as a whole appealing only to prurient interest, (2) portrayed patently offensive acts, and (3) lacked any serious literary, artistic, political, or scientific value. The state can be more strict in regulating such materials that portray children.

The ultimate answer to pornography and obscenity is not to pass enough laws to be rid of it or to define it clearly enough to identify it unmistakably and make it illegal. The answer will come when Christian people refuse to have anything to do with it and when people's hearts are changed so that they don't want to hear it or read it. As long as Christians and others listen to it and buy it and pay for tickets to see it, there will be those who are happy to provide it.

This freedom of speech is true for print media, movies, and other artistic expressions. Broadcast media are another matter. The Federal government began regulating broadcasting with the creation of the Federal Communications Commission (FCC) in 1933. Through FCC regulations, the government has imposed certain standards on radio and television broadcasting, especially with regard to obscenity and decency. Stations that broadcast material in violation of these rules run the risk of losing their license. The FCC has allowed more offensive television broadcasting with the adoption of a ratings system for television programs.

Radio Broadcasters, 1929

One rule related to political speech was the FCC's Fairness Doctrine, which it imposed from 1949 until 1987. Under this rule broadcast outlets had to devote some time to a discussion of public issues, and they had to make a reasonable attempt to present varying viewpoints. Failure to do this could mean that a station would lose its license. In 1987, the FCC decided that the increasing number of broadcast outlets through the cable and satellite industries made the Fairness Doctrine obsolete. The doctrine also served to limit free discussion of issues since many broadcasters chose not to be controversial rather than to attempt an open discussion and possibly face an FCC complaint. Thus the doctrine was dropped.

Another question regarding the free speech clause is what constitutes speech. For instance, in 1989 the Supreme Court ruled that burning the American flag was a form of political expression that was protected by the First Amendment right of free speech. According to the Court's 5-4 decision, "the Government may not prohibit the expression of an idea simply because society finds the idea itself offensive or disagreeable."

"Or the right of the people peaceably to assemble, and to petition the Government for a redress of grievances."

The British government had largely ignored the grievances of the American colonists. This was a major factor in the revolution of 1776. The framers of the Constitution wanted to guarantee the American people that they could take their complaints to the government without fear of recrimination. When enough people petition the government to rectify what they think is wrong, the government might be moved to act. How this petitioning is to take place is not defined in the First Amendment.

People are free to assemble peaceably. They are not free to riot. Also, some assemblies can be forbidden if the outcome is not expected to be peaceable. Sometimes the racist organization Ku Klux Klan applies to a local government for permission to hold a public rally. Outright denial of the permit is usually an infringement of free speech and the right of assembly. Most of the time Klan rallies occur peaceably. However, localities can place strict limits on the place, time, and nature of the rally, such as whether guns will be permitted, in keeping with existing local ordinances. Counter-demonstrations are common at Klan rallies. If local authorities believe that a clear and present danger to community peace is possible because of a Klan rally, the authorities must conduct a public hearing (with sufficient notice given to the Klan) in order to decide whether the rally should be held.

This lesson mentions just a few of the numerous and complicated issues related to our First Amendment right of free speech. Freedom of speech is an ongoing question as new angles are constantly brought forth to test how the First Amendment gives freedoms and protects the people at the same time.

[P]roclaim liberty throughout all the land
unto all the inhabitants thereof. . . .
Leviticus 25:10 KJV

Reading

- "The Liberal Assault on Freedom of Speech" by Thomas G. West (*WHTT*, p. 141)

Lesson 44—Amendments 2-10

If they outlaw guns only the outlaws will have guns.

– Popular saying

(Read the Second through the Tenth Amendments to the U.S. Constitution.)

Second Amendment: The Right to Keep and Bear Arms

The Founding Fathers understood the importance of the right to own and use guns. Thomas Jefferson, for instance, wrote, "No free men shall ever be debarred the use of arms." The historical context for this amendment is important. As Noah Webster pointed out in 1787, European kingdoms routinely took guns away from the populace. This meant that only the army had such weapons, which gave the government the upper hand in any confrontation or civil dispute. (Much later in history, Adolph Hitler confiscated the guns, including hunting rifles, of private citizens in Nazi Germany.) When the government or only one part of society has all the guns, the society is not free.

The United States did not depend on a standing army for its defense. Instead, the mainstay of defense and public order was the militia. This was a force of average citizens who were organized into companies and who engaged in military exercises, but who pursued their daily lives unless called upon to preserve order or to defend against an aggressor. The government maintained no stockpile of weapons for the militia to use. Instead, each man was expected to own his own gun and to use it when serving in the militia. The militia was not a roving band of self-appointed peacekeepers. They were well-regulated.

As a result of this dependence on the militia and the experience of other countries, Congress passed and the states ratified the Second Amendment, which guarantees to the people the right to keep and bear arms. This assumes (1) the need for security and (2) the illegality of using firearms in crime. Today the threat to our domestic security comes mostly from criminals, although there could be a threat from insurrection or external attack. The right to keep and bear arms is still vital to maintaining peace and safety in our country.

South Carolina Boy with a Hunting Rifle, 1908

Because of an increase in the amount of crime committed with firearms, laws have been passed to regulate gun ownership. Certain categories of people are not able to purchase a gun, such as convicted felons, illegal drug users, illegal aliens, and those under a restraining order to prevent domestic violence. Gun purchases require a criminal background check, which usually only takes a few minutes. About 2% of purchasers are disqualified through these background checks. States have imposed various laws requiring gun registration. Laws have also restricted the kinds of weapons that may be purchased.

Committing a crime while using a firearm has been made a more serious charge to discourage the wrong use of a gun. Still, despite these safeguards, people have been able to purchase guns by using fake IDs.

The political battle over the Second Amendment is between advocates of stricter gun control and those who want to limit or roll back gun control laws. Advocates of greater controls cite the number of crimes committed with guns, the ease with which even criminals can obtain guns, and the number of incidents in homes involving firearms, including accidents and domestic violence. Those who urge greater freedom for legal gun use point out that criminals will obtain guns illegally if they choose to and that law-abiding citizens need a way to defend themselves and to enjoy legal activities such as hunting and target-shooting. Gun rights advocates see no need to penalize people who do not commit gun crimes because of the actions of those who use guns illegally. Trying to maintain a safe and sane balance between these conflicting interests is what keeps the debate alive. The Supreme Court has generally deferred to the traditional gun-ownership statement of the Second Amendment.

> *James Brady was President Ronald Reagan's press secretary who was shot and permanently disabled in the assassination attempt on Reagan in 1981. John Hinckley, the would-be assassin, used a false address to buy a handgun at a pawn shop in Texas and took immediate possession of the gun he used to shoot the President and Brady. Brady and his wife have become leading gun-control advocates. After many years of consideration in Congress (amid stiff opposition by the National Rifle Association and other pro-gun ownership interests), new gun purchasing restrictions passed Congress and went into effect in 1994. The legislation was called the Brady Law. A mandatory waiting period for a purchaser to take possession of his or her gun was part of the law, but that part of the law expired in 1998.*

Third Amendment: No Quartering of Troops

One of the irritations connected with Britain's rule over the American colonies was the practice of requiring colonists to house British troops. Not only did the colonists have to pay taxes to support the army, but they also had to house the troops when the commanding officer demanded it. The Third Amendment assured Americans that the new government would not resort to this practice.

The amendment gives two exceptions. First, the owner of the house can agree to it. Second, quartering troops in private homes can occur in wartime but only according to regulations passed by Congress. The structure of today's military forces and the number of military bases around the country that provide housing for troops make this problem unlikely to occur again.

Fourth Amendment: Protection Against Unreasonable Search and Seizure

This amendment protects a person's privacy. It limits what law enforcement agents can do when searching a person's property and possessions as part of an investigation into possible criminal activity. A legal search must be reasonable, it must be supported by a search warrant issued by a judge or magistrate, and the warrant must state who or what is being sought at what particular place. A warrant can only be issued if the judge believes that there is probable cause, that is, the likelihood exists that evidence will be found which will lead to an arrest. In certain circumstances, law enforcement agents do not need a warrant. For instance, if a person is being actively pursued or arrested for a crime, a search of that person and his possessions is appropriate.

Evidence that is found in violation of the Fourth Amendment's provisions may not be used in court, unless the discovery of the evidence was an error made in good faith.

The operative word in the amendment is "unreasonable." Many times defense lawyers have challenged evidence that was uncovered in what they said was an unreasonable search. Law enforcement searches of automobiles, for instance, are debated as to whether they are reasonable given their circumstances.

Amendments Five through Eight: Rights of the Accused

These four amendments list the rights granted to those who are accused of crimes. In our system, a person is assumed innocent until proven guilty in a court of law. Travesties of justice can occur in many ways. A person can be accused falsely, or the police or the justice system might feel pressure to obtain a conviction at whatever cost to the truth, or the weight of the system can be unfairly brought to bear against an accused individual. It is a great country that grants rights and protections to someone accused of a crime. The justice system has the responsibility to respect the accused and his assumed innocence.

The rights provided in these amendments include:

The requirement of an indictment by a grand jury for a person to stand trial for a capital (involving the death penalty) or other infamous (serious) crime. The grand jury is a step that protects a citizen from having to go through a trial when sufficient evidence to convict that person cannot be found. Cases involving the military are excepted.

The right to avoid "double jeopardy" —being tried for the same offense twice in the same jurisdiction. If a person is found not guilty in a trial, the state cannot try the same case again. This prevents the government from persecuting someone by repeatedly putting him or her on trial.

The right not to be forced to testify against oneself in a criminal trial. This includes a ban on any coerced confession that the authorities might try to produce during questioning.

The right to due process of law before being deprived of life, liberty, or property. "Due process" means essential fairness in providing all persons the same legal process, including

Courtroom Scene, 1909

all procedures and safeguards. The courts cannot treat blacks or repeat offenders or the city mayor any differently from the way anyone else is treated.

The right that prevents the government from taking private property without equitable compensation. We will discuss issues related to this topic in a later lesson on eminent domain.

The right to a speedy and public trial by an impartial jury in the state and district where the crime was committed. The government cannot keep a person in jail awaiting trial forever, perhaps hoping that he will confess. A public trial provides a greater likelihood of a fair trial. The prosecution may not stack the jury with people who have already decided that the defendant is guilty or who would be more likely to side with the prosecution (perhaps because they are government employees). Conducting the trial in the locality of the crime gives each side the same chance and does not work a hardship on the defendant by taking him away from friends and family.

The right to know with what crime a person is being charged. The state cannot hold a man indefinitely without any charges filed against him.

The right of a defendant to cross-examine in court witnesses who testify against him.

The right to compel (by subpoena) witnesses to appear in court who might testify on behalf of the defendant. Otherwise, the state might find it convenient only to subpoena witnesses for the prosecution.

The right to an attorney, even at the government's expense if the defendant cannot afford to pay an attorney himself.

The right to a jury trial in a civil case whenever the value being contested is over twenty dollars.

The right that prevents a judge from throwing out the verdict of a jury, unless he determines (1) the case was improperly submitted to a jury or (2) the verdict of the jury was unreasonable given the evidence and testimony provided.

The right not to have excessive bail imposed. Bail cannot be set at a high figure unless the judge determines that the accused person is a threat to public safety or is likely to run away. The Eighth Amendment is an almost exact quote from the English Bill of Rights from 1689. Several states had included this right in their constitutions.

The right to avoid excessive fines. The general rule is that the punishment must fit the crime. English law as well as the legal codes of other countries sometimes called for ridiculously high fines for mere misdemeanors.

The right to avoid imposition of "cruel and unusual punishments." This was understood by the founders to mean such actions as mutilation or extreme torture. The Constitution assumes that the death penalty is not cruel and unusual punishment and is therefore acceptable (note the reference to being deprived of life in the Fifth Amendment). However, a contemporary school of thought holds that the death penalty is cruel and unusual and that it should be outlawed. The Supreme Court in *Furman v. Georgia* (1972) placed great emphasis upon a phrase written by Chief Justice Warren in 1958 in *Trop v. Dulles*:

> The [Eighth] Amendment must draw its meaning from the evolving standards
> of decency that mark the progress of a maturing society.

In other words, what used to be acceptable punishment might now be considered cruel and unusual. This view rejects the idea of permanent, absolute standards. It says that criminal punishment can and should be determined by what is socially acceptable. If it is the judgment of society (however that is determined, perhaps only in the minds of five Supreme Court justices) that the death penalty is cruel and unusual, then society can only punish wrongdoers because what they did was socially unacceptable, not because it was absolutely morally wrong.

The 1972 *Furman* decision did note that the way the death penalty had been administered was cruel and unusual. Those who are convicted of capital crimes wait for many years on Death Row. In addition, statistics show that the vast majority of those who are executed are poor and black. Whites convicted of capital crimes are much less likely to be executed. Moreover, in some states, the law allowed for discretion by the judge or the jury on whether execution or life in prison was to be the sentence; and this was seen as leading to inconsistent application of the death penalty. Because of the *Furman* decision, states had to rewrite sentencing requirements in capital crimes to make application of the death penalty less a matter of discretion and less open to charges of racial and economic bias.

Ninth Amendment: Enumerated Rights Do Not Disparage Other Rights

Alexander Hamilton disapproved of a Bill of Rights because he knew that all possible rights could not be included. He was afraid that government in the future might assume that if a right was not specifically listed it was not held by the people. Because of this concern, the Ninth Amendment was proposed and adopted as one of two blanket amendments.

This amendment says that the listing of specific rights in the Constitution (which is what the Bill of Rights was doing) was not to be taken to mean that rights not stated did not remain with the people. The rights in question were the generally understood rights of citizens as reflected in American legal practice at the time.

Tenth Amendment: Powers Reserved To The States And To The People

This second blanket amendment provides that powers not specifically delegated to the Federal government by the Constitution nor specifically denied to the states by the Constitution remained with the states or the people. This embodies the principle of a limited government which has specifically delegated powers. The Federal government can only do what it has been given the authority to do in the Constitution, while the states can do whatever has not been denied to them by the Constitution.

This amendment is largely ignored today. It is rare that the Supreme Court strikes down a Federal law because it oversteps the powers enumerated for the Federal government in the Constitution. In addition, Americans are not overly concerned about whether the Federal government is overstepping its bounds. Most people seem only interested in what the government—Federal, state, or local—can do for them. The detail of who is doing it for them is of little concern.

You shall do no injustice in judgment;
you shall not be partial to the poor nor defer to the great,
but you are to judge your neighbor fairly.
Leviticus 19:15

Courtroom in Chicago, Illinois

Lesson 45—Amendments 11-27

But every amendment to the Constitution, if once established, would be a single proposition, and might be brought forward singly.
—*Alexander Hamilton,* The Federalist *Number 85 (1788)*

(Read the Amendments of the U.S. Constitution that are discussed in this lesson.)

We have already discussed several amendments earlier in this text. These include the Eleventh (Lesson 37), the Twelfth (Lesson 26), the Seventeenth (Lesson 17), the Twentieth (Lessons 18 and 27), the Twenty-Second (Lesson 27), the Twenty-Fifth (Lesson 27), and the Twenty-Seventh (Lesson 18). This lesson examines the remaining amendments.

Thirteenth Amendment

The Thirteenth, Fourteenth, and Fifteenth Amendments are called the Civil War Amendments because they came about as a result of that conflict. The Thirteenth Amendment outlawed slavery and involuntary servitude except as punishment for crime. Congress borrowed the wording of Article VI of the Northwest Ordinance of 1787 to ban slavery nationwide.

President Lincoln had issued the Emancipation Proclamation on January 1, 1863; but some questioned its legitimacy and whether it would stand up in the complicated process of readmitting states. Some political leaders thought that Congress could abolish slavery by simple legislation, but again many thought the law on the issue would need more force. Thus an amendment to the Constitution was proposed. The Amendment passed Congress in early 1865, before the war had ended. Ratification of it was a condition that Congress placed on the former Confederate states before they would be readmitted to the Union. It became a part of the Constitution in December of 1865.

The Amendment seems simple and straightforward enough, but it played a part in the Supreme Court's decision in the Civil Rights Cases of 1883. In those cases the majority of the Court held that the Amendment not only abolished slavery but also gave Congress the authority to outlaw the "badges and incidents of slavery"—that is, the continuing realities of segregation and discrimination:

> . . . It is assumed that the power vested in Congress to enforce the article by appropriate legislation, clothes Congress with power to pass all laws necessary and proper for abolishing all badges and incidents of slavery in the United States.

However, the Court took a narrow view and did not apply the amendment to state law until many years later in *Jones v. Mayer* (1968). This case involved the refusal of a real estate company to sell a house to a black man, which was allowed under Missouri state law. In their opinion, in this case, the Court said:

. . . Whatever else they may have encompassed, the badges and incidents of slavery—its "burdens and disabilities"—included restraints upon "those fundamental rights which are the essence of civil freedom, namely, the same right . . . to inherit, purchase, lease, sell and convey property, as is enjoyed by white citizens" [quoting from the Civil Rights Cases]. Just as the Black Codes, enacted after the Civil War to restrict the free exercise of those rights, were substitutes for the slave system, so the exclusion of Negroes from white communities became a substitute for the Black Codes. And when racial discrimination herds men into ghettos and makes their ability to buy property turn on the color of their skin, then it too is a relic of slavery.

Fourteenth Amendment: Citizenship, Equal Rights in State Actions

Congress passed a Civil Rights Act in 1866 that included essentially the provisions of this Amendment. President Andrew Johnson vetoed the bill, and Congress overrode his veto; but Congress wanted these provisions to be beyond the reach of any further interference. Therefore, Congress passed and the states eventually (in 1868) ratified this Fourteenth Amendment. All the former Confederate states except Tennessee rejected the Amendment at first. Their ratification of it became another step in the Reconstruction process that Congress required.

This is probably the most significant amendment adopted since the Bill of Rights. The two main provisions are included in Section 1: (1) The Amendment defines citizenship on both the state and national levels (overturning the finding of the *Dred Scott* decision), and (2) the Amendment forbids states from denying anyone life, liberty, or property without due process of law. States had to provide equal protection under the law to all citizens. This has been interpreted to mean that any governmental action on any level has to be within these provisions. The amendment does not apply to purely private transactions.

Section 2 replaced the three-fifths clause of Article I by providing for representation in the House to be determined by a straight population count of the states. However, if states prohibited some people over twenty-one years old from voting, their representation would be reduced by the proportion that group was to the entire population of the state over twenty-one.

Section 3 forbade all former Federal and state office holders who had participated in the rebellion of the Confederacy from holding office on both the Federal and state levels. This section was intended to remove many leading Confederates from the political process. Congress did have the right to pardon these people with a two-thirds vote of each house.

Section 4 said that the United States government would honor debts incurred by the Union during the Civil War but would not honor Confederate debts.

Fifteenth Amendment: Right to Vote

This amendment was ratified in 1870 in response to many state laws that forbade black Americans from voting. After 1870, states no longer blatantly discriminated on the basis of race; but they found new ways to limit the voting rights of blacks, such as requiring literacy tests and poll taxes. Many blacks could not read, and state voting officials often gave more difficult literacy tests to blacks than they did to whites. Payment of a poll tax was difficult for many poor blacks.

Sixteenth Amendment: Income Tax

Congress enacted an income tax during the Civil War, which the Supreme Court found to be constitutional in 1880. Congress passed another income tax law in 1893, which took effect in 1894; but the Supreme Court struck it down as unconstitutional in 1895. The Court declared that a tax on income was a direct tax which Congress could only impose by apportioning it by population among the states.

A progressive income tax, which provides for higher tax rates for those with greater incomes, was one of the reforms proposed by the Progressive movement in the late nineteenth and early twentieth centuries. It was presented as a way to generate revenue for the government and to equalize the distribution of wealth. This amendment passed Congress in 1909 and was ratified by the states in 1913. The original rates set by Congress were low and the exemptions were high. Those who made less than $4,000 a year (roughly equivalent to $65-70,000 today) paid no tax. The tax rate for those making up to $20,000 worked out, with deductions, to be 1%. Those in the highest bracket paid a tax of six percent.

Over the years, tax rates have increased, the tax law has become much more complicated, and the Federal government has become dependent on revenue from personal income tax for the bulk of its ever-growing expenditures. We will discuss taxation and budgeting issues in a future lesson.

Eighteenth and Twenty-First Amendments: Prohibition and Its Repeal

Another popular cause in the late 1800s and early 1900s was the prohibition of the production, sale, and transportation of alcoholic beverages. Supporters of Prohibition cited the harmful effects of alcohol on individuals, families, and society. Opponents did not want to pass laws that regulated private behavior. Lobbyists for the liquor industry gave money to elected officials to persuade them to oppose a ban on liquor. The subject was a hot political issue. In Nashville, Tennessee in 1908, a gun battle between men on different sides of the issue left Edward Ward Carmack, a prominent politician and newspaper editor, dead.

Several states had outlawed alcohol before Congress passed the Eighteenth Amendment. It was ratified by the states in 1919. One result of national Prohibition was widespread disregard of the ban, especially in large cities, and a law enforcement nightmare as a result of organized crime developing a lucrative industry out of the illegal production and distribution of liquor. The popular image of the Roaring Twenties is in large part a result of the underground disobedience to Prohibition.

The Twenty-First Amendment, ratified in 1933, repealed the Eighteenth Amendment and national Prohibition. It left enforcement of liquor laws to the states.

Poster Encouraging Prohibition

Nineteenth Amendment: Women's Right to Vote

Passage of the Nineteenth Amendment in 1920 was the culmination of decades of campaigning by women's suffrage proponents. Some states had given women the right to vote before this Amendment was ratified.

Twenty-Third Amendment: Electoral Votes for the District of Columbia

This amendment, ratified in 1961, gave more political power to residents of the District of Columbia. By this amendment the District is guaranteed the same number of electoral votes as the least populous state (which has always been three electoral votes).

Twenty-Fourth Amendment: Outlawing of the Poll Tax

Passage of this amendment was part of the Civil Rights movement of the 1950s and 1960s. African Americans were proportionally more affected by the poll tax than white Americans. It became part of the Constitution in early 1964, about two months after President Kennedy's assassination.

Twenty-Sixth Amendment: Lowering the Voting Age to Eighteen

This amendment, which lowered the voting age nationally from 21 to 18, required the shortest period in U.S. history for an amendment to be ratified. It was proposed on March 23, 1971, and was ratified 107 days later, on July 1, 1971. One motivation for the speed was to avoid any problems in the 1972 election.

The involvement by eighteen-year-old American draftees in the Vietnam War prompted many to argue that if men were old enough to fight they ought to be considered old enough to vote. During World War II, legislators in Georgia and Kentucky had agreed with this reasoning and had lowered the voting age in those states. Part of a 1970 law passed by Congress lowering the voting age to eighteen in all elections had been ruled unconstitutional by the Supreme Court, and the Court's decision had left the situation unclear with regard to state elections. To avoid confusion, Congress proposed this amendment to the Constitution; and it was quickly adopted by the states.

U.S. Air Force Personnel Voting on the Field, 1996

The conclusion, when all has been heard, is:
fear God and keep His commandments,
because this applies to every person.
Ecclesiastes 12:13

Reading

- "Constitutional Myths and Realities" by Stephen Markman (*WHTT*, p. 149)

Part 3

State and Local Government, Taxes, and Budgets

10 State Government

We now turn to the workings of state governments. This unit surveys state constitutions and the three branches of government on the state level: legislative, executive, and judicial. We also include a lesson about controversial incidents regarding prayer in state legislatures.

Lessons in This Unit

Lesson 46—State Constitutions
Lesson 47—State Legislatures
Lesson 48—Controversial Legislative Prayers
Lesson 49—State Governors
Lesson 50—State Bureaucracies and State Courts

Activity Idea

Reflect on the changes that the United States is experiencing: from rural to urban, the aging of the Baby Boomer generation, and our increasing ethnic diversity. Is our diversity a strength or a weakness? How can we bring our diverse nation together yet allow for individual freedom? How should government on all levels respond, and how should Christians respond? Write a five-minute speech addressing a group of ministers and Christian businessmen in your community.

If you are using the optional *Quiz and Exam Book*, answer the questions for each lesson after you have completed the lesson and read any assigned readings in *We Hold These Truths*. After you have completed Lesson 50, take the quiz for Unit 10 and the second exam, which covers Units 6-10.

Lesson 46—State Constitutions

That all power is inherent in the people, and all free governments are founded on their authority, and instituted for their peace, safety, and happiness; for the advancement of those ends they have at all times, an unalienable and indefeasible right to alter, reform, or abolish the government in such manner as they may think proper.
—Article I, Section 1, Tennessee State Constitution

The actions of the Federal government receive the most media coverage, but the workings of state government are of vital interest to every American. We should not let the influence of the national media blind us to the importance of knowing what happens in government on the state and local levels. State governments oversee most law enforcement operations; they have the most authority about education issues; they are responsible for road building and maintenance; and they enforce laws having to do with business operations, marriage and divorce, and other matters directly relevant to all citizens.

America has one national government, but we have fifty state governments. This means that America has fifty state constitutions, fifty state chief executives, fifty state legislatures, and fifty state court systems. Each state has its own unique arrangement for governing the people. These state systems have many similarities to each other but also

Missouri State Capitol

important variations. We will not attempt to detail all of these differing systems. Instead, we will survey what is generally true about state government. We hope to point you toward issues that you will want to investigate on your own regarding your state government.

State Constitution History

The fundamental law of a state, like that of the nation, is the constitution. Even before the United States declared its independence, the Continental Congress urged each state to develop a government that would best bring about the well-being of its citizens. In doing so, most state governments gave the people little direct voice.

The earliest state constitutions vested most governmental power in the hands of the legislatures. Reacting to the experience with colonial governors who were appointed by and represented the king, state governorships were usually weak positions. Many state constitutions established property qualifications for voting and holding office. A few states had established churches.

The Connecticut and Rhode Island state assemblies transformed their colonial charters into state constitutions with few changes. These states did not adopt new constitutions until well into the nineteenth century. Six other state legislatures drew up new constitutions and declared them to be in effect. Four state legislatures called conventions to draw up new constitutions. Only in Massachusetts was a convention elected by the people. The convention met in 1780 and formulated a constitution which was ratified by popular vote. This became the pattern for later constitutions and for new states that were admitted into the Union later. However, the members of Tennessee's constitutional convention were in such a hurry to achieve statehood in 1796 that they sent their new constitution directly to Congress without bothering to get a vote from the people.

As just noted, the transition from colonial status to statehood led to the development of new state constitutions. Another event that had a similar effect was the Civil War. The eleven states that seceded to form the Confederacy were required by Congress to write new constitutions as a condition for being readmitted to the Union. The states had to remove all defenses of slavery, and they had to promise their allegiance to the Union.

Comparisons to the U.S. Constitution

State constitutions are similar in many ways to the United States Constitution. Most begin with a listing of the rights of the people—similar to the Bill of Rights—and all of them include such a list at some point. All state constitutions establish three branches of government—executive, legislative, and judicial—and define a separation of the powers that are distributed among the branches.

The major differences between state constitutions and the Federal Constitution are: (1) the state documents are much longer and more detailed, and (2) state constitutions have been rewritten and amended much more often. The U.S. Constitution has about 7,000 words. The Rhode Island and Connecticut constitutions are about the same length. However, the California state constitution has over 90,000 words. Before Louisiana adopted a new constitution in 1974, its constitution ran to over 200,000 words! The average length of a state constitution is 26,000 words, almost four times the length of the U.S. Constitution.

Unlike the Federal Constitution, all fifty state constitutions specifically make reference to God.

Rewriting and Amendments

The national Constitution was written once, in 1787. States, by contrast, have rewritten their foundational documents much more often. On average, each state has had three constitutions. Alabama has had six, Georgia has had ten, and Louisiana is using its eleventh. Fewer than twenty states operate under their first and only constitution. Only six constitutions now in use were written prior to 1850. About one-fourth were drafted after World War II.

While the Federal Constitution has been amended 27 times (and the first ten of those came at the same time), the average state constitution has been amended about 100 times. California has seen about 425 amendments, and Alabama's constitution carries over 600 amendments. About 70% of the Alabama amendments are actually local laws that had to be made part of the constitution. The state constitution of Alabama concentrates power at the state level and leaves relatively little authority for counties and cities. Thus many amendments were voted on by people across the state who had no personal stake in whether the amendment passed or not. The Oregon state constitution has been amended about 120 times. It has two Article VIIs (dealing with the state court system, designated Original and Amended), and twelve Article XIs, which touch on various subjects and are designated XI-A, XI-D, XI-E, XI-F(1), XI-F(2), and so forth.

Some reasons can be identified for the longer state constitutions, the greater number of amendments, and the frequency of rewriting the basic constitution. As indicated above, the vast majority of state constitutions do not come from the revolutionary period. As a result, a different purpose was in view in most cases when the state constitution was written. The state constitutional conventions wanted to specify and limit the powers of state government in a great number of areas. States have often included in their constitutions provisions that might be expected to be embodied in regular legislation. When provisions have been included that addressed issues relevant only at a given point in history, in later years those provisions became meaningless or a hindrance. In addition, special interest groups have been able to influence the writing and amending process at the state level, so a greater number of provisions have been included that are favorable to particular groups.

Tennessee's original constitution was written in 1796. In 1834, a convention met to rewrite the document. The delegates in 1834 changed the way property was taxed. Before, all land had been taxed at the same rate. From that point, land used to produce income as well as city property were taxed at a higher rate. In addition, the property requirement for voting was removed. However, perhaps in reaction to the 1831 Nat Turner rebellion in Virginia and the increased activity of abolitionists across the country, the right of free black citizens to vote was taken away. Tennessee's third constitution was drafted in 1870. It declared slavery to be illegal and gave black people the right to vote. However, it also imposed a poll tax, which kept many African Americans from voting.

A constitutional convention was called in Tennessee in 1953 to consider several amendments. The amendments changed the length of the governor's term and of state senators' terms. It also eliminated the poll tax. By then, the poll tax was being paid on behalf of individual voters by big city political machines to encourage people to vote for the candidates the machine supported. Repeal of the poll tax was an attempt to lessen the influence of political machines.

Another reason for the large number of amendments in state constitutions is the ability of the public to be involved in the process. Every state legislature may call a constitutional convention to consider amendments. A few states require the question of calling a convention to be put before the voters every few years. In almost all states, the legislature may place amendments before the voters. In addition, several states give the citizenry the right of initiative in proposing amendments. This means that if enough voters sign petitions to place an amendment on the ballot, it has to appear and be voted on, regardless of what the legislature does. On the other hand, some states limit the number of amendments that can be proposed at one time. Having too many amendments to consider at once can be confusing to the voters, especially when they are written in language that is hard to understand. Generally speaking, fewer people vote on amendments than vote for contested races because many voters do not

Vermont State Capitol

understand the amendments and because they do not see them as relevant to their lives. The voters of Georgia in 1962 deserve our sympathy. They were faced with an astounding 132 proposed amendments that year!

The process involved in amending the constitution varies from state to state. In most states, the legislature can propose an amendment with a simple majority vote. Some legislatures require a super-majority (two-thirds or three-fifths) of both houses. About a fourth of the states require that an amendment be approved in two successive sessions of the legislature before it is put on the ballot. In most states, a simple majority of popular votes cast on the question is sufficient to pass the amendment. However, a few states have special rules, such as requiring a majority of the total votes cast in the election.

New York State Capitol

Tennessee has one of the most difficult amendment processes. A proposed amendment must receive a majority in both houses of the state legislature in one session and a two-thirds majority in both houses in the next session. It then is placed on the ballot, but it must receive a majority of the number of votes cast in the governor's race (or most recent governor's race) in order to be ratified and added to the constitution. As you can see, a proposal might receive more yes than no votes but fall short because it did not get enough yes votes when compared to the votes cast in the governor's race.

Is All of This Good or Bad?

The overall effect of state constitutions is probably a mixture of good and bad. It is good that state governments have specific and limited powers. It is not good if the state constitution is so long and complex that few people are familiar with it and if its wording can be twisted by various interests. It is good that popular initiative can help mold state law and bypass a legislature that is satisfied with the status quo. It is not good if the process can be controlled by a relatively few people or by special interest groups with money to influence legislators and to swamp voters with persuasive ads.

The American people have to be involved in government at the state level, first to exercise our rights and freedoms in a way that can really make a difference, and second to make sure that state government is responsive to the people.

But beyond this, my son, be warned: the writing of many books is endless,
and excessive devotion to books is wearying to the body.
Ecclesiastes 12:12

Reading

- The time has come to find a comfortable chair, get a good snack, and read your state constitution. You might not be able to do this in one sitting, but you need to spend some time getting to know the foundational law of your state. Many states publish a Blue Book or other similar book about state government in which the state constitution will be printed. You can also find your state constitution online through an Internet search. Happy reading!

Lesson 47—State Legislatures

What Makes You Think We Read the Bills?
—Title of a book by former California State Senator H.L. Richardson

The law-making powers of state government are vested in the legislature, which is known by various names in different states: State Legislature, General Assembly, Legislative Assembly, or (in Massachusetts and New Hampshire) the General Court. Every state except Nebraska has a bicameral (two-house) legislature. Every upper house is called the State Senate. The lower house, depending on the state, is called the House of Representatives, the Assembly, or (in Maryland, Virginia, and West Virginia) the House of Delegates.

State Senators generally serve four year terms while State Representatives are elected to two-year terms. Most states hold legislative elections in even-numbered years, coordinating with presidential and Congressional elections. Two states elect their legislators in odd-numbered years. A session of the legislature is for two years.

The number of elected servants in each state chamber varies widely from state to state. On average, a state senate has about 39 members and a state house has around 108. The Alaska State Senate has only twenty members. California, the most populous state, has 40 senators and 80 representatives. Indiana has 100 representatives and 50 senators. The largest body, by far, is the lower house of the New Hampshire legislature. It has 400 members for a state with a population of about 1.3 million. New Hampshire is the 41st most populous state in the Union, but the New Hampshire House is one of the largest legislative bodies in the world. Based on the population represented, it is the most representative body in the world. The New Hampshire Senate, by the way, has 24 members.

As of 2006, about 23% of state lawmakers were women, about eight percent were African American, and about 3% were Hispanic. The average age of a state legislator was 53.

Fifteen states have term limits for members of the state legislature. These limits are usually eight or twelve years for both the state House and the state Senate. Since the push for limits began in 1990, twenty-one states have adopted term limits; but the courts in four states ruled that the measures were not constitutional, usually for technical reasons, and the legislatures in two states repealed the measures. The implementation of term limits has taken place gradually. In 2000, half of the membership of the Florida and Ohio lower houses was ineligible to run again. Two years later, 71% of Michigan's state Senate was turned out due to term limits.

Same and Different

State legislative bodies are organized in much the same way that Congress is. Each chamber selects its presiding officers (although the Lieutenant Governor chairs the State Senate), and each body (except Nebraska) has majority and minority party organizations. The presiding officers and the Calendar Committees have significant power in deciding what bills reach the floor for debate and vote. The legislature has standing committees on a variety of subjects that hold hearings on proposed legislation and conduct investigative sessions on topics that relate to state law and policy. The majority party in the chamber usually names the chairman and the majority of seats on each committee. Some state legislatures have dozens of committees that create plenty of work for the elected officials and staff.

The process by which a bill becomes law is generally the same as that followed by the U.S. Congress. A bill is introduced and assigned to a committee. That committee studies it and either tables it or votes it out to the floor. The bill is then debated and voted on. If it passes, it is sent to the other chamber for the same process. When a bill passes both houses in the same form, it is sent to the governor for his signature. The governor can either sign the bill or veto it and send it back to the legislature. Lobbyists for special interest groups are a significant presence in state legislative work. Sometimes lobbyists help write the laws that are introduced.

> *Some states have a referendum provision which allows for a proposal to become law by a vote of the people. In these states, citizens can mount a petition drive to get a proposal on the ballot. If enough voters sign the petition, and if the proposal wins a majority in the election, it becomes law. The referendum is a way for the people to bypass the typical legislative procedure and to enact laws in a more purely democratic process.*

Despite these similarities, state legislatures are different from Congress in significant ways. Perhaps the most obvious difference is that legislatures generally meet for a much shorter period than Congress does. Most legislatures begin their sessions in January and complete their business by April or May. Legislatures are generally restricted by state constitution or state law on the number of days they can meet. This is the number of days when both chambers are in official session. Legislators work many more days than that, however, attending committee meetings, investigating bills, handling requests by their constituents, and carrying out other responsibilities.

The legislatures of six states meet only every other year. They meet in odd-numbered years following November elections that occur in even-numbered years. Of the forty-four that have annual sessions, six of them limit the topics that the legislature can consider in one of the years, usually to budget or other fiscal issues. However, even when the legislature meets only every other year, legislators still attend committee meetings and fulfill other functions in the

> *Nebraska's one-house state legislature is the only unicameral legislative branch among the fifty states. It was formed in 1937 after the tireless campaigning of George Norris and others on its behalf. The body is called the Nebraska Senate. It is also distinctive in that it is nonpartisan. Nebraskans run for state Senate seats without party affiliation. The top two vote-getters in each district's primary face off in the general election. Before the transition was made in 1937, the Nebraska legislature had two houses and each chamber was divided along party lines.*
>
> *The unicameral approach has cut down on administrative costs and has made the deliberations more open to the public. Fears of poorly considered legislation have not been borne out in Nebraska. Some other states have investigated the unicameral approach, but no other state has adopted it. Few legislators want to vote themselves out of a job.*

Nebraska State Capitol

off-years. These every-other-year sessions are the exception now, but for many years they were the rule. In the early 1960s, only nineteen states had annual sessions.

As a result of this limited schedule, the role of a legislator in most states is a part-time job. Only about a dozen legislatures work full-time or almost full-time. Elected officials in the rest of the states consider their work to be about one-half to two-thirds of a full time job. Most legislative staff personnel work full-time.

This part-time situation is reflected in the compensation that legislators are paid. Most states provide a salary plus an additional per diem (per day) expense amount for every day that the legislature is in session. Pay scales vary widely. In California (one of the full-time states), a

In 2005, the Nissan Corporation announced that it was moving its North American operations headquarters from the Los Angeles area to suburban Nashville, Tennessee. The state of Tennessee offered Nissan financial incentives to encourage the company to choose Tennessee for its new location. In May of 2005, the state legislature voted to reimburse Nissan employees up to $50,000 each to make the move. The inducement could cost the state up to $64 million. A consultant hired by Nissan helped to shape the bill granting this reimbursement before it was considered by the legislature. State and local incentives to the company totaled almost $200 million. (Source: "Nissan shaped incentive bill while legislators in dark," The (Nashville) Tennessean, December 4, 2005)

legislator receives $110,880 annual salary plus $138.00 for expenses each day the legislature is in session. In New York, the yearly salary is $79,500 with expense reimbursement tied to the Federal rate. Pennsylvania lawmakers are paid $69,647 annually plus $128.00 per diem. In Missouri, legislators receive $31,351 per year and $76.80 per diem. Montana members receive $76.80 per legislative day and $90.31 per day for expenses. New Hampshire state senators and representatives rake in a big $100 per year with no per diem rate for expenses—only mileage reimbursement. One result of state legislators being part-time is that, as with Congress, hourly or salaried workers are not generally able to fill these positions. Legislators are usually attorneys, business owners, retirees, or others who can maintain flexible schedules. Lawyers account for about 15% of legislators nationwide. (All figures were accurate as of 2006.)

Apportionment and State Senate Districts

Two long-standing issues regarding how state legislators are elected were resolved in the 1960s. These issues involved legislative reapportionment and the drawing of state senate districts. During the twentieth century, population shifts caused significant growth in urban areas and smaller growth (sometimes even declines) in rural areas. However, state legislatures often did not want to reapportion legislative districts in keeping with population changes. Rural representatives were often fearful that legislators from urban areas would not be interested in protecting the traditional interests of farmers.

In Tennessee, legislative districts were not reapportioned on the basis of the U.S. census for sixty years after 1901, even though the state constitution required it. As a result, by 1960 the legislative district in which Charles Baker lived in Shelby County (which is largely the city of Memphis and its suburbs) had about ten times the population of some rural districts in the state. Baker and others sued Tennessee Secretary of State Joe Carr (who oversaw elections but who was not responsible for apportionment) in Federal court, claiming that they did not have equal protection under the law as guaranteed by the Fourteenth Amendment to the U.S. Constitution.

Federal courts denied the suit on the grounds of a long-standing tradition that courts avoided political questions. This was first stated in an 1849 Supreme Court decision (*Luther v. Borden*) and reaffirmed as recently as 1946 in *Colegrove v. Green*. In the latter case, the Court declined to become involved in a congressional redistricting case in Illinois. Associate Justice Felix Frankfurter said that courts should not get involved in the "political thicket" of apportionment problems. Baker appealed to the Supreme Court, and the decision in *Baker v. Carr* was announced in 1962. The Court reversed its position and said that reapportionment cases were justiciable controversies appropriate for Federal courts. This led to lawsuits all over the country regarding reapportionment of state legislatures. Some legislatures got the message and redrew district lines without court cases being filed. In a series of decisions, the Court said that malapportionment was a denial of equal protection, since the votes of some people were "debased and diluted" just because of where they lived.

The 1964 case *Reynolds v. Sims* involved the state senate of Alabama. Under a reapportionment plan drawn up in 1962, each of Alabama's counties was to send one senator to the upper house, even though the population of the counties ranged from about 15,000 to over 600,000. In his decision, Chief Justice Earl Warren wrote,

Alabama State Capitol

> In *Baker v. Carr*, we held that a claim asserted under the Equal Protection Clause challenging the constitutionality of a State's apportionment of seats in its legislature, on the ground that the right to vote of certain citizens was effectively impaired since debased and diluted, in effect presented a justiciable controversy subject to adjudication by Federal courts. The spate of similar cases filed and decided by lower courts since our decision in *Baker* amply shows that the problem of state legislative malapportionment is one that is perceived to exist in a large number of the States. . . .

> Legislators represent people, not trees or acres. . . . We hold that, as a basic constitutional standard, the Equal Protection Clause requires that the seats in both houses of a bicameral state legislature must be apportioned on a population basis. Simply stated, an individual's right to vote for state legislators is unconstitutionally impaired when its weight is in a substantial fashion diluted when compared with votes of citizens living in other parts of the State. . . .

> Much has been written since our decision in *Baker v. Carr* about the applicability of the so-called Federal analogy to state legislative apportionment arrangements. After considering the matter, the court below concluded that no conceivable analogy could be drawn between the Federal scheme and the apportionment of seats in the Alabama Legislature under the proposed [state] constitutional amendment. We agree with the District Court, and find the Fed-

eral analogy inapposite and irrelevant to state legislative districting schemes. Attempted reliance on the Federal analogy appears often to be little more than an after-the-fact rationalization offered in defense of maladjusted state apportionment arrangements. The original constitutions of 36 of our States provided that representation in both houses of the state legislatures would be based completely, or predominantly, on population. And the Founding Fathers clearly had no intention of establishing a pattern or model for the apportionment of seats in state legislatures when the system of representation in the Federal Congress was adopted. Demonstrative of this is the fact that the Northwest Ordinance, adopted in the same year, 1787, as the Federal Constitution, provided for the apportionment of seats in territorial legislatures solely on the basis of population.

As a result of this decision, both houses of all state legislatures (as well as the Nebraska Senate) are apportioned on the basis of population and are reconsidered after every ten-year U.S. census.

The Importance of State Legislatures

As we noted in the previous lesson, state government should be of vital interest to every citizen. Consider just some of the topics of legislation which state bodies address: taxation, inheritance, mortgages, corporations, the operation of a state lottery, major crimes, and childhood vaccinations. Another reason to take an interest in state legislatures is that, in some states, the minimum age to be elected is lower than that required to be a U.S. Congressman or Senator. In Oregon and South Dakota, for instance, a person can be elected to either house at the age of 21. Moreover, if you have your eye on Federal office, holding a state office can be an excellent training ground for learning about the operation of government.

Calling them to Himself, Jesus said to them,
"You know that those who are recognized as rulers of the Gentiles lord it over them;
and their great men exercise authority over them.
But it is not this way among you,
but whoever wishes to become great among you shall be your servant;
and whoever wishes to be first among you shall be slave of all.
For even the Son of Man did not come to be served, but to serve,
and to give His life a ransom for many."
Mark 10:42-45

Lesson 48—Controversial Legislative Prayers

After calling the House to order, the order of business for the day shall be as follows:
   1. Roll Call
   2. Prayer by the Chaplain, followed by the Pledge of Allegiance
   3. Approval of Journal
   . . . .

—*Rules of the Idaho State House of Representatives*

Each chamber of a state legislature customarily opens its meetings with a prayer. Usually these prayers are led by a minister who is invited to come for the day. Sometimes the prayer is led by a member of the legislative body. This is a long-standing custom that predates even the U.S. Constitution. Most of the time this practice arouses little controversy. When this tradition has been challenged in court, it has been upheld. On a few occasions, however, spiritual sparks have flown.

Marsh v. Chambers (1983)

The Nebraska legislature named a chaplain, a Presbyterian minister, and paid him a little over $300.00 per month while the body was in session. The chaplain led a prayer at the opening of each day's session. One member of the Nebraska legislature objected to this practice as a violation of the Establishment Clause of the First Amendment to the U.S. Constitution. The Supreme Court rejected this claim in its 1983 *Marsh v. Chambers* decision:

> On September 25, 1789, three days after Congress authorized the appointment of paid chaplains, final agreement was reached on the language of the Bill of Rights. Clearly the men who wrote the First Amendment Religion Clauses did not view paid legislative chaplains and opening prayers as a violation of that Amendment, for the practice of opening sessions with prayer has continued without interruption ever since that early session of Congress. . . . It can hardly be thought that in the same week Members of the First Congress voted to appoint and to pay a chaplain for each House and also voted to approve the draft of the First Amendment for submission to the states, they intended the Establishment Clause of the Amendment to forbid what they had just declared acceptable. . . .
>
> In light of the unambiguous and unbroken history of more than 200 years [in Congress and in state legislatures], there can be no doubt that the practice of opening legislative sessions with prayer has become part of the fabric of our society. To invoke Divine guidance on a public body entrusted with making the laws is not, in these circumstances, an "establishment" of religion or a step toward establishment; it is simply a tolerable acknowledgment of beliefs widely

held among the people of this country. As Justice Douglas observed, "[w]e are a religious people whose institutions presuppose a Supreme Being" (*Zorach v. Clauson*, 1952). . . .

[T]here is no indication that the prayer opportunity [in Nebraska] has been exploited to proselytize or advance any one, or to disparage any other, faith or belief. That being so, it is not for us to embark on a sensitive evaluation or to parse the content of a particular prayer.

Joe Wright's Prayer

On January 23, 1996, Joe Wright, pastor of Central Christian Church in Wichita, Kansas, opened a meeting of the Kansas House of Representatives in Topeka with this prayer:

Heavenly Father, we come before you today to ask your forgiveness and seek your direction and guidance. We know your Word says, "Woe to those who call evil good," but that's exactly what we've done. We have lost our spiritual equilibrium and inverted our values.

We confess that we have ridiculed the absolute truth of your Word and called it moral pluralism. We have worshipped other gods and called it multiculturalism. We have endorsed perversion and called it an alternative lifestyle. We have

Kansas State Capitol

exploited the poor and called it the lottery. We have neglected the needy and called it self-preservation. We have rewarded laziness and called it welfare. We have killed our unborn and called it choice. We have shot abortionists and called it justifiable. We have neglected to discipline our children and called it building esteem. We have abused power and called it political savvy. We have coveted our neighbors' possessions and called it ambition. We have polluted the air with profanity and pornography and called it freedom of expression. We have ridiculed the time-honored values of our forefathers and called it enlightenment.

Search us O God and know our hearts today; try us and see if there be some wicked way in us; cleanse us from every sin and set us free. Guide and bless these men and women who have been sent here by the people of Kansas, and who have been ordained by you, to govern this great state. Grant them your wisdom to rule and may their decisions direct us to the center of your will. I ask it in the name of your son, the living savior, Jesus Christ. Amen.

Some legislators walked out during the prayer. Wright's prayer stirred a nationwide controversy. The story was picked up by national radio newscaster Paul Harvey, who told about it and read it on one of his broadcasts. Harvey said that the story generated the largest response of any he had ever done. Wright's church received thousands of phone calls, almost all of them supportive.

"Too Much 'In Jesus' Name'" in Indiana

In 2005, four citizens of Indiana—two Roman Catholics, a Quaker, and a retired Methodist minister, in conjunction with the Indiana Civil Liberties Union—filed suit in U.S. District Court to require the Speaker of the Indiana House of Representatives to forbid any prayer that is part of the official proceedings of the chamber to be sectarian in nature, specifically, that uses or is offered in the name of Christ. The plaintiffs claimed standing in court because, as taxpayers, state revenue was used to send letters to the ministers who were invited to offer prayers, to have the ministers' pictures taken and sent to them, and to have the invocations broadcast on the Internet. The total cost to the state was estimated to be $448.38 per year.

Indiana State Capitol

In its decision on *Hinrichs et al. v Bosma*, issued on November 30, 2005, the court analyzed the prayers from the 2005 session of the Indiana House:

Fifty-three opening prayers were offered in the House during the 2005 legislative session. Forty-one of those invocations were delivered by clergy identified with Christian churches; nine were delivered by Representatives; and one each was delivered by a lay person, a Muslim imam, and a Jewish rabbi. Transcripts are available for forty-five prayers. Of these, twenty-nine were offered in the name of Jesus, Jesus Christ, the Savior, and/or the Son. In the majority of these invocations, the officiant did not indicate that he or she was personally praying in the name of Jesus or Christ. Some officiants explicitly stated that the prayer was offered for all those assembled or for persons other than the legislative body.

The judge went on to quote a few comments from some of the prayers. One prayer ended, "In the Strong name of Jesus our Savior, Amen." Another closed by saying, "We ask You to bless these leaders in the name of Jesus, Your Son, and our Lord who reigns forever and ever. Amen." Another prayer included the following petition: "We look forward to the day when all nations and all people of the earth will have the opportunity to hear and respond to messages of love of the Almighty God who has revealed Himself in the saving power of Jesus Christ." Another prayer used the name of God, YHWH, that Jews do not pronounce, a usage that is offensive to Jews.

In the view of the court, the pattern of prayers in the Indiana House amounted to an endorsement of Christianity, which violated the Establishment Clause of the First Amendment. The court ruled in favor of the plaintiffs. It admitted the right of the legislature to open its meetings with prayer, but it issued a permanent injunction against the Speaker,

[B]arring him from permitting sectarian prayer as part of the official proceedings of the Indiana House of Representatives. If the Speaker chooses to continue any form of legislative prayer, he shall advise persons offering such a prayer (a) that it must be nonsectarian and must not be used to proselytize or advance any one faith or belief or to disparage any other faith or belief, and (b) that they should refrain from using Christ's name or title or any other denominational appeal.

The Indiana decision claimed that the prayers in the state House violated the last section of the *Marsh* decision quoted above. The case was appealed to the U.S. Seventh Circuit Court of Appeals, which dismissed the case in October of 2007 in a 2 to 1 vote on the grounds that the plaintiffs lacked standing to file the suit. The prayer practice, said the Appeals Court, was a tradition of House rules and not a law enacted by the legislature; therefore the plaintiffs could not claim loss as a result of the practice. No decision was given on the question of whether prayers or certain words in prayers were acceptable. The decision effectively ended this suit, but some other state legislatures reconsidered their practice of opening sessions with a prayer out of a desire to avoid similar lawsuits.

First of all, then, I urge that entreaties and prayers, petitions and thanksgivings,
be made on behalf of all men, kings and all who are in authority,
so that we may lead a tranquil and quiet life in all godliness and dignity.
This is good and acceptable in the sight of God our Savior,
who desires all men to be saved and to come to the knowledge of the truth.
1 Timothy 2:1-4

Soldier Preparing the Flagstaff for the National Prayer Service at the National Cathedral
in Washington, D.C., in Honor of President George H. W. Bush, 1989

Lesson 49—State Governors

My fellow Americans, this is an amazing moment for me. To think that a once-scrawny boy from Austria could grow up to become Governor of California and stand in Madison Square Garden to speak on behalf of the President of the United States—that is an immigrant's dream. It is the American dream.
— Arnold Schwarzenegger, governor of California,
at the 2004 Republican National Convention

As we mentioned in Lesson 46, the history of governors in America is a checkered one. The first governor was of the Jamestown colony in 1607, and each of the British colonies had a royal governor who represented the king. In the new nation, state legislatures limited the powers of governors, often to no more than a figurehead role. Most governors were elected by the legislature, and only two were given veto power. Many state governors served only a one-year term.

Over time, Americans realized that this was an imbalance of power. Legislatures did not always do what they should, and the absence of the checks and balances system that was in the national government left many states with an unhealthy political climate. The result was that, as state constitutions were amended and rewritten, governors gradually gained more power.

The Role of the Governor

The governor is the chief executive of the state. He or she oversees the workings of the state bureaucracy with its many departments and agencies. The governor delivers an annual State of the State address (similar to the president's State of the Union speech), in which he or she reviews the state's government and economy and proposes new laws for the legislature to consider. The governor also prepares a proposed

George Ervin (Sonny) Perdue III, Governor of Georgia,
Addressing Members of the Georgia Army National Guard, 2006

state budget for the legislature to consider and enact. Governors can veto legislation and return it to the legislature. In 43 states, governors can exercise the line-item veto, in which they can reject only part of a bill and return it for reconsideration.

Most governors have the power to call the legislature into special session to deal with specific issues. Governors sometimes use the threat of this power to get the legislature to deal with an item that is high on his agenda.

A state governor is an *ex officio* (Latin for from the office) member of many official state boards and commissions. He receives official visitors to the state and delivers many speeches to civic groups and other meetings. Governors have become active in recruiting businesses to their states, often traveling overseas to meet with representatives of foreign companies. The governor is head of the state National Guard, although the state adjutant general actually oversees day-to-day operations. A governor can call out the National Guard to help in times of natural disaster or civil unrest. When the Guard is Federalized by the president, the governor's role is set aside for the stated period. The governor also has broad powers of pardon for inmates in state prisons. He can reduce sentences; he can commute sentences to time served and thus release prisoners; he can issue pardons; and he can issue a stay or delay of execution if a person is facing the death penalty, in order to give the legal process more time.

> *In 2000, Illinois Governor George Ryan imposed a moratorium on any further executions of Death Row inmates in the state until a commission could investigate the cases and the state's application of the death penalty. Ryan, a long-time supporter of the death penalty, was deeply affected by the large number of Death Row inmates who were exonerated after further research into their cases. In January 2003, a few days before he left office, Ryan pardoned four men who had confessed to murder after being victimized by police brutality. He also commuted the sentences of all other Death Row inmates in the state to life in prison.*

Terms, Salary, Qualifications

Governors serve a four-year term in all but two states. Most governorships have term limits imposed on them. In 35 states, governors may serve a maximum of two four-year terms. Some of these two-term limits have variations. In Indiana, a person may serve as governor for only two terms over a three-term period. In Montana and Wyoming, the limit is two terms over a four-term period. Some states set a two-term limit in a person's life, while others limit service to two consecutive terms. The limit in Utah is three consecutive terms. A governor of Virginia serves one term and may not run for re-election. Vermont and New Hampshire governors have two-year terms, but neither state imposes term limits. In eleven states, the governor is elected to a four-year term and has no term limits.

Many more states have term limits for governor than have them for state legislators. The tradition in American politics is to limit the service of the chief executive but not of legislators, partly out of fear of one person acquiring too much power.

States have a minimum residency requirement (often five years as a resident of the state) and a minimum

> *A different kind of term limit is the recall provision in some state constitutions, which allows the removal from office of an elected official if enough people sign a petition and if the recall initiative passes in the succeeding election. In 2003, California voters turned Governor Gray Davis out of office and replaced him with actor Arnold Schwarzenegger.*

age requirement to be governor (usually 30). The average governor is in his or her late 50s. Governors' salaries currently range from Maine's low of $70,000 per year to the $179,000 paid to the governor of New York. All governors have a staff and are provided with expense accounts. Almost all of the states provide the governor with an official residence. However, like the presidency, no one runs for governor for the money. People want to be governor to serve the public or to promote their agenda or to have political power. Many governors became wealthy in private business before becoming a state's chief executive. Some governors, such as Massachusetts' Mitt Romney and Arnold Schwarzenegger of California, have served without taking their salary.

> *A one-term limit does not always open up the governor's election. Tennessee once had a one-term limit. At the time, state politics were controlled by the Democratic Party. Democrat Frank Clement was elected to a four-year term in 1954, then Democrat Buford Ellington was elected in 1958. Clement ran and won again in 1962, then Ellington ran and won again in 1966. This process was called leap-frogging. In another instance, after George Wallace of Alabama served his one-term limit in the 1960s, his wife was elected governor to succeed him. Everyone knew who really ran the state government while she was governor.*

Lieutenant Governor

In all but six states, the person who holds the Number Two position in state government is called the lieutenant governor. He or she becomes governor if the position of governor becomes vacant. Some states provide for the lieutenant governor to serve as acting governor (being able to exercise only caretaker powers) if the sitting governor is out of the state. The methods for choosing the lieutenant governor are not at all consistent. In twenty-five states, candidates for governor and lieutenant governor run for election together as a ticket. In eighteen states, the office of lieutenant governor is an entirely separate race. This can mean that the governor and lieutenant governor can be of different political parties.

Six states do not have a lieutenant governor. In three of these, the Secretary of State is the next in line for the governorship, while in the other three the Speaker of the Senate is next in line. In states where the lieutenant governor serves as Speaker of the Senate, he or she has considerable influence in determining what legislation is considered by that body.

> *Zell Miller served four four-year terms as the elected lieutenant governor of Georgia (1975-1991). As Speaker of the state Senate, he played an important role in Georgia politics and government. He then was elected governor for two terms. After a brief retirement from politics, he served in the U.S. Senate from Georgia.*

The Power of the Governor

The power of the governor to influence legislation and to affect the operation of state government varies to some degree from state to state. How the state's government is organized by the state constitution and by legislation impacts a governor's power. Here are some of the factors involved.

Length of term and nature or absence of term limits. In the two states where the governor serves only a two-year term, it probably seems as though he is always running for re-election. This gives the office somewhat less security. In states where the governor has no term limits, the legislature cannot know if the governor is a lame duck (on his way out of office) unless he announces that he will not be seeking re-election. The absence of term limits gives the governor more political power.

Frequency of legislative sessions. When the legislature meets only every other year, the executive branch is given more responsibility for carrying out the functions of government. If the legislature can work only a limited amount of time, the governor has relatively more power.

Veto power and vote needed to override. All governors have veto power, although the North Carolina governor has been able to exercise a veto only since the state constitution was amended in 1996 to allow it. Governors who have the line-item veto have comparatively more power to get the legislation they want without having to accept catch-all bills that have provisions he must accept in order to get what he really wants.

In addition, the legislative vote required to override a veto affects the governor's power. In most states, the legislature can override the governor's veto with a two-thirds majority of both houses. Some legislatures need only a three-fifths majority (60%) to override. In those states, a veto is more likely to be defeated. In Tennessee, the legislature can override the governor's veto with a simple majority of the membership of both houses. Since the bill probably got that majority to pass, a veto by the governor in Tennessee is relatively

meaningless, unless he simply wants to make a personal statement or if he hopes to influence a few legislators to change their votes if the bill passed with a narrow majority.

Other statewide elective offices. Most states have other positions in addition to the governorship that are filled in statewide elections. In Georgia, for instance, the positions of attorney general; secretary of state; the state superintendent of schools; the state commissioners of agriculture, labor, and insurance; and members of the Public Service Commission (a

Linda Lingle, Governor of Hawaii, 2007

body that oversees utilities that operate in the state) are all elected in statewide contests. Although they oversee what are normally considered executive branch departments, they do not answer to the governor. They answer to the people, just as the governor does. The state government framers who made these offices to be elective believed that their work was too important to be left to a political appointee of the governor.

States also vary in the number of positions on boards, agencies, and commissions that are filled by the governor's appointment. When positions are filled by the legislature or by independent commissions, this limits the power of the governor. The governorship of Texas is considered to be one of the weakest in the country because of the large number of officials that either are elected or are appointed by someone other than the governor.

Where the lieutenant governor is elected separately from the governor, and especially when he or she is Speaker of the state Senate, this arrangement takes some degree of power away from the position of governor. In Tennessee, the governorship is the only position in state government that is filled by a statewide election (except for state supreme court justices,

President Jimmy Carter at a Press Conference, 1977

who run unopposed). No one in Tennessee state government besides the governor can claim a statewide mandate to accomplish his or her desired goals.

A Steppingstone to Higher Office

We indicated in an earlier lesson that several U.S. presidents have previously served as state governors. Four recent presidents served as governor before being elected president (Jimmy Carter, Ronald Reagan, Bill Clinton, and George W. Bush). Serving as chief executive of a state can be good training for the role of chief executive of the country. The similarities between the two positions include overseeing a large government bureaucracy, dealing with a legislative body that has its own will and agenda, and trying to put forth a vision for what is best for the people.

Ronald Reagan had a long career in acting, but he was also interested in politics. He was a long-time Democrat and was at one time the president of a union, the Screen Actors' Guild. In 1962, Reagan switched parties and became a Republican because he thought the Republicans offered the best hope for the nation. He supported Republican Barry Goldwater's candidacy for president in 1964.

Reagan was urged to run for governor of California in 1966 against long odds. Goldwater's huge defeat had left the Republican Party weakened in California and in other parts of the country. What is more, another Republican, former Vice President Richard Nixon, had suffered a bitter loss in his campaign for governor of California in 1962. However, Reagan won his election and was re-elected in 1970. He compiled a strong record as governor and received the Republican nomination for president in 1980. He defeated the incumbent President, former Georgia governor Jimmy Carter, in that election and was re-elected President in 1984.

Scenes from Ronald Reagan's Presidential Campaigns, 1980 and 1984

Then they delivered the king's edicts to the king's satraps and to the governors in the provinces beyond the River, and they supported the people and the house of God.
Ezra 8:36

Reading

- "The Late, Great Doctrine of States' Rights" by Ray Notgrass (*WHTT*, p. 155)

Lesson 50—State Bureaucracies and State Courts

We ought to consider, what is the end of government, before we determine which is the best form. Upon this point all speculative politicians will agree, that the happiness of society is the end of government, as all Divines and moral Philosophers will agree that the happiness of the individual is the end of man. From this principle it will follow, that the form of government, which communicates ease, comfort, security, or in one word happiness to the greatest number of persons, and in the greatest degree, is the best.

—*John Adams*, Thoughts on Government (1776)

A state government provides many services for the people of the state. How well those services are provided depends on several factors: the leadership of department heads, the work ethic established in those departments, the presence or absence of complicated channels of communication (sometimes called "red tape"), and the desire of the workers to serve and not simply to occupy a position and draw a paycheck.

The departments, offices, agencies, and other bodies of state government are organized in different ways depending on the state. For illustrative purposes, we will use the system in the state of Tennessee. You might want to investigate how your state government is organized, the names of the various departments and agencies, and the relationship these offices have to the governor and to the legislature.

View from the Tennessee State Capitol, 1864

Constitutional Offices

Three offices in Tennessee are known as constitutional offices because they are called for by the state constitution. Those who fill these positions are chosen by the General Assembly (the state legislature) in joint session. Thus, they answer to the legislature and not to the governor.

The Secretary of State is elected by the General Assembly for a four-year term. He or she is not involved in diplomatic relations as is the U.S. Secretary of State. Instead, the state Secretary of State maintains the official records of the state. His office publishes the laws and administrative regulations of the state and keeps corporate charters and other legal documents. The State Election Commission and the State Registry of Election Finance work with the Secretary of State in maintaining financial records dealing with candidates and elections. The Secretary is an *ex officio* member of about twenty boards and agencies, including the State Building Commission, the Tennessee Housing Development Agency, the State School Bond Authority, and the Higher Education Commission.

The State Treasurer is elected by the General Assembly for a two-year term. The main work of the Treasurer is the collection of state revenue and the payment of state obligations (bills, payroll, and so forth). The office also oversees the retirement system for state workers and the responsible investment of funds received by the state. The Treasurer is an ex officio member of many boards and agencies.

The Comptroller of the Treasury is also elected by the legislature for a two-year term. This person's main work involves auditing the finances of the state government and local governments and helping to determine how well the state bureaucracy is operating.

The Governor's Cabinet

The executive branch of Tennessee's government has twenty-two departments. Each department is headed by a commissioner who is nominated by the governor and confirmed by the legislature.

The Department of Agriculture encourages the state's number one industry by administering grants, overseeing state forests, and building markets for Tennessee farm products. The department regulates food and dairy quality, animal health, pesticides and other farm-related chemicals, and the accuracy of gasoline pumps.

Tennessee Farm

The Department of Children's Services handles state foster care and adoption programs, licenses child welfare agencies, and oversees programs for delinquent youths and probation for youths convicted of crimes.

The Department of Commerce and Insurance registers and regulates professions, businesses, and insurance companies operating in the state. It also is responsible for fire inspections. Another program helps consumers avoid being defrauded by unscrupulous businesses.

The Department of Correction oversees the operation of the state's penal institutions and rehabilitation programs.

The Department of Economic and Community Development encourages companies to open or build facilities in Tennessee and helps communities plan economic growth.

The Department of Education oversees the state's public school system, adult education and GED programs, school nutrition, local textbook adoption, and other matters related to public education. The State Board of Education sets policy while the Department carries it out. The Board has nine members, one from each congressional district (nine-year terms) plus a student member (one-year term). All are nominated by the governor and confirmed by the legislature. The Tennessee Higher Education Commission coordinates post-high school education. Higher education in the state has two systems: (1) the University of Tennessee and its branches, overseen by the UT Board of Regents, and (2) everything else, organized as the State University and Community College System, which includes four-year colleges (other than the UT system), community colleges, and technical institutes.

The Department of Environment and Conservation enforces anti-pollution laws, oversees the Tennessee Historical Commission, and operates the system of state parks.

The Department of Finance and Administration is primarily an in-house operation for the state government itself. It leads in the development of the state budget and oversees the financial operations of state government.

The Department of Financial Institutions charters and regulates banks, credit unions, loan companies, check cashing businesses, and other finance-related businesses.

The Department of General Services is another department that works primarily to help state government. It oversees obtaining equipment for state agencies, maintains state buildings and the state motor vehicle fleet, and provides printing services, food services, and other service agencies.

The Department of Health licenses health care professionals, operates clinics for low-income residents, maintains birth and marriage certificates, and encourages a healthy lifestyle through many services and agencies.

The Department of Human Services is involved with the food stamp program and other avenues of assistance and determines eligibility for the state medical assistance program.

The Department of Labor and Workforce Development provides training and information for people seeking better employment opportunities and handles applications for unemployment assistance.

The Department of Mental Health and Mental Retardation provides services to those with mental illness and other mental and developmental disabilities.

The Department of the Military oversees the Tennessee Air and Army National Guard and is responsible for the Tennessee Emergency Management Agency.

The Department of Personnel is another department that serves other state departments by overseeing employment laws and regulations and handling applications for state positions.

The Department of Revenue collects almost all of the state's tax revenues and enforces the state's tax and revenue laws.

The Department of Safety oversees the Tennessee Highway Patrol (called the State Police in many other states), issues drivers' licenses, and enforces laws regarding commercial vehicles and school buses.

The Department of Tourist Development promotes the lucrative tourist industry (second-largest industry in the state behind agriculture) with national and international publicity efforts and maintains welcome centers on interstates.

The Department of Transportation plans, builds, and maintains the state road system.

The Department of Veterans Affairs provides services for the state's veterans and maintains veterans' cemeteries in the state.

The executive branch is also responsible for several independent agencies, such as:

- the Alcoholic Beverage Commission, which licenses and regulates the sale of liquors;

- the Arts Commission, which awards grants and encourages broader participation in artistic endeavors;

- the Tennessee Bureau of Investigation, the agency that investigates serious crimes;

- the Tennessee Housing Development Agency, which makes affordable mortgages available for first-time home buyers and maintains a rental housing program;

- the Human Rights Commission, which insures that Tennesseans are treated without discrimination in employment, housing, and public accommodations;

- the Tennessee Wildlife Resources Agency, the body that manages, protects, and enhances the state's wildlife resources and oversees boating safety.

Roaring River in Middle Tennessee

The Judicial Branch

Tennessee's court system has four levels. The first level is made up of courts of limited jurisdiction. Every county has a General Sessions Court, which hears cases involving certain kinds of offenses and monetary losses. General Sessions judges are elected for eight-year terms. General Sessions Courts handle cases involving juveniles except in counties where the legislature has created a separate Juvenile Court. Municipal or City courts handle cases involving alleged violations of city ordinances.

The second level is made up of the state trial courts. Tennessee's 95 counties are divided into 31 judicial districts. Each judicial district has Circuit Courts and Chancery Courts, and some districts also have Criminal Courts and Probate Courts that have been created by the legislature. Circuit Courts have general jurisdiction and hear civil and criminal cases. They also handle appeals from courts that are on the first level. Chancery Courts hear cases of equity when someone has a complaint of some kind and seeks legal relief. Criminal Courts have been established to ease the burden on Circuit Courts where the case load is heavy. Probate Courts deal with matters involving wills, estates, conservatorships, and guardianships. Judges in these courts are also elected to eight-year terms.

The third level involves courts of appeal. Tennessee has separate courts for appeals in civil cases and appeals in criminal cases. Each court has twelve judges which hear cases in groups of three. Appeals Court judges are elected on a yes or no vote every eight years (the ballot reads, "Shall So-and-So continue as a justice on the Tennessee Court of Criminal Appeals?"). The process of filling a vacancy involves a judicial commission recommending three names to the governor, who then appoints one of the three to serve until the next state election. At that point, the justice must face a yes or no vote to continue serving.

Finally, the Tennessee Supreme Court is a five-member panel that hears appeals from lower courts. The Court can choose to review any and all cases except that it is required to review capital punishment cases. Justices on the state Supreme Court stand for a yes or no vote every eight years. A case can be appealed from the state Supreme Court to a Federal court if it involves a Constitutional question.

The state Attorney General is appointed by the state Supreme Court for an eight-year term. Tennessee is the only state where the Attorney General is not elected. He provides legal opinions when asked to do so by the governor, state agencies and departments, or the legislature. His office also represents the state in civil trials.

Each judicial district in the state has a District Attorney who is popularly elected for an eight-year term. The office of the District Attorney prosecutes criminal cases for the state. The state also funds public defenders in each district for defendants who cannot afford to pay an attorney themselves. The District Attorneys are not overseen by the Attorney General; but the Attorney General decides which cases to appeal. His office also handles the appeals process, which involves writing a brief and appearing before the appeals court.

You, Ezra, according to the wisdom of your God which is in your hand,
appoint magistrates and judges
that they may judge all the people who are in the province beyond the River,
even all those who know the laws of your God;
and you may teach anyone who is ignorant of them.
Ezra 7:25

Tennessee State Capitol, c. 1943

11 Local Government

This unit focuses on local government. We look first at county and city government. Then we offer three case studies of the meaning of government on the local level. First we consider a rapidly growing community in the South. Then we look at the response that government made to the suffering caused by Hurricane Katrina. Finally, we examine the issue of eminent domain and the impact of a ruling by the U.S. Supreme Court on the issue.

Lessons in This Unit

Lesson 51—Counties, Townships, and Special Districts
Lesson 52—Municipal Government
Lesson 53—Government in Action: Spring Hill, Tennessee
Lesson 54—Government Inaction: The Response to Hurricane Katrina
Lesson 55—Government Action: The Issue of Eminent Domain

Activity Idea

Many government social services are called entitlements. Are we entitled to individual assistance by the government? President James K. Polk in the 1840s believed that government should not help individuals. If it did, he argued, people would vote for candidates based on what the people thought those candidates might give them from the public purse instead of on the basis of the character of the candidates and the policies they would pursue. Have too many people become dependent on government assistance in one form or another? Write two pages on the topic, "Are We Entitled?"

If you are using the optional *Quiz and Exam Book,* answer the questions for each lesson after you have completed the lesson and read any assigned readings in *We Hold These Truths.* After you have completed Lesson 55, take the quiz for Unit 11.

Lesson 51—Counties, Townships, and Special Districts

[M]unicipal institutions constitute the strength of free nations. Town meetings are to liberty what primary schools are to science; they bring it within the people's reach, they teach men how to use and how to enjoy it. A nation may establish a free government, but without municipal institutions it cannot have the spirit of liberty.
— *Alexis de Tocqueville,* Democracy in America *(1835)*

In Anglo-Saxon England, kings utilized administrative districts called shires to give them greater control over local areas. The king's representative in the shire was the earl, a large landowner who commanded the local militia when the king needed troops. The peace officer was called the reeve, who also served as tax collector.

With the Norman Conquest of England in 1066 and the introduction of French terms and ways, the local representative of the king was no longer the earl but the count. The region in which he had authority was not the shire but the county. The name of the peace officer remained the same, but the pronunciation changed over time from shire-reeve to sheriff.

When English settlers came to America, they set up local governments the way they had known them in England. Thus, the colonies were divided into counties and the law enforcement officer was the sheriff. The county as a basic unit of local government has continued to this day.

Counties in the U.S. are the creation of the state government. They are formed by the state legislature passing a bill that sets out its boundaries. Counties exist to serve the purposes of the state government. As a result, county officials carry out such state-mandated functions as administering state laws, issuing marriage licenses, selling hunting and fishing licenses, conducting elections, and (in many places) operating schools. A county government can enact its own laws that work best for that county's particular needs, but its reason for existence is to assist the state government.

The Development of County Government

In England, the chief executive of a county and the official before whom accused persons had to appear was the justice of the peace. Some counties had several justices of the peace, and their jurisdictions were sometimes a matter of conflict. This confusing situation was also transferred to America, with the result that county government has often taken many forms and has not always been well organized. This situation has changed in

The fifty United States have a total of 3,066 counties. Delaware and Hawaii have three counties each, while Texas has 254. Louisiana calls its counties parishes, while in Alaska they are known as boroughs. Rhode Island and Connecticut have geographic areas called counties, but the counties in these two states do not have distinct, functioning governments. Counties range in size from Virginia's Arlington County, which measures 26 square miles, to the North Slope Borough in Alaska, which covers 87,860 square miles. Loving County, Texas contains 67 people, while Los Angeles County, California has over 9.5 million residents. Three-fourths of American counties have a population under 50,000.

recent years, and county governments are now more regularized in their structure and function.

Currently, almost all county governments take one of three forms. The most common, used in over half of the nation's counties, is an elected commission or board of supervisors. In Louisiana, the body is called the parish police jurors, while in New Jersey the panel is called the board of chosen freeholders. These county commissioners usually serve for a two- or four-year term. They are elected from separate districts within the county. In some places each district elects two or

Courthouse in Jackson County, Missouri

three commissioners. This form of government does not have a separate executive for the county. The commission not only passes the budget and enacts new laws but also fulfills the executive function by overseeing the county bureaucracy.

The two other forms, which together comprise about forty percent of counties, have a separate executive. The commission-administrator form uses an administrator appointed by the commission. The administrator oversees the daily operation of the county government, including the hiring and firing of personnel. The third form is the commission-executive/ mayor format. Under this plan the county executive (sometimes called the county mayor) is an elected position. In some places he can even veto ordinances passed by the commission.

Other county officials are either elected by the people or appointed by the commission. The functions of county government and the officials and personnel who are elected or hired to do these jobs vary depending on the needs of the county. The most common elected official is the county clerk, who oversees elections, handles marriage licenses, and issues license plates, among other duties. Another common elected position is the register of deeds. With the importance of land development, and since the buying and selling of property is a major decision for all citizens, accurate recording and transferring of deeds in a county is essential. Other elected officials might include:

- county treasurer or trustee, who is responsible for collecting and disbursing county funds;

- county auditor, who keeps a check on the books of county government;

- property assessor, who computes the value of property for property tax purposes;

- road supervisor, who oversees road maintenance and construction.

The county coroner or medical examiner is usually appointed. This person performs an inquest to investigate the cause of someone's death when something other than natural causes is suspected. He or she often works with law enforcement officials because criminal activity might be involved. The medical examiner can conduct hearings and subpoena witnesses if he believes such actions are necessary. Medical examiners are almost always physicians.

Other county officials who are usually appointed include the surveyor, engineer, health officer, and members of the zoning commission. In times past, the pay for some county positions was based on fees that the officials collected. This sometimes led to corruption. Now county officials receive salaries.

Education

About one-third of a typical county's revenue comes from property taxes and from a sales tax that the county imposes on top of the state sales tax. The rest comes mostly from funds provided by the state government or the Federal government.

The largest single expense for many counties is public education. Many counties operate all of the public schools within those counties, although in many places cities have their own separate school districts or a special school district has been formed. The school system is overseen by a board of education and a school superintendent or director. Members of the board of education are elected by the public. The board of education is subject to the oversight of the

The city or town where the county courthouse and government offices are located is called the county seat. The county seat is usually the largest city in the county, but not always. If a once-smaller town experiences population growth, it might surpass the county seat in size. The informal rule that was followed when most counties were created in the 1800s was that the county seat should not be more than a day's wagon ride away from all county residents. Many counties were quite large when they were established. As the population grew, new counties were formed, which gave more people easier access to a county seat.

county commission. This means, for instance, that the board of education in most places can only request a budget from the county commission and does not have the power to raise its own tax revenues.

The superintendent or director of schools might be elected or appointed. In Tennessee for many years, county superintendents were appointed by the county commission. A few years ago, the trend developed for county superintendents to be elected. However, this caused some problems. Sometimes the most popular person was not the best person to oversee education. In addition, if a conflict developed between the board and the superintendent, both parties could claim that they represented the people. Now, the county school director is once again appointed by the county board of education. This has enabled trained professionals to be hired for the position through the application and interview process and has lessened the likelihood that Good Ol' Joe whom everybody has known since he was a kid would win a popularity contest in an election.

Rural Texas School, 1943

Township Government

In twenty states, the township is a level of government for an area that is larger than a town or city but smaller than a county. Townships are most common in New England, Mid-Atlantic, and Midwestern states. They began when New England communities delineated the areas for which the local government was responsible. In fact, in New England the term township is more commonly used than the term town.

The elected township leadership is a group called the selectmen, the board of supervisors, or the board of trustees. Those who work full-time in township offices are generally appointed by the board. Townships perform a wide variety of functions, depending on the traditions of government in those regions. A township government might be responsible for maintaining

Blaine's Schoolhouse, Greenfield Township, Ohio, c. 1884

roads and bridges, operating fire and rescue squads, enforcing zoning and code regulations, maintaining libraries, providing water service and other public utilities, and collecting taxes for itself and for cities and counties. In some Illinois townships, residents apply for U.S. passports at the township office.

When an area within a township becomes populous enough to become a town or city, the people there can submit a request to the state legislature to be incorporated, in keeping with that state's constitution or laws. This change allows a city to become more autonomous and to provide more services for that locality than the township might be willing or able to provide.

Special Districts

Another level of government that is not quite a county but not quite a city is the special district. A special district is formed to meet one specific need for an area, such as providing fire protection, clean water, sanitation, library services, and sometimes schools. The district is usually overseen by an elected board. The special district sometimes can tax the residents and businesses that are within it, or it might merely be able to propose a tax rate for its needs to the county or city in which it is located.

A special district is formed for any number of reasons. The need might extend over an area that includes several small communities or rural areas, none of which has a large enough population to provide for the need. Alternatively, communities that are near to each other might want to coordinate their efforts instead of each developing its own program. A special district might be formed to provide greater control over an issue or to avoid political wrangling that would hinder the service from being provided at all. Over 35,000 special districts have been formed in the United States. In addition, about 13,500 special school districts exist in the U.S. In thirty-three states, this is how public schools are organized and governed as opposed to being simply a function of the county government.

If a king judges the poor with truth,
His throne will be established forever.
Proverbs 29:14

Lesson 52—Municipal Government

People ask where I get my energy. Well, it's really simple. It comes from you. It comes from here. What I mean by that is that my strength and energy comes entirely from the people of the City of New York. And it comes from a place like this, St. Paul's Chapel. This is a House of God, and it's one of the homes of our Republic. . . . When I walked in here from City Hall. . . on September 11, when the Twin Towers were viciously attacked and came crashing to the ground, . . . this chapel remained, not only not destroyed, but not a single window was broken. And I think there's some very special significance in that. This is the place where George Washington prayed when he first became President of the United States. It also stood strong, powerful, untouched, undaunted by the attacks of these people who hate what we stand for. What we stand for is so much stronger than they are. So this chapel stands for our values. It's a very important place and I hope you return here often to reflect on what it means to be an American and a New Yorker.
—Rudolph Giuliani, Farewell Address as
Mayor of New York City, December 27, 2001

Los Angeles, California: population, about four million.
Providence, Rhode Island: population, about 175,000.
Minot, North Dakota: population, about 36,000.
Castleberry, Alabama: population, about 600.

These and over 19,000 other municipalities in the United States have one thing in common: they all need city government. Beyond that, the needs of America's cities are very different. For instance, Minot does not have to deal with issues related to being an ocean port while Los Angeles does not have to deal with being prepared for snow removal. A city situated on the seacoast has to deal with erosion of the shore. In the Idaho farming region, which might only get ten inches of rain per year, water usage by cities can be a major issue. As a result of these differences, city governments take different forms and carry out widely different functions.

Los Angeles, California

The population of the United States was once predominantly rural. Most people lived in small towns or in unincorporated rural areas. Now the U.S. is predominantly an urban country. About seventy percent of the population lives in incorporated areas: cities, towns, and incorporated suburbs. Thus, municipal government is a major part of the lives of most Americans.

The Nature of Municipal Government

Villages, towns, and cities are incorporated by the state legislature as legal bodies and thus are to a degree dependent on the state government. However, they generally operate as autonomous units of government and are not expected to carry out the functions of the state the way that county governments do. Municipalities are formed to govern, protect, and provide services for the people of those localities.

Local governments are created according to the guidelines set forth in the state constitution or in state laws. When a locality is incorporated, it is granted a charter and is expected to maintain a government and provide certain services for the people according to that charter. A village or a town is not expected to provide the same level of services that a city must offer. The city charter is something like its constitution. For a charter to be amended (for example, to change the way the office of mayor is filled if it becomes vacant between elections), the city has to ask the state government for permission to change it. Some cities are given the power of home rule. A municipality with home rule can amend its charter through local action, such as a referendum or a simple vote of the city council, depending on what the state

City Hall and Courthouse, Juneau, Alaska, c. 1915

government and the city's charter allows. If a municipality is governed badly (for instance, if it gets too deeply in debt because of poor management), the state can revoke its charter and the city has to start all over again to reconstruct its government.

The Forms of Municipal Government

The earliest form of city government in America was the democratic town meeting. The adult male residents who owned property or paid taxes met regularly to decide issues that needed to be addressed. They sometimes elected a board of supervisors to oversee the operation of the city government between meetings and to hire people to carry out the work of the city. Because of city growth, such town meetings are rare today.

Three-fourths of American cities elect their officials on a non-partisan basis. In other words, candidates run on their own merits and not as candidates of political parties.

At one time, the most common form of city government was the mayor-council arrangement. In this plan the city is governed by a mayor, who is elected city-wide, and a council of representatives (sometimes called aldermen) elected by districts. Four-year terms for mayors and city council members are common. The mayor is the city's chief executive. He oversees the operation of the city's work force while the council is the legislative body that considers the annual budget and new ordinances or laws for the city. As cities grow larger, the position of mayor is more likely to become a full-time position. In smaller cities, he might be a local businessman who holds the position of mayor on a part-time basis. Just under forty percent of American cities have a mayor-council government.

The third form of city government is the commission plan. Commissioners are elected by the voters of the city, and they form the city council. However, they also each head one or more departments of city government, such as public safety, finance, parks and property, and street maintenance. Sometimes candidates run for specific posts, while in other places the council divides up the responsibilities once they are elected. The mayor might be the commissioner who gets the most votes, or he might be chosen by the council of commissioners. This system combines the legislative and executive functions into one body. While this streamlines government operations, it violates the principle of separation of powers. A commission government can devolve into five or seven little governments, each competing for more of the city's limited budget. The commission plan was first implemented in Galveston, Texas in 1901 after the city was almost destroyed by a hurricane and tidal wave the year before. The mayor-council city government there had become corrupt and was unable to cope with the massive devastation, so the commission plan was instituted to provide more accountability for what the city government did. Today, however, only a small percentage of municipalities use the commission form.

The most common city government today, utilized by just under sixty percent of American municipalities, is the council-manager plan. In this arrangement council members are elected by districts and have the primary responsibility for city government. A mayor might be elected also, while in some cities the council candidate who receives the most votes becomes mayor. However, the mayor does not really run the city government in this plan. That job is performed by a professional city manager who is hired by the council and answers to it. College courses of study and professional training programs have helped people learn the work of managing a city. The goal of the city manager plan is to raise city government above petty politics and to enable city employees to do their jobs well.

These basic forms of city government can have many variations. For instance, the mayor-council form that has often allowed politics as usual to hold sway has become more accepting of professional public administrators in city government. On the other hand, the supposedly professional and scientific approach of the council-manager form can have its share of petty politics. The city manager might believe that city worker Good Ol' Bob isn't doing his job and needs to be fired; but if Bob is the nephew of one of the council members, the city manager's days in office might be numbered also.

Weak Mayor, Strong Mayor

The traditional understanding of city government is that the mayor is the head of government like the president of the country and the governor of a state. However, the office of mayor can be strong or weak depending on the makeup of a city's governing structure. A strong mayor can push for his agenda and has considerable influence on the votes of council members and on what happens in city government on a day to day basis. A weak mayor might chair council meetings, but he lacks any real authority to promote his ideas. His primary functions might be to sign proclamations and to cut the ribbon when a new business opens.

New York City Mayor Michael Bloomberg, 2006

In the commission form of government, the mayor is fairly weak. His main function is to chair the meetings of the council. The council-manager form also tends to have a weak mayor. The real power is vested in the council, and the city manager has the most authority over the daily operation of the municipality. If a city has many administrative boards and commissions, the power of the mayor to influence what happens can be limited.

*Parade by Town Hall,
Southington, Connecticut, 1942*

In a city whose charter calls for a mayor who is more than a figurehead, he or she really is the chief executive of the city. The mayor in such a city can hire and fire the heads of city departments. Some mayors can veto the actions of the city council. Strong mayors are usually full-time positions, while council members usually serve on a part-time basis.

Of course, even though the formal structure of a municipal government might call for a weak mayor or strong mayor, the informal structure might enable just the opposite. If the mayor is widely respected and has a great deal of personal influence in a city, he or she can have considerable influence in the direction that the city government takes, even though his official position does not give him much power in the practical operation of the city. On the other hand, even if a mayor holds a strong official position, someone else in city government, such as an influential council member or even a powerful businessman in the community, can exert considerable influence in what happens in the city and can thwart the mayor's plans.

City governments sometimes appoint special boards and commissions to handle particular needs. The beer board, for instance, reviews applications from retailers for permission to sell alcoholic beverages and considers charges of violations of city ordinances governing such sales. A stadium authority might be created by the government of a large city to plan, implement, finance, and operate the construction of a major sports facility. The airport authority oversees the operation and expansion of the city's airport. Such issues as these could dominate a city council's time, so the special authority is created to provide government oversight while enabling the council to maintain perspective on all of the issues facing the municipality.

Consolidated Governments

Of the over three thousand counties in the United States, thirty-three have a consolidated city-county government. In these places, the county is considered to be the city and vice versa (though in some of these counties, small communities continue to function as independent entities). Lexington-Fayette County, Kentucky; Denver-Denver County, Colorado; and Jacksonville-Duval County, Florida are examples of consolidated or metro governments. In these places, functions of county government on behalf of the state and the functions of a city in governing the locality are all handled by the same government entity.

Denver, Colorado

The idea of consolidating government generates arguments both pro and con. Supporters say that a consolidated government eliminates duplication of services and provides better coordination of services and of planning for growth. It also eliminates the adversarial positions that cities and counties sometimes take. Opponents claim that consolidation does away with smaller communities and their cherished identities. They also say that city dwellers and the rural population will likely not share the same needs and expectations of government. In the ongoing contest for every government dollar, opponents say that the demands of the city (for such services as better streets and more modern equipment) will drown out the needs of the county (which might include better roads and better rural law enforcement).

Many Levels of Government

As you can see, the individual citizen is subject to many different levels of government at the same time. He is subject to the Federal, state, and county governments. He might also be subject to a city government, a township government, and one or more special service districts. All of these governments offer certain services and make certain demands on the individual. In addition, all of them want some of his money, usually in the form of taxes.

City governments can give permission for private companies to provide services to the population in an action called franchising. For instance, cable television companies might bid to receive the contract to offer this service to people living in the city. It is often not profitable for several cable companies to compete for customers in the same municipality. If one company can get the exclusive franchise for a city, however, they are more likely to make a profit. In exchange for this monopoly on a service, the company's operations are examined by the city and rate increases must receive city approval. If customers complain about poor service or too many price increases, the city council might decide to award the contract to someone else.

However, cities can decide to allow competition for services. In Urbana, Illinois, for example, garbage collection is provided by private companies who compete for customers instead of by a department of the city government. This competition can hold down prices, but it also means that heavy garbage trucks from several companies rumble down the same streets almost every day of the week.

Should I not have compassion on Nineveh, the great city
in which there are more than 120,000 persons
who do not know the difference between their right and left hand,
as well as many animals?
Jonah 4:11

Lesson 53—Government in Action: Spring Hill, Tennessee

A blend of commerce, history, and country living.
—Spring Hill, Tennessee slogan

In this lesson we present a case study of city government by looking at a small town that has experienced phenomenal growth over the last few years. We will consider the issues that the community has had to confront because of the population growth, the economic changes it has experienced, and how the government has handled these issues. In this way we show how local government works in a real situation.

Background

The town of Spring Hill, Tennessee is located in northern Maury County, near Williamson County in Middle Tennessee. It began with land grants to Revolutionary War soldiers. Settlers first came there in the early 1800s. The city of Columbia, about twelve miles to the south, was founded in the same era. Since Columbia is located on the Duck River and is in the center of Maury County, it grew faster and was designated the county seat when the county was formed in 1807.

In the 1960s, Columbia was a town of about 20,000 people experiencing slow to moderate growth. Spring Hill was a tiny community of perhaps a thousand residents. It had one main road going through it (the highway between Columbia and Nashville) and two traffic lights.

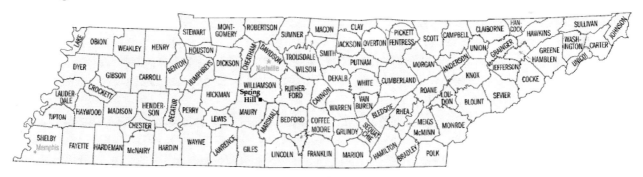

Tennessee

The Impact of Saturn

This scenario began to change dramatically in the mid-1980s. In 1985, General Motors announced that it would locate a new automobile manufacturing plant just south of Spring Hill. The Saturn Corporation would be an entirely new division of GM, and thousands of employees were expected to work there. Almost immediately land prices around Spring Hill shot up. Landowners and realtors made a great deal of money as buyers and investors speculated on how the land might be developed for new homes and other businesses. Many in Columbia expected a huge economic boom in their city also, with new jobs being created and new Saturn-related businesses starting up.

Then reality set in. Land prices settled back to more realistic levels, and some people found themselves in possession of land that was worth less than what they had paid for it. GM announced that current GM employees would have the first option of moving from Detroit or their other facilities to work at the Saturn plant, so the huge hiring boom for Maury County did not happen. As workers moved to the area, the majority of them bought homes in Williamson County or in other places closer to Nashville, since they wanted to be near a larger city and didn't mind a slightly longer commute to work. Meanwhile, the Saturn plant caused a great strain in providing public services (such as electricity, water, sewers, and roads) to the area. The first Saturn vehicle rolled off the assembly line in 1990. Spring Hill and Columbia experienced moderate growth, and long-time residents of the area coped with their big new industrial neighbor.

Growth from the North

Within a few years, another factor began to impact Spring Hill, this time from the other direction. The city of Nashville was growing rapidly. As the center of a huge music industry and with many other qualities attractive to business (such as good weather, historic sites, major banking offices, tourism attractions, relatively inexpensive cost of living, favorable land sites for building, several colleges, and growing retail activity), Nashville began to boom. The U.S. Census Bureau defines a Metropolitan Statistical Area (MSA) as consisting of a city and the counties around it that have a significant social and economic connection to the city. The Nashville MSA, consisting of Davidson County and seven surrounding counties, grew by 15.8% between 1980 and 1990. It grew 25% between 1990 and 2000. Williamson County, just to the south of Nashville-Davidson County, is part of the Nashville MSA but Maury County is not.

Williamson County experienced much of this Nashville-related growth. Large new shopping areas were built in the northern part of the county, and many new residential developments were undertaken. The county became one of the fastest growing counties in the country. As developers looked for places where they could build, they moved further and further away from Nashville and began building in the southern part of the county, just north of little but growing Spring Hill.

The leaders of Spring Hill decided to respond to the situation by annexing areas across the county line in Williamson County as part of the city. The town's growth was so significant that the community of Thompson's Station, a few miles north of Spring Hill in Williamson County, incorporated as a town in 1990 to avoid being annexed by Spring Hill. Spring Hill also began annexing areas to the south of it into the city, and Columbia responded by annexing to its north. Now, the city limits of Spring Hill and Columbia meet a few miles south of the Saturn plant.

The Numbers and the Future

The 1990 census for Spring Hill showed 1,464 residents. In 2000, the census was 7,105. This significant increase was the result of both more people living in the city and more area being annexed into the city limits. The city has taken frequent special censuses to measure its growth. Newer censuses also allow the city to receive additional funds from state programs. In 2003, the population was measured at 12,242. At the end of 2005, the count was 21,168.

The Williamson County side of the city has been growing faster than the Maury County side. Maury County has seen significant growth, but the growth in Williamson County as a whole has been much greater. Columbia's population is now about 33,000. The Spring Hill and Columbia high schools now compete against each other in sports, and Spring Hill has scored victories against the school that was once in an entirely different size classification.

The growth of Spring Hill shows no signs of slowing down. Large retailers such as Home Depot, Lowe's, and Target are locating in Spring Hill. New housing and business developments are under construction in and near the city. The mayor of Spring Hill predicted in late 2005 that the city could grow to over 40,000 residents in the next five years and could surpass the population of Columbia. Also in 2005, the automaker Nissan announced plans to move the headquarters for its North American operations from Los Angeles to northern Williamson County (a Nissan truck factory is located in nearby Rutherford County). Many of the 1,300 jobs involved with the operation were filled by people who move from Los Angeles. This spurred more demand for housing in the county.

Near Spring Hill and Columbia, Tennessee

Amazingly, Spring Hill accomplished this growth while lowering the city property tax rate to zero. Revenue from the state government plus fees from new businesses have meant that the city was able to eliminate the city property tax altogether. Spring Hill residents still pay county property tax, but they do not pay an additional tax for property in the city.

Urban Planning

Growth such as that experienced by Spring Hill presents many challenges. One challenge is to balance personal freedom with community well-being. We live in a free country that gives individuals the opportunity to enjoy success in their personal endeavors; but if urban growth is not guided in some way, the result can be detrimental to personal, family, community, and business success.

Urban planning is a profession that helps communities, counties, states, and regions anticipate (as much as possible) what growth and changes are possible and best for a region. Urban planners study long-range population and business trends, predict what the impact of growth might be, and advise communities on what steps the government can take to maintain and improve the quality of life for the residents. Smaller cities might utilize the services of a private planning consulting company. As municipalities become larger, they are more likely to need a full-time city planner. County governments also need the services of planners. A planning commission is a board whose members are citizens appointed by the city council or county commission to recommend the course of growth for a unit of government.

Planning can involve many areas of community life. Land use planning considers what tracts of land would be best suited for commercial, residential, or public uses (the latter involving, for example, parks and schools). Transportation planning examines traffic patterns and addresses such topics as road improvement (Should this road be widened to four lanes or kept to two? Do we need to build a bypass around the city?). Larger cities might have to consider beginning or expanding mass transit lines such as buses, subways, or commuter trains. Water use planning will look at whether a city will be able to provide clean water to a growing population and how a city on a river or seacoast can best expand its port facilities. Natural resources planning might consider how to preserve the environment and how best to utilize minerals, lumber, and other natural resources.

Annexation

Cities do not grow merely by residents having children or new residents moving into the city. A municipality can also grow by annexing or taking in areas adjacent to the city and thus expanding the city limits. State governments have established guidelines for how annexation is to happen.

Annexation is a trade-off for all parties involved. Many city dwellers move out of the city to escape high taxes, heavy traffic, and the problems associated with city life. A family moving to an urban area might want to live in a suburb in order to have a yard and access to better schools, while Dad drives into the city to work. However, along with these advantages, those who live outside of the city might not have access to garbage pickup, fire protection, or sanitary sewer service that are provided within the city limits. A special water services district might provide pure water to the homes and businesses in the suburb. However, suburban dwellers use city streets, for which they pay no city taxes; and they will probably want to use the city library, also funded by taxes, as well as other city services. The city government might want to annex a growing area into the city to broaden the tax base. At the same time, with annexation the city has to provide more services to a larger number of people. Residents who live in an area being considered for annexation might want additional services, but they might fear the commercial development that might come into what had been an exclusively residential area. They might also think that increased services would not be worth the increased taxes they would have to pay.

Cities have the right to annex adjacent land, within the restrictions set by the state. For instance, a city cannot annex another incorporated area without that other area's permission. Some states do not let a city annex vacant land. An area has to have a certain population density before it can be annexed. A city must provide certain services if it annexes land. It cannot just make a vague promise that services will be provided someday. Residents of an area being considered for annexation might want to be annexed and can petition to be annexed. On the other hand, residents might fight annexation by submitting a petition to the planning commission or hiring an attorney to initiate legal action against the city. The city government then has to decide whether the benefits to the city outweigh the ill will generated by the efforts to annex.

Zoning

Ken and Nancy Greene purchased a ten-acre tract on a county road twelve years ago. Their dream was to build a home there someday and move out of the city. By careful saving, they were finally able to accomplish their dream. They built a home just like they wanted, with a pretty yard and a beautiful view. One afternoon, as they were sitting on their front porch, a pickup truck drove past their house and stopped just down the road. A man got out and erected a sign on the neighboring tract of land. The sign said, "Coming soon: Bob's Auto Salvage Lot. Pick a wreck and find the part you need." As the pickup drove back by their house and the driver gave a friendly wave, Ken and Nancy looked at each other in horror. Their twelve-year dream had suddenly become a nightmare.

This is a free country. What is to prevent such a scenario from happening? Why can't someone build a convenience store in the middle of a residential subdivision? What prevents a large, smelly factory from going up next to an exclusive golf course that has large, expensive homes surrounding it? What keeps these things from happening is the process called zoning, by which a city or a county regulates how various areas of property are used.

The zoning commission is another appointed board that oversees the zoning process. The city planner or other official might chair the commission. Typical zones are residential, commercial, and industrial. These are subdivided into more specific kinds of use. A residential zone might be restricted to single-family dwellings, or it might allow two-family dwellings (duplexes), mobile homes, or multi-family dwellings in the form of apartments. Commercial zones might allow certain kinds of businesses but forbid others; for instance, a bookstore might be permitted on the town square but not a lumber yard. Industrial zones can be designated light industrial or heavy industrial. A small tool and die shop would be in a different zone from a large auto parts manufacturer.

Zoning regulations create a pleasant and coordinated community environment and help to maintain property values. For instance, it would be difficult to sell a house that is located next to a factory. Many people would be reluctant to buy a home if a liquor store might be built next to it. Zoning separates business areas, industrial areas, and residential areas to help with traffic flow and personal safety. In addition, when a piece of property is sold, the seller can impose covenants and restrictions on how the property can be used for a certain period of time into the future.

Few cities were zoned from the time they were established. As a result, when zoning is initiated it has to pick up with the status quo and go on from there. In addition, zoning is not a one-time process. Zoning designations can be changed. A county might change a farm or residential zone to industrial if it wants to create an industrial park. A property owner can petition to have his or her site rezoned to another designation. If the owner of an empty warehouse wants to build apartments on the site, he would apply for a zoning change. Public notice has to be given on the proposed change, and a public hearing is held to allow input from citizens on the proposal. Some Spring Hill residents, for instance, opposed a zoning change request from someone who wanted to build a small shopping center in an area that had been designated residential.

Zoning and planning have been used longer for cities than for counties. More counties are seeing the need for staying ahead of growth and avoiding problems before they surface. Those who oppose zoning want the freedom to do what they want with their property. Those who support zoning want to regulate growth and development and want to avoid the situation faced by Ken and Nancy Greene. Planning, annexation, and zoning are all areas in which local governments try to maintain a balance between personal freedom and community interests.

Special Issues

Any city or county will have special situations that have an impact on life and government there. Spring Hill, for instance, straddles a county border. Residents of the Williamson County side of the city pay Williamson County taxes and receive services from Williamson County, while those who live on the Maury County side of the city pay Maury County taxes and receive Maury County services. Many larger urban areas spill over county lines. While few cities cross those lines the way Spring Hill does, it can be a complex process to know the governments and special districts to which a resident is responsible.

Near Spring Hill and Columbia, Tennessee

Not all communities are growing. Some urban areas, small cities, and counties are shrinking in population and business output. When a factory or military base closes, the tax base and the economy of the locality can be seriously affected. Dealing with decline can be a difficult problem for governments to handle. Closed factories and empty apartment buildings generate no income for the city and can invite criminal activity. A city will often recruit families and businesses to move into the community, and it might offer tax incentives to the businesses to encourage them to do so. However, residents and businesses who have remained in the community usually do not get offers of tax abatements and might resent the benefits offered to newcomers. Revitalization can be a long process that requires widespread community commitment to the goal of renewal.

In this lesson we have considered some of the issues that local governments face in dealing with long-term, developmental challenges. In the next lesson, we will look at how government responded to the challenges that occurred with a single, dramatic event.

By the blessing of the upright a city is exalted,
But by the mouth of the wicked it is torn down.
Proverbs 11:11

Lesson 54—Government Inaction: The Response to Hurricane Katrina

It has become increasingly clear that local, state, and federal government agencies failed to meet the needs of the residents of Louisiana, Mississippi, and Alabama. . . . Our investigation revealed that Katrina was a national failure, an abdication of the most solemn obligation to provide for the common welfare. At every level—individual, corporate, philanthropic, and governmental—we failed to meet the challenge that was Katrina.

—A Failure of Initiative, *Report of the U.S. House of Representatives Select Bipartisan Committee to Investigate the Preparation for and Response to Hurricane Katrina, February 2006*

Early on the morning of Monday, August 29, 2005, Hurricane Katrina slammed ashore along the Louisiana and Mississippi Gulf Coast with winds measuring 125 miles per hour. A few hours later, the levees protecting New Orleans from the waters of Lake Pontchartrain and the Mississippi River gave way, releasing additional flood waters onto the city that is mostly below sea level. About 80% of the city was flooded, in some places with water 20 to 25 feet deep. In addition to the destruction caused in Louisiana, a storm surge drove ten miles into Mississippi, in some places up to 34 feet deep. Over half of Mississippi was without electrical power and experienced storm-related damage. Months later, some Mississippi coastal towns were still deserted. Neighboring Alabama also suffered property loss and casualties. Over 1,400 confirmed deaths were blamed on the storm. Estimates of property losses are over $75 billion, making Katrina the costliest natural disaster in U.S. history.

Flooding in New Orleans after Hurricane Katrina

The suffering experienced by survivors of the storm was played out on national television. Tens of thousands were sheltered in the New Orleans Superdome and the Morial Convention Center. These people were eventually evacuated to Texas, Arkansas, Oklahoma, and other states. Countless numbers were rescued from rooftops and flooded structures. Medical personnel set up temporary facilities at the New Orleans airport and other locations and worked desperately to help the sick and injured. About 1.2 million people were under evacuation orders. Some 1.5 million were displaced at least temporarily; and about 3 million were without electricity for some period of time, some for several weeks. Displaced persons eventually found shelter in all 50 states and in half of the nation's zip codes, although most were housed within 250 miles from their homes. Many vowed never to return to New Orleans.

As the hours and days unfolded following Katrina's landfall, it became clear that governments on every level were not adequately prepared to respond to such a major disaster or to work together to create an appropriate response. The blame game started early, with government officials pointing the finger at each other and rarely taking personal responsibility for the failures. The scenario has been analyzed repeatedly in the media and by several government bodies. A special committee of the U.S. House of Representatives issued its report in February 2006, and the White House published its analysis a few weeks later.

This lesson is a case study in the government's disaster management and response capabilities. We will discuss the responsibilities of different levels of government and what can be changed by the public and private sectors to prevent another inadequate response to a national calamity. We will also consider the long-term effects of the storm on American government. It is probably impossible to be completely prepared for a disaster as big as Katrina was, and it is easy to say after the fact what people should have done. We must, however, evaluate the performance of our governments to be sure that the common welfare is served.

A Member of the U.S. Coast Guard Rescuing a New Orleans Resident after Hurricane Katrina

Many government workers, military personnel, volunteers, and charitable organizations responded heroically and sacrificially. Many volunteers served or contributed because of their Christian faith. The Salvation Army collected the second highest total of donations after the American Red Cross. These responses were the works of God that people performed without stopping to ask why the storm had hit (see John 9:1-5).

Preparations for the Storm

After forming in the South Atlantic, Katrina cut across southern Florida in late August and gained strength in the Gulf of Mexico as it headed toward the Gulf Coast. The National Weather Service and the National Hurricane Center tracked the storm and predicted its strength and landfall with amazing accuracy. Government response agencies had plenty of warning about the storm thanks to the Federal government's weather service.

Federal, state, and local officials participated in mock exercises in the summer of 2004 that tried to anticipate a catastrophic hurricane striking the New Orleans area. The exercise was called Hurricane Pam and anticipated levee failures, massive evacuations, and huge casualties. Numerous articles appeared in major publications that raised questions about whether the government was prepared for such an eventuality. Whatever plans were developed for responding to such a scenario, apparently not enough was done.

Evidently the levee system protecting New Orleans was not adequately designed or maintained to handle the excess water brought on by a large hurricane. A canal connecting New Orleans with the Gulf of Mexico has also been cited by some observers as contributing to the presence of excess water around the city. These failures suggest inadequate government planning or a faulty appraisal of the physical features near New Orleans.

Government procedures that were set up to prepare for a crisis of this magnitude were obviously inadequate. Supplies and response personnel were not in place, even though the most likely area of landfall had been known several days in advance. The New Orleans mayor had ordered an evacuation of the city, but how the evacuation was supposed to take place was not clear. Transportation for hospital patients, nursing home residents, and citizens without personal vehicles was not provided for. All those who could not leave the city were told to use the Superdome as temporary shelter. Tens of thousands of residents and tourists were left in the city, unable or unwilling to leave.

Louisiana governor Kathleen Blanco declared a state of emergency on August 26. President Bush declared a state of emergency the next day, two days before the storm struck. On August 28, New Orleans mayor Ray Nagin ordered a mandatory evacuation of the city after advising evacuation over several previous days (New Orleans and its parish have a consolidated government, so a separate county government was not involved). These three officials were in contact with each other, but it is a matter of dispute what concrete actions took place as a result of their conversations.

After the Storm Hit

The combination of Katrina's hit and the breach of the levees caused terrible problems in New Orleans and along the coast. Law and order broke down in New Orleans as the city police force for the most part simply vanished. Widespread looting took place in the city. National Guardsmen from Louisiana and most other states responded as they could over the next several days. Order was restored in the city over the following week. Guard, military, and law enforcement personnel (many of whom also came from other states) were involved in rescuing people from their homes. The Superdome was damaged by the storm, and utilities failed in the building that housed up to 60,000 persons. The Convention Center was broken into, and some 20,000 people made their way there. Desperate pleas were broadcast on national television for supplies to be sent to the Convention Center, but response was slow since it was not part of the rescue plan. Accounts of violent crime in the two large arenas were common but were apparently greatly exaggerated.

New Orleans Residents Seeking Shelter at the Superdome after Hurricane Katrina

When it was obvious that the vast human needs could not be met in New Orleans, plans were implemented to move the displaced persons elsewhere. About 230,000 were taken to Texas, where they were sheltered temporarily in the Houston Astrodome and in other facilities in San Antonio, Dallas, and elsewhere. Some 40-50,000 more were bused to Arkansas and Oklahoma. The Morial Convention Center was emptied by September 3 and the Superdome by September 6. Then many of these evacuees were taken to other states to spread the impact of such large numbers of needy people.

Meanwhile, the Federal response was mired in its own bureaucratic red tape. No clear response plan was followed, and urgent requests for supplies were commonly lost or rejected. The accusation was made that the Department of Homeland Security (DHS) was not geared to respond to a natural disaster since it had been focusing on terrorist threats. The Federal Emergency Management Agency (FEMA) had been placed in the DHS when the department was formed, and in the Katrina crisis FEMA was stuck down the government chain of command. The official procedure that FEMA follows involves responding to requests from states and localities, but with communication snarled the formal procedure could not be followed. As a result, much of FEMA's resources sat unused.

FEMA finally began responding by issuing debit cards worth $2,000 each to those affected by the storm. Some of these, of course, were used for purposes other than to pay for food and shelter. Fraud, abuse, and duplicate payments were commonplace. The Federal government received some 700,000 applications for housing assistance. In response, the government ordered tens of thousands of temporary housing units to be

Buildings Along the Gulf
Damaged by Hurricane Katrina

built and moved to the Gulf region and other places. However, some were poorly constructed and many remained empty far from New Orleans as distribution was not accomplished smoothly.

Causes of the Problems

A major contributing factor to the poor response to Katrina was that the channels of procedure needed to bring about an appropriate government response were either poor or absent altogether. If you have ever written a letter or made a phone call to a government agency, you have learned that government bureaucracy responds slowly. The military has a ready response capability, but government desk workers are used to taking their time. What Katrina victims did not have was time. Following routine procedures does not work when food, medical supplies, and shelter are needed immediately. Moreover, the power to order an evacuation is one thing, but the ability to carry it off is another. One-fourth of New Orleans households did not have personal vehicles, and about 38% of the city's residents lived below the poverty level. These

FEMA Undersecretary Michael Brown and Louisiana Governor Kathleen Blanco at a Press Briefing after Hurricane Katrina

people, along with the medically infirm, needed to have a way out of the city when the evacuation was ordered. Issuing an evacuation order too soon can present problems, but Katrina demonstrated the problems that can come from issuing such an order too late.

Another major problem with the Katrina response was communication. Emergency communication links were not in place when routine channels failed. The sharing of information among various agencies (the military, FEMA, and the Red Cross, for instance) and especially among Federal, state, and local authorities was haphazard. Unverified information competed with accurate information and created a cloud of uncertainty, even on the ground in New Orleans and the Gulf Coast area. The Red Cross was forbidden to enter New Orleans for a time. Governor Blanco refused to release state funds to provide medical assistance until she was sure that the Federal government would reimburse the state.

A third problem involved personal failings. Those in positions of leadership did not lead; they merely responded, and often poorly at that. Compare the actions of elected and appointed officials affected by Katrina to the leadership provided by New York City mayor Rudolph Giuliani following the September 11 attacks. Giuliani won widespread praise for his proactive and involved leadership during that crisis. One cannot imagine Giuliani responding to a question several days after the attacks occurred with a confused look and saying, "Well, we're still looking into that." Typical bureaucratic answers simply do not work in a time of crisis. Giuliani understood that, but most of those charged with responding to Katrina did not.

Another category of personal failings involved the response of many citizens. Those who could have evacuated the city but chose not to do so have to bear the responsibility for what

The review of the Federal government's response issued by the White House in the spring of 2006 called for a regional response structure as opposed to a single national bureaucracy, better use of the National Guard, improved preparation by public health agencies, and the development of an attitude of preparedness among the citizenry as a whole.

happened to them. It is, to be sure, too simplistic just to blame the poor for their poverty (for instance, if someone can't get work because he is black or physically disabled, that is not his fault). However, we have created a culture in which many people expect the government or someone else to provide for them; and this is wrong. People can exercise personal initiative and improve their circumstances, but they must be willing to do so. It is easy to say that everything is the government's fault, but such a charge is rarely accurate.

Finally, we cannot think that government as usual will take care of our problems. It is wrong to think that simply creating a new department/agency/commission/office or shuffling the boxes on the organizational flow chart will adequately address a problem. The quick and effective response of thousands of volunteers and dozens if not hundreds of charitable organizations (many of which were Christian) shows that actions, not words and charts, will get the job done. In addition, a problem will not be solved merely by throwing money at it. The Federal government appropriated over $62 billion for Katrina relief by the spring of 2006. When you have that much money floating around with little accountability, some of it is likely to be used inappropriately. A large appropriation makes for a good press release, but the often awkward and messy follow-through rarely gets reported. Even the handling of some Red Cross funds and materials came into question. The state of Texas responded in a far superior way to the needs of the displaced persons who went there, even considering the fact that the state's utilities and other services were not destroyed the way they were in the New Orleans area. Texas government had studied how it should respond to a disaster and was able to make a huge difference. Let us hope that the Katrina experience will cause policy-makers to realize that fundamental, systemic changes need to take place.

Baby Items Donated to Hurricane Katrina Victims through a Christian Charity Organization

Looking to the Future

The effects of Hurricane Katrina will likely be felt for years and will involve governments at every level.

- How can a community start over with almost nothing—few workers, few jobs and businesses, destroyed housing, and a damaged infrastructure—as many small communities along the Gulf Coast must do? Will the answer be found in Federal grants?

- What will be the long term effect in New Orleans, especially if many former residents do not return? What will this population shift mean for New Orleans' tax base and for political representation in state and Federal government—and what will it mean for those areas that have gained population as a result of this shift?

- What bureaucratic red tape can be cut between states and cities and between the Federal government and states and localities in order to handle emergencies? How can this happen while still respecting the sovereignty and the responsibilities of each level of government?

- What will happen to the natural environment of the Gulf Coast? Wetlands have been destroyed, some species of wildlife disappeared from the region at least temporarily, and industries such as oyster harvesting may take a long time to recover. Oil, chemicals, sewage, and polluted water have been released into the environment. If the Mount St. Helens recovery is any indication, God can bring back the natural resources; but the effects on humans from this environmental damage might be significant.

- The response to Hurricane Katrina illustrates the difficult relationship between Federal, state, and local governments. It appears that in some ways states and cities can't live with the Federal government but at the same time they can't live without it. Will states and cities look even more to the Federal government, since it has the most resources? Will this mean an even bigger Federal bureaucracy and Federal debt? Will this lessen the already eroding sovereignty of the states?

And His disciples asked Him, "Rabbi, who sinned,
this man or his parents, that he would be born blind?"
Jesus answered, "It was neither that this man sinned, nor his parents;
but it was so that the works of God might be displayed in him.
We must work the works of Him who sent Me as long as it is day;
night is coming when no one can work."
John 9:2-4

Volunteers from a Louisiana Church Distributing Water and Other Supplies to Hurricane Katrina Victims

Lesson 55—Government Action: The Issue of Eminent Domain

[Nor] shall private property be taken for public use, without just compensation.
—Fifth Amendment, U.S. Constitution

Eminent domain is the power of government to use or take private property for public purposes without the owner's permission. It is a right that governments have claimed since kings considered themselves to be owners of all the property in their realms.

This power can be exercised in several ways. For instance, when the utility company sends trucks and workers onto private property to repair a power line, it does not need to get the landowner's permission. The utility personnel can come onto the property by the power of eminent domain. The term eminent domain is more commonly applied to situations in which the government wants to purchase property for a project that is deemed to be for the public good. Highway and railroad construction projects are examples of a typical use of eminent domain by governments. The declaration by a government that it plans to exercise eminent domain on a piece of property is called the condemnation of that property.

The government's power of eminent domain is a limitation on the right of private ownership of property. A property owner usually cannot stand in the way of a government project merely because he does not want to sell his land. However, in the United States certain safeguards have traditionally kept a check on the process. The Fifth Amendment says that the government must want the land "for public use" and that it must provide "just compensation" to the owner. This is often called the Takings Clause of the Fifth Amendment. Typically the process of acquiring land for public projects in the name of eminent domain requires public hearings and careful appraisals of the property. Lawsuits are common over the parcels of land that are to be taken and over the price offered for them by the government.

Eminent domain has generally been seen as a right of the government to acquire land for public use and not for private development. However, the definition of "public use" has gradually expanded to include economic development, even by a private entity, that will supposedly benefit the public at large. In the 1920s, the U.S. Supreme Court upheld the condemnation of urban slums to allow private developers to use the land for their projects, reasoning that such projects would benefit the public. In 1954, the Court reaffirmed this power in a case involving a blighted area in the District of Columbia (*Berman v. Parker*). A store owner in the area in question stated that his business was not blighted and thus should not be condemned, but the Court ruled that the overall plan required that all property owners sell their land. The Court deferred to the legislative intent of Congress by declaring that the plan was carefully drawn and would be for the public good. In 1981, the Michigan Supreme Court, using the same reasoning, upheld the condemnation of slum property in Detroit for General Motors to build a factory.

In a 5-4 decision announced in June of 2005, the U.S. Supreme Court ruled against property owners in New London, Connecticut, who objected to having to sell their land to private developers because a city agency had decided that developing the land would bring greater economic benefit to the community than would be derived from the land remaining

Justice John Paul Stevens, 1976

as it was. This lesson examines the *Kelo, et al. v. City of New London, et al.* decision, as well as the dissents written by the minority of the Court. Most of the remaining text of this lesson consists of quotations from the majority and minority opinions. Legal footnotes and citations have been omitted to make reading easier. Justice John Paul Stevens wrote the majority opinion, which is quoted first. (In this lesson, the long block quotations from Court decisions are in italics.)

Background

In 2000, the city of New London approved a development plan that, in the words of the Supreme Court of Connecticut, was "projected to create in excess of 1,000 jobs, to increase tax and other revenues, and to revitalize an economically distressed city, including its downtown and waterfront areas." In assembling the land needed for this project, the city's development agent has purchased property from willing sellers and proposes to use the power of eminent domain to acquire the remainder of the property from unwilling owners in exchange for just compensation. The question presented is whether the city's proposed disposition of this property qualifies as a "public use" within the meaning of the Takings Clause of the Fifth Amendment to the Constitution. . . .

The city council approved the plan in January 2000, and designated the [New London Development Corporation, or] NLDC as its development agent in charge of implementation. The city council also authorized the NLDC to purchase property or to acquire property by exercising eminent domain in the City's name. The NLDC successfully negotiated the purchase of most of the real estate in the 90-acre area, but its negotiations with petitioners failed. As a consequence, in November 2000, the NLDC initiated the condemnation proceedings that gave rise to this case.

Petitioner Susette Kelo has lived in the Fort Trumbull area since 1997. She has made extensive improvements to her house, which she prizes for its water view. Petitioner Wilhelmina Dery was born in her Fort Trumbull house in 1918 and has lived there her entire life. Her husband Charles (also a petitioner) has lived in the house since they married some 60 years ago. In all, the nine petitioners own 15 properties in Fort Trumbull—4 in parcel 3 of the development plan and 11 in parcel 4A. Ten of the parcels are occupied by the owner or a family member; the other five are held as investment properties. There is no allegation that any of these properties is blighted or otherwise in poor condition; rather, they were condemned only because they happen to be located in the development area.

In December 2000, petitioners brought this action in the New London Superior Court. They claimed, among other things, that the taking of their properties would violate the "public use" restriction in the Fifth Amendment. After a 7-day bench trial, the Superior Court granted a permanent restraining order prohibiting the taking of the properties located in parcel 4A (park or marina support). It, however, denied petitioners relief as to the properties located in parcel 3 (office space).

After the Superior Court ruled, both sides took appeals to the Supreme Court of Connecticut. That court held, over a dissent, that all of the City's proposed takings were valid. It began by upholding the lower court's determination that the takings were authorized by chapter 132, the State's municipal development statute. That statute expresses a legislative determination that the taking of land, even developed land, as part of an economic development project is a "public use" and in the "public interest." Next, relying on cases such as [previous Supreme Court decisions] Hawaii Housing Authority v. Midkiff *(1984) and* Berman v. Parker *(1954), the court held that such economic development qualified as a valid public use under both the Federal and State Constitutions. . . .*

We granted certiorari to determine whether a city's decision to take property for the purpose of economic development satisfies the "public use" requirement of the Fifth Amendment.

The Thinking of the Majority

Two polar propositions are perfectly clear. On the one hand, it has long been accepted that the sovereign may not take the property of A for the sole purpose of transferring it to another private party B, even though A is paid just compensation. On the other hand, it is equally clear that a State may transfer property from one private party to another if future "use by the public" is the purpose of the taking; the condemnation of land for a railroad with common-carrier duties is a familiar example. Neither of these propositions, however, determines the disposition of this case. . . .

[T]his is not a case in which the City is planning to open the condemned land—at least not in its entirety—to use by the general public. Nor will the private lessees of the land in any sense be required to operate like common carriers, making their services available to all comers. But although such a projected use would be sufficient to satisfy the public use requirement, this "Court long ago rejected any literal requirement that condemned property be put into use for the general public." . . . [W]hen this Court began applying the Fifth Amendment to the States at the close of the 19th century, it embraced the broader and more natural interpretation of public use as "public purpose." . . .

The disposition of this case therefore turns on the question whether the City's development plan serves a "public purpose." Without exception, our cases have defined that concept broadly, reflecting our longstanding policy of deference to legislative judgments in this field. [The decision here refers to opinions issued by the Court that were mentioned in the first part of this lesson as well as other decisions.] . . .

Those who govern the City were not confronted with the need to remove blight in the

Fort Trumbull area, but their determination that the area was sufficiently distressed to justify a program of economic rejuvenation is entitled to our deference. The City has carefully formulated an economic development plan that it believes will provide appreciable benefits to the community, including—but by no means limited to—new jobs and increased tax revenue. As with other exercises in urban planning and development, the City is endeavoring to coordinate a variety of commercial, residential, and recreational uses of land, with the hope that they will form a whole greater than the sum of its parts. To effectuate this plan, the City has invoked a state statute that specifically authorizes the use of eminent domain to promote economic development. Given the comprehensive character of the plan, the thorough deliberation that preceded its adoption, and the limited scope of our review, it is appropriate for us, as it was in Berman, *to resolve the challenges of the individual owners, not on a piecemeal basis, but rather in light of the entire plan. Because that plan unquestionably serves a public purpose, the takings challenged here satisfy the public use requirement of the Fifth Amendment.*

To avoid this result, petitioners urge us to adopt a new bright-line rule that economic development does not qualify as a public use. Putting aside the unpersuasive suggestion that the City's plan will provide only purely economic benefits, neither precedent nor logic supports petitioners' proposal. Promoting economic development is a traditional and long accepted function of government. There is, moreover, no principled way of distinguishing economic development from the other public purposes that we have recognized. . . .

In Dissent

Justice Sandra Day O'Connor wrote the lead dissenting opinion for the four-justice minority.

Over two centuries ago, just after the Bill of Rights was ratified, Justice Chase wrote: "An act of the Legislature (for I cannot call it a law) contrary to the great first principles of the social compact, cannot be considered a rightful exercise of legislative authority. . . . A few instances will suffice to explain what I mean. . . . [A] law that takes property from A and gives it to B: It is against all reason and justice, for a people to entrust a Legislature with such powers; and, therefore, it cannot be presumed that they have done it." Calder v. Bull *(1798).*

Today the Court abandons this long-held, basic limitation on government power. Under the banner of economic development, all private property is now vulnerable to being taken and transferred to another private owner, so long as it might be upgraded—i.e., given to an owner who will use it in a way that the legislature deems more beneficial to the public—in the process. To reason, as the Court does, that the incidental public benefits resulting from the subsequent ordinary use of private property render economic development takings "for public use" is to wash out any distinction between private and public use of property—and thereby effectively to delete the words "for public use" from the Takings Clause of the Fifth Amendment. Accordingly I respectfully dissent. . . .

Petitioners are not hold-outs; they do not seek increased compensation, and none is opposed to new development in the area. Theirs is an objection in principle: They claim that the NLDC's proposed use for their confiscated property is not a "public" one for purposes of the Fifth Amendment. While the government may take their homes to build a road or a railroad or to eliminate a property use that harms the public, say petitioners, it cannot take their property for the private use of other owners simply because the new owners may make more productive use of the property.

The Fifth Amendment to the Constitution, made applicable to the States by the Fourteenth Amendment, provides that "private property [shall not] be taken for public use, without just compensation." When interpreting the Constitution, we begin with the unremarkable presumption that every word in the document has independent meaning, "that no word was unnecessarily used, or needlessly added" Wright v. United States *(1938). In keeping with that presumption, we have read the Fifth Amendment's language to impose two distinct conditions on the exercise of eminent domain: "the taking must be for a 'public use' and 'just compensation' must be paid to the owner"* Brown v. Legal Foundation of Wash. *(2003).*

These two limitations serve to protect "the security of Property," which Alexander Hamilton described to the Philadelphia Convention as one of the "great obj[ects] of Gov[ernment]." (Records of the Federal Convention of 1787, p. 302, M. Farrand ed. 1934). *Together they ensure stable property ownership by providing safeguards against excessive, unpredictable, or unfair use of the government's eminent domain power—particularly against those owners who, for whatever reasons, may be unable to protect themselves in the political process against the majority's will. . . .*

New London does not claim that Susette Kelo's and Wilhelmina Dery's well-maintained homes are the source of any social harm. Indeed, it could not so claim without adopting the absurd argument that any single-family home that might be razed to make way for an apartment building, or any church that might be replaced with a retail store, or any small business that might be more lucrative if it were instead part of a national franchise, is inherently harmful to society and thus within the government's power to condemn.

In moving away from our decisions sanctioning the condemnation of harmful property use, the Court today significantly expands the meaning of public use. It holds that the sovereign may take private property currently put to ordinary private use, and give it over for new, ordinary private use, so long as the new use is predicted to generate some secondary benefit for the public—such as increased tax revenue, more jobs, maybe even aesthetic pleasure. But nearly any lawful use of real private property can be said to generate some incidental benefit to the public. Thus, if predicted (or even guaranteed) positive side-effects are enough to render transfer from one private party to another constitutional, then the words "for public use" do not realistically exclude any takings, and thus do not exert any constraint on the eminent domain power. . . .

[W]ho among us can say she already makes the most productive or attractive possible use of her property? The specter of condemnation hangs over all property. Nothing is to prevent the State from replacing any Motel 6 with a Ritz-Carlton, any home with a shopping mall, or any farm with a factory.

The Court [in its majority opinion] suggests that property owners should turn to the States, who may or may not choose to impose appropriate limits on economic development takings. This is an abdication of our responsibility. States play many important functions in our system of dual sovereignty, but compensating for our refusal to enforce properly the Federal Constitution (and a provision meant to curtail state action, no less) is not among them. . . .

"[T]hat alone is a just government," wrote James Madison, "which impartially secures to every man, whatever is his own."

Justice Clarence Thomas wrote a separate dissenting opinion.

Long ago, William Blackstone wrote that "the law of the land . . . postpone[s] even public necessity to the sacred and inviolable rights of private property." The Framers embodied that principle in the Constitution, allowing the government to take property not for "public necessity," but instead for "public use." Defying this understanding, the Court replaces the Public Use Clause with a "Public Purpose" Clause, (or perhaps the "Diverse and Always Evolving Needs of Society" Clause, capitalization added), a restriction that is satisfied, the Court instructs, so long as the purpose is "legitimate" and the means "not irrational." This deferential shift in phraseology enables the Court to hold, against all common sense, that a costly urban-renewal project whose stated purpose is a vague promise of new jobs and increased tax revenue, but which is also suspiciously agreeable to the Pfizer Corporation, is for a "public use."

I cannot agree. If such "economic development" takings are for a "public use," any taking is, and the Court has erased the Public Use Clause from our Constitution, as Justice O'Connor powerfully argues in dissent. I do not believe that this Court can eliminate liberties expressly enumerated in the Constitution and therefore join her dissenting opinion. Regrettably, however, the Court's error runs deeper than this. Today's decision is simply the latest in a string of our cases construing the Public Use Clause to be a virtual nullity, without the slightest nod to its original meaning. In my view, the Public Use Clause, originally understood, is a meaningful limit on the government's eminent domain power. Our cases have strayed from the Clause's original meaning, and I would reconsider them. . . .

The most natural reading of the Clause is that it allows the government to take property only if the government owns, or the public has a legal right to use, the property, as opposed to taking it for any public purpose or necessity whatsoever. . . .

The Takings Clause is a prohibition, not a grant of power: The Constitution does not expressly grant the Federal Government the power to take property for any public purpose whatsoever. Instead, the Government may take property only when necessary and proper to the exercise of an expressly enumerated power. . . . In other words, a taking is permissible under the Necessary and Proper Clause only if it serves a valid public purpose. [Justice Thomas then cites state and Federal precedents that support the limited and careful application of the Takings Clause and questions the reasoning used in the earlier Supreme Court decisions.] . . .

For all these reasons, I would revisit our Public Use Clause cases and consider returning to the original meaning of the Public Use Clause: that the government may take property only if it actually uses or gives the public a legal right to use the property.

The consequences of today's decision are not difficult to predict, and promise to be harmful. So-called "urban renewal" programs provide some compensation for the properties they take, but no compensation is possible for the subjective value of these lands to the individuals displaced and the indignity inflicted by uprooting them from their homes. Allowing the government to take property solely for public purposes is bad enough, but extending the concept of public purpose to encompass any economically beneficial goal guarantees that these losses will fall disproportionately on poor communities. Those communities are not only systematically less likely to put their lands to the highest and best social use, but are also the least politically powerful. If ever there were justification for intrusive judicial review of constitutional provisions that protect "discrete and insular minorities," surely that principle would apply with great force to the powerless groups and individuals the Public Use Clause protects. The deferential standard this Court has adopted for the Public Use Clause is therefore deeply perverse. . . .

The Debate Continues

The debate over a government's appropriate use of the eminent domain power continues, but the effect of this decision is a practical one that affects all property owners. The  government cannot force a property owner to sell his property to another person, and a seller must receive just compensation if his land is condemned for a public project. However, apparently a government can condemn property and force its sale if the government believes that the property can be used to generate more revenue by other private owners.

The majority opinion encourages petitioning state governments for strict guidelines on eminent domain procedures. However, state legislatures will likely be persuaded by the arguments of developers that a broad takings policy will generate more revenue for the state. A few states forbid condemnation of private property for economic redevelopment unless the property is defined as blighted. Most states either allow takings for private development or have no legislation forbidding it. The best hope for property owners will be to persuade state legislatures to protect private property or to trust a future Supreme Court to reverse this decision.

*He who oppresses the poor to make more for himself
or who gives to the rich, will only come to poverty.*
Proverbs 22:16

12 Taxing and Spending

This unit considers government and money: how government gets money and how government spends it. We look at the budget process, typical government expenditures, sources of revenue for government, and what government tax policies can and should do.

Lessons in This Unit

Activity Idea

Should property ownership play any role in who has a voice in government? In the early days of the republic, voting rights and qualifications for holding office were based on property ownership. It was believed that those who owned property had a vested interest in doing what was best for society and that only they were responsible enough to be trusted with the right to vote and to hold office. Those who did not own property could be too immature or too irresponsible to have an interest in the well-being of society. Daniel Webster warned that if non-propertied citizens could vote, they might think that they ought to get a share of what the propertied people had and might vote accordingly. Is there any truth to this idea? How might this principle of responsibility in government be maintained when the only significant requirement for voting is that a person be eighteen years old? Write a two-page response.

If you are using the optional *Quiz and Exam Book*, answer the questions for each lesson after you have completed the lesson and read any assigned readings in *We Hold These Truths*. After you have completed Lesson 60, take the quiz for Unit 12.

Lesson 56—Government Budgets

Republics are created by the virtue, public spirit, and intelligence of the citizens. They fall, when the wise are banished from the public councils, because they dare to be honest, and the profligate are rewarded, because they flatter the people, in order to betray them.
—Supreme Court Justice Joseph Story (1833)

Budgets, Income, and Expenses

A budget is a plan of income and expenses, usually for a year's time. Responsible families plan their income and expenses. If an individual family's expenses exceed their income, they have to borrow money, find other sources of income, or reduce their spending.

A government budget is in many ways the same as a family budget. Every government entity, from the smallest agency to the entire Federal government, operates on the basis of a budget. The government tries to anticipate the revenues it expects to receive in the coming year. It also makes an estimate of the expenses it will have for salaries, equipment, and programs. Generally speaking, a government, like a family, should try to make its expenses about equal to its revenues. If revenues far exceed expenditures, the government is collecting too much money that could be staying in the pockets of its citizens. If expenses far exceed revenue, the government is spending beyond its means and should reassess its priorities to bring expenses in line with revenue or find additional sources of revenue.

A family has necessary expenses and discretionary or optional expenses. Most families find it necessary to spend money to provide housing, utilities, food, clothes, and medical care. Examples of optional expenses might include a new car, a vacation, or a new computer. Admittedly, sometimes the line between necessary and optional is hard to determine. If the old family car is constantly breaking down, buying a newer car might be the wiser choice. Internet service can be seen as optional; but if the family operates an Internet business, then Internet service is essential for what the family wants to do. This illustrates how family priorities are reflected in the family budget.

A government makes choices about how it spends its revenue. Spending for defense is the most essential expense, since without a defense budget the country might cease to exist. Law enforcement is essential for state and local governments, since a society must have peace and order to be able to function. Many Federal programs involve what is called mandatory spending because the government chose at some point to guarantee that those programs would be available. This is a choice or a priority that government makes which is reflected in its budget. The government also has discretionary expenses, meaning budget priorities that are not mandated by law but are reconsidered to some extent every year, at least in terms of how much money will be allocated for those programs.

Many people want the government to spend money on them or on their favorite projects; and since government does not have unlimited revenue, government decision-makers have to decide which ones it will approve. This too is like what a family experiences. A family receives advertisements from companies that want to sell them things and requests from people or groups who want the family to donate to them. The family has to decide what they can and want to do. In the same way, governments receive hundreds of requests each

282

year, from day care centers, schools, universities, the military, the space program, farmers, veterans, the poor, the elderly—and the list goes on and on. Elected government officials often sincerely believe that the government should spend money on what they believe to be high and valid priorities. At the same time, these office holders also usually want to be re-elected; and so they do not want to tell people, "The government cannot or should not pay for your request. You will have to find another source of money or do without." Government programs are often enacted so that elected officials can say to the voters, "See what I did for you? This is why you should re-elect me."

However, the government cannot say yes to every request for funding without exceeding its revenues. When a family spends more than it receives, it experiences a deficit and has to borrow money. The amount that a family owes is called debt. When a deficit occurs month after month, the debt grows. The family has to develop a plan to pay off the debt, which might include generating more income and/or cutting expenses. If the family does not do this, it will be overcome by debt. More and more of the family's income will have to be allocated to paying off the debt, which usually involves paying interest on the debt. In the worst case scenario, the family is unable to pay its debts and must declare bankruptcy. It must then go through a process to decide what debts can be canceled or reduced and what long-term plan will enable them to pay off the remaining debts. Those to whom the family owes money may receive less than the amount they have loaned the family. These creditors will want to regain what they have lost by forcing the family to sell off some assets, such as a car or other valuables. Another way that a creditor might compensate for his loss is by increasing interest charges to other debtors.

Government finds it difficult to say no to requests or perceived needs. As a result, it is easy for a government to go into debt. It is possible for cities, states, and countries to default on indebtedness and go bankrupt; but this is an extreme case. What is more likely is that the government will try to raise taxes or borrow money. If it borrows a great deal of money, its budget can become increasingly dominated by payments on the debt. Either way, the economy of the state or nation becomes increasingly influenced by the demands made by the government for more revenue.

> *Department or agency budgets are estimates of what they think they will need in the coming year. Sometimes the agency does not spend as much as it had anticipated before the budget year started. However, government agencies want to spend all of what has been appropriated for them this year lest they lose some of their appropriation next year. This means that government workers sometimes look around for something to buy or a conference to attend—even thought they don't strictly need it—just so they will spend all of their appropriation.*

The Budget Process

The process for developing and adopting a budget by a government is roughly the same whether it is the local, state, or Federal government. First, the various executive departments and agencies prepare their estimates for expenses for the coming year. Many times this will include what the department sees as a minimum essential budget as well as a wish list for what the department would like to have. Second, the estimates are collected and reviewed by a central budget office. This office compares desired expenditures with expected revenues and comes up with a final budget proposal. Third, the executive (the president, governor, county executive, mayor, or city manager) presents the budget to the legislative body (Congress, legislature, county commission, or city council). The president submits his budget proposal to Congress in February, and most other governmental budgets are also submitted in the spring for the upcoming fiscal year. The Federal budget year or fiscal year runs from October 1 of one calendar year to September 30 of the following year. Some states and localities use a July 1 to June 30 fiscal year.

The legislative body then considers the budget, usually by breaking it down for review by various committees. Congress makes a distinction between the budget resolution (the overall plan) and specific appropriations, through which money is actually committed to programs. Governments on lower levels do not necessarily make this distinction. As the proposed budget is being considered, the committees and other members of the legislative body will probably have their own ideas about department budgets and programs they would like to see implemented, so the figures in the executive's budget proposal will likely be changed before final passage.

Budget considerations in the legislative branch usually bring forth the same debates year after year. For instance, conservatives almost always say that we need more money for defense and point out the waste and fraud that occur in social programs. On the other hand, liberals almost always say that we need to spend more on social programs and point out the waste and fraud that occur in defense spending. What happens too often is that both defense and social programs receive more funding and little is done to stop the waste and fraud anywhere.

After the budget is adopted, procedures are followed to oversee the accurate expenditure of and accounting for government funds.

State government budgets are formulated under stricter guidelines than the Federal budget. The national government does not ever have to balance its budget, but forty-nine states have balanced budget requirements. These state requirements take different forms. Thirty-five state constitutions require a balanced budget, while the other states only have a law or resolution that can be easily amended from year to year to allow deficit spending. Another variation in state budgeting is that fifteen of them pass budgets for two years at a time. Some prepare a two-year budget, while others pass two separate annual budgets for the two-year cycle.

You can see that budget planning is a major part of what government departments do. In the next lesson we will look at sample budgets from various levels of government.

Sunshine, Sunset

It is easier to get a government program started than it is to get one stopped. Some states and localities have adopted what are called sunset laws for certain programs. This means that authorization for the program will end at a stated point in the future. The program must be reconsidered for it to continue. The sunset provision is intended to make programs have accountability. If an agency or program is not accomplishing what it was created to do, it needs to be changed or abolished.

Sunset provisions are not the same as sunshine laws. Sunshine laws require government bodies to hold their meetings in public, especially when votes are taken. They also require freedom of access to most government documents. This prevents secret or backroom deals that are attempts to avoid accountability.

*I give my opinion in this matter,
for this is to your advantage,
who were the first to begin a year ago not only to do this,
but also to desire to do it.
2 Corinthians 8:10*

Lesson 57—Sample Government Budgets

A billion here, a billion there, and pretty soon you're talking about real money.
—Attributed to twentieth century Republican Senator Everett Dirksen of Illinois
(The statement reflects his attitude toward government spending,
though many doubt that he ever actually said it.)

The elements of a family budget are usually easy to identify. Income is recorded on the W-2 form (or equivalent) issued by the employer or by careful record keeping if the family's income is from self-employment. Expenses can be fairly accurately recorded as well. The family spends so much on the house payment, so much on utilities, so much on food, so much on clothes, so much on medical care, and so forth. Some purchases might be difficult to classify. For example, do cleaning supplies come out of household expenses or out of groceries? Does eating with another family at a restaurant count as food or as entertainment? Nevertheless, most families can determine the best way to break down their spending accurately.

Government budgets, by contrast, are terribly difficult to nail down. They involve huge amounts of money in a large number of categories. The information is not easy to find or to break down line by line. This is exactly what many government officials want. They have less accountability this way.

- For instance, do Social Security payments come out of the regular budget or are they a separate item? Are benefits paid to veterans to be considered military expenditures or social program expenditures?

- In addition, government budgets are difficult to examine. You may have a hard time finding a copy, and budgets are such huge and complicated documents that studying them is a frustrating experience. The budget and tax levy document for a rural county, for example, might contain 50 pages with many lines of figures in small print. The budget for the Federal government runs to hundreds of pages.

- Finally, state and local governments have become so dependent on Federal funding for much of what they do that it is difficult to determine what is actually state or local revenue and what is provided by Federal grants. State officials like to talk about how much they are spending on certain programs, but they might not mention that much of what they are spending comes from the Federal government.

In the 2000 election, candidates George W. Bush and Al Gore argued about the Social Security "lock box," meaning a guarantee that Social Security taxes will only be spent on Social Security expenses. However, there is no such lock box. There is a trust fund of excess Social Security tax collections from the past. The trust fund is used to buy government bonds as investments to increase the funds available for Social Security payments. Social Security contributions by individuals and employers are taxes, and payments to recipients come out of the Federal budget. If Social Security payments ever exceed Social Security revenue, the trust fund will have to be used to help make Social Security payments.

In addition, government budgets rarely decrease. Governments do not usually spend less one year in actual dollars than they did the previous year. A major part of the increase in the Federal budget is because of entitlement programs that are automatically increased year by year with at least a cost of living adjustment if not an actual increase in appropriations. When elected officials talk about budget cuts, they are often talking about a smaller increase than had been proposed, not a truly lower dollar amount from the previous year.

The chart shows the growth of the Federal budget from the 1960s. Major increases took place with Lyndon Johnson's Great Society programs in the 1960s and at other times. Even though Republicans have often complained about runaway government spending, the Federal budget continued to increase under Republican presidents and a Republican-controlled Congress.

The Federal Budget

The Federal budget for fiscal year 2007 that President Bush submitted to Congress in February 2006 called for $2,770,000,000,000.00 (that's $2.77 trillion) in spending. The general categories were as follows:

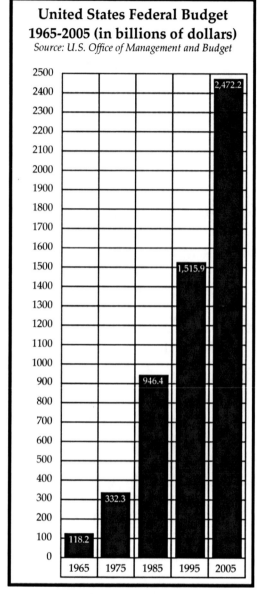

United States Federal Budget 1965-2005 (in billions of dollars)
Source: U.S. Office of Management and Budget

- Social Security: $586 billion or 21%

- Defense: $466 billion or 17%

- Medicare: $394.5 billion or 14%

- Unemployment and welfare assistance: $367 billion or 13%

- Medicaid and other health expenses: $276.4 billion or 10%

- Interest payments on the national debt: $244 billion or 8%

- Education and Training: $90 billion or 3%

- Transportation: $77 billion or 2.8%

- Veterans benefits: $72.6 billion or 2.6%

- Everything else (including justice, environment, agriculture, community development, energy, and governmental expenses—a $20.1 billion budget line in itself): the remaining 8.6%

All categories were increased over the previous budget except foreign affairs and energy.

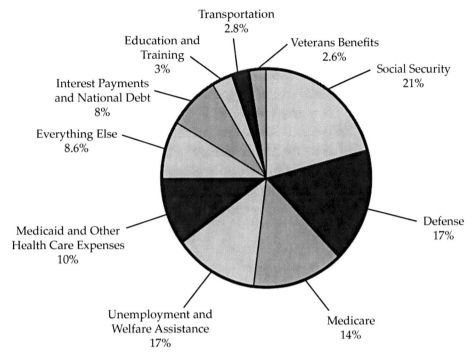

Within these general categories lie expenses for an almost endless list of programs. Here is one example. The community of Mt. Pleasant, Tennessee saw the construction of a community center that cost $1.2 million and was funded by the U.S. Department of Agriculture Rural Development Agency (*The [Columbia] Daily Herald*, February 10, 2006, page 1). If the Federal government is spending over a million dollars for one project in one small town in one county in Tennessee, we can begin to see why the entire Federal budget amounts to over two and three-quarters trillion dollars.

State Budgets

The budgets for state governments vary widely. The state government of New York planned to spend $110.7 billion in fiscal 2007. California's proposed 2007 budget called for almost $98 billion in spending. The Wyoming state budget, by contrast, was about $2.4 billion. Once again, we will consider the Tennessee state government's budget in more detail as our example.

The 2005-2006 budget for the state of Tennessee called for $25,927,600,600 in spending. Of this amount, 47% was on health and social services. The major part of this category, over $8 billion, was for the TennCare health care program (Tennessee's form of Medicaid) that provides health coverage for the poor and many others who do not have

Tennessee State Budget
Total Expenditures: 2005-2006

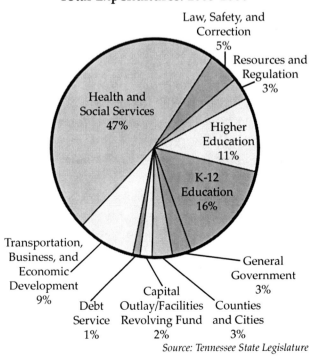

Source: *Tennessee State Legislature*

traditional health insurance. Another 27% (almost $7 billion) was allocated to education, from kindergarten through college. Transportation, business, and economic development received a total of 9% of the state's expenditures. Law, safety, and correction accounted for 5% of the state's spending. The expenses of operating state government totaled 3% of the budget. Another 3% was money sent to county and city governments.

The state's expenditure picture was a bit more complicated than this, however, because of the money provided by the Federal government. Of the $25.9 billion state outlay, a little less than $9.8 billion or about 37% came from the Federal government. Tennessee collects 45% of its funds through state taxes. The rest of its funds come from fee-based services and sale of long-term bonds. Of the Tennessee tax dollar, 41% is spent on education; 31% on health and social services; and 9% on law, safety, and correction. Since Tennessee receives significant Federal funds to help pay for the TennCare health program, proportionally more of the tax revenues generated by the state goes to education.

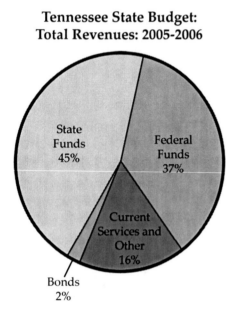

Tennessee State Budget:
Total Revenues: 2005-2006

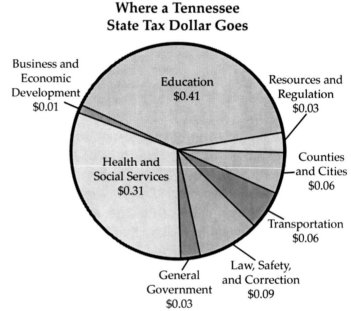

Where a Tennessee
State Tax Dollar Goes

Source: Tennessee State Legislature

> *Some of the revenue that a state receives from the Federal government is called "pass through" money, because it enters the state treasury but is earmarked for specific purposes and passes through directly to that expense. The state has no discretion on how it spends this money.*

County Budgets

Jackson County, Tennessee is a rural area. The county population is about 11,000 people. The largest community is Gainesboro, which has a population under 1,000. For the period July 1, 2005 to June 30, 2006, Jackson County government planned to spend just over $18 million. Of this amount:

- $10.6 million was for schools and another $903,000 was for cafeteria services.

- $3.3 million was earmarked for the broad category of general services, which includes county offices, the sheriff's department, and most other county expenses.

- $2.1 million funded the county's roads and public works departments.

- $577,000 was designated for the county's debts (such as school construction bonds)

- $354,000 paid for the county's solid waste and sanitation programs.

As with the state, an examination of the county's expenditures has to take into account funding from other sources. Fifty-nine percent ($9.4 million) of the county's revenue came from the state. Direct Federal grants accounted for just under one million dollars. Only 35%, or just over one-third of expenditures ($5.7 million), came from the county itself. Of the county's portion, over half was provided by the county property tax, while the rest came from the county's general fund that had $6.5 million in reserve (expenditures exceeded income in this budget by about $2 million). Thus, some of the state budget was included in the Federal budget, and some of the county budget was included in the state budget. These figures came from the Jackson County 2005-2006 budget document.

City Budgets

Finally, we look briefly at budget averages for municipalities. According to the National League of Cities, across the country cities spend:

- 21% of their budgets for safety (including police and fire protection)

- 21% for housing, waste disposal, and other environmental issues

- 14% for transportation (such as street repair and subsidizing city bus service)

- 12% for education (a lower figure than in a typical county since many cities depend on county or special district school systems)

- 11% for health, hospitals, and welfare

- 7% for administration costs.

The other 14% covers various smaller programs which might vary from city to city.

As with a family, a government's budget reflects its needs and priorities. To spend money, a government has to receive money. In the next lesson, we will analyze from where government revenues are derived.

Those deputies provided for King Solomon and all who came to King Solomon's table,
each in his month; they left nothing lacking.
They also brought barley and straw for the horses
and swift steeds to the place where it should be, each according to his charge.
1 Kings 4:27-28

Lesson 58—Sources of Federal Revenue

Our Constitution is in actual operation; everything appears to promise that it will last; but in this world nothing is certain but death and taxes.

—Benjamin Franklin (1789)

When a family needs more money, the father might change jobs to one that pays better, or he might take on a part-time job. Other family members might go to work or produce things in the home to sell. When a government needs more money, however, it cannot go out and govern more. Governments obtain more revenue by increasing taxes, enacting new taxes, or finding new sources of revenue such as imposing fees for certain services or creating a state lottery.

The sharp increase in government spending in recent years has meant that more and more money earned by Americans is being taken for government revenues. Americans have not always shouldered this heavy tax burden. In the early years of the country, the Federal government collected domestic taxes only on the production and sale of certain items such as alcoholic beverages, tobacco, carriages, and slaves. The War of 1812 was partly financed by a national sales tax on certain luxury items such as silverware, jewelry, and watches. In 1817, Congress ended internal taxes and financed the Federal government with tariffs imposed on imported goods. Since 1913, the Federal government has collected taxes on personal and corporate incomes.

Filing Income Taxes, c. 1920

The Federal Income Tax

The greatest single source of revenue for the Federal government is the income tax. It provides about sixty percent of Federal revenue.

The income tax is collected on the honor system. For most Americans, payment of the income tax begins with the process called withholding. Workers tell their employers at what rate they want their taxes withheld from their paychecks. The employer saves that money and sends that amount to the U.S. Treasury on behalf of the employee every three months. After the year ends, the employer gives the employee a statement, called the W-2 form. The W-2 tells how much the employee has earned and how much has been withheld and sent to the government.

The Tax Foundation computes what the average American pays in all taxes each year, including income tax, Social Security tax, sales tax, corporate taxes that are passed on to the consumer, and so forth. Based on the average American's income, the foundation annually announces Tax Freedom Day, the day when the average American has earned enough to pay all of his taxes based on a five-day work week. In 2005, Tax Freedom Day was April 17. Everything that the average American worker earned from January 1 to April 17 went to pay his taxes for the year. After that, he was able to work for himself.

Each individual is responsible to file a tax return by April 15. The return reports the individual's income, amounts that can be deducted from taxable income, and how much he owes in taxes. If too much has been withheld, the taxpayer is entitled to a refund. If too little has been withheld, he must pay the government the difference.

Withholding eases the burden on taxpayers by letting them pay their taxes throughout the year instead of forcing them to come up with the entire amount at tax filing time. It also lets the government be sure that it will in fact receive the taxes that are due. The government does not pay interest on the taxpayer's money that it holds until the tax returns are filed.

Self-employed persons have to maintain their own records and must make their own quarterly estimated tax payments to the government. Corporations file profit and loss statements with the government showing their income or loss for the year. On the basis of that information, corporations pay corporate income taxes.

The government assumes that a business honestly reports its profit or loss and the salaries that it pays to workers. The government also assumes that self-employed persons report all of their income and that hourly and salaried workers report all of their outside income that is not subject to withholding (such as tips received by restaurant servers and income from craft fairs and mowing lawns). Employers must send copies of the W-2 to the Internal Revenue Service (IRS). Banks and investment companies send copies of earnings statements both to investors and to the IRS. The information reported by employers is matched with the information reported by employees on their tax returns. When someone does not tell the truth to the IRS, they are subject to fines, the payment of back taxes with interest, and in some cases prison terms.

Members of the U.S. Air Force Work on an Income Tax Return at a Military Base in Germany, 2001

The Federal tax code is a dizzying assemblage of forms, requirements, exemptions, percentages, and loopholes. When an individual taxpayer reports his earnings, he does so on the IRS Form 1040 (or variations of it) with accompanying forms that provide relevant information such as interest income, self-employment income, rental income, and legitimate deductions. The taxpayer is entitled to a personal exemption of a certain amount of income each year on which he does not have to pay income tax. He or she can also claim an exemption for his dependents, the people for whom he provides most of the financial support. This most often refers to a taxpayer's children. The taxpayer can also claim certain deductions to be subtracted from his income before his tax is calculated. Deductions include medical expenses paid during the year, property taxes, interest on a home mortgage, and charitable contributions. He can take the standard deduction that the government offers or he can itemize (list) his deductions if the itemized total is higher.

When all of the exemptions and deductions have been subtracted from a person's gross income, what remains is taxable income. The tax rate is greater on higher incomes. This policy is called a progressive tax. It is based on the assumption that those with greater incomes can afford to pay a greater percentage in taxes and still be able to live comfortably.

This philosophy has been carried to an extreme in the past. The highest tax rate in the early 1960s was 91%. After a series of reductions, the top rate is now 28%. Still, the wealthiest Americans pay the majority of income taxes and the poorest pay no income taxes at all.

Social Security and Medicare Taxes

As we showed in an earlier lesson, Social Security and Medicare are a major part of what the Federal government does. Taxes to support these programs are listed separately but are withheld along with income tax. Social Security and Medicare taxes are paid by both the employee and the employer. The worker and the employer each pays 6.2% of the employee's income, up to an income of $94,200 per year, in Social Security (or FICA, Federal Insurance Contribution Act) taxes. Each also pays 1.45% in Medicare tax on all income (there is no income ceiling with Medicare as there is with Social Security). The employer portion is the government's way to make businesses contribute to retirement benefits for its workers and for all Americans. Thus a total of 15.3% of a person's income is paid to the government for Social Security and Medicare taxes (6.2% plus 1.45% of the worker's salary sent in by the employer; and 6.2% plus 1.45%—plus what he owes in income taxes—withheld from the employee's paycheck and sent to the government).

Keeping Individual Old-Age Insurance (Social Security) Records, 1930s

Self-employed persons must also pay Social Security and Medicare taxes, in accordance with the Self-Employment Contributions Act (SECA). At one time, self-employed persons paid a lower rate, but now a self-employed person is responsible for the entire 15.3% rate that covers both Social Security and Medicare. However, to ease the burden on self-employed persons, they pay this 15.3% rate on only 92.35% of their income, and they can subtract one-half of their self-employment tax as a deduction from their income before they figure their income taxes. I told you the Federal tax code was complicated!

Excise or luxury taxes are as close as we have come to a national sales tax. Countries such as the United Kingdom and Canada have a national sales tax called the Value Added Tax or VAT that can be as high as 18% of the purchase price. Supporters of a U.S. national sales tax (the rate of 23% has been suggested) to replace the income tax system say that it would be simpler than the complicated system we now have. A sales tax taxes consumption, not income. The more you buy, the more you pay. Most plans provide for poorer families to receive a rebate of the national sales taxes they pay. It would also be a way to tax the underground economy. No income tax is collected on illegal drug transactions, for instance; but when the persons involved in such activity make purchases, they would pay their fair share of taxes. One problem with creating a new avenue for the government to collect taxes is that the old avenues are still there. At some point both old and new will likely be used to generate revenue.

Other Sources of Federal Revenue

The Federal income tax provides most of the national government's revenue. The other 40% is generated by a wide array of sources.

- The government collects taxes on the sale of certain items, such as alcoholic beverages and tobacco products, gasoline, furs, jewelry, and guns.

- Customs or tariff duties are collected on items being imported into the country for sale.

- The capital gains tax is collected on the increased value that long-term investments acquire for the investor. This applies primarily to things like stocks and real estate owned for investment purposes. For many years, the increased value of a family home was taxed as a capital gain when the home was sold. This was quite a burden for the average American until the capital gains tax on the sale of residences under $500,000 for a married couple (under $250,000 for a single person) was repealed in 1997. The capital gains tax is seen by many as a way to generate tax revenue from people who have excess income to invest. Opponents of the tax say that it discourages investment.

- Estate or inheritance taxes are collected when an heir receives an inheritance from a deceased person in excess of $2 million. Most inheritances are below this amount. The rate on taxable estates is about 45%. Supporters of this tax say that a person who receives income in this way should be taxed for it. Opponents say that the estate has already had taxes paid on it as the deceased person built his wealth over his lifetime and therefore it should not be taxed again when someone inherits it.

- A gift tax is to be paid by the giver when he or she gives someone over $10,000 in one year. This tax is intended to prevent a person from shifting his wealth to someone else in order to avoid paying taxes on it or to avoid having it used to pay for such things as nursing home expenses. Some gifts are protected from taxes by certain laws, such as those governing education funds established by parents or grandparents.

- A Federal tax is charged on telephone service to help pay for Internet connections in public schools.

- A major source of Federal revenue is borrowing. For fiscal 2007, the government expected to spend $354 billion more than it would receive in revenues. This money was mostly borrowed by the sale of government bonds. This policy provides money for the short term, but it pushes the Federal government deeper in debt over the long term.

The rich rules over the poor,
and the borrower becomes the lender's slave.
Proverbs 22:7

Reading

- "The Moral Case for the Flat Tax" by Steve Forbes (*WHTT*, p. 158)

Aerial View of Washington, D.C., Showing the
Old Executive Office Building, the White House, and the U.S. Treasury

Lesson 59—State and Local Taxes

The truth is that all men having power ought to be mistrusted.

—James Madison

State and local governments need revenue to carry out the services that they render to the public. To raise this revenue, these governmental units employ a wide variety of taxes and fees.

State Income Tax

Forty-one states have imposed a state income tax on the regular earned income of residents and corporations. Two states, New Hampshire and Tennessee, only tax dividend and interest income above a certain amount. Seven states—Alaska, Florida, Nevada, South Dakota, Texas, Washington, and Wyoming—do not have a personal state income tax.

Just as with the Federal income tax, state income tax is withheld from paychecks and self-employed persons are required to make quarterly estimated payments of their tax liability. Residents (and others who earn income in the state, such as those who own rental property in one state but live in another state) send to the state department of revenue tax returns that are due the same time that Federal returns are due. States have lower income tax rates than the Federal income tax rate, and state returns are generally simpler to complete than the Federal forms. Montana's progressive rate runs between 2% and 11% of taxable income. California collects from 1% to 9.3% depending on the amount of income. Rates of 2% to 6% are common.

State Sales Tax

Taken as a whole, the fifty states collect about as much from personal income taxes as they do through state sales taxes. States that do not have a personal income tax rely more heavily on the sales tax for revenue. Sales taxes are collected at the time of purchase

Prudhoe Bay at the Northern End of the Trans-Alaska Pipeline

The state of Alaska receives substantial revenue from the sale of minerals exported from the state. The largest portion of this revenue comes from the oil sent through the Trans-Alaska Pipeline. A permanent fund has been created to invest and manage this income. Each year, the state gives a dividend from the fund's profits to every adult who has lived in the state for at least one year. In 2005 the dividend was about $845.00 each. The highest dividend so far was $1,963.86, which was the dividend paid for 2000.

by the seller, and the seller sends payments to the state revenue department once a month or once a quarter. Thus, those who conduct business in a state do the bulk of the work of collecting sales tax on behalf of the state government.

In most states, the state legislature sets a statewide rate but allows counties and cities to add an additional amount on sales occurring within their borders. Colorado collects only a 2.9% state sales tax, but localities can add up to 7% additional sales tax. Oklahoma's state rate is 4.5%. Local communities can add up to 6%, making a total possible tax rate of 10.5%. The Arkansas rate is 5.125% state and up to 5.5% local, giving a maximum combined sales tax of 10.625%. Counties receive all of the local sales tax plus a portion of the state sales tax collections. Hawaii has the lowest sales tax rate, charging a flat 4% statewide. The rate in Maine, Maryland, and Massachusetts is a flat 5% statewide. Alaska does not have a state sales tax, but localities may impose up to a 7% sales tax.

Grocery Store in Lincoln, Nebraska, 1942

Several exemptions to the sales tax are provided by the states. Churches and other charitable organizations are not generally charged sales tax on purchases they make. Some items, such as food and prescriptions, are in some states exempted from the sales tax or taxed at a lower rate. Professional services (doctor visits, plumbing calls, and so forth) are not taxed in all states, however some states do collect tax on certain services. Wholesale purchases (when a retail company buys something from a manufacturer or distributor to sell to the public) are not subject to sales tax, since sales tax will be paid by the retail customer.

Sales made in interstate commerce (a company in one state selling to someone who lives in another state) have traditionally not had to include sales tax, but this is changing. The practice of not charging sales tax on interstate sales has caused states to lose significant revenue from interstate sales made on the Internet. Because of this, some states have made an agreement to collect sales taxes on interstate Internet sales between participating states. Businesses will have to collect the sales tax for the customer's state of residence and send those revenues to the respective states on a regular basis.

The sales tax is often considered a regressive tax because it is not based on the person's ability to pay. Wealthy people pay the same sales tax on a loaf of bread or compact disc that poor people pay, but the sales taxes paid by a poor person make up a larger portion of their income than they do for wealthy people. This is why some states have exempted food and prescriptions from sales tax.

Other State Taxes

The next largest source of state revenue, after income tax and sales taxes, has to do with automobiles. Since vehicles play a big part of American life, and since they are such major purchases, states give special attention to how they can generate revenue from the sale, ownership, and use of vehicles.

States may impose their own sales tax on gasoline on top of the Federal gasoline tax. These revenues are generally used to help pay for road maintenance and construction. In addition, states charge a fee for registering vehicles and obtaining license plates. States assume that if you can afford to buy a car, you must be able to afford to register it with the state. This process not only raises revenue for the state, but it also gives the state a record of the vehicle in case it is stolen or is involved in an accident or traffic violation.

State governments can be quite creative when it comes to generating revenue through their citizens' ownership of cars. For instance, in Mississippi, the cost of license plates or annual renewal stickers is based on the value of the car. This is called an ad valorem tax (from the Latin for "to the value"). Thus, owners of newer and more expensive cars can expect to pay several hundred dollars for their license plates. The ad valorem tax that a car owner pays each year decreases over time as the value of the car decreases.

Other taxes that generate a significant amount of revenue for states include taxes on the sale of alcohol and tobacco and taxes paid by utilities and insurance companies to do business in the state. Taxes that have become popular with state and local governments in recent years are an amusement tax that is charged at theme parks and restaurants and a hotel/motel tax that is added to the price of a motel room. In some cases the taxes for staying in a motel room can add 15-18% to the basic rate. Some cities impose these taxes whether the state does or not. These taxes are attractive to governments because they are often collected from tourists who come from out of state or from business persons who have expense accounts and therefore do not feel the tax personally. Thus, a government can benefit from visitors without having to impose another tax on its residents.

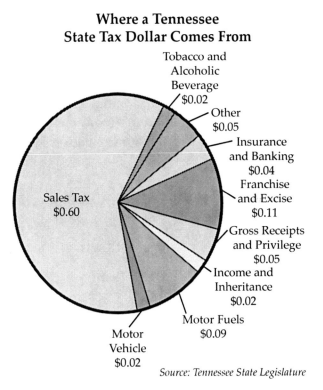

Where a Tennessee State Tax Dollar Comes From

Tobacco and Alcoholic Beverage $0.02
Other $0.05
Insurance and Banking $0.04
Franchise and Excise $0.11
Gross Receipts and Privilege $0.05
Income and Inheritance $0.02
Motor Fuels $0.09
Motor Vehicle $0.02
Sales Tax $0.60

Source: Tennessee State Legislature

County and Municipality Revenues

The major portion of a county's revenue comes from the property tax (some states charge property taxes also). Real property is a community's most valuable asset, and since it is protected by the local government it is taxed according to its value. The property assessor must consider every parcel of land and determine a value for it. Usually this assessed evaluation is somewhat less than the fair market value of the property (the price for which the property could be expected to sell). If a property owner believes the assessment is too high, he can request a hearing before the board of equalization, which will reconsider the assessor's decision.

A portion of the property's assessed worth, perhaps 25%, is taxed at the rate set by the county government for each hundred dollars of taxable assessed value. For instance, the property tax rate for a rural county might be $2.61 for each $100 of taxable assessed value. A person who owns a home assessed at $100,000 would pay $652.50 in property taxes for the year ($100,000 x 25%= $25,000, then $2.61 x 250 = $652.50). This rate is low compared to many counties in the country. Property tax rates in some places are three or four times this much.

Property taxes are always collected in arrears, or at the end of the period in question. In other words, the 2005 property tax was paid at the end of 2005 or the beginning of 2006.

Many home mortgages include an amount for property tax in each month's payment, and the lending institution pays the property tax on behalf of the property owner when it comes due.

Business property is also taxed. A store owner pays a higher property tax than a residence since the property is used to generate income. Business equipment (such as computers and printers) is taxed as real business property. Counties and cities might also collect a business tax, which is a small percentage of the total sales a business has during the year. Cities and counties can charge for a business license or a professional license, which is a fee for the right to conduct business in the locality.

Cities and counties can be imaginative in how they collect taxes. For example, several years ago in Lexington, Kentucky, the city could not impose a city income tax (the state already had a state income tax). However, to generate more revenue, the city imposed what was called a licensing fee, which was a fee of 2% of a person's income for the privilege of having a job in the city. It wasn't an income tax, they said, but it taxed a person's income.

According to the National League of Cities, the average municipality in the U.S. receives 29% of its revenue from charges and fees, 21% from property taxes, 21% from the state government, 5% from the Federal government, and the rest from other taxes and fees.

For the love of money is a root of all sorts of evil, and some by longing for it have wandered away from the faith and pierced themselves with many griefs.
1 Timothy 6:10

Harrisburg, Pennsylvania

Lesson 60—Tax Policy Issues

When more of the people's sustenance is exacted through the form of taxation than is necessary to meet the just obligations of government and expenses of its economical administration, such exaction becomes ruthless extortion and a violation of the fundamental principles of free government.

—President Grover Cleveland, 1886

It is generally assumed that a government will collect taxes and provide services. In this lesson, we will take a second look at what might be the best taxing and spending policies for a government to pursue.

What Should the Government Do?

It seems like the faint echo of a distant day and time to suggest that the Federal government was intended to be limited in its scope and powers and that it cannot do whatever Congress and the president might want to do. A few facts give us some historical perspective:

- A program of "internal improvements" (Federally-funded roads and canals) was hotly debated in the early nineteenth century as to whether it was an appropriate and constitutional undertaking by the Federal government.

- The establishment of a national bank was repeatedly a matter of political conflict during the same period. Its opponents (including President Andrew Jackson) believed that such a bank was unconstitutional since it was not specifically mentioned in the Constitution.

President Grover Cleveland

• President Grover Cleveland vetoed an appropriation of $10,000 in 1887 to help farmers in Texas who were suffering from a drought. In his veto message he said,

I can find no warrant for such an appropriation in the Constitution; and I do not believe that the power and duty of the General Government ought to be extended to the relief of individual suffering which is in no manner properly related to the public service or benefit. A prevalent tendency to disregard the limited mission of this power and duty should, I think, be steadily resisted, to the end that the lesson should be constantly enforced that, though the people support the Government, the Government should not support the people.

- Cleveland believed that private charities should and would assist the struggling farmers. He was right. The farmers received ten times more financial assistance from private sources than they would have received through this Federal appropriation. Perhaps the charitable impulse has been squelched today because many people believe the government will take care of everyone.

- When the Great Depression hit in 1929, the Federal government under Herbert Hoover provided assistance to states but not to individuals because Republicans did not believe such individual assistance to be an appropriate function of the Federal government.

Today, few question whether a government should undertake the programs that it does. With this outlook, it is no wonder that our taxes are getting higher and higher.

President Herbert Hoover
Signing the Farm Relief Bill, 1929

What Is a Taxable Event?

Here again, it seems that government generally will try to tax anything it is not specifically prevented from taxing (for example, states are not permitted to tax Federal lands, and export tariffs are specifically prohibited in the Constitution). The earning of income by private citizens is accepted as a taxable event. The purchase of most retail items is seen as a taxable event. The inheritance of a large estate is seen as a taxable event. The increase in capital worth (as in stocks and, until recently, the rise in property value of a home) is seen as a taxable event.

Does Lowering Taxes Help the Economy?

When President John Kennedy proposed cutting taxes to stimulate the economy, he justified the proposal by saying that a rising tide lifts all boats. Cutting taxes would seem to hurt the government's ability to generate revenue, but in fact cutting taxes has been shown to stimulate the economy so much that the government actually receives more revenue. This was demonstrated with the tax cuts enacted under Presidents Reagan and George W. Bush.

The answer to economic problems and personal difficulties is not always more government spending. Many times more government spending means more government bureaucrats but little help reaching those in need. What will help most is less government spending, which enables people to save, invest, and spend more of their own money as they see fit.

What Should Be the Goal of Tax Policy?

The government's collection of taxes should be undertaken to provide revenue for government to render necessary services: military defense, police and fire protection, and so forth. However, governments often use taxing and spending policies to regulate the economy and to accomplish other goals. For instance, high import tariffs do not just raise revenue. They provide protection for domestic companies against cheaper imported goods. This appears to be a good thing, but the result can be that domestic companies might not be motivated to produce goods economically or of high quality if they have no fear of foreign competition.

Tax policies should not attempt to reward or punish certain segments of the economy. The tax code is huge and complex because so many special provisions have been enacted that reward certain businesses and those with a certain level of income. What those businesses and individuals don't pay, average Americans (who don't have a strong lobby in Congress or luxury resorts to offer Congressmen) wind up paying. Sometimes attempts to punish by taxes backfire. As part of the tax increases enacted under President Clinton, a luxury tax was added to the price of yachts. This would seem a fair enough tax to the average American, but the added tax severely hurt the yacht-building industry and caused layoffs that wound up costing the government because it had to pay unemployment benefits.

Sometimes states, counties, and cities offer tax breaks to big companies in an effort to attract them to a particular location. The county government might offer to waive the business property tax for ten years, for instance. In return for this, the county hopes that having the business or industry there will create jobs and generate revenue in other ways. Places that are competing for businesses to come can get into bidding wars to see how attractive they can make the package offered to a prospective business. Some large companies have been known to demand such concessions and tax abatements before they will consider building in a locality. Of course, smaller businesses and local property owners do not get offers of tax cuts. In fact, they have to pay more for the services that the big company uses. Some companies make payments in lieu of taxes, and the Federal government makes payments if a large amount of county land is owned by the Federal government (such as a military base) and thus cannot be taxed by the local authority.

When the policy is complicated and is used to accomplish purposes other than generating needed revenue, it can adversely affect many people.

Fort Gillem Military Base near Atlanta, Georgia

How Big Should Government Spending (and Deficits) Be?

Indebtedness can be a heavy weight for a family to bear. It can come to dominate the thinking of the family and make a calm, peaceful life almost impossible. The debt of a home mortgage can be less of a problem, since most homes increase in value. However, buying too much house, being saddled with a huge mortgage payment, or having a long-term mortgage that requires paying the purchase price two or three times in interest can be financially paralyzing situations.

Yearly budget deficits and a constantly increasing debt would be indicators of fiscal irresponsibility for a family. It is no different with the government. We all should be willing to get by with less so that the government can regain fiscal soundness. Our government should not consistently spend more than it takes in. This means that hard choices have to be made and not every government program might be able to continue, but government action is not the only way to get things done. Some other countries, such as Ireland, New Zealand, and Slovakia, have found that cutting government spending greatly helps the economy.

President Warren Harding
Addressing Budget Committee, 1923

On the other hand, Federal spending in the U.S. is about one-fifth of the gross domestic economy, and the deficit is an even smaller percentage. Government spending in the U.S. is a much smaller part of the economy than is the case in European countries. The situation in the U.S. is not as dire as it could be, but the trend is not favorable.

Should Churches Be Tax-Exempt?

The exemption that churches receive from paying most taxes has been an element of the freedom of religion that we enjoy in this country. As John Marshall pointed out, the power to tax involves the power to destroy. However, the tax-exemption of churches has allowed certain individuals to build huge financial empires from which they derive enormous personal gain (which is usually taxed). Some religious groups own valuable pieces of property and pay no taxes on them. To have churches pay their fair share of property taxes and sales taxes might help spread the burden of taxation more evenly among the populace, but admittedly it might also cause a strain on smaller congregations. As difficult as having to pay taxes might be for churches, it is worth noting that the church has grown most in times and places where it was not privileged but in fact was persecuted.

These questions invite us to look again at the underlying assumptions of our system of taxing and spending. To change the direction that government has been going for decades would mean a major change in our thinking, our expectations of government, and our personal initiative and responsibility. However, if we want the direction of government to change, the change has to start somewhere. If we keep doing what we are doing now, we will continue getting what we already have.

He who is faithful in a very little thing
is faithful also in much;
and he who is unrighteous in a very little thing
is unrighteous also in much.
Therefore if you have not been faithful in the use of unrighteous wealth,
who will entrust the true riches to you?
Luke 16:10-11

Issues Facing American Government Today

13 International Relations

A major role of the United States government today is as a participant in the community of nations. This unit considers the topic of diplomacy in general and then presents four issues in contemporary foreign policy: trade, terrorism, the United Nations, and the difficult subject of human rights in other countries.

Lessons in This Unit

Activity Idea

In his speech in *We Hold These Truths*, Mark Steyn presents arguments for the United States withdrawing from the United Nations. What do you think? Is the UN hopelessly corrupt and in the pocket of anti-American forces, or is the UN our best hope for world peace—or is there a middle way? Discuss in a two-or-three page paper what you think America's role in the world—and particularly in the UN—should be.

If you are using the optional *Quiz and Exam Book*, answer the questions for each lesson after you have completed the lesson and read any assigned readings in *We Hold These Truths*. After you have completed Lesson 65, take the quiz for Unit 13.

Lesson 61—Diplomacy

Wars were too common in diplomacy to disturb the habits of the diplomat. . . . If the American Minister was in trouble today, the Russian Ambassador was in trouble yesterday, and the Frenchman would be in trouble to-morrow. It would all come in the day's work. There was nothing professional in worry. Empires were always tumbling to pieces and diplomats were always picking them up.
—Henry Adams, The Education of Henry Adams *(1907)*

The United States has always been involved with other nations. Our country began by breaking away from Great Britain, from where most colonists had come. A key factor in the American victory in the War for Independence was the recognition and assistance given by France during the war. Not many years later, America fought Great Britain again in the War of 1812. Then came the Mexican War from 1846 to 1848. In addition to being in these conflicts, the United States has always carried on trade and diplomatic relations with many countries of the world.

> *The word diplomacy comes from a Greek word meaning a folded paper. The word diploma comes from the same root. Diplomats usually try to portray their own country and other countries in as positive a light as possible. Trying to be tactful and choosing one's words carefully in any context is called being diplomatic.*

From the time of the Spanish-American War of 1898, the pace of American involvement in the world increased dramatically. The United States was drawn into World War I, but then we tried to pull back to a position of isolation from the rest of the world during the 1920s and 1930s. The growing threat of aggression in Europe and Asia in the late 1930s led the U.S. to become involved in world affairs once again. Beginning with our participation in World War II and continuing through the founding of the United Nations, the rise of the Communist threat around the world, and the war against terrorism, international relations have been a major issue for the United States government.

Embassy Row is the informal name of an area in the Georgetown portion of the District of Columbia in which foreign embassies are located. This photograph shows the Embassy of Niger.

The Process of Diplomacy

The president is head of state for the United States. This means that he is responsible for conducting relations with other countries. According to Article II, Section 2 of the U.S. Constitution, the president is responsible for nominating ambassadors, public ministers, and consuls (with the Senate's consent) to be our country's official representatives in other nations. Section 3 declares that the president shall receive ambassadors and other public ministers who are official representatives of other countries.

Diplomatic relations between two countries begin with an announcement of formal recognition, a decision for which the president is responsible. After formal recognition, the two countries exchange ambassadors. Ambassadors and consuls are appointed by the president with the approval of the Senate. An ambassador is the highest ranking official representative of one country in another country. His office is called the embassy. The president chooses people to be ambassadors for a number of reasons. The nominee might know the country well, or he might be a skilled negotiator, or he might be someone for whom the president would like to do a political favor. Sometimes a major financial contributor is named to be an ambassador to a country that has a peaceful relationship with the United States. Countries where problems exist need more skilled diplomats.

A consul is a representative of a foreign government that assists individuals and businesses who are from the consul's home country. The consulate office might issue travel visas or assist a business wanting to do work in the consul's home country. Consulate offices might be in any major city, not necessarily the nation's capital. Full diplomatic recognition is not required before establishing a consulate office.

The president also sometimes receives other official representatives from foreign countries for meetings. These official meetings might also include the Secretary of State and other representatives of the U.S. Government.

> *Diplomatic tradition recognizes two roles: the head of state and the head of government. In the United Kingdom, the monarch is the head of state while the prime minister is the head of government. Several European nations also make this distinction. In the United States, the president is both head of state and head of government. This distinction has been described as the difference between reigning and ruling. In Great Britain, for instance, the monarch reigns, but the prime minister rules.*

The Importance of Diplomatic Recognition

Diplomatic recognition says that one government believes the government of another country is legitimate. Withholding recognition says that a government does not believe those holding power in another country are the legitimate rulers. Events in other countries sometimes make the decision to extend recognition a difficult one. For instance, when a revolution occurs in a country and the military seizes control, the president has to decide whether to recognize the new government as legitimate or to continue to maintain that the deposed government was legitimate and should be restored.

The importance of diplomatic recognition can be seen in two examples from American history. France's recognition of the United States during the War of Independence was important in giving the new American government legitimacy in the world community of nations. Years later, the U.S. government worked hard to keep other countries from granting official recognition to the Confederacy during the Civil War. This would have legitimized the rebellion of the Southern states in the eyes of the world and perhaps drawn other countries into the conflict if they had provided assistance to the Confederacy. The Confederate states never received official diplomatic recognition from another country and did not exchange ambassadors with any other nation, although Confederate negotiators were sent to Great Britain and other countries.

Diplomatic recognition can sometimes be used for economic and political advantage. In the early 1900s, the French company that had the rights to build a canal through the isthmus of Panama sold the rights to the United States. At the time, Panama was part of the country of Colombia. The Colombian government placed huge demands on the United States for the U.S. to be able to work on the canal. At this point, a group of people in the province of Panama declared their independence from Colombia (with the help and encouragement of President Theodore Roosevelt) as the new nation of Panama. Roosevelt recognized the new Panamanian government as legitimate in 1903 and signed a deal with it to build the canal. This arrangement was more favorable to the U.S. than the terms that had been demanded by Colombia.

Diplomatic recognition (or the withholding of it) can also make a statement of approval or disapproval. The Communist revolution took place in Russia in 1917, but the United States did not grant formal diplomatic recognition of that government until Franklin Roosevelt did so in 1933. When Communists took control of China in 1948, the United States continued to recognize the Nationalist government that had fled to the island of Taiwan as the real government of China. It was not until 1979 that the American government recognized the Communist government of China as legitimate. The U.S. has never recognized the legitimacy of the Castro regime in Cuba. This withholding of recognition has been a way for the United States government to express formal disapproval of the Communist regimes in these countries. However, recognition does not necessarily imply approval of a government. Formal recognition can simply be the admission that a particular government holds legitimate authority in the country.

If the United States does not recognize a government, it can still carry on relations with that country through a third country that both countries do recognize. However, those relations are usually strained. American travel to and trade with the unrecognized country are difficult if not impossible.

Relations between governments that recognize each other can sometimes deteriorate. When serious conflict develops, the president can call an ambassador home or order a foreign ambassador to leave the U.S. The next step is to sever diplomatic relations and close the embassy.

The Intricate Nature of Diplomacy

A basic principle that usually is at work in foreign relations is that a nation will generally act out of its own self-interest. France, for instance, did not form an alliance with the United States during the American Revolution because of any French commitment to the cause of democracy and freedom. France was

The U.S. Ambassador to Pakistan and the Chairman of the Joint Chiefs of Staff Meet with the Pakistani President, 2008

still a monarchy at the time. France was willing to help the U.S. because France and Britain were traditional enemies, and the French government was willing to do anything it could to weaken Great Britain.

The United States government sends billions of dollars in foreign aid to many countries. Some of this is provided to long-time allies and to poor countries out of a sincere desire to do good for people in need. In other situations, however, the aid has some strings attached. During the Cold War between the U.S. and the Soviet Union, both powers sent aid to smaller countries in order to win their support or to keep those countries from officially aligning with the enemy. The American aid that is sent is to be used to fund specific programs in the smaller country, such as agricultural development or the construction of schools. Often, however, at least some of the money has gone into the pockets of government leaders.

At times, international diplomacy and the complicated nature of world relations has made for some interesting alignments. In the 1930s, Adolph Hitler of Germany and Josef Stalin of the Soviet Union signed a treaty promising that neither country would attack the other. Hitler later invaded the Soviet Union. Since Stalin was now an enemy of Germany and the U.S. was an enemy of Germany, this made the U.S. and the Soviet Union allies fighting together. However, the U.S. had deep suspicions about the Soviets; and almost immediately after the war the U.S. and the Soviet Union became adversaries. Once their common enemy was gone, the two former allies found more reasons to oppose each other than to continue their alliance.

In the late 1970s, the revolutionary government of Iran was strongly anti-American, largely because the U.S. had supported the deposed Shah of Iran. Iranian militants took over the U.S. embassy in Tehran and held Americans hostage for over a year. That crisis was eventually resolved, but then neighboring Iraq attacked Iran for its own purposes. Since Iraq was fighting an enemy of the U.S., the American government gave support to Iraq and Saddam Hussein in its war against Iran. After that war was over, Iraq drew closer to other enemies of America in the Middle East, so the U.S. found itself opposing a country that it had once assisted.

The different countries of the world have varying interests and various ways of pursuing their interests. The government of Switzerland, for instance, will pursue its goals differently from the way that the government of North Korea does. Leaders of nations have various motives for what they do. Sometimes a leader is facing domestic opposition, so he will create or magnify conflict with another country to try to get his people to rally around his leadership. Diplomatic relations are intended to prevent wars whenever possible, to produce mutual benefits for all countries involved, and to provide assistance for a country when it is attacked by another country. One reason why the United States encourages democracy in other countries is that, generally speaking, democracies do not go to war against each other. Considering the high stakes that are involved, foreign relations are an important function of American government.

Now it happened afterwards that the king of the Ammonites died, and Hanun his son
became king in his place. Then David said, "I will show kindness to Hanun
the son of Nahash, just as his father showed kindness to me."
So David sent some of his servants to console him concerning his father.
But when David's servants came to the land of the Ammonites, the princes
of the Ammonites said to Hanun their lord, "Do you think that David
is honoring your father because he has sent consolers to you? Has David not
sent his servants to you in order to search the city, to spy it out and overthrow it?"
2 Samuel 10:1-3

Reading

- "Morality and Foreign Policy: Reagan and Thatcher" by Edwin Meese III (*WHTT*, p. 163)

Lesson 62—Trade

Free trade consists simply in letting people buy and sell as they want to buy and sell. Protective tariffs are as much applications of force as are blockading squadrons, and their objective is the same: to prevent trade. The difference between the two is that blockading squadrons are a means whereby nations seek to prevent their enemies from trading; protective tariffs are a means whereby nations attempt to prevent their own people from trading.

—Henry George, Protection or Free Trade *(1886)*

Trade starts out simply. I have something, and you have something else. I want some of what you have and you want some of what I have. We decide on what is a fair trade. Mine is twice as valuable as yours because it took twice as long to make. I give you one of mine, you give me two of yours, and the trade is done. After I go away from the trade, I might trade what I got in the exchange to another person for something else, or I might trade something else I made to another person for the item he has, or I might return to you as a repeat customer.

Beyond this level, matters can get complicated. Instead of the barter exchange described in the first paragraph, we might decide to buy or sell items for amounts of money. People called agents, salesmen, or middlemen might do the trading for us and charge a fee for their services. Trade can involve several steps if we go to one source for raw materials, another source for the machinery to make the goods, outsource part of it to another manufacturer, and then sell it at a wholesale price to someone else who will then sell it at retail. I might be set up to make the goods but not to sell them, while the retailer is set up to sell goods but not make them.

Then the government gets involved. I have to register my business and pay a license fee. The government can make regulations about how the goods are made (no child labor, safe working conditions in the factory, accurate information on the label and in advertising, for instance) and how they are transported to market (in safe and registered trucks, that pay taxes for using the roads). The government can decide to tax the sale of the goods and tax the income that I make from selling them.

When trade is conducted between countries, it gets even more complicated. Each country has its own regulations for buying and selling. The company that transports the goods has to be registered. A country's government can decide that certain items may not be imported into it (no fresh fruit or meat from a particular country, for example). If the shoe industry in a country, for instance, makes a good enough case for protection to its government, the government might forbid the importation of shoes or impose an import tariff so high that imported shoes will not find many buyers. The government of another country might subsidize its shoemakers so that, even with the tariff, its shoes can be priced low enough to compete with shoes made in the target country.

International trade involves private American companies providing goods and services to other countries and our receiving goods and services from those other countries or from companies in those countries. The role of the U.S. government is to allow and encourage trade, or, alternatively, to hinder or forbid trade with countries that the government does not want to help.

Trade Agreements

Before World War II, the United States trade policy primarily involved setting tariff rates for imported goods. Whenever the tariff schedule was up for a vote in Congress, intense debate took place on the relative merits of free trade versus protectionism. Tariff rates would be raised or lowered according to which party was in power and what the accepted wisdom of trade policy was at the time. American business and labor tried to influence Congress to favor the American economy, which often meant encouraging higher tariffs and a policy of protectionism.

In 1944, representatives of the 45 Allied nations in World War II met at Bretton Woods, New Hampshire, to formulate a plan for postwar recovery and trade. An international bank was organized to finance reconstruction of war-ravaged countries. In addition, the International

Representatives at Bretton Woods, 1944

Trade Organization (ITO) was created to establish regulations for trading between nations. The ITO agreement was not ratified by the U.S. Senate; but what came out of that organization was the General Agreement on Tariffs and Trade (GATT), rules that governed trade for countries who signed on to it. In 1995, the World Trade Organization (WTO) took over administration of the GATT. The United States has participated in GATT and the WTO. The WTO now has 150 member countries.

The WTO encourages countries to erect as few trade barriers as possible. Its member countries are to be as free of discrimination as possible (that is, not having policies that treat countries unfairly because of religious, ethnic, or racial differences). WTO members want predictable trade conditions so that political unrest will not interrupt trade agreements. Member nations are also encouraged to accommodate poorer or developing nations by granting them more favorable terms when making trade agreements with them.

Today, U.S. trade policy primarily involves individual agreements with various countries and with united blocs of countries such as the European Union (EU). The goal that countries have in trading with the U.S. is to receive Most Favored Nation (MFN) status from the American government. A country that is declared to be an MFN is guaranteed to receive trade considerations that are the best that the U.S. gives to any other country. Today about 180 countries (almost all the countries of the world) have MFN status with the United States. This status is also called Normal Trade Relations, since only a few countries do not enjoy this status with the U.S.

NAFTA

The North American Free Trade Agreement (NAFTA) was passed by Congress in 1993. It created a free-trade zone among the U.S., Canada, and Mexico. Canada and the U.S. already had a free-trade agreement, and tariffs placed by Mexico on U.S. products shipped there are being phased out over several years.

The NAFTA proposal was a major issue in the 1992 U.S. presidential campaign. Incumbent Republican President George H. W. Bush (who oversaw the drafting of the agreement) and Democratic candidate Bill Clinton both supported the agreement, but Reform party candidate Ross Perot warned of a "giant sucking sound" that would be caused by jobs being pulled away from American workers to Mexico if NAFTA were ratified. Labor unions generally opposed the agreement, fearing the loss of jobs for American workers. Businesses generally supported the measure, thinking that removing tariffs and being able to build factories in Mexico where labor costs are cheaper would increase their profits.

What has come about since NAFTA was ratified has been a combination of effects. More factories are being built in Mexico by American companies, but the economies of all three countries have actually grown. The U.S. unemployment rate has remained relatively low, although some American workers have lost their jobs because of companies moving production facilities to Mexico. Mexican farmers and farm workers have been hurt because U.S. farm goods can be sold more cheaply in Mexico than goods grown in Mexico.

A similar agreement called CAFTA (Central American Free Trade Agreement) was passed by Congress in 2005. It deals with trade between the U.S. and the Central American countries of Costa Rica, El Salvador, Guatemala, Honduras, Nicaragua, and the Dominican Republic. Many political liberals and environmentalists opposed CAFTA, expressing fears of low wages for workers, a lack of government regulation in the Central American countries involved, and damage to the environment of Central America where factories were to be built.

Technically, these two agreements were not proposed as treaties but are considered part of U.S. law. This way, they needed only a simple majority vote in Congress instead of the two-thirds majority that the Constitution requires for treaties.

Trade with China

The People's Republic of China was established in 1949, when Communist forces overthrew the government of Nationalist Chinese leader Chiang Kai-shek. Chiang and his followers fled to the island of Taiwan off the Chinese coast, and they continued to declare themselves to be the legitimate government for all of China. The Taiwanese government continues to make this claim today, while the mainland government believes Taiwan is simply part of China.

The United States recognized the Taiwan government for many years but began to establish contacts with the Communist government in 1972. In 1979, the U.S. formally recognized the People's Republic of China as the legitimate government. The United States does not recognize the Taiwanese government, but Americans are still able to travel to and trade with Taiwan (by going through a third country first). Communist China was granted MFN status in 1980. This status was renewed each year by the President, although Congress could have voted to rescind it. In 1999, Congress voted to give China permanent Normal Trade Relations or MFN status. This enabled China to join the WTO.

American trade with Communist China has skyrocketed in recent years. In 1985, the U.S. exported $3.856 billion to China and imported $3.862 billion, resulting in a slight trade deficit. In 2000, our exports to China were $16.1 billion while we imported about $100 billion, leaving a deficit of $84 billion. In 2005, the U.S. exported almost $42 billion in goods to China and imported $243.5 billion in goods from China, resulting in a trade deficit with China of over $200 billion for the year.

Defenders of this increased trade with Communist China say that it has opened China to American products and introduced a greater understanding of capitalism there. In many cases, the products we import from China were not once made in America but instead were once imported from other countries. Detractors of trade with China say that the trend puts the U.S. at an economic disadvantage which might develop into a political and military disadvantage if the U.S. becomes dependent on Chinese goods. Our exports to China have not kept pace with our imports from there because Americans are more likely to purchase inexpensive Chinese goods than the Chinese are to purchase more expensive American goods. Critics also say that wages are low and working conditions are often poor in China, and increasing our trade with China simply endorses this situation. We will discuss the role of trade in the context of the issue of human rights later in this unit.

Is Truly Free Trade Possible?

If I want what you have and you want what I have and we make a trade, that is the essence of free trade. Ideally, the countries of the world would impose no trade restrictions or artificial tariffs; and goods would flow freely among the nations. The rising tide of economic growth, technological advancement, and government fairness and compassion would lift all national boats and improve the material well-being of all people in those nations.

However, that does not happen. When I impose a tariff, that interrupts free trade. When you underbid my price by holding wages low for your workers and refusing to give them the right to protest, that interrupts free trade. When a government subsidy to an industry enables the selling price of an item to be lower, that interferes with free trade. Free trade often has a cost, and sometimes that cost is the job of a worker you know who becomes unemployed because his factory closes and production is moved to another country. However, this displacement can be temporary as new industries develop and a new kind of factory opens in the U.S. What could be happening in the long run is a leveling of economic conditions around the world.

The goal of the American government is to promote trade that is as free as possible around the world, based on the belief that this will bring about the most benefit for the most people with as little government interference as possible. This will likely be an ongoing process, with greater or lesser degrees of freedom in various countries instead of a once-and-for-all accomplishment of completely free trade.

Come now, you who say,
"Today or tomorrow we will go to such and such a city,
and spend a year there and engage in business and make a profit."
Yet you do not know what your life will be like tomorrow.
You are just a vapor that appears for a little while
and then vanishes away. Instead, you ought to say,
"If the Lord wills, we will live and also do this or that."
James 4:13-15

Lesson 63 — Terrorism

Maybe the purpose of all this is to find out if America today is as strong as when we fought for our independence or when we fought for ourselves as a Union to end slavery or as strong as our fathers and grandfathers who fought to rid the world of Naziism and communism. The terrorists were counting on our cowardice. They've learned a lot about us since then. And so have we.

—Rudolph Giuliani, at a funeral for a friend following the September 11, 2001 terrorist attacks on the U.S.

Remains of the World Trade Center

Our world changed on September 11, 2001. Perhaps it shouldn't have. We had seen the use of terror many times, especially in the Middle East. American military personnel had been the victims of terrorist attacks in Lebanon in 1983 and on the USS Cole in Yemen in 2000. We had even seen a terrorist bomb explode in the underground garage of the World Trade Center in 1993, killing and injuring innocent civilians. The 9/11 attacks, however, brought the threat of terrorism into our consciousness with full force. It also triggered a war on the forces of terrorism in other parts of the world, especially in Afghanistan and Iraq. The work of the American government today includes countering the forces of terrorism. This effort has several facets.

Elements of the War on Terrorism

The first step in the war on terror is to understand the thinking of the terrorists. Islamic terrorists believe that they are doing the will of Allah and that they are promised blessings in Paradise when they give their lives to kill those whom they see as enemies of Allah. People are seen as enemies of Allah for at least two reasons. (1) Enemies of Allah are Christians and Jews and those who help Christians or Jews. Islamic terrorists especially hate the nation of Israel and her allies, which include the U.S. and Great Britain. Muslims believe that they have the right to control the land of Palestine and that the existence of Israel stands in the way of their claiming that right. (2) Muslim terrorists hate what they see as enemies of the standards of Allah. To them, the West, with its impure movies and scantily-dressed women, is a cultural force that is in conflict with the way of Allah and should be destroyed.

It is not at all the case, however, that those who plan and encourage terrorist activity are motivated by noble ideas for the betterment of society. Israel, the United States, and Western culture are handy scapegoats for those who want to exercise control over their people and who want to shirk their responsibility for bettering the lives of their people.

A second part of the war on terror is recognizing who the terrorists are. Not all Muslims are terrorists. In most cases terrorists are organized into underground, widely-scattered cells of activists who maintain a loose network of communication and support. Generally they are not agents of a recognized government. However, governments can give them aid and protection. The result when governments do assist terrorists is called state-sponsored terrorism. It is assumed, for instance, that terrorists are living in the U.S. and Great Britain; but the governments of these countries oppose terrorists and want to stop their activities. On the other hand, the governments of such countries as Syria, Iran, and (until Saddam Hussein was removed from power) Iraq have been known to give assistance to terrorists. The al-Qaeda terrorist operations in Afghanistan were aided by the government of that country until the Afghan government was overthrown in 2001 as a result of the U.S.-led invasion.

Third, governments who oppose terrorists want to identify any individuals, groups, or governments who give any assistance to terrorists. Terrorists need supplies and weapons. They can obtain these in a number of ways. Sometimes government funds are given to terrorists in a way that will be difficult to trace. In addition, wealthy individuals might use their resources to help fund terrorists. It is also generally believed that illegal activities in many places around the world such as drug trafficking are a way terrorists obtain money. Governments who oppose terrorists have to use diplomatic efforts and secret investigations to discover who might be supporting terrorists and how they are doing it.

U.S., Canadian, and Afghani Soldiers Join Forces on a Mission Which Includes Searching for Osama Bin Laden, 2002

Fourth, governments must use military force to oppose terrorists and to stop their planning and activity. This is what the United States and its allies have accomplished in Afghanistan and Iraq. The usual rules of diplomacy cannot work against people who are willing to blow up themselves and others. They must be stopped by force before they can act. This involves not only responding when terrorists strike but also, ideally, locating and stopping terrorists before they strike.

How the Government Opposes Terrorism

The United States government pursues many lines of activity to oppose, limit, and eliminate terrorists. It engages in diplomacy to encourage the governments of other nations to join with us in working against terrorism. The U.S. also confronts governments that are suspected of or are involved in state-sponsored terrorism. Our government uses secret operations, including the work of informants, to find out where the underground cells are located and who the specific individuals are that are involved in these activities. A major part of the work of the U.S. military is engaging in operations against terrorists.

Somehow the nineteen men who hijacked the four planes on September 11, 2001 got into the country and had been living here for some time. The government wants to keep this from happening again. To accomplish this, the government must closely monitor those who enter the country and what foreign nationals do once they are in the country. Sometimes these foreign nationals have contact with American citizens who are sympathetic to their cause. To obtain as much information as possible, the government might sometimes have to invade the privacy of American citizens by intercepting mail, phone calls, emails, and other data regarding personal activities. American law has established channels by which this can be done. The Bush administration has engaged in such surveillance and has been criticized for violating personal rights and privacy. It is not always easy to determine who a terrorist is or whether the people he communicates with are innocent or complicit. If we have to choose, it does seem better for government investigators to read a few irrelevant emails than to allow another 9/11 to happen.

The war on terrorism includes having an intelligent and effective immigration policy that keeps potential terrorists out of the country. It also involves investigations into the transfer of money and weapons. After all, a leader of a foreign government or a wealthy Arab is not going to hand a terrorist leader an envelope of money while they are standing on a street corner.

Our government is also involved in gathering intelligence in other countries. The governments of those countries might harbor terrorists or they might simply look the other way (especially if they are threatened by the terrorists themselves). The U.S. also works with the intelligence departments of other countries and international agencies such as INTERPOL (the International Police Organization) in gathering relevant information.

A Difficult Mission

When the United States was at war with Germany and Japan, our military, diplomatic, and intelligence-gathering efforts were focused ultimately on Berlin and Tokyo. We knew where the headquarters of our enemies' operations were located, however far-flung and complicated those operations were. In the war on terror, tracking down the enemy and his lines of

> In the spring of 2006, the Bush administration announced a deal to sell the operations at six major U.S. ports to a company owned by the government of the United Arab Emirates (UAE). The UAE has been linked to terrorists. The administration gave assurances that security standards would not be compromised at the ports, but critics sharply questioned the deal as being unwise because of the possibility of terrorist infiltration at American ports and because of the appearance of compromising domestic security. The ports deal was eventually canceled.

communication and supply is a more complicated task. Terrorist leaders usually remain in hiding. Their support may come from countries with whom we are officially at peace. The terrorist network is purposefully loose and secretive. Our military and our homeland security forces must be constantly on the alert for an unexpected attack in an unsuspected place. Many Americans, for example, have had to submit to more thorough security measures in airports.

The effort against terrorism is huge and will not be easily won. We have to be willing to support a long-term battle in order to achieve greater physical security within our country and around the world. Our government has a heavy responsibility to protect our freedoms and our personal rights while at the same time tracking down those who threaten those freedoms and rights. We cannot live in fear and let the terrorists win by paralyzing our way of life. We can trust above all else the One who knows all things and who will accomplish righteousness and justice in the end.

The real answer to terrorism and hatred is the changing of hearts by the gospel of Jesus. This is an especially difficult challenge in countries where it is illegal to evangelize in the name of Jesus; however, amazing and encouraging reports of Muslims being converted to Christ are trickling out of the Muslim world. The war on terror is another example of how government can be helpful but is not the source of ultimate power. The Lord can accomplish amazing things through governments and even in spite of governments. We must pray for the Prince of Peace to continue His work in the world.

Air Force Chaplain Praying before a Memorial Service at a U.S. Air Base in Germany, September 14, 2001

*Do not fear those who kill the body
but are unable to kill the soul;
but rather fear Him who is able to destroy
both soul and body in hell.
Matthew 10:28*

Reading

- "American Unilateralism" by Charles Krauthammer (*WHTT*, p. 168)

Lesson 64—The United Nations

Observe good faith and justice towards all nations; cultivate peace and harmony with all. Religion and morality enjoin this conduct; and can it be, that good policy does not equally enjoin it? . . . Can it be that Providence has not connected the permanent felicity of a nation with its virtue? . . .

In the execution of such a plan, nothing is more essential than that permanent, inveterate antipathies against particular nations, and passionate attachments for others, should be excluded; and that, in place of them, just and amicable feelings towards all should be cultivated. The nation which indulges towards another a habitual hatred or a habitual fondness is in some degree a slave. It is a slave to its animosity or to its affection, either of which is sufficient to lead it astray from its duty and its interest. . . .

Against the insidious wiles of foreign influence (I conjure you to believe me, fellow-citizens) the jealousy of a free people ought to be constantly awake, since history and experience prove that foreign influence is one of the most baneful foes of republican government. . . . The great rule of conduct for us in regard to foreign nations is, in extending our commercial relations, to have with them as little political connection as possible. So far as we have already formed engagements, let them be fulfilled with perfect good faith. Here let us stop. Europe has a set of primary interests which to us have none, or a very remote, relation. Hence she must be engaged in frequent controversies, the causes of which are essentially foreign to our concerns. Hence, therefore, it must be unwise in us to implicate ourselves by artificial ties in the ordinary vicissitudes of her politics, or the ordinary combinations and collisions of her friendships or enmities. . . .
—George Washington in his Farewell Address (1796)

The warnings that George Washington voiced in his Farewell Address against permanent alliances were meant to keep the U.S. out of entangling commitments to help other countries when the U.S. had no direct interest in what was going on. For instance, if the U.S. had a mutual defense treaty with France and France was attacked by Germany, the U.S. would be drawn into a conflict in which it had no real interest. Washington also warned against relations with a country that were based on prejudices instead of objective judgment. If the U.S. disliked anything British, America could wind up opposing Britain in a war for no good reason and paying dearly for its mistake.

The United States today is involved in permanent alliances. Following World War II, the American government established alliances with other nations in an effort to stop Communist aggression. American leaders believed that a Communist threat anywhere was a threat to our own security. At the same time, we were in permanent opposition to the Communist Soviet Union, which for seventy years had as a stated goal the destruction of democracy and capitalism. Another permanent arrangement in which the United States is currently involved is our membership in the United Nations.

The History of the UN

President Woodrow Wilson had a strong desire to establish an international League of Nations after World War I, in an attempt to prevent another terrible conflagration from engulfing the globe. His dream, however, was not shared by many in the U.S., including the Republican leadership in the U.S. Senate. The treaty calling for the League of Nations was rejected in the Senate, and the United States never became a member of the League. As a result, the League was never a powerful force in international relations.

As World War II was drawing to a close, the Allied nations (this time including the U.S.) agreed to create a new international body, the United Nations. It was formed in 1945, and its permanent headquarters are in New York City. The General Assembly of the UN is where all 191 member nations are represented. The only two countries not in the General Assembly are Vatican City and Taiwan. The most powerful body in the UN is the Security Council. The Council consists of five permanent members (the U.S., Great Britain, the Russian Federation, France, and China) and ten other rotating member nations that each serve two-year terms. Each of the five permanent members has a veto over any action or resolution before the Council. In other words, no major action is taken by the UN unless these five nations agree.

United Nations Building in New York City

Since 1948, the UN has sent peacekeeping forces on over fifty missions in many places around the world. Other operations, including the Korean War and the Persian Gulf War, were endorsed by the Security Council but were not carried out by UN personnel. The UN sponsors many agencies, such as the United Nations Children's Fund (UNICEF), the World Health Organization (WHO), and the International Court of Justice. United Nations agencies have conducted scientific and humanitarian projects in many places around the world.

American membership in the UN has brought us assistance at times. The confrontation between the U.S. and the Soviet Union during the Cuban Missile Crisis of 1962 was partly played out in the forum of the United Nations, and this might have helped bring about the peaceful resolution of this standoff. Our membership in the United Nations also helped to generate world support for efforts against Saddam Hussein in 1990-1991 and again in 2003. However, our membership in the UN has also been a factor in bringing about our involvement in foreign wars. Our participation in the Korean War was the result of UN resolutions against the North Korean invasion of South Korea.

The United Nations has been a costly alliance for the U.S. in several ways. Many member nations accuse the U.S. of being the real threat to world peace. Smaller nations have often looked to the United States as a source for financial assistance. In addition, the UN is top-heavy with bureaucracy and has been accused of serious corruption. In 1996, with backing from the Clinton administration, the UN began what was called the Oil-for-Food

Program. This allowed Iraq to sell oil on the world market in exchange for food and other humanitarian supplies that were scarce in Iraq because of a world trade embargo against the country. Funds from the sale of oil were also used to pay war reparations from the Persian Gulf War and to pay for UN weapons inspections in Iraq. The program ended in 2003 with the U.S.-led invasion of Iraq. Critics said that the program helped Saddam Hussein stay in power and that it was riddled with corruption. An investigation showed that much of the food shipped to Iraq was unfit to eat and that Saddam and top UN officials received large amounts of money illegally through the program.

NATO, SEATO, and Rio

The United States has been involved in other permanent alliances as well. The North Atlantic Treaty Organization (NATO) was formed in 1949 as a mutual defense system for twelve countries. The NATO treaty states that an attack on one member will be seen as an attack on all member countries. Its intended purpose was to discourage and, if necessary respond to, an attack by the Soviet Union. That attack never happened. NATO military forces were employed for the first time in 1994 in the fighting that took place in the Balkan peninsula as a result of the complicated ethnic and national conflict that emerged after the end of Soviet domination there and the collapse of Communist governments in the region. The first time that the mutual defense provision was invoked was on September 12, 2001, in response to the terrorist attack on the U.S. Other nations have joined NATO from time to time over the years. Since the fall of Communism in Europe, several nations that were members of the Soviet sphere of influence and even of the U.S.S.R. itself have become members of NATO.

Members of NATO at a Defense Ministers Meeting in Lithuania, 2008

The Southeast Asia Treaty Organization (SEATO) was formed in 1954 and consisted of the United States, France, the United Kingdom, Australia, New Zealand, Pakistan, Thailand, and the Philippines. It was modeled after the NATO agreement. Conflicts arose in Southeast Asian countries that were not members of SEATO (most notably Vietnam), but military action was never initiated under terms of the SEATO treaty because the required unanimous agreement was never reached. The alliance was dissolved in 1977.

The United States and twenty other countries in the Western Hemisphere signed the Inter-American Treaty of Reciprocal Assistance in 1947 in Rio de Janeiro. It is also called the Rio Treaty and is actually older than NATO. The Rio treaty stated that an attack on one of the signatories would be considered an attack on all of them. The Rio Treaty was another effort to resist possible Communist aggression. Three other countries joined the agreement in later years.

The Rio Treaty was invoked several times in the 1950s and 1960s, but no significant military action came from it. Generally, the Rio agreement has not been as strong as NATO. In 1982, Argentina seized the Falkland Islands that Great Britain had long claimed as one of its territories. The British military attacked Argentine positions on the islands and drove them off, but the Rio Treaty was not invoked during this conflict. The U.S. did invoke the treaty after the 9/11 attacks in 2001. Mexico withdrew from the Rio agreement in 2002, effective in 2004. The Mexican President said that he wanted to see a new agreement among the countries of the Americas that dealt with modern issues, such as security against terrorism, economic cooperation, and ways to provide assistance in times of natural disasters.

As George Washington warned, permanent alliances with and permanent enmities toward other countries can bring problems. A policy of isolation from the world as it was once practiced by the American government is not a viable option for the U.S. today. However, America must always act on the principles of justice, freedom, and defense of our legitimate national interests. Our alliances and our stances of opposition must serve these ends and not compromise them.

For a child will be born to us, a son will be given to us;
and the government will rest on His shoulders;
and His name will be called Wonderful Counselor,
Mighty God, Eternal Father, Prince of Peace.
Isaiah 9:6

Reading

- "America and the United Nations" by Mark Steyn (*WHTT*, p. 175)

Lesson 65 — Human Rights

The care of human life and happiness, and not their destruction, is the first and only object of good government.

—Thomas Jefferson (1809)

The freer the flow of world trade, the stronger the tides of human progress and peace among nations.

—Ronald Reagan (1986)

What is the best way to get a friend to stop smoking?

One way is to say, "Friend, you ought to stop smoking. It is killing you and hurting people around you. I want you to stop smoking so much that I am going to have nothing to do with you until you stop."

Another way is to say, "Friend, you ought to stop smoking. It is killing you and hurting people around you. But I love you and I know that stopping smoking is a difficult thing to do. I will be with you and will be your friend whether you stop or not, but I hope that my friendship, influence, and example will encourage you to stop."

It will probably not help to say nothing to that friend. Continuing to be a friend but never addressing the topic will likely cause your friend to think that smoking is not a problem. On the other hand, withdrawing from the person without saying anything at all about the matter will likely only leave the person hurt and confused.

A Member of the U.S. Air Force Holding a Refugee Child, Kabul, Afghanistan, 2007

If you withdraw from your friend, whether or not you tell him why, he may find other friends who will either smoke with him or communicate in some way their approval or acceptance of his habit.

What is the best way to get a national government to protect the human rights that its people deserve?

One way is for other nations to have nothing to do with that government until it changes. If this happens, the government being boycotted might find other countries that will do business with it; or it might engage in black market trade. Another way is for other countries to carry on relations with the offending government in order to have an avenue of influence with it, while regularly bringing up the issue of human rights as a matter of concern.

There is no debate that national governments sometimes fail to honor the human rights that their people deserve. Governments put political opponents in prison, and government leaders abuse their citizens for personal gain. Government persecution of Christians is common in China and in Muslim countries. In extreme situations, when leaders of one ethnic or tribal group gain power in a country, they sometimes engage in genocide against an opposing group, leading to thousands of deaths and millions of refugees.

The debate that does exist and that becomes quite heated centers on the question of whether and how the United States and other countries should address the violation of human rights when it occurs. Is a policy of engagement or a policy of isolation the best way to bring about change?

Human Rights and How to Protect Them

Human rights are rights and freedoms that are generally recognized as being what every person deserves. Among these are life, freedom from slavery and torture, freedom of religion and expression, an adequate standard of living, freedom of movement, and the right of political self-determination (being able to vote for the government under which one lives).

The United Nations published a Declaration of Human Rights many years

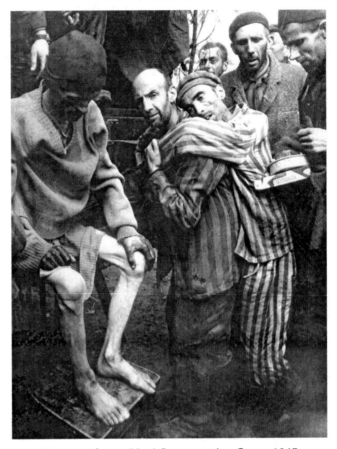

Prisoners from a Nazi Concentration Camp, 1945

ago, and it sponsors an on-going Human Rights Commission. However, the UN has done little to lessen the suppression of human rights. In some ways, the foxes are in charge of the UN chicken coop. Some of the worst offending nations are occasionally selected to serve on the Human Rights Commission. The United Nations has not brought its entire weight and influence to bear on the problem of human rights violations.

The goal of U.S. policy is to eliminate human rights abuses. We want to pursue that goal in the most effective way possible. The approach that has proven most effective is that of engagement with the offending country while maintaining pressure on the offending government to change its practices. The issue is a genuine moral and spiritual struggle, since carrying on trade and diplomatic relations with human rights violators appears to send the signal that such practices do not matter or can be ignored.

Previous Policies

The United States government has not followed a consistent policy on this issue. For instance, since the Communist takeover of Cuba in 1959, the United States has had a policy of allowing as little contact with Cuba—diplomatic, economic, cultural, or humanitarian—as possible. The U.S. has called on its allies to join in this embargo. Our government has hoped by this policy to weaken the Communist regime in Cuba and to force it to give up power. A few tentative steps have been taken toward better relations with Cuba in recent years, but the quarantine still applies. As yet, despite the economic hardships endured by the Cuban people, the Communist regime is still in power and is still popular with the people.

The overall effect of the policy of isolation can be negative. The oppressive leader can portray himself as the victim of unfair treatment by other countries, thus strengthening his position with his people. The offending government can find other countries with which to trade and can often get at least some of what it needs by covert, illegal trade. The people might suffer, but the leader usually does not.

On the other hand, after sixteen years of isolation, the United States recognized the Soviet Union in 1933. There is no question that the Soviet Communist government had one of the worst human rights records in history. Millions of people were killed or imprisoned for their political beliefs. Christianity was severely restricted and many Christians lost their lives. The U.S. and other countries carried on relations with the Communists, all the while expressing concern for the Soviets' human rights violations. Eventually, the Communist government fell and greater freedoms emerged in the former Soviet Union.

For many years the white minority government of South Africa followed a policy of racial apartheid or segregation. The South African government imprisoned Nelson Mandela and other critics for several years. Many nations refused to have any contact with South Africa as a way to protest this policy. The United States, however, continued to have

South African President Nelson Mandela, 1994

relations with the South African government. Eventually, after years of violent protests and political unrest, the white government stepped aside. New elections were held, and the leadership of South Africa now reflects the black majority of the population.

Biblical Principles

If the analogy of interpersonal relationships with which we started this lesson has any validity, some teachings of the New Testament might help us understand the best approach. The Bible does not directly address how one government should influence another government to protect human rights, so we can only try to make application of Biblical principles.

Jesus said in Matthew 18:15-20 that a Christian should approach a brother who sins against him and point out his fault. If the sinning brother refuses to listen to the Christian, to two or three witnesses, or to the church, he is to be treated as a Gentile and a tax collector, i.e., as an outcast from the fellowship. 1 Corinthians 5:1-5 says that a sinning brother should be delivered to Satan "for the destruction of his flesh, so that his spirit may be saved in the day of the Lord Jesus." Galatians 6:1 says that if a brother is entangled in sin, another Christian should seek to restore him in a spirit of gentleness, remembering how easily he himself can give in to temptation.

However, these all have to do with an erring Christian within the fellowship. Later in 1 Corinthians 5, Paul says that when he told the Corinthians not to associate with immoral people, he was referring to so-called brethren who were immoral. He did not expect them to leave the world in order to avoid contact with immoral outsiders (1 Corinthians 5:9-13). Jesus lived among sinners in order to influence them for good. First Peter encourages Christians to live good lives before outsiders so that unbelievers will glorify God (1 Peter 2:12, 3:15-16).

We cannot draw a direct parallel between any of these Biblical passages and how nations of the world should conduct their relations. However, we can learn some principles that can help us identify the best policy. First, we should not ignore violations of human rights. The Bible teaches that God's people must stand up for what is right. Second, we cannot ignore human rights violations in the name of greater trade and profit. This would be putting riches before speaking the truth on behalf of God. Third, we should not give direct aid to regimes that ignore human rights. This is a different question from whether we should trade with such countries.

The Question of China

Perhaps the most pressing human rights dilemma facing the United States is how to approach trade with Communist China. The Chinese government has suppressed all political opposition. It has imprisoned and tortured Chinese Christians. The Chinese people do not enjoy freedom of expression. Many of those who work in Chinese manufacturing plants receive low wages and live in squalid conditions. What is the best way to change all of these realities and help to bring about a greater respect for human rights in China?

A refusal to do business with an oppressive government often results in greater oppression of the people by that government. This outcome only hurts those we are trying to help. On the other hand, trade with an offending country promotes contact with the West, lessens the people's dependence on their government, and introduces the possibilities of democracy and a

A Chinese Christian Pastor and His Family, c. 1900

higher standard of living. Without question, China is changing. People are gaining more economic independence and the Chinese economy is becoming more capitalistic. It has changed more since we have been carrying on trade than it did when we did not recognize the Communist government. It is fair to say that China is not changing fast enough; but as we continue to pray and work, the day may come when Communism will fall in China just as it did in the Soviet Union and Eastern Europe.

The policy that Ronald Reagan followed gives us a good model. Reagan did not cut off all contact with the Soviet Union. He did not say, "Mr. Gorbachev, tear down this wall or I will have nothing to do with you." He engaged in continuing negotiations with the Soviet leaders. However, as he carried on talks and engaged in relations with the Soviet Union (1) he negotiated from a position of American strength, and (2) he was willing to point out the failings of the Communist system.

Children in Shanghai, China, 1986

An improvement in the human rights conditions in China, including greater religious freedom, might well require grave personal sacrifice from the Chinese people. If Chinese workers try to organize labor unions to improve their wages and the conditions in factories, some may lose their lives. Those of us in the West should be willing to make sacrifices ourselves to support their cause, such as doing without goods made in China if such a boycott can be effectively tied to an effort to improve working conditions. More than anything, we can pray for God to continue to work in China to bring about His will.

He says, "It is too small a thing that You should be My Servant
to raise up the tribes of Jacob
and to restore the preserved ones of Israel; I will also make You a light of the nations
so that My salvation may reach to the end of the earth."
Isaiah 49:6

14 Contemporary Questions

This unit presents issues that confront the American people and American government at the present time: the economy, immigration, health care, education, and abortion. We look particularly at what the role of government is and what it should be in each of these issues.

Lessons in This Unit

Lesson 66—Government and the Economy
Lesson 67—Immigration
Lesson 68—Health Care
Lesson 69—Education
Lesson 70—Abortion

Activity Idea

Select one of the issues discussed in this unit, or one of your own choosing, and write a three-page paper outlining the questions involved in it and what you think government on all levels should do about it.

If you are using the optional *Quiz and Exam Book*, answer the questions for each lesson after you have completed the lesson and read any assigned readings in *We Hold These Truths*. After you have completed Lesson 70, take the quiz for Unit 14.

Lesson 66—Government and the Economy

There is nothing wrong with America that the faith, love of freedom, intelligence and energy of her citizens cannot cure.

—Dwight D. Eisenhower

An economy can be defined as the structure and functioning of the production, distribution, and use of goods and services of a people. A town has an economy, a state has an economy, a country has an economy, a region of the world has an economy, and the world has an economy.

In a strong economy, wages are high and increasing, prices are kept low, businesses make profits, unemployment is low, inflation is kept at a low rate, and the general population has enough to live comfortably and to save a portion of their income. In a weak or struggling economy, the opposite factors are present: wages are low and are insufficient for people to be able to buy what they need, unemployment is relatively high, the prices for goods are higher than many people can afford, businesses frequently fail because they cannot make a profit, and the general population is struggling to get by.

Advertisement for Detroit

Many factors can affect an economy. The farm economy, for instance, can be affected by the weather, such as a drought in the Midwest or cold temperatures in a citrus growing region. In the case of Hurricane Katrina, weather can devastate the economy of an entire area. War can interrupt normal business activities such as production and transportation. On the other hand, a new invention or new technology can boost the economy. This is what happened with the development of the auto industry in and around Detroit in the early twentieth century and with the development of computer technology in the area known as Silicon Valley in California in the 1980s.

One major influence on an economy is the government. In this lesson we outline classic government-economy relationships and mention several specific ways that government actions influence the economy.

Classic Government-Economy Arrangements

The two main kinds of economic systems are *capitalism* and *socialism*. In capitalism, the means of production are owned by private individuals. The economy is driven by the investment of private capital (monetary resources) to create businesses and to make profits. In socialism, the means of production are owned by the government in the name of society as a whole. What the government thinks is best for society drives the economy. These are the two main categories of economic systems; however, the national economies of the world today actually cover a spectrum of varying degrees of government involvement in the economy.

At the capitalist end of the spectrum, *mercantilism* was the economic philosophy in which government gave active assistance to private business. This was the philosophy that lay behind the development of colonies by English businessmen and settlers in the sixteenth and seventeenth centuries. The governments in countries such as Taiwan and Singapore encourage private businesses in a similar way today.

Another approach is for the government to take a hands-off policy toward business with minimal regulations and as few taxes as possible. The typical phrase for this policy is *laissez-faire* (French for "allow to be"). Laissez-faire economics is an ideal theory. Few if any governments have ever practiced a completely hands-off policy.

A more complex mix of free enterprise with government regulation and taxation of private business is called a *regulated private economy*. The economy is still capitalist, but businesses have to deal with government rules and regulations. Government laws and policies can either encourage or hinder such private endeavors as energy production (by allowing or regulating oil wells or the building of nuclear power plants), industry (with laws that regulate workplace safety and the minimum wage), or foreign trade (by placing tariffs on imported items that might compete with items produced within the country).

Capitalists have shown themselves to need regulation. They are subject to the same sins of selfishness and greed that everyone faces. Without government regulation, companies are likely to harm and pollute the environment because being careless is cheaper than being responsible for the waste that is produced by an industry or dealing responsibly with the effects of strip-mining. Nineteenth-century industrial towns in England and experiences in twentieth century America show that this is true. Companies have in the past hired children as workers because they could pay them less than what adults were paid. Businesses sometimes make false claims in advertising and produce unsafe goods unless the government makes them stop (they sometimes engage in these acts even with government regulations).

Young Boys at Work in a Glass Factory, 1908

The next step on the spectrum is an economy in which the government takes an active role, from subsidizing businesses that are not profitable to taking over some of the means of production in the economy. At this point the economy begins to take on aspects of socialism. The Amtrak passenger rail service is an example of the American government operating a business.

Governments in other countries, especially in Europe, have taken over more areas of their economies than has the United States government. The British government, for instance, took over the operation of the country's mines many years ago. This move was called nationalization, when the nation became responsible for the operation of what had been a private industry. The British government has also nationalized the country's health care system. The arrangement is called socialized medicine. Almost all doctors who practice in Great Britain work for the government and receive a salary, and almost all hospitals there are owned by the government. We will say more about the issue of health care in Lesson 68.

At the other end of the spectrum is the completely socialist economy in which all business endeavors are run by the government. The extreme form of socialism is the planned economy, in which bureaucrats and not businessmen make the decisions. Bureaucrats do not necessarily have good business ideas; instead, they work to support the government system. The former Soviet Union had a planned economy. For instance, farmers were to begin their spring plowing on May 1 because that was the date set by government planners. The ground might be muddy or have a foot of snow on it, but the farmers were still supposed to start plowing according to the plan. A country might have a socialist economy but still also have free elections, free speech, and so forth. *Communism* is full socialism in economics with the additional factor of total government control over all aspects of life, including politics, religion, what speech is permitted, and so forth.

U.S. Soldiers on an Anti-Black Market Mission in Iraq

As you can see, an economy planned from the top down is subject to inefficiency and poor results. Workers and industries in a socialist economy have little incentive to do a better job, since they have no competition and will get paid the same whether the widgets they make work well or fall apart. A planned, socialist economy encourages the development of an underground black market, through which goods that are desired but not produced by government efforts are made available, often at exorbitant prices. Black market goods might include anything from alcoholic beverages to electronics to prescription drugs. Sometimes government agents accept bribes or receive a percentage of the profits to let the black market operate.

These government-economy relationships exist on a spectrum because no economy that has been in operation for very long is exclusively one kind. The United States has a capitalist economy, even though the government issues many regulations and operates some businesses. Communist China is officially socialist, but in the last few years a few individuals have been permitted to begin capitalist enterprises.

Government Influences on the Economy

The government is always a factor in an economy, in one way or another. This influence can take any number of forms.

- If a country experiences political turmoil and the government is not functioning, farmers might be forced to leave their land and become refugees. Transportation is unsafe and goods are not shipped from one area to another. People might be unwilling or unable to travel to their places of work.

- In Mississippi in the early 1980s, the state was one of the few in the country that did not have a state-funded kindergarten program. Many in the state believed that this made Mississippi unattractive for economic development, since it was assumed that many workers would prefer to live where a state kindergarten program existed.

- High taxes can discourage workers and businesses because a large portion of what they earn goes to the government. Often workers do not see how they themselves benefit from many of the government programs which they help finance.

- A large number of government regulations can discourage business. For instance, if a business has to spend a great deal of money to meet pollution regulations or safety requirements, it might have to charge more for its goods or choose to locate somewhere else. On the other hand, a lack of sufficient regulations can hurt the economy also. If industrial pollution renders an area unsafe and uninhabitable, residents and businesses will have to locate elsewhere and people will have to spend more on medical care.

- The Tennessee Valley Authority (TVA) was a New Deal government program that encouraged the economic development of the region surrounding the Tennessee River. Many homes in the region did not have electricity, and opportunities for work during the Depression were limited. The Federal government spent money to build dams on the Tennessee River that generated electricity at low cost. This encouraged businesses to build factories in the area, which provided employment for people who lived there. It also created a market for home electrical appliances, from light bulbs and radios to stoves and refrigerators. On the other hand, TVA also drove small, private electric companies out of business because they could not compete with TVA's lower, government-subsidized rates.

Carpenter at Work on a TVA Dam, 1942

Creating and Redistributing Wealth

It is important to remember that government does not produce wealth. A government may have millions of workers, but those workers are paid from the wealth produced by business and industry that generates tax revenues. All of the people who receive some kind of financial benefit from the government (scholarships, welfare assistance, research grants, military expenditures, etc.) receive money that for the most part comes from taxes and fees on business activity. Even in socialist countries, government revenue comes from the business activity, not the bureaucrats who oversee the business activity.

Instead of creating wealth, government is primarily involved in redistributing wealth. Property taxes paid by landowners are used to pay teachers in public schools. The wages of soldiers are paid by taxes from the citizens whom those soldiers protect. People whose incomes are considered poverty level receive food distribution and rental assistance paid for by the work of people whose income is above the poverty line.

A society decides through its elected representatives to redistribute wealth in this way. We prefer having soldiers and government food inspectors to the alternative of not having them. With the growth of government, however, comes the by-products of more government workers, more government involvement in our lives, and a greater demand for revenue on the private economy.

The Biblical alternative to government redistribution of wealth is for Christians to redistribute their wealth voluntarily to those who have needs. The pattern in the New Testament is for believers to give to others to the point of self-sacrifice. When this is done, little or no government bureaucracy is needed. The money goes to those in need and not to governmental costs. Assistance is personal, not impersonal. Those who receive help are people you know, not nameless "recipients."

The Goal of the Government-Economy Relationship

History has shown time and again that economic freedom works while too much government involvement causes problems. Capitalist nations generally have growing economies because people are motivated to work hard, are able to save and make their own decisions, and can utilize their abilities to improve their economic conditions. Socialist economies struggle because people are not motivated to work hard and are not encouraged to let their individual talents flourish.

At the same time, government plays an important role in a capitalist economy by defending truth and justice. Laws protect workers, the public, and the environment from abuse. The best arrangement is a free economy in which people are guided by Biblical principles of fairness, honesty, and justice, with government protecting those who are hurt when people do wrong.

For even when we were with you we used to give you this order:
if anyone is not willing to work, then he is not to eat, either.
For we hear that some among you are leading
an undisciplined life, doing no work at all, but acting like busybodies.
Now such persons we command and exhort
in the Lord Jesus Christ to work in quiet fashion and eat their own bread.
2 Thessalonians 3:10-12

Lesson 67—Immigration

The Democratic Party looks at massive immigration, legal and illegal, as a source of voters. . . . The Republican Party looks at massive immigration, legal and illegal, as a source of cheap labor, satisfying a very important constituency. . . . I have to tell you that we are facing a situation, where if we don't control immigration, legal and illegal, we will eventually reach the point where it won't be what kind of a nation we are, balkanized or united, we will actually have to face the fact that we are no longer a nation at all.

—Tom Tancredo, Republican Congressman from Colorado

The United States is a nation of immigrants. Our forefathers came to these shores from many distant lands. Throughout our history, millions of immigrants have come to escape poverty and persecution or to get a new start in life. Our country has been enriched in countless ways by the cultural diversity, the hard work, and the hopes and dreams of immigrants. My mother was from England. She married my father during World War II, came to this country after the war, and became an American citizen. Thus, I am not just the descendant of immigrants; I am the son of an immigrant.

People in other lands have long seen the U.S. as a beacon of freedom and opportunity. There are good reasons why those millions of immigrants left everything, sometimes risking their lives, to come here. Our richly blessed country offers what no other country on earth offers. Critics will justly point out particular failings, but overall and in many specific ways the United States is a shining light to people who are looking for something better.

Today, however, our country faces an immigration crisis. The fact that most of those now coming to the U.S. illegally are non-whites does not make it a crisis. Race has nothing to do with it. Instead, it is a crisis of security, economy, law, and justice. Security is involved because people have come to the United States illegally and done us harm. The economy is an issue because many have

Polish Immigrant Boarding a Ship, 1907

come to the United States to work and as a result have had an impact on our economy. It is an issue involving the law because some have come to the United States in flagrant violation of our laws and have engaged in criminal activity while here. Finally, immigration is a crisis of justice because people who play by the rules must sometimes wait for years before they are permitted to come, while those who break the rules come and live here with impunity.

Immigration is a serious issue confronting governments on all levels—national, state, and local. The Federal government is responsible for establishing and enforcing immigration policy and for making sure that terrorists and criminals do not gain entry into our country. State governments usually provide services that illegal immigrants want and need, services that legitimate citizens have to pay for with their taxes. Local governments have to deal with sometimes crowded housing conditions and with law enforcement issues that arise due to the activities of some illegal immigrants. Enforcing immigration law is an overwhelming job, but ignoring the problem will only make matters worse.

Official U.S. Immigration Policy

Foreign nationals who wish to come to the United States must obtain a visa from the U.S. government, although the citizens of certain countries can come to the U.S. temporarily simply by having a valid passport. Visas are issued in several categories. Most are tourist visas for those who want to come for a vacation. Another large category is student visas, which are issued to those who want to come to this country to go to school. Many foreign nationals come on a work visa, which is issued for a set period of time so that the person can fill a specific job. Visa applicants must provide personal information and must go through a background check. Approval for a visa can take thirty days if there are no questions or problems. A much longer time is required in more complicated situations.

The next step for someone who wants to live in the United States is to apply for an Alien Registration Receipt Card and become a legal permanent resident. This document is often called a Green Card. A Green Card is usually issued for a period of ten years. After a period of time, a permanent resident can apply to become a citizen.

For many years, the United States has set an official limit on the number of persons who can come to the country in any given year for the purpose of becoming a permanent resident. Currently, the annual limit is set at 675,000 persons. This total is broken down into three categories:

- family-sponsored immigrants (family members of those who are already legal residents in the U.S.)

- employment-based immigrants (those who come to the U.S. to work at a job that has already been offered)

- diversity admissions (those from certain countries who participate in a lottery that determines who gets admitted; applicants must meet certain education or work experience requirements)

However, the admission policy is actually more complicated than this. There is no limit on the number of spouses, children, and parents of U.S. citizens that can be admitted to the country. Those seeking political asylum and those who are refugees also do not count against one of the above categories. If the quota in one category is not met in a year, that shortfall can be applied to another category the following year. The standard percentage rule says that no one country can send more than 7% of the immigrants admitted into the United

States in any given year; however, this rate is flexible depending on unused quotas as well as asylum and refugee admissions.

About two-thirds of the people who receive permanent resident status each year are those who make family-related applications. Mexico is by far the country of origin for most of those applying for legal permanent resident status. The number of Mexican applications is three times as great as that from India, which has the second highest total. China, the Philippines, and Vietnam round out the top five. The process for being admitted to the U.S. on a permanent basis is slow. Foreign nationals who are brothers and sisters of U.S. citizens routinely wait up to ten years after making application before their case is reviewed. Even the process for adopting a child from another country is slow and involved.

Illegal Immigration

As you can see, following the legal route to becoming a permanent resident in the U.S. is complicated and frustrating. The course that many people take instead is that of making an illegal, secret crossing of the border into the U.S. It is impossible to know how many undocumented immigrants are in the United States, but the figure of ten million is a good estimate. Many of these come across the Mexican border, but they are not all Mexicans. Some illegal immigrants come through Florida or other ports of entry. Most of these people wind up living in large cities and in states along the southern tier of the states from California to Florida. However, immigrants work in many places throughout the country: the potato fields of Idaho, the Christmas tree farms of North Carolina, and poultry processing plants in Arkansas, to name just a few.

The problems associated with illegal immigration are many. First, our government cannot know the background of these people. It is widely assumed that some countries send criminals to the U.S. to get rid of them. It is also suspected that officials and border agents of other countries take bribes to let people leave those countries illegally. Second,

A Military Policeman Searching an Illegal Alien Found on a Train in California, 1986

the conditions along our borders are often chaotic and dangerous. Gun battles have broken out between U.S. border officers and illegal immigrants or those giving assistance to the illegals. On occasion, immigrants hiding in a truck suffocate or are killed in an accident. Illegal immigrants are often taken into custody and then released with no consequences, since the government law enforcement agencies are not equipped to handle many detainees. Third, an underground network of contacts can be involved in recruiting undocumented workers to come across the border. For instance, an American might pay a legal or illegal immigrant to recruit other workers from his home country. Part of this money might go to finance the bribes paid to foreign officials mentioned earlier. Those brought into the country work at jobs while using either no documentation or fake documents. Whether these illegal immigrants take jobs from Americans or are taken advantage of by unscrupulous employers is a matter of much debate.

Once in the country, these undocumented workers and their families can become a drain on schools, public health services, and other government programs. They do pay sales taxes on purchases, but they often do not pay income tax. One estimate of the cost of illegal immigration to the U.S. is $45 billion. Many illegals do not speak English, so they develop a separate society and do not fully integrate into the American culture. Occasionally they engage in criminal activity, such as burglary and the sale and use of illegal drugs. The situation undermines the rule of and respect for law since immigration laws are ignored. The greatest fear is that some undocumented immigrants might be terrorists who plan to inflict great harm on American lives and property.

What Can We Do?

The United States can and should continue to be an open door for legal and legitimate immigrants. This maintains our historic policy of welcoming to our shores the needy and those willing to work. However, the government must get a handle on illegal immigration, since it is affecting our economy and our social fabric.

U.S. Navy Ship Sailing Past the Statue of Liberty, 2006

We should make it clear to foreign governments that we must have their cooperation in providing the proper screening of those who want to come to the U.S. We must strengthen our patrolling and enforcement efforts along the borders and send back all who do not have legitimate documentation. We must also be willing to pay the salaries of enough government workers to provide the proper handling of immigrants already within the United States. If they want to become permanent residents, there are procedures and screenings that can accomplish this step for those who have legitimate requests. Our economy should not be dependent on an illegal workforce. Those who want to live in the U.S. must be willing to be integrated fully into American life and not just take jobs and use government services. We must do all we can to prevent our country from being attacked from within by those who have entered illegally.

America needs to be compassionate toward those who come here in need. Many illegal workers are desperate to be able to feed their families back home. Many families that have come illegally need medical care and educational opportunities for their children. However, these needs must be met in the context of a respect for the rule of law. One suggestion that has been made is to implement a kind of reverse documentation by investigating illegal immigrants already here and then either certifying them for a work visa or sending them back to their countries of origin. Another idea is for employers to take the responsibility of going to other countries, recruiting and screening applicants, and then closely overseeing them during their time in the U.S.

Any steps will be difficult to take. Implementing them will require time, wisdom, and political courage. Politicians will find it hard to address these issues, so the voters must demand it of candidates and office-holders. We do not need to act on the basis of fear or prejudice. We need to act out of a sense of compassion and justice for all. America can still be a beacon of hope for those from other countries, but it will not be such by disregarding the law and by making life difficult for law-abiding American citizens.

After these things I looked, and behold,
a great multitude which no one could count,
from every nation and all tribes and peoples and tongues,
standing before the throne and before the Lamb,
clothed in white robes, and palm branches were
in their hands; and they cry out with a loud voice, saying,
"Salvation to our God who sits on the throne, and to the Lamb."
Revelation 7:9-10

Reading

- "Immigration, the War on Terror, and the Rule of Law" by Michelle Malkin (*WHTT*, p. 182)

- "Frank Talk About 'Mexifornia'" by Victor Davis Hanson (*WHTT*, p. 189)

Mexican Immigrant, c. 1912

Lesson 68—Health Care

Nobody spends somebody else's money as carefully as he spends his own. Nobody uses somebody else's resources as carefully as he uses his own. So if you want efficiency and effectiveness, if you want knowledge to be properly utilized, you have to do it through the means of private property.

—*Milton Friedman, economist*

Paying for Health Care

When you or your parents go shopping, the prices that stores charge for items is one of the factors you consider when deciding where to shop. If a store nearer to your home charges a higher price than a store farther away charges for the same item, you will probably go to the store farther away, provided that the difference is worth your time and expense to go there. You might pay more for an item if it is of higher quality than similar ones you are considering; but if it is exactly the same item offered at different prices, you will likely want to pay as little as you can. However, if someone else—perhaps your grandparents, or the government—tells you just to buy the item wherever you wish and they will pay for it, you will likely go to the nearer store and pay the higher price, since you are not spending your own money for it.

This illustration shows how paying for health care has changed in recent years. Before the mid-1960s, payment for health care was largely a private matter between the patient and the doctor or hospital. Health insurance was available, but it was not the major topic of concern that it is today. People paid their medical bills the same way they paid other bills. Those who could not afford to pay either did not go to the doctor or received some kind of charitable assistance (the doctor or hospital wrote off the expense or charged less, or the patient received help from a church or other group).

When the Federal government entered the health care field with the Medicare and Medicaid programs in the mid-1960s, the rules of the game changed. For people over 65 who pay a small monthly premium, Medicare provides government payments for health care services. Medicaid is a Federally-funded program administered by the states that pays health care costs for the poor and others who cannot afford or cannot obtain traditional health insurance coverage. People covered by Medicare and Medicaid receive heath care, and the government pays for most of it. When the government began paying a large percentage of health care costs, those costs skyrocketed. Exorbitant medical charges, mismanagement, and corruption became common. Efforts to reform Medicare and Medicaid have been going on since shortly after the programs began.

Health Care Costs

In 1960, Americans paid about $28 billion for health care. By 1970, the total had almost tripled to $75 billion. Twenty years later still, the total had increased over nine times more, so that in 1990 the national health care tab was $717 billion. The rate of increase has slowed since 1990, but the figures are still astounding. In 2004, national health care costs totaled two trillion dollars. Health care now accounts for 16%, or about one-sixth, of the country's gross domestic product (or GDP, another way of saying the economy). This share of the GDP is three times greater than it was in 1960. Health care costs consistently rise each year at a rate higher than the annual overall increase in the cost of living.

Prescriptions are a larger percentage of health care costs and hospitalization is a lower portion than in previous years. Providers have learned that it is cheaper to prescribe medication than it is to build and maintain a hospital, pay a staff, and incur all of the other costs of a facility. Prescription costs have also risen rapidly, and drug companies now have large advertising and marketing budgets to encourage patients and doctors to use their medicines.

Today local, state, and Federal governments pay one-half of all health care bills in the United States. Overseeing and paying for health care has become a major function of government. This fact helps to push the cost of health care higher for all Americans, including those who have private insurance and who pay their own medical expenses.

TennCare

In 1994 the state of Tennessee initiated TennCare, a public health care system that was a trial program to replace Medicaid. TennCare uses Managed Care Organizations (MCOs, which are mostly private health insurance companies) to pay for services that patients get from doctors, hospitals, pharmacies, and other providers who participate in the program. The state government reimburses the MCOs for what they pay to providers. TennCare provides coverage for the poor and for those considered uninsurable by private insurance companies. Most TennCare recipients do not pay anything for the services they receive, although a small percentage of those covered by TennCare pay premiums and co-payments for office visits and other services. Payments for medical services under TennCare are usually less than what providers receive from regular insurance companies, and payments to providers are often slow in coming.

TennCare has seen the same explosion of costs that has characterized American health care as a whole. As of 2005, 1.35 million Tennesseans were covered by the program, out of a state population of almost 6 million. Just under one-half of those covered were children under the age of twenty-one. The program cost $8.7 billion in 2005, which means that the program paid out an average of over $6,400.00 per covered person that year. Two-thirds of the funding for TennCare came from the Federal government, while the other third was paid for by the state. The total TennCare bill included a considerable amount that went for bureaucratic expenses in the state government and in the MCOs. Of the $8.7 billion, $2.9 billion went to the MCOs. $2.55 billion went for pharmaceuticals, $1.7 billion for long-term care, and $455 million for Behavioral Health Organizations (mental health services).

The program has experienced higher-than-expected costs, charges of mismanagement, and complaints from both health care providers and patients. TennCare has had five different directors, and the original director who lasted just over a year in 1994-1995 returned in 2002 to head the program again. Counting acting and interim directors, TennCare had eight leadership changes between 1995 and 2002. In 2005 several thousand TennCare patients were dropped from the program in an effort to save money. All of those cut from the program were over nineteen. No coverage for children was eliminated.

What's The Problem?

The United States has a good health care system. We have good medical schools, good hospitals, good doctors and nurses, and a good level of availability of drugs and medical tests. I would rather have a medical need in the U.S. than anywhere else in the world. Generally speaking, if you need medical attention in the U.S., you can get it.

The problem is paying for it. The costs are too high and the administration of health care involves too much bureaucracy. It is a complicated problem, and all of the parties in

the system usually blame the other players for the situation. Greed is a major component. Doctors play a part by wanting everything they do to be above question. Insurance companies want to call the shots. Medical malpractice insurance is terribly expensive, but doctors pay for it because they do not want to be ruined by a lawsuit, however frivolous it might be. A major part of medical practice today involves the prescribing of drugs, and pharmaceutical companies want as much profit as possible. Government oversight can be unreasonable and complicated. The addition of prescription coverage as a Medicare option was difficult for many users to understand.

Consider the way that charges are calculated. When someone has a medical bill, say a test or an office visit, the charge is submitted to the payer, which is usually Medicare or an insurance company. This is called a third-party payment, the third party being someone other than the two parties directly involved, the doctor and the patient. The charge for the service is usually ridiculously high: perhaps $60.00 or $75.00 for a brief office visit, several hundred dollars for a test, or several thousand dollars for a hospital stay. The payer then uses a standard known as the "usual and customary" charge for such a service. Using that standard, Medicare or the insurance company approves a portion of the bill and pays the provider on behalf of the covered person. The provider says thank you for that partial payment and goes on to the next patient.

If a person does not have insurance, he is stuck with that inflated bill and has to either pay it, negotiate a lower price, or risk damaging his credit rating or declaring bankruptcy by not paying it (it is estimated that as many as half of all personal bankruptcies involve at least some medical debt). One reason for the high medical charges is to cover the expense incurred by providers by those who do not pay. Doctors who receive government payments, which has come to be just about all of them, have their billing practices for all patients critiqued by the government.

All of this adds up to a system that is complex, costly, and inefficient.

Finding Answers

The health care delivery system needs fixing, but developing a completely government-run system of socialized medicine is not the answer. The goal of such tax-supported systems, which are used in the United Kingdom and Canada and some other countries, is to make health care equally available to all regardless of one's ability to pay. The result, however, has been that less health care is available for everyone. Care becomes not more available but more limited and rationed. The system is inefficient, and it is not unusual for people to wait months and sometimes years for procedures that would take place within a few days in the United States. The government bureaucracy has no motivation to do a good job since it has no competition.

Socialized medicine is driven by the bureaucracy and by the government's desire to control health care. A better approach is for health care to be patient-centered and driven by competition, with government's role being to enable and encourage effective serving of health care needs. Some steps toward this goal have included the following:

- The ability of workers to carry their health insurance coverage with them when they change jobs has given people more freedom. Continuing medical coverage through an employer is one reason why many people continue to work for a company or are reluctant to retire.

- Medical savings accounts allow individuals to set aside a certain amount of their income tax-free to pay for medical costs.

- Insurance companies are currently regulated by the states, but national competitiveness might give consumers more choices.

It is a humane and compassionate policy for people to be able to receive an adequate level of health care even if they cannot afford to pay for all of it. However, recipients of such care should also be expected to pay some of the cost. They need to bear the responsibility for a co-payment and for making lifestyle changes when that is needed. It is not right for taxpayers to bear all of the responsibility for the medical bills of people who do not take care of themselves. It it also a good policy to provide local clinics for those who receive subsidized care. This is more cost-efficient than simply having them go to an emergency room, which is the most expensive way to deliver health care. Ideally, Christians should be willing to help pay the medical expenses of those who need assistance.

In April 2006, the state of Massachusetts became the first state to require all citizens to have health insurance coverage, in much the same way that states require auto owners to carry auto insurance. Several different plans and levels of coverage were offered, and the state helped to pay the premiums of those who could not afford to do so themselves. The plan enabled the government to help some of the people but kept health care delivery in the private sector.

The health care system has grown in piecemeal fashion, and all of the players want more of the pie. To make the needed changes, everyone will have to give up something; but with proper planning and execution, individuals and organizations in the health care field will still be able to earn a comfortable living and more people will be able to get the medical care they need.

For bodily discipline is only of little profit, but godliness is profitable for all things,
since it holds promise for the present life and also for the life to come.
1 Timothy 4:8

Lesson 69—Education

The fundamental theory of liberty upon which all governments in this Union repose excludes any general power of the state to standardize its children by forcing them to accept instruction from public teachers only. The child is not the mere creature of the state; those who nurture him and direct his destiny have the right, coupled with the high duty, to recognize and prepare him for additional obligations.
—Pierce v. Society of Sisters *(1925 U.S. Supreme Court decision)*

The training of children is one of the most important functions that a family performs. Parents who bring children into the world are responsible for teaching those children to live well and to use their lives to serve the Lord. In the nineteenth and twentieth centuries, a philosophy of education arose in which the state was put forth as an important player in the training of children. Now the government is seen by many as the primary educator of

children. The government's role in education raises many important issues, some of which we will discuss in this lesson.

A Brief History of Education

Formal schools for the training of children were rare for most of human history. Most children lived at home and learned from their parents until they got married and started their own home. Wealthy families often provided tutors for their children or sent their children to small, private academies, where usually a single teacher guided a handful of students. Young men were sometimes apprenticed to a master craftsman in order to learn a trade.

The earliest schools in the American colonies were local schools, organized by local communities. A committee or board was formed to oversee the school; and the board hired a teacher, whose salary was paid by local taxes or by subscriptions (fees) paid by participating families. Such schools were small; they were intimately connected with the community; and they included Biblical, religious, and moral teaching as part of the curriculum since that is what most parents wanted and expected.

Since the early 1800s, social and government leaders have taken an increasing interest in promoting the training of children in formal school settings. Horace Mann was named secretary of the new Massachusetts State Board of Education in 1837. He was an activist in promoting public education and improving teacher preparation. Mann and other progressive leaders said that education was the key to a young person's success in life. However, the definition of success that Mann and others used was largely a secular one. The proper purpose they saw for public education was to create a population that fit in with social expectations and that would be trained to work in the growing number of factories in the country. The goals of encouraging children to excel and to enrich society with their individual talents were downplayed. Mann also urged the exclusion of religious teaching from public schools. The approach that Mann promoted began the process of severing education from community

The first compulsory school attendance law was passed in Massachusetts in 1852. The law required children between the ages of eight and fourteen to attend school for a minimum of three months each year. At least six weeks of their required three months had be consecutive. Some places did not have compulsory school attendance laws until the twentieth century. Today, the standard school year in all states is about 180 days.

values, from the importance of spiritual truth, and from close parental oversight.

Two key factors that increased the importance of public schools and decreased parental influence in their children's lives were compulsory attendance laws and state funding of education. Compulsory attendance laws require children between certain ages to attend school. These laws were promoted as serving the best interests of the children, but they also served to take control of a child's training away from the parents. Formal schooling became not an option provided to families but something that was required by law.

States increasingly encouraged counties and communities to establish schools, but state governments did not always back this encouragement with dollars. In some cases in the late nineteenth century, cities and counties received authority from the state to establish schools; but no state revenue was provided. The schools that were established were mostly small academies that served local communities and that were funded by tuition. State funding did not come about in these areas until school attendance was made compulsory by law in the 1900s. The combination of a compulsory attendance requirement and state funding proved to be the death knell of small, tuition-supported academies. Most parents opted to send their children to state-funded schools instead of paying school tuition in addition to paying state taxes. Private schools continued to operate, but often they were accessible only to the wealthy.

States have increasingly taken public education as a major function since the early years of the twentieth century. The Federal government got into the education act in the late 1950s, when Congress appropriated funds for the teaching of math and science education after the Soviet Union launched Sputnik in 1957 and the U.S. was embarrassed at being technologically behind the Communists.

Today, public education is big business. The total outlay for education by governments on all levels is around $450 billion per

Public School in Washington, D.C., c. 1900

year. State revenues account for over half of the money, local governments contribute about one-third, and the Federal government adds just under ten percent.

Formal schooling also takes more and more of a person's life. Before World War II, eight years of education were the norm in many states. Only a small percentage of children went on to high school. Now, public education encompasses kindergarten through grade twelve. Pre-K and programs for even younger children are growing in popularity in many states.

The broader reach of education also extends beyond high school. About half of American high school graduates go to college, and in many professions a master's degree is becoming a standard requirement. Thousands of students earn doctoral degrees each year, and some pursue post-doctoral studies.

The education establishment controls teacher training requirements, and this funnels students through college undergraduate and graduate programs so that they can be certified to teach in public schools and in accredited private schools. In addition, grade schools have increased their staffing requirements. Guidance counselors, reading specialists, technology officers, and other positions have become commonplace. However, the performance of schools in their primary job—the training of children—is dismal. The only answer offered by educators is that more money needs to be spent.

Kindergarten at Horace Mann School, Tulsa, Oklahoma, 1917

The Role and Rights of Parents

For most of history, parents were understood to have the primary responsibility for training their children. This began to change with the growth of public education in the early twentieth century, as the state came to play an increasing role in the training of children. Sometimes this zeal for state control of education went too far. For instance, Oregon's compulsory attendance law, passed in 1922, required all students to attend a public school with only a few exceptions (for example, if the student had completed the eighth grade, or if the child had special needs). The Society of Sisters was a Roman Catholic charitable organization that cared for orphans and provided private schooling for children. The Society sued the State of Oregon over the compulsory attendance law, claiming that enforcement of it would put the Society out of business.

The U.S. Supreme Court heard the case in 1925 and agreed with the Society that the Oregon law was too intrusive into the rights of parents to educate their children as they saw fit. This included the parents' right to send their children to a private school. The quotation at the beginning of this lesson indicates how the Court supported parental rights and responsibilities in this decision.

The Supreme Court also supported parents in the 1923 case *Meyer v. State of Nebraska*. Nebraska state law forbade any school from teaching a foreign language to a child who had not completed the eighth grade. The purpose of the law was to integrate the children of immigrants (many of whom were German or Scandinavian) into American life. State educators wanted the schools to teach only English until students completed the eighth grade, at which point most students would end their formal education. An instructor in a private school was arrested for teaching German to a ten-year-old student; and, as the saying goes, the case went all the way to the Supreme Court. The Court struck down the Nebraska law as overly broad. The court said:

> That the state may do much, go very far, indeed, in order to improve the qual-
> ity of its citizens, physically, mentally and morally, is clear; but the individual
> has certain fundamental rights which must be respected. The protection of the
> Constitution extends to all, to those who speak other languages as well as to

those born with English on the tongue. Perhaps it would be highly advantageous if all had ready understanding of our ordinary speech, but this cannot be coerced by methods which conflict with the Constitution.

. . . The desire of the Legislature to foster a homogeneous people with American ideals prepared readily to understand current discussions of civic matters is easy to appreciate. Unfortunate experiences during the late war and aversion toward every character of truculent adversaries were certainly enough to quicken that aspiration. But the means adopted, we think, exceed the limitations upon the power of the state and conflict with rights assured to plaintiff in error. The interference is plain enough and no adequate reason therefor in time of peace and domestic tranquility has been shown.

In other words, if parents wanted to send their child to a school that taught German below the eighth grade, they had the right to do so.

However, the Court has since ruled that the rights of parents to train their children as they see fit is limited. In *Prince v. Massachusetts* (1944), the Court ruled in a case involving a Jehovah's Witness mother who had been arrested for taking her children out onto the streets in the evening to sell tracts and to teach Witness doctrine. The Court opinion said:

To make accommodation between these [personal and religious] freedoms and an exercise of state authority always is delicate. It hardly could be more so than in such a clash as this case presents. On one side is the obviously earnest claim for freedom of conscience and religious practice. With it is allied the parent's claim to authority in her own household and in the rearing of her children. The parent's conflict with the state over control of the child and his training is serious enough when only secular matters are concerned. It becomes the more so when an element of religious conviction enters. Against these sacred private interests, basic in a democracy, stand the interests of society to protect the welfare of children, and the state's assertion of authority to that end, made here in a manner conceded valid if only secular things were involved. The last is no mere corporate concern of official authority. It is the interest of youth itself, and of the whole community, that children be both safeguarded from abuses and given opportunities for growth into free and independent well-developed men and citizens. . . .

[T]he family itself is not beyond regulation in the public interest, as against a claim of religious liberty. And neither rights of religion nor rights of parenthood are beyond limitation. Acting to guard the general interest in youth's well being, the state as parens patriae [literally, parent of the country; a phrase that means government as parent] may restrict the parent's control by requiring school attendance, regulating or prohibiting the child's labor, and in many other ways.

Today, the rights of parents regarding their children's education are being even more sharply limited. In the case *Fields v. Palmdale School District*, parents sued a school system in California over a survey given to seven- to ten-year-old public school students that asked questions about highly personal and sensitive issues. Parents had received letters notifying them of the survey, but the letter said nothing about questions involving sexuality. The Ninth Federal Circuit Court of Appeals upheld the actions of the school system in its 2005 ruling. The Circuit Court said:

> [We] hold that there is no fundamental right of parents to be the exclusive provider of information regarding sexual matters to their children, either independent of their right to direct the upbringing and education of their children or encompassed by it. We also hold that parents have no due process or privacy right to override the determinations of public schools as to the information to which their children will be exposed while enrolled as students. . . .
>
> [O]nce parents make the choice as to which school their children will attend, their fundamental right to control the education of their children is, at the least, substantially diminished. . . .
>
> [W]e affirm that the *Meyer-Pierce* right [the right of parents as stated in the two cases discussed above] does not extend beyond the threshold of the school door. . . .
>
> [E]ducation is not merely about teaching the basics of reading, writing, and arithmetic. Education serves higher civic and social functions, including the rearing of children into healthy, productive, and responsible adults and the cultivation of talented and qualified leaders of diverse backgrounds.

What This Means

The implications of these trends are many. First, public schools, which once reflected community values and beliefs, have been taken out of the hands of local parents who pay for them. The policies and practices of public schools and professional educators are largely untouchable, as far as the courts are concerned.

Second, this control over education is increasingly flowing to the Federal level. The Federal government is spending more money for education than ever before. The No Child Left Behind Act (NCLB), signed into law in January of 2002, gives the greatest control yet by the Federal government over local schools. The purpose of the law was to make schools more accountable for their results by measuring yearly progress in standardized reading and math test scores. Schools are required to close the achievement gaps between different groups of students (for example, white, black, Hispanic, economically disadvantaged, and disabled students). If a school does not make the required progress two years in a row, parents can

U.S. Air Force Master Sergeant Visiting a First Grade Class, Culver City, California, 2002

decide to send their children to another school from choices selected for them by the school district. States can adapt NCLB standards to their own situations to some degree. Many professional educators do not like the NCLB law, complaining that the law sets standards but does not give enough funding or guidance to states to enable them to reach those standards. The primary issue in the debate, however, is not really the students but the control of school operations. It is a shame that so much of our tax money goes to an institution that often attacks the most deeply held beliefs that Christians have.

Third, public education has reached this point for many reasons; but one main reason is that Christian parents and teachers have let it happen. Christians who teach in the public schools have compromised their beliefs in order to keep their jobs and to go along with cultural practices. If Christian schoolteachers had said, "We're not going to muzzle our faith in the schoolroom—fire us if you wish" and if Christian parents had supported them, things would be different. Either expressions of faith and the exalting of truth and purity in public schools would still be allowed, or Christians would have long ago abandoned public education and developed a more vibrant and effective system of training children.

Learning at Home

Fourth, Christian families are increasingly considering either Christian schools or homeschooling for the training of their children. Both of these options provide a viable alternative to secular, public education.

Public education has provided much that is good. Without a doubt, many Americans have used their education to better themselves financially. The GI Bill has enabled millions of veterans to attend college and provide for their families probably better than they would have otherwise. The moral and spiritual effects of public education, however, are another matter. Christians schools and homeschooling are attempts to provide the benefits of education without compromising the spiritual training of children.

Beware of the false prophets, who come to you in sheep's clothing,
but inwardly are ravenous wolves.
Matthew 7:15

Lesson 70—Abortion

Abortion is advocated only by persons who have themselves been born.
—Ronald Reagan

Is it a human being, deserving the rights and protection of the Constitution, or is it merely something that is subject to the decisions of someone else?

Is the Constitution the final answer, or should we appeal to a higher law?

Is the core issue what one side says it is, or is the core issue what the other side says it is?

Should we view the matter as the most important moral, spiritual, and political issue of the day, or is it a settled issue that should be left alone?

These are questions that swirl around the subject of abortion today. However, they are also some of the questions that swirled around the subject of slavery before the Civil War. The numerous parallels between the two issues help us to see what is at stake in the abortion

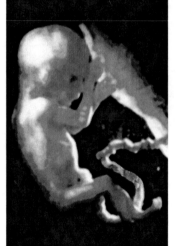

debate, what those who oppose abortion can do about it, and what the proper actions of government are.

Much can and should be said about abortion as a moral and spiritual issue. For the purpose of this curriculum, however, we will focus on government policies regarding abortion. Suffice it to be said that abortion is a great moral wrong which God-fearing people should oppose.

The *Roe* and *Casey* Decisions

Before 1973, states had various laws regarding abortion. Many states outlawed the procedure altogether, while some, such as Texas, allowed it only when a doctor found that the mother's health was at risk because of the pregnancy. Jane Roe was the pseudonym of a woman who was unable to obtain an abortion because of the restrictive Texas law. The case was argued twice before the Supreme Court, which announced its 7-2 decision in 1973.

The Court declared that the right of a woman to obtain an abortion was protected by what it called the right to privacy, a right that the Court had declared in *Griswold v. Connecticut* in 1965. This right, though not stated in the Constitution, was described in *Griswold* as being within the penumbra of the provisions of the Bill of Rights. Basing its decision on the medical knowledge of the day, the Court declared that the right

Jane Roe was eventually identified as Norma McCorvey. McCorvey eventually disassociated herself from the Roe *decision. She became a Christian and worked against abortion. McCorvey herself never had an abortion.*

to an abortion was affected by the trimesters of a woman's pregnancy. In the first trimester, the right to an abortion was virtually unlimited. States could restrict the right to an abortion during the second trimester to cases involving the mother's health. Finally, states could restrict and even ban abortions during the final trimester except when the health and life of the mother were clearly at risk.

The majority of the Court determined that the original intent of the Constitution did not include extending Constitutional rights to the unborn. In addition, the Court declined to address the issue of when life begins:

> We need not resolve the difficult question of when life begins. When those trained in the respective disciplines of medicine, philosophy, and theology are unable to arrive at any consensus, the judiciary, at this point in the development of man's knowledge, is not in a position to speculate as to the answer.

Roe v. Wade affected the abortion laws of 46 states.

The *Roe* decision was upheld in the 1992 case *Planned Parenthood v. Casey*. This case involved limitations that Pennsylvania law placed on a woman's right to obtain an abortion. For instance, the state law required that a woman be told what would happen during an abortion and that she agree to the procedure in a process called informed consent. The state also required a 24-hour waiting period after a woman requested an abortion before it could be performed. A minor who wanted to have an abortion had to have the consent of one parent, although she could obtain a judge's permission instead in some cases. A married woman had to inform her husband of her intention to obtain an abortion.

Over 47 million abortions have been performed in the United States since the Roe v. Wade *decision in 1973. Abortions were already taking place in some states before the decision. Over one million abortions are performed every year in the U.S., or about 3,600 every day.*

The *Casey* decision upheld all of the Pennsylvania restrictions except the one requiring that the husband be notified. More significantly, however, the 5-4 decision upheld the basic right to an abortion that had been stated in *Roe*.

The Issues Surrounding Slavery

Let us review some of the issues that surrounded slavery in the period leading up to the Civil War. Slavery was seen by abolitionists as the most important moral, spiritual, and political question of the day. How America dealt with slavery, they said, communicated the most important truths about who and what America was. Those who supported slavery, on the other hand, saw it as a settled issue. They said that the "peculiar institution" was protected by the Constitution and should be left alone. Most pro-slavery spokesmen wanted the right to extend slavery into the territories beyond the states where it already existed.

The main question in the slavery debate involved determining whether slaves were human beings who deserved equal protection under the Constitution or mere property that was subject to the decisions of their owners. Defenders of slavery saw slaves as property. The *Dred Scott* decision of the Supreme Court upheld the view that slaves were not citizens and thus did not have rights under the Constitution. Opponents of slavery, on the other hand, pointed to the obvious reality that slaves were human beings. Senator William H. Seward said in 1850 that the country should look to "a higher law than the Constitution" (namely, the teachings of the Christian faith) to determine government policy regarding slavery.

The core issue in the slavery question, according to abolitionists, was how the country treated slaves. Were they human beings? Was it not hypocrisy to claim to be the land of the free while millions were enslaved? Proponents of slavery, by contrast, said that the core issue was states' rights. States ought to be able to govern their own internal practices without interference by the Federal government, and the Constitution nowhere gave the Federal government the power to legislate on slavery.

The Issues Surrounding Abortion

The parallels between the slavery debate and the abortion debate are amazing. Opponents of abortion believe that it is the most important spiritual, moral, and political issue of the day. How America handles the issue of abortion, they say, provides the most telling evidence about who we are as a people. Defenders of abortion say that it is a settled issue and should be left alone just as it is, except perhaps that access to abortion should be even more readily available.

Pro-abortion forces say that the unborn child is a fetus, a blob of tissue, and not a human being that deserves protection by the Constitution. Pro-life advocates say that

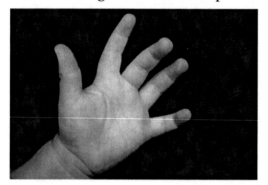

the unborn child is a human being, with a distinct DNA identity. Although the Constitution does not specifically address the rights of the unborn, pro-life groups refer to a "higher law than the Constitution," namely God's law, that tells of the human identity and eternal value of the unborn child.

Advocates of abortion say that the main issue involves the rights of women: reproductive choices, the right to control their own bodies, and the supposed Constitutional right of privacy that the *Roe* decision affirmed. To abortion advocates, the unborn child does not have any rights. Opponents of abortion say that the fundamental issue involves the rights of the unborn child to life and to due process of law.

What Government Can Do

Government is made up of people. Elected officials lead government and create laws. Voters should insist on knowing how candidates stand on the issue of abortion and what the candidates promise to do about it if they are elected. The populace should hold elected officials accountable for what they actually do on this issue.

Congress and the state legislatures could abolish all funds that support the performing of abortions. Even though abortion has not been outlawed, it does not have to be supported by the taxes of people who oppose it. This move would be controversial because abortion is big business, and the loss of public funds would be vigorously opposed by the abortion industry.

The Supreme Court could reverse the *Roe v. Wade* decision, just as the Court eventually reversed the *Plessy v. Ferguson* decision that legitimized racial segregation. The *Roe* decision was based on faulty logic and on the medical capabilities that were known in 1973. Those capabilities have advanced dramatically since then, but even more important is the need to recognize the rights of the unborn child.

A constitutional amendment guaranteeing the rights of all people from the moment of conception could be passed by Congress and ratified by the states. This is how the Thirteenth Amendment permanently outlawed slavery even after the Emancipation Proclamation and other wartime steps greatly reduced the practice of slavery. Laws are helpful, but laws can be overturned by five members of the Supreme Court.

Those who oppose abortion need first to exemplify and to encourage God's plan for having children within marriage. In addition, we need to develop realistic and compassionate plans to care for expectant mothers and their children. This does not necessarily mean government assistance. In fact, it would be better if such help came from churches and other private sources. Giving birth to a child needs to be more attractive to an expectant mother than aborting it. Fathers need to bear the responsibility for their children. Mothers need to be encouraged in caring for their children. Families that are willing to adopt also need support. Many families are eager to adopt children, but the slow-moving bureaucracies of state child services departments and the high cost of private and foreign adoptions make the process difficult. It is not enough to oppose abortion. Abortion foes must provide a workable way to care for the greater number of God's treasures who will be born when abortion is made illegal.

Recent Developments

In 2003, Congress passed and President Bush signed into law a ban on partial birth abortions. This is a procedure used in late-term abortions in which part of the baby's body is delivered and then the baby is put to death by the abortionist. However, the law has never been enforced. Several Federal district and appeals courts have ruled that the law is unconstitutional because it does not provide an exception if the health of the mother is at risk. The U.S. Supreme Court agreed in 2006 to hear an appeal of one of the cases.

In February of 2006, South Dakota enacted a ban on almost all abortions in the state. The bill passed both houses of the legislature by large majorities and the pro-life governor signed it into law. Supporters of the measure said that it was intended to be a direct challenge to the *Roe v. Wade* decision. They hoped that the two new Supreme Court justices appointed by President Bush would help to overturn *Roe*. However, South Dakota's anti-abortion law was overturned in a November 2006 referendum by a 56% to 44% vote.

About a half dozen other state legislatures confronted abortion either by passing restrictive laws or by proposing amendments to the state constitution that would fully or virtually outlaw abortion.

Taking the Moral High Ground

For centuries adults have abused and taken advantage of children. In the United States, it used to take the form of slavery and child labor. Today, one form it takes is abortion. This makes abortion the key moral, spiritual, and political issue of our day.

Before government will act, however, more of the American people will have to take up the cause of life. Christians need not only to oppose abortion but also to be leaders in standing up for children and others who do not have a voice in the political and social system. This includes opposing the commercial exploitation of children by advertisers and others who want to target children for the purpose of financial gain. Christians should remember that Jesus said a willingness to receive children is a requirement for entering the kingdom of God (Mark 10:15).

Another way that Christians can show compassion and take the higher moral ground is in how we treat those who support abortion. If the parallel with the slavery-abolition controversy is valid, we should remember that some great Americans whom we respect today owned slaves. George Washington and Thomas Jefferson, among many other leaders in the early nation, owned slaves. Daniel Webster opposed slavery, but in 1850 he was willing to let it continue for the sake of preserving the Union. We must help others see God's truth about the meaning and value of human life, but to do this effectively we must have a gentle and loving attitude even toward those with whom we disagree on this most important issue.

Those who oppose abortion need to find some way to move the hearts of the American people against abortion the way that Harriet Beecher Stowe moved hearts against slavery with her book *Uncle Tom's Cabin*. If the American people really understand what actually happens to a baby in an abortion, how abortion abuses women as well as children, and the profit motive involved in continuing the abortion industry, perhaps there is enough decency still left among us to put an end to this practice and to gain a new appreciation of the gift of life that God gives to each of us.

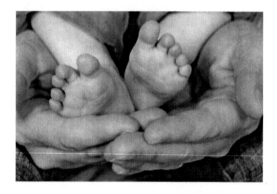

For You formed my inward parts; You wove me in my mother's womb.
I will give thanks to You, for I am fearfully and wonderfully made;
wonderful are Your works, and my soul knows it very well.
Psalm 139:13-14

Reading

- South Dakota 2006 Law Regarding Abortion (*WHTT*, p. 94)

15 Toward a Better America

In this last unit, we consider how our country can become more of what it ought to be. We look first at church and state issues from the perspective of the First Amendment. What constitutes the establishment of religion, and what does the free exercise of religion mean? We then suggest ways that reform might come about, including the possibility of your running for public office. We conclude with a survey of the rights and responsibilities of every American Christian.

Lessons in This Unit

Lesson 71—Avoiding the Establishment of Religion
Lesson 72—Freedom of Religious Expression
Lesson 73—Reforming Government
Lesson 74—Running for and Holding Public Office
Lesson 75—A Citizen's Rights and Responsibilities

Activity Idea

How is government the solution, and how is it the problem? In whose hands does your future lie—your own hands, the hands of powerful people and institutions, or God's hands? Write two or three pages on where you think America should go from here and what you plan to do about it.

If you are using the optional *Quiz and Exam Book*, answer the questions for each lesson after you have completed the lesson and read any assigned readings in *We Hold These Truths*. After you have completed Lesson 75, take the quiz for Unit 15 and the third exam, which covers Units 11-15.

Lesson 71— Avoiding the Establishment of Religion

Congress shall make no law respecting an establishment of religion . . . .
—First words of the First Amendment to the U.S. Constitution

The plain, original meaning of this clause of the First Amendment is clear. Congress is not to establish an official national religion, the way that European countries had done

Savannah, Georgia

for centuries. At the same time, the First Amendment also says that Congress may not prohibit the free exercise of religion. The amendment does not mean that the government cannot acknowledge God in any way. The houses of Congress have paid chaplains. Church services were held in the House chamber on Sundays for many years. Presidents have issued Thanksgiving proclamations that confessed our nation's dependence on God. Congress passed resolutions calling for days of fasting and prayer. Congress made the phrase "In God We Trust" the official national motto; and the motto appears on all U.S. coins and currency.

The First Amendment creates a delicate tightrope that Congress must walk. On one hand, Congress must avoid establishing a religion; but a too stringent application of this clause can prohibit the free exercise of religion. On the other hand, the free exercise of religion can create the possibility of government recognition of religious beliefs, which can be challenged as an establishment of religion. Supreme Court decisions dealing with issues related to this clause have attempted to define this tightrope.

Jefferson's "Wall of Separation"

In 1801, the Danbury (Connecticut) Baptist Association wrote a letter to the new President, Thomas Jefferson. The Baptists believed that their rights in the state were limited because the Congregationalist church was the established church in Connecticut. The Baptists asked for Jefferson's endorsement of the idea that people should be free to worship God in any way they choose without interference from the state. In his reply, Jefferson said that the First Amendment made a "wall of separation between Church and State." In other words, the wall was to protect the church from the state. The state was not to interfere with the activities of a church.

Jefferson's phrase "wall of separation," which expressed his personal opinion in a private letter, has become the standard for dealing with church and state issues. It has been quoted in Supreme Court opinions even though the phrase is not used in the Constitution. The phrase is now interpreted by many to mean that the state must not condone or participate in any religious expression whatsoever. In other words, the wall is now seen as protecting the state from the church and from any and all religious expression.

In considering the meaning of the establishment/free exercise clause, we must try to delineate (1) what is right and proper according to the letter of the Constitution and the intention of its authors (that is, what ought to be) and (2) what the Supreme Court has said is the meaning of the clause (in other words, what the law is that we must deal with). These two are not always the same thing, but the decisions of the Court are what we must live by unless we are willing to violate the law of the land.

The First Amendment was originally meant to limit the actions of Congress. The Court later interpreted the Fourteenth Amendment to mean that the provisions of the Constitution applied to state and local governments also. The bulk of cases that have come before the Supreme Court have dealt with state and local rather than Federal laws. In this lesson we will look at Court cases that emphasize the non-establishment clause. We will consider freedom of religious expression cases in the next lesson.

Government Association with Religion

Many cases that have come before the Court have dealt with state assistance to or involvement with private, church-related schools. In considering this area of American life, the Court has expressed certain principles.

The Supreme Court has recognized the essential religious nature and religious needs of the American people. In the mid-twentieth century, some churches wanted to provide religious instruction to students who were enrolled in public schools. The Champaign, Illinois schools adopted a policy that allowed non-school employees (often ministers) to teach these classes to interested students in available classrooms in school facilities during the school day. In 1948, the Court struck down this policy as a violation of the separation of church and state. Four years later, the Court upheld a New York City school policy that allowed students to go off-campus to receive religious instruction. This policy was called released time instruction. In writing for the majority, Associate Justice William O. Douglas (who usually took a liberal stance) wrote:

We are a religious people whose institutions presuppose a Supreme Being. We guarantee the freedom to worship as one chooses. We make room for as wide a variety of beliefs and creeds as the spiritual needs of man deem necessary. We sponsor an attitude on the part of government that shows no partiality to any one group and that lets each flourish according to the zeal of its adherents and the appeal of its dogma. When the state encourages religious instruction or cooperates with religious authorities by adjusting the schedule of public events to sectarian needs, it follows the best of our traditions. For it then respects the religious nature of our people and accommodates the public service to their spiritual needs. To hold that it may not would be to find in the Constitution a requirement that the government show a callous indifference to religious groups. That would be preferring those who believe in no religion over those who do believe. Government may not finance religious groups nor undertake religious instruction nor blend secular and sectarian education nor use secular institutions to force one or some religion on any person. But we find no constitutional requirement which makes it necessary for government to be hostile to religion and to throw its weight against efforts to widen the effective scope of religious influence. The government must be neutral when it comes to competition between sects. It may not thrust any sect on any person. It may not make a religious observance compulsory. It may not coerce anyone to attend church, to observe a religious holiday, or to take religious instruction. But it can close its doors or suspend its operations as to those who want to repair to their religious sanctuary for worship or instruction. (*Zorach v. Clauson*, 1952)

The Supreme Court has made a distinction between the state giving assistance to students who attend religious schools and giving assistance directly to the schools. In *Everson v. Board of Education of Ewing Township* (1947), the Court upheld a New Jersey state law that provided reimbursement to parents who incurred transportation costs in sending their children to school, whether the school was public or private. The Court declared:

[W]e cannot say that the First Amendment prohibits New Jersey from spending taxraised funds to pay the bus fares of parochial school pupils as a part of a general program under which it pays the fares of pupils attending public and other schools. It is undoubtedly true that children are helped to get to church schools. There is even a possibility that some of the children might not be sent to the church schools if the parents were compelled to pay their children's bus fares out of their own pockets when transportation to a public school would have been paid for by the State. The same possibility exists where the state requires a local transit company to provide reduced fares to school children including those attending parochial schools, or where a municipally owned transportation system undertakes to carry all school children free of charge. . . . This Court has said that parents may, in the discharge of their duty under state compulsory education laws, send their children to a religious rather than a public school if the school meets the secular educational requirements which the state has power to impose. It appears that these parochial schools meet New Jersey's requirements. The State contributes no money to the schools. It does not support them. Its legislation, as applied, does no more than provide a general program to help parents get their children, regardless of their religion, safely and expeditiously to and from accredited schools.

The Court later required a state to pay for a sign-language interpreter to accompany a deaf student to a religious school, since Federal and state law required the school district to provide such services to students (*Zobrest v. Catalina Foothills School District*, 1993). This principle is also why students attending a religious college may receive government grants or loans. The religious college benefits indirectly from the government money, but the money goes to individual students and not the school.

The Court has devised a three-part test to determine whether a law respects the establishment clause.

First, the statute must have a secular legislative purpose; second, its principal or primary effect must be one that neither advances nor inhibits religion; finally, the statute must not foster "an excessive government entanglement with religion." (*Lemon v. Kurtzman*, 1971)

This ruling came in a decision that considered two state laws which (1) gave private school teachers a pay supplement if their schools' per-pupil expenditure was below the state public school average and (2) allowed local school districts to "purchase secular educational services" from non-public schools, such as the teaching of math, science, and foreign languages. The Court struck down these laws as creating an excessive government entanglement with religion. This three-part screen came to known as the *Lemon* test.

Religious Expression in Government-Sponsored School Settings

The New York State Board of Regents, "a governmental agency created by the State Constitution to which the New York Legislature has granted broad supervisory, executive, and legislative powers over the State's public school system," composed a prayer which it required to be recited "aloud by each class in the presence of a teacher at the beginning of each school day:

> 'Almighty God, we acknowledge our dependence upon Thee, and we beg Thy blessings upon us, our parents, our teachers and our Country.'"

A group of parents sued to have the practice stopped in the school district where their children were enrolled. In *Engel v. Vitale* (1962), the Supreme Court struck down the practice as a violation of the establishment clause. The Court said, "[W]e think that the constitutional prohibition against laws respecting an establishment of religion must at least mean that in this country it is no part of the business of government to compose official prayers for any group of the American people to recite as a part of a religious program carried on by government."

In a similar vein the next year, the Court ruled against a Pennsylvania law which required that, "At least ten verses from the Holy Bible shall be read, without comment, at the opening of each public school on each school day. Any child shall be excused from such Bible reading, or attending such Bible reading, upon the written request of his parent or guardian" (*Abington School District v. Schempp*, 1963). These two decisions are the ones frequently cited by critics of the Supreme Court when they say that the Court has taken prayer and Bible reading out of public schools.

The 1985 case *Wallace v. Jaffree* challenged an Alabama law providing for a one-minute period of silence at the beginning of each public school day "for meditation or prayer." The Court ruled this law to be unconstitutional because it mentioned prayer and thus was seen by a majority of the Court as promoting religion. Concurring opinions suggested that a law which authorized simply a moment of silence might be acceptable. Then in 1992, the Court ruled in *Lee v. Weisman* that a school-sponsored prayer at a public high school graduation ceremony violated the establishment clause. School officials planned for prayers to be included in the program, selected the religious officiant, and gave him guidelines on what should be said in the prayer. Since non-participation in a graduation exercise is not a realistic option, the Court said that the practice had the effect of coercing students to engage in a religious activity.

The Pledge of Allegiance: "One Nation Under God"

In June 2004, the Court issued its opinions in the case *Elk Grove Unified School District et al. v. Newdow et al.* Mr. Newdow, a parent of a child enrolled in the school district and an atheist, sued to stop the practice of schoolchildren reciting the Pledge of Allegiance because it contains the phrase "one nation under God." Newdow is divorced from the child's mother, who is the child's only legal custodian.

Pledging Allegiance to the Flag, New York City, 1958

The Ninth Federal Circuit Court of Appeals (the same circuit that ruled against parents' objections to an inappropriate survey; see Lesson 69) ruled that the phrase "under God" in the Pledge was a violation of the separation of church and state. However, the Supreme Court dismissed the case in a rare, unanimous opinion (the vote was 8-0 because Justice Antonin Scalia did not participate). The majority opinion, written by Justice John Paul Stephens, held that Newdow did not have legal standing to bring the suit and was not himself harmed by the school district's policy. A concurring opinion, written by Chief Justice Rehnquist, also addressed the issue of the phrase "one nation under God" itself. Rehnquist wrote:

I do not believe that the phrase "under God" in the Pledge converts its recital into a "religious exercise" of the sort described in *Lee* [*v. Weisman*]. Instead, it is a declaration of belief in allegiance and loyalty to the United States flag and the Republic that it represents. The phrase "under God" is in no sense a prayer, nor an endorsement of any religion, but a simple recognition of the fact noted in [a House resolution]: "From the time of our earliest history our peoples and our institutions have reflected the traditional concept that our Nation was founded on a fundamental belief in God." Reciting the Pledge, or listening to others recite it, is a patriotic exercise, not a religious one; participants promise fidelity to our flag and our Nation, not to any particular God, faith, or church.

There is no doubt that respondent is sincere in his atheism and rejection of a belief in God. But the mere fact that he disagrees with this part of the Pledge does not give him a veto power over the decision of the public schools that willing participants should pledge allegiance to the flag in the manner prescribed by Congress. There may be others who disagree, not with the phrase "under God," but with the phrase "with liberty and justice for all." But surely that would not give such objectors the right to veto the holding of such a ceremony by those willing to participate. Only if it can be said that the phrase "under God" somehow tends to the establishment of a religion in violation of the First Amendment can respondent's claim succeed, where one based on objections to "with liberty and justice for all" fails. Our cases have broadly interpreted this phrase, but none have gone anywhere near as far as the decision of the Court of Appeals in this case [which had upheld Newdow's complaint]. The recital, in a patriotic ceremony pledging allegiance to the flag and to the Nation, of the descriptive phrase "under God" cannot possibly lead to the establishment of a religion, or anything like it.

When courts extend constitutional prohibitions beyond their previously recognized limit, they may restrict democratic choices made by public bodies. Here, Congress prescribed a Pledge of Allegiance, the State of California required patriotic observances in its schools, and the School District chose to comply by requiring teacher-led recital of the Pledge of Allegiance by willing students. Thus, we have three levels of popular government—the national, the state, and the local—collaborating to produce the Elk Grove ceremony. The Constitution only requires that schoolchildren be entitled to abstain from the ceremony if they chose to do so. To give the parent of such a child a sort of "heckler's veto" over a patriotic ceremony willingly participated in by other students, simply because the Pledge of Allegiance contains the descriptive phrase "under God," is an unwarranted extension of the Establishment Clause, an extension which would have the unfortunate effect of prohibiting a commendable patriotic observance.

Ten Commandments and Nativity Displays

Roy Moore, a West Point graduate and Vietnam veteran, earned a law degree and then in 1992 became an Alabama state circuit court judge. While in that position he displayed a copy of the Ten Commandments in his courtroom and occasionally led prayer from the bench. The ACLU sued Judge Moore over these practices, but the cases were dismissed. In 2000 he was elected Chief Justice of the Alabama Supreme Court. The next year, Moore had installed in the rotunda of the state judicial building a granite monument displaying the religious heritage of U.S. law and government. Included on that monument was a copy of the Ten Commandments. Moore was sued by the ACLU and other groups in Federal district court, which ordered the monument removed. Moore refused to do so. The case was appealed to the Eleventh Federal Circuit Court of Appeals, which upheld the district court's decision. The U.S. Supreme Court declined to review the case. The rest of the Alabama Supreme Court suspended Moore, and the Alabama Court of the Judiciary (a review panel) removed him from office in 2003.

In 2005, the U.S. Supreme Court issued two different rulings on what appeared to be similar cases. A stone monument, one of many monuments in a park adjacent to the Texas State Capitol in Austin, displays the Ten Commandments. It had been placed there forty years earlier by a private civic group to recognize the text's influence on American law and to encourage godly living by Texas citizens. A petitioner complained that the presence of the monument violated the First Amendment's establishment clause. The Court ruled 5-4 that the display did not violate the First Amendment. Chief Justice Rehnquist said,

Of course, the Ten Commandments are religious—they were so viewed at their inception and so remain. The monument, therefore, has religious significance. According to Judeo-Christian belief, the Ten Commandments were given to Moses by God on Mt. Sinai. But Moses was a lawgiver as well as a religious leader. And the Ten Commandments have an undeniable historical meaning, as the foregoing examples demonstrate. Simply having religious content or promoting a message consistent with a religious doctrine does not run afoul of the Establishment Clause.

There are, of course, limits to the display of religious messages or symbols. For example, we held unconstitutional a Kentucky statute requiring the posting of the Ten Commandments in every public schoolroom (*Stone v. Graham*, 1980). In the classroom context, we found that the Kentucky statute had an improper and plainly religious purpose. . . .

The placement of the Ten Commandments monument on the Texas State Capitol grounds is a far more passive use of those texts than was the case in *Stone*, where the text confronted elementary school students every day. Indeed, Van Orden, the petitioner here, apparently walked by the monument for a number of years before bringing this lawsuit. . . . Texas has treated her Capitol grounds monuments as representing the several strands in the State's political and legal history. The inclusion of the Ten Commandments monument in this group has a dual significance, partaking of both religion and government. We cannot say that Texas' display of this monument violates the Establishment Clause of the First Amendment.

At the same time, in *McCrary County, Kentucky, et al. v. American Civil Liberties Union of Kentucky*, the Court held that displays in public facilities of the Ten Commandments and other documents from American history that emphasized our religious roots were a violation of the Establishment Clause in that they were promoting religion. Actually, a succession of displays had been created; and changes that had been incorporated in the display were attempts to deal with objections.

Justice David Souter, writing for the majority, emphasized the importance that the Founders placed on the government being religiously neutral. "[T]he divisiveness of religion in current public life is inescapable. This is no time to deny the prudence of understanding the Establishment Clause to require the Government to stay neutral on religious belief, which is reserved for the conscience of the individual."

> The Supreme Court has upheld Sunday closing laws as a legitimate action by governments to encourage rest, even though making Sunday a special day has religious roots (McGowan v. Maryland, 1961). Also, the Court has sustained tax exemptions for churches because churches contribute to the cultural well-being of a community the way that libraries, museums, and other tax-exempt institutions do (Walz v. Tax Commission of City of New York, 1970).

In dissent, Justice Scalia emphasized the importance of faith in the American system and in American history and expressed his belief that the displays in question were within the previous judgments of the Court and the traditions of the United States.

The first displays did not necessarily evidence an intent to further religious practice; nor did the second displays, or the resolutions authorizing them; and there is in any event no basis for attributing whatever intent motivated the first and second displays to the third. Given the presumption of regularity that always accompanies our review of official action, the Court has identified no evidence of a purpose to advance religion in a way that is inconsistent with our cases. The Court may well be correct in identifying the third displays as the fruit of a desire to display the Ten Commandments, but neither our cases nor our history support its assertion that such a desire renders the fruit poisonous.

More recently, Federal Circuit Courts of Appeal have upheld displays of historic documents that do not give particular emphasis to the Ten Commandments. The Supreme Court has also decided differently in 5-4 votes on two similar cases involving Christmas displays on public grounds. In 1984, *Lynch v. Donnelly* held that inclusion of a nativity scene in a city's Christmas display was not an establishment of religion. Instead, it was a recognition of the historic background of what had become a national holiday. On the other hand, in *Allegheny County v. Greater Pittsburgh ACLU* (1989), the Court ruled against a nativity scene that was set up by itself on a central staircase inside a county courthouse. The scene was accompanied by a sign indicating that it was a gift from a Roman Catholic group and by a banner which said, "Gloria in Excelsis Deo" (Latin for "Glory to God in the highest.")

Nativity Scene Displayed in Centennial Park in Nashville, Tennessee, c. 1960

We can see the narrow tightrope on which government and the supporters of religious expression walk, as well as the frequency with which opponents of religious expression charge that any such expression in a public setting is a violation of the First Amendment. The propriety of such expressions with reference to the First Amendment is decided on a case-by-case basis, although the Supreme Court has established general principles by which such expressions are judged.

Blessed is the nation whose God is the Lord,
the people whom He has chosen for His own inheritance.
Psalm 33:12

Reading

- Exchange of Letters between Danbury (Connecticut) Baptist Association and President Thomas Jefferson (*WHTT*, p. 65)

- "The Ten Commandments Controversy" by Michael Novak (*WHTT*, p. 195)

Lesson 72—Freedom of Religious Expression

. . . or prohibiting the free exercise thereof. . . .
—First Amendment to the U.S. Constitution

The free exercise of religion is more than just having personal beliefs. It involves spoken words and physical actions. The purpose of this second religion clause in the First Amendment is to prevent the state from interfering with or criminalizing the legitimate expression of religious faith. Just as we saw with the previous question of what constitutes the establishment of religion, the issues surrounding the freedom of religious expression involve defining precisely what that phrase means.

School Activities and Peaceful Assemblies

As with the Establishment Clause, battles over the Free Expression clause have often been centered in activities that involve public schools. In 1940, the Supreme Court

Saluting the Flag, Juneau, Alaska, 1915

ruled in *West Virginia Board of Education v. Barnette* that the state Board of Education could not require public school students to give a raised-hand salute to the United States flag. The court case came about because Jehovah's Witnesses believed that giving such a salute constituted the worship of a graven image, which in their view violated the second of the Ten Commandments. Witnesses' children had been expelled from school and their parents had been prosecuted for violating state law. The Court declared that the state could not compel an action that interfered with a person's free exercise of religion.

The Court determined in *Wisconsin v. Yoder* (1972) that the State of Wisconsin could not compel the children of the Old Order Amish faith to attend public school beyond the eighth grade. The state contended that its interest in educating the children of the state outweighed any discomfort that Old Order Amish children might have by attending public school. However, the Court agreed with the arguments of the Amish, that such compulsory attendance beyond the eighth grade threatened the social order and customs of the Amish as well as their religious beliefs.

They [the Old Order Amish] object to the high school, and higher education generally, because the values they teach are in marked variance with Amish values and the Amish way of life; they view secondary school education as an impermissible exposure of their children to a "worldly" influence in conflict with their beliefs. The high school tends to emphasize intellectual and scientific accomplishments, self-distinction, competitiveness, worldly success, and social life with other students. Amish society emphasizes informal learning-through-doing; a life of "goodness," rather than a life of intellect; wisdom, rather than technical knowledge; community welfare, rather than competition; and separation from, rather than integration with, contemporary worldly society.

Formal high school education beyond the eighth grade is contrary to Amish beliefs, not only because it places Amish children in an environment hostile to Amish beliefs with increasing emphasis on competition in class work and sports and with pressure to conform to the styles, manners, and ways of the peer group, but also because it takes them away from their community, physically and emotionally, during the crucial and formative adolescent period of life.

The compelling factors that the Court considered in this case were: (1) whether the religious belief was sincere, (2) whether the government's action imposed a burden on the free exercise of that belief, and (3) whether the government's interest could be achieved by a less restrictive means. These factors are sometimes called the *Yoder* test.

The Court has consistently ruled that public facilities which are available to the public must also be made available to religious groups. Doing so upholds the Free Exercise clause (and the free speech clause) without violating the Establishment clause. If a school sponsors a chess club, scuba club, and so forth, it cannot forbid the organizing of a Bible club. If public facilities are available for groups to rent or use, they must be made available to religious groups. In *Widmar v. Vincent* (1981), the Court held that a university could not bar a religious group from meeting in school facilities simply because it was religious if it allowed other groups to meet in those facilities. Such a ban would violate the free speech and free expression of religion clauses in the First Amendment. In avoiding the establishment of religion, the Court has said that the government must not be an enemy of the free expression of religion.

Other Issues

The Court has held that a church may discriminate on the basis of religious faith in the hiring of workers for even its non-religious functions. It ruled that a church may require that someone hired to work in a non-profit gymnasium open to the public be a member of that church (*Corporation of the Presiding Bishop v. Amos*, 1983). This control over hiring is a legitimate use of the Free Expression clause that overrides laws which forbid discrimination in hiring practices.

In *Gillette v. United States* (1971), the Court ruled that conscientious exemption status may be granted to someone who has been drafted for military service but objects to a particular war (in this case, the Vietnam War), and not necessarily to war in general. The broader restriction had been the standard used by Congress in providing for conscientious objector status. When someone states his conscientious objection to a particular war, it must be based on religious teachings that seek to define whether or not a war is just.

The Court found that a provision in the Maryland constitution requiring a "declaration of belief in the existence of God" for public officials violated the First Amendment (*Torcaso v. Watkins*, 1961). Some years later, the Court ruled that a Tennessee law barring ministers and priests from serving in a called state constitutional convention wrongly infringed on their freedom of religious expression (*McDaniel v. Paty*, 1978). In other words, they should not have been barred simply because of their ministerial profession. Since the Tennessee state constitution has a similar provision barring clergy from the state legislature, the Court's ruling is taken to mean that this provision is also an abridgment of a person's freedom of religious expression.

Limitations to Free Exercise

The right to free exercise of religion is not absolute. In 1968, the Court ruled that a person could not engage in acts that were otherwise illegal in the name of a religious exercise. The Court decided against a man who claimed that using illegal drugs was a part of his religious expression. The Court later upheld a state court finding that two men who were fired from their jobs for using illegal drugs in a Native American religious ceremony were not entitled to state unemployment benefits (*Oregon v. Smith*, 1990).

In 1983, the Court ruled that Bob Jones University was not entitled to tax-exempt status because its admission policies discriminated on the basis of race (*Bob Jones University v. United States*). BJU admitted as students unmarried blacks or blacks married to blacks, but it denied admission to a partner in an interracial marriage or to someone who supported interracial dating and marriage. The school's policy was based on the belief held by the school's leaders that such practices violate the teachings of the Bible. The Court held that the compelling state interest in preventing racial discrimination outweighed BJU's religious expression that included this racial discrimination.

> When the Government grants exemptions or allows deductions all taxpayers are affected; the very fact of the exemption or deduction for the donor means that other taxpayers can be said to be indirect and vicarious "donors." Charitable exemptions are justified on the basis that the exempt entity confers a public benefit—a benefit which the society or the community may not itself choose or be able to provide, or which supplements and advances the work of public institutions already supported by tax revenues. History buttresses logic to make clear that, to warrant exemption under 501(c)(3), an institution must fall within a category specified in that section and must demonstrably serve and be in harmony with the public interest. The institution's purpose must not be so at odds with the common community conscience as to undermine any public benefit that might otherwise be conferred.

> . . . The governmental interest at stake here is compelling. As discussed [above], the Government has a fundamental, overriding interest in eradicating racial discrimination in education—discrimination that prevailed, with official approval, for the first 165 years of this Nation's constitutional history. That governmental interest substantially outweighs whatever burden denial of tax benefits places on petitioners' exercise of their religious beliefs.

Bob Jones University later dropped its policy against interracial dating, but the school has not tried to regain its tax-exempt status.

Depend on God

The Supreme Court has declared unconstitutional several practices that have been part of American life for years: prayer and Bible reading at school, prayers at high school graduation exercises, and (in certain circumstances) the display of nativity scenes in public facilities during the Christmas season. The Court began by striking down mandatory prayer and Bible reading but then broadened its scope to ban other religious traditions.

School Children in San Francisco, California, 1942

On the other hand, the decisions of the Court have not all been against the expression of religion in the public forum. The Pledge of Allegiance is still used and stands unaltered. Christians can meet in public facilities that are open to other groups. The traditional role of faith in American life still has a place. We are no longer able to expect favorable treatment in the public arena, but we should be able to receive fair treatment there.

In one sense, the Court's rulings are helpful. Christians do not need to think that the survival and growth of our faith are dependent on governmental decrees and approval. Throughout its history, the church has grown most when it is opposed by government. However, the rulings have not made America a better or more moral nation. In fact, it could be said that many of our social problems began to increase when these religious influences were removed. Since this is the case, the church needed to be alerted to the fact that it was depending on the slender reed of government support to accomplish its mission of helping God to transform lives in Jesus Christ.

Christians should not expect the state to do the job that the church is to do. The church should not be surprised when the secular state acts against what the church believes and what the Bible teaches. Whatever support we get from the government is a reason to give thanks, but we must look beyond government for reliable help in living the Christian life. We are first and foremost dependent on God, not on the Supreme Court.

But Peter and the apostles answered,
"We must obey God rather than men."
Acts 5:29

Lesson 73—Reforming Government

I don't make jokes. I just watch the government and report the facts.
—Will Rogers, American humorist

The Trends of Government

Over the last two-thirds of the twentieth century, the size, spending, and power of the Federal government grew at an enormous rate. The Federal budget for 1933 was about $4.6 billion. For 2007, Federal spending exceeded $2.7 trillion, a figure that is 600 times greater than the 1933 budget.

It is common for government to do poorly many things that it attempts to do. Stories have abounded for years of waste, mismanagement, and corruption. Civil service workers generally get paid whether they do a good job or not. Different departments develop programs that are almost duplicates of each other. It is often frustrating to try to get an answer from a government worker about a question or a need.

The Republican Opportunity

The usual cry of Republicans has been that the Democrats are the tax and spend party. It is a fact that the Democrats have controlled Congress for most of the time since 1933, the period during which the Federal government has seen dramatic growth. During the sixty-two years between 1933 and 1995, the Democrats controlled the U.S. Senate for all but ten years (1947-1949, 1953-1955, 1981-1987). During that same sixty-two year period, the Democratic party controlled the U.S. House of Representatives for all but four years (1947-1949, 1953-1955). The Republicans did not control both houses of Congress at any time from 1955 until 1995. In the 1994 election, Republican House candidates offered a Contract with America in which they promised to make significant changes if Republicans gained the majority in Congress. Strong campaigning coupled with some unpopular moves by President Clinton enabled the Republicans to gain control of both the House and the Senate. The Republicans maintained this control except for a brief period when the Senate was evenly divided and then a Republican declared himself an independent, giving control to the Democrats for two years (2001-2003).

In 1994, the American voters handed the Republican party the opportunity to change the philosophy and direction of government; but the Republican-led revolution did not happen. The Republicans failed to lead the way they always said they would. Republican control of Congress did not lead to a major change in the size and spending of government. Expenditures keep going up every year. Programs continue to increase in number.

It is true that the Republican Congress has supported the war on terrorism and has passed legislation banning partial-birth abortion and supporting traditional marriage. However, Republicans in power have shown themselves to be subject to the same moral failings and political corruption that were seen among Democrats for years. Obviously just changing the majority party in Congress did not turn the ship of state around.

How Can We Accomplish Real Reform?

Is it possible truly to reform government? Will we ever see the day when governments spend only as much as they receive in revenues—and when the revenues collected are less than they were the previous year because of tax cuts? Will the national debt ever be paid off? Will a Cabinet department ever be eliminated? Will any government programs ever end?

These changes will not happen by replacing the majority party in Congress, nor will they happen by merely reducing the rate at which government spending increases. Real reform in government will take some hard choices and some radical (meaning at the root) changes in what we expect of government and how government operates.

Being free of government needs to be more attractive than being dependent on government. Elected officials make promises and wave checks in front of voters, and voters re-elect them. Real reform involves supporting candidates who say they will reduce the size of government, and then holding them accountable to follow through on their promises. But cutting programs will only cut loose the many people who have become dependent on government. We need a way to help those people rethink how they should be living.

We need to encourage Americans to live responsibly, and we also need to encourage employers and large companies not to be greedy for more profits and not to create bigger pay and benefit packages for top management. The American economy is not a limited pie which has to be divided up among workers, bosses, and recipients of government aid. By working together, we can have an unlimited pie, the benefits of which can extend to more and more Americans. As long as receiving government checks is more attractive to people, financially and philosophically, we will not be able to reverse the trend of government.

We need to tell government, "I don't want government money; I just want to be left alone." So many people are employed by government and are dependent on government that a large percentage of the population has a major interest in maintaining the status quo. This needs to change. Smaller government will mean fewer government workers, but we can trust that they will be able to find better jobs in a private sector that is energized by a smaller government.

The biggest government programs need the biggest cuts. We will not revolutionize government by nibbling at the edges of government spending. All wasteful and duplicate programs should be eliminated, but we need to take aim at the biggest budget lines. The military is essential, but that is no excuse for the military being wasteful. Many entitlement programs can be phased out so that people will not feel entitled to taxpayers' money. The Federal education budget is not a huge slice of the pie, but it is getting bigger. That money can be returned to the state and local level, along with real control of educational policy.

Parents, communities, and states—not isolated bureaucrats in Washington—need to be in charge of training children.

The American people deserve accountability from the government. It is impossible for the American people to know what big government is doing. We cannot keep track of millions of workers and trillions of dollars. But to know what government is doing, government needs to become smaller and more open. Programs need to have clearly stated objectives, and those programs need to end if the objectives are not being met—and some programs need to end even when the objectives are met! The Food and Drug Administration, for instance, should not have cozy ties to the food industry and to pharmaceutical companies. Regulators cannot protect the public if they are in the pockets of big companies. The purpose of education will not be accomplished by spending more money and trying out this or that new fad. Schools need to be accountable to parents and taxpayers. If the job is not getting done, the approach needs to be changed.

We need a simpler government with fewer regulations. Basic personal and American rights need to be protected from those who would treat people unfairly, but America is over-regulated by government. A real, dramatic change would be to radically reform the tax structure in America. We should not simply let special interest groups receive loopholes and meekly go along with the complicated tax code under which the little guy suffers and the big guy (who can hire accountants and lawyers) skates. This is the twenty-first century, but we have a tax system that is built on procedures almost a century old. Elected officials need to muster the courage to simplify the tax system and make it more just and fair. It is possible, and we should demand it.

Start Somewhere

The problem has become so huge that it is hard to know where to start. It is like trying to figure out which part of an avalanche needs to be stopped first. But we have to start somewhere or we will get nowhere. If we are not willing to help bring about a real change in the direction of government, then we should quit complaining and we should change what we talk about with others. If we take the easier route and do nothing, we will be shirking our responsibility. We are the people of the U.S. government.

*Brethren, I do not regard myself as having laid hold of it yet; but one thing I do:
forgetting what lies behind and reaching forward to what lies ahead,
I press on toward the goal
for the prize of the upward call of God in Christ Jesus.
Philippians 3:13-14*

Reading

- "Rolling Back Government: Lessons from New Zealand" by Maurice P. McTigue (*WHTT*, p. 201)

Lesson 74— Running for and Holding Public Office

Many forms of Government have been tried, and will be tried in this world of sin and woe. No one pretends that democracy is perfect or all-wise. Indeed, it has been said that democracy is the worst form of government except all those other forms that have been tried from time to time.

—Sir Winston Churchill (1947)

Government is not just a subject to study in school. It is not just something that some people do to the rest of us. In America, the government is the servant of the people. Government is something in which we can take part. We can support and vote for candidates and we can let our elected representatives know what we think. We can also seek to serve in government, either in an appointed position or in an elected office. Running for and holding an elected government position is probably the best way to get an education about government, and it can give you the opportunity to put your beliefs into action and to do something good for others.

President Calvin Coolidge Campaigning with His Family, c. 1924

Observing Government

The easiest way to begin taking an active role in government is to attend a meeting of your city council, county government, or state legislature. The activities you see there might look boring, and the subjects and comments might be difficult to understand; but they affect you and your family and involve the spending of thousands and millions of citizens' tax dollars. You will learn the political pressures that elected officials feel. In attending these meetings you will get a good first-hand view of government at work.

Many state homeschool organizations sponsor a rally day or a homeschool day at the state capitol. At these events, hundreds of homeschoolers and their families meet together to hear one or more speeches and then disperse to meet their legislators. Sometimes groups set up displays to show legislators what homeschoolers have been doing. These events are a good way to get to know elected officials and to communicate a positive message about homeschooling.

You might also think about writing a letter to your Congressman or Senator.

Our family visited Washington in the fall of 1995. At the time, Congress and the President were battling over the Federal budget. Important votes were being taken, so when we sat in the House and Senate galleries, we were able to see many well-known members of Congress. Near the end of our visit, the government shut down as a result of the budget standoff. We missed seeing a few sites because of the closures, but the traffic was much lighter!

Use the correct form, keep your letter short and respectful, and discuss one specific issue. Members of Congress want to hear from their constituents, and a letter carries considerable weight with them.

Appointed Positions

One way that a student can take part in government is by serving as a page in the state legislature. A page runs errands for a state legislator or legislative committee, often just for a single day so that many young persons can have the experience. You might be told to get some photocopies made, or you might be asked to bring some water to a committee meeting. You might sit in the back of the legislative chamber and be ready to run an errand for a legislator. Contact your state representative or state senator to let him or her know that you would like to serve as a page. He or she will tell you what you need to do. If you are given this opportunity, make a good appearance and do a good job. This will let you have the most influence that you can in this position.

A few students get the opportunity to serve in a more responsible fashion. You might be chosen to be on a commission that studies a topic and presents a report to the governor or legislature. The Tennessee agency that oversees higher education has a student member that serves a one-year term. To be involved in this way, you would have to be known by or recommended to the person or agency that forms the committee. Making yourself known to your state legislator is a good way to help this happen.

Most of the people who work in government are not elected. They serve as staff members for an elected official or as an employee of a government agency or office. Governments at all levels have hiring procedures to fill the jobs that are authorized by the legislative body. You might have to start on the bottom rung and work your way up to a more responsible position. A person simply has to jump in somewhere and get his or her feet wet to serve in government.

Running for Office

You might dream of becoming the president or a U.S. Senator, but most likely you will have to start small to be able to accomplish that dream. The best way to begin in elective politics is by running for a seat on the county commission or the city council. To do this, you don't just start putting signs by the road and handing out fliers. Candidates must meet certain qualifications, such as age and residency requirements. You must contact the local election commission and fill out the proper forms. In most places, a candidate must get the signatures of a small number of voters on a petition and pay a small fee to be able to have his or her name on the ballot. Filing deadlines are several months prior to the election.

States and the Federal government have strict rules about how campaigns are organized and run, how contributions are collected and spent, and how financial records are to be maintained during the campaign and turned in after the election. You must follow the laws regarding any fundraising that you do. Anyone is free to spend any amount of his or her own money on a campaign.

You will need to meet people and to give them information about yourself and what you believe in. You might want to organize meetings at which you give a short speech. Chili suppers and live entertainment may sound corny, but they do draw crowds. Signs and bumper stickers do not give a great deal of information about a candidate, but they can improve name recognition and can give the sense of a bandwagon developing on behalf of a candidate. Volunteers can help distribute information about your candidacy.

Publicity is all important in a campaign. People must know about you and what you stand for if you want them to vote for you. You, your family, and your friends know what a wonderful and intelligent person you are; but you need the support of many total strangers in order to win an election. Sending press releases to the local newspaper and radio station about your campaign events is a good form of publicity. Paid advertisements can help voters know more about you, but remember that people will be swamped with advertisements and that this can be a very expensive part of a campaign. Developing a website, even for a local race, is a convenient and increasingly essential way to let people know about you. As you campaign, don't talk down to people, and don't make promises that you cannot keep. Don't talk about the Federal deficit or the war in Iraq if you are running for county commission. Address issues that you will have to deal with in the body for which you are running. Be aware that it is illegal and in poor taste to campaign in church settings and to ask churches to support you officially. Churches can lose their tax-exempt status if they campaign for

candidates. You also do not want to give the impression that the only choice that a faithful Christian has is to vote for you. And after the election, win or lose, please be a good citizen and remove the signs that have been placed on your behalf (but not the signs of other candidates!).

Most local elections are non-partisan, but political parties are heavily involved in state and national offices. If you want to run for the state legislature, the state political parties will have their own procedures for being a candidate in a party primary. There are at least two important notes to remember about partisan elections. First, you will probably have to put in a few years of legwork on behalf of the party in order to get the party's support for your own campaign. Parties reward loyalty, and party leaders are more likely to support someone they know and who has paid his dues as opposed to a fresh-faced youngster who shows up and acts as though he has all the answers. Second, the electoral process is heavily weighted in favor of the Republican and Democratic parties. Third parties and independents have a much tougher job of even getting on the ballot, much less getting elected. Independents are rarely elected, and if they are elected they rarely get important committee assignments. Legislatures are organized along party lines, and independents do not fit easily into that scheme. If you cannot go along with either of the major parties, hold to your principles and run as an independent or as a third party candidate. The status quo can only be shaken up by changes in the current system.

And the Winner Is. . .

If the Lord grants you a victory in your campaign, give the glory to Him and do your best to be His servant and the servant of the people who elected you. It is a gracious gesture to put an advertisement in the local paper thanking the voters for their support and pledging your best efforts to serve all of the people while you are in office. If you lose, place an ad to thank those who supported you and to pledge your support to the winner.

As an elected official, you are a servant of the people, not their master. You have made a solemn commitment to helping all of the people the best way you can as you serve in the office. Attend every meeting of the council, commission, or legislature and any committee meetings that you are supposed to attend. Stay informed on the issues. Read the budget and the proposals that come before the body. Listen respectfully when people call or stop you on the street to give you their input. Learn from your critics. Be ready to be confronted with widely divergent ideas, most of which have at least some logic behind them. Also be ready to be confronted with politics as usual, where people behave as if tradition and political connections mean more than good sense and fairness.

Always decide that your family comes first. If you lose your relationships with your family while you are involved in politics and government, you have lost what is really important. Someone else can carry the cause to victory, but no one else can be the member of your family that you need to be.

Federal Elections

When it comes to elections, money talks. About four billion dollars was spent on the 2004 presidential and Congressional campaigns. A small portion of this was the personal wealth of candidates. The overwhelming majority of it was donated to candidates, political parties, or groups formed to promote certain issues. Individuals and organizations contribute this money to candidates not only because they believe in what the candidates say but also in the hope of influencing elected officials to promote the causes that they believe in. The costs of advertising, personnel, travel, and other expenses of a campaign on the Federal level (and

Gerald Ford During the 1976 Presidential Race

for state governorships) have come to mean that usually only those with a large bankroll have a chance of winning—and only those who have a legitimate chance of winning will be able to collect significant contributions.

On Federal income tax returns, each filer has the option of earmarking three dollars of his or her taxes to a Federal presidential campaign fund. This fund is distributed to candidates in the primary season and again for the general election, according to certain guidelines. A candidate can choose to reject these Federal funds and spend as much of his or her own money as he wishes, but if the candidate accepts Federal matching funds he or she has to follow Federal guidelines. The fund was established to try to keep candidates from being dependent on donations from special interest groups and to lessen the advantage that incumbents have, but it has not accomplished these goals. Instead, it has merely helped to increase the amount of money spent on campaigns.

Election and fundraising reforms have been enacted at various times in the past; but candidates, parties, and supporters have always found a way around the laws. After the Watergate scandal in the early 1970s, new laws restricted the money that could be given to candidates. As a result, organizations called political action committees (PACs) were formed that had no restrictions. These groups were organized around specific issues in such a way that it would be obvious what candidate a PAC supported. A labor union PAC, for instance, would almost always support a Democrat. A Family and Freedom PAC would likely support a Republican. Later, other issue groups were formed that also had clear allegiances. Citizens Concerned About Crime, for instance, would buy ads that criticized the Democratic candidate without mentioning the Republican. Americans for Personal Liberty would make charges against the Republican without mentioning the Democratic candidate. These groups were not official parts of the candidate's campaign, but they tried to influence voters just the same. Now a candidate has to approve an ad and the ad has to carry his or her picture if it is paid for by the candidate's official organization.

Contributions to a candidate's campaign are called hard money, and such contributions have limitations and guidelines on how they can be spent. Contributions to issue groups and other such organizations are called soft money because they have not been subject to stringent regulations. The McCain-Feingold Campaign Finance Reform Act of 2002 was an attempt to limit the influence of money in Federal campaigns. A ban was placed on soft money donations, and groups may not run issue ads for a period of time before an election. The law was upheld by the Supreme Court in 2003. Supporters of the law say that it will lessen candidates' dependence on money and make the playing field more level in campaigns. Opponents charge that it is a restriction on legitimate free speech. They say that individuals and groups should be able to support whom they wish and run the ads that they wish. Opponents also say that it will give incumbents a greater advantage, since challengers will have a more difficult time getting their message across to voters.

Almost all candidates for Federal office have considerable personal wealth and have a long track record of being active in state and party politics. Obviously only a relatively few people will ever run for and get elected to a Federal office. However, you can be involved in a Federal campaign as a volunteer and make a considerable difference. A major factor in the re-election victory of George W. Bush in 2004 was the work of volunteers in key states such as Ohio and Florida in getting likely Republican voters to the polls.

Therefore, brethren, select from among you
seven men of good reputation, full of the Spirit and of wisdom,
whom we may put in charge of this task.
Acts 6:3

Reading

- "Something Higher Than Incumbency" by James Rogan (*WHTT*, p. 208)

Lesson 75—A Citizen's Rights and Responsibilities

The fate of the country. . . does not depend on what kind of paper you drop into the ballot box once a year, but on what kind of man you drop from your chamber into the street every morning.

—*Henry David Thoreau (1854)*

The only thing necessary for the triumph of evil is for good men to do nothing.

—*Edmund Burke (1795)*

We live in a great country. America is great for many reasons. It is founded on a carefully considered belief in God, personal freedom, the rights and worth of humans, and the rule  of law. Along with the rights and freedoms we enjoy, however, come responsibilities. We must consider both our rights and our responsibilities to get an accurate assessment of what it means to be an American.

America is great, but America is not perfect. Our history has been marked by the abuse of racial minorities by the white majority. We have sometimes been the bully in world affairs. Some of our leaders have failed the people's trust. Because our country is not perfect, each generation has the responsibility to make our nation more of what it can and should be.

Whatever you believe about politics, the proper sphere of government activity, and the relationship of government to its citizens, you are involved with government. You are affected by it and, in one way or another, you contribute to how it operates. You either help or hinder the process of government by taking part or by letting others act in government without your participation.

Our Greatest Right and Responsibility

Our greatest right, which is at the same time our greatest responsibility, is to pray for our government leaders (1 Timothy 2:1-4). Prayer is a recognition of the ultimate and sovereign power of God to rule over the affairs of men. It is also an appeal to this ultimate Power to accomplish His will through the minds and hearts of those who wield the powers of government. Governments, like nations, are not inanimate objects. They are made up of people, created in the image of God and capable of wonderful good and terrible evil. Prayer brings together the greatest Power for good in the universe with those who guide the nations on an everyday basis.

Praying for our leaders is a precious right that God has given to us. We can do it privately in our own homes and hearts; but we also have the freedom to do it in public, in our churches, and in other settings. Prayer is a responsibility because God has given us this instruction and this ability, and to fail to use it would be to fail God. Never think that you have no say in government. By exercising your right and responsibility to pray, you can exert the greatest influence any human being can have on the workings of government.

> *More things are wrought by prayer than this world dreams of.*
>
> *– Alfred, Lord Tennyson, "Idylls of the King"*

Our Rights

Among the rights we have as Americans:

- We have the right to worship God without interference from the state according to our individual conscience.

- We have the right to participate in the choosing of our elected leaders by voting, by participating in campaigns, and by running for office ourselves.

- We have the right to speak and publish our opinions freely and to assemble peaceably to voice our concerns.

- We have the right to keep and bear arms.

- We have the right to the fair and equitable due process of law: no unreasonable search and seizure, no imprisonment without knowing why, no requirement to testify against oneself, a speedy trial by jury, and no fear of having to be tried more than once for the same charge.

- We have the right to live anywhere in the country and to move about freely from place to place.

- We have the right to educate our children in the way we think best.

- We have the right to work in a job or run a business of our choice.

- We have the right to privacy and confidentiality in our personal and business activities.

Our Responsibilities

Among the responsibilities we have as Americans:

- We have the responsibility to live as Christians because in this way we will do the most good for our country.

- We have the responsibility to influence others for good while not allowing ourselves to be influenced by the world.

- We have the responsibility to pay the taxes that we legitimately owe.

- We have the responsibility to serve when called upon, such as on juries and in times of emergency.

- We have the responsibility to obey the laws and to face the consequences when we do not.

- We have the responsibility to respect our leaders, whether or not we support them and voted for them.

- We have the responsibility to inform our leaders of our opinions for the purpose of helping and not for tearing down.

- We have the responsibility to engage in civil debate on the issues and to consider other points of view respectfully.

- We have the responsibility to use our freedoms, such as the right of free speech and the right to keep and bear arms, in a way that shows respect for other people and for our society as a whole.

Taking Exception

"The faith which you have, have as your own conviction before God" (Romans 14:22a). As Christians, our first responsibility is to God (Acts 5:29). The faith of some Christians has led them to believe that it is best for them not to be involved in the workings of government. Some Christians choose not to vote or to participate in political campaigns or to serve on juries. Some Christians have conscientious objections to serving in the military. These are wonderful rights that we have in the United States. Christians who exercise these rights must be willing to pay the civil consequences for doing so (such as having to render alternative service instead of serving in the military).

Governments will, from time to time, engage in policies with which you disagree. You must decide before God how you will respond to this. The apostles did not counsel the early Christians to ignore laws with which they did not agree. We have the freedom to inform our elected officials of our opinions regarding policies with which we disagree. We are also free to organize petition drives and to employ other means to demonstrate to the government that we disagree with certain policies or proposals.

At times in our history, some have objected to certain laws and were not willing to accept them. The non-violent civil disobedience that characterized the Civil Rights movement challenged laws which enforced racial segregation and discrimination. Henry David Thoreau refused to pay taxes as a protest against the Mexican War. Thousands of Americans protested in various ways our involvement in the Vietnam War. The actions of these dissenters brought their convictions regarding government policies before the public. Those who protest existing laws and policies have to be willing to accept the consequences of their actions as the price they have to pay for making their statement.

It could be that some Christians are convicted of the need to oppose abortion in some way, such as by refusing to pay a portion of their Federal and state taxes. If they do this, they also have to be willing to face the consequences of their actions. However, the publicity surrounding their decision and its consequences might convict legislators to change abortion law, in the same way that civil disobedience helped to change civil rights laws.

Helping America to Be a City on a Hill

> You are the light of the world. A city set on a hill cannot be hidden; nor does anyone light a lamp and put it under a basket, but on the lampstand, and it gives light to all who are in the house. Let your light shine before men in such a way that they may see your good works, and glorify your Father who is in heaven.
>
> —Matthew 5:14-16

After a large number of Jews had been taken into exile in Babylon, Jeremiah sent to them the word of the Lord concerning how they were to live. The prophet told them to go about their lives with hard work and noble purpose. "Seek the welfare of the city where I have sent you into exile, and pray to the Lord on its behalf; for in its welfare you will have welfare" (Jeremiah 29:7). The Lord also warned them against listening to false prophets. God gave them these instructions because He had a plan for them, "plans for welfare and not for calamity to give you a future and a hope" (verse 11). His plan was that in due time He would bring them out of exile and return them to their homeland.

> *Of the sons of Issachar, men who understood the times, with knowledge of what Israel should do, their chiefs were two hundred; and all their kinsmen were at their command.*
>
> *—1 Chronicles 12:32*

Christians live today as aliens and strangers in the world (1 Peter 2:11). This world is not our home because "our citizenship is in heaven" (Philippians 3:20). Nevertheless, we are to live well as God's light to the world. As we seek the welfare of the city where we live, we will bless others and ourselves. We have the opportunity and the responsibility to do good for God's glory and to further His kingdom in the world. Because God has given us "a future and a hope," we can bless our nation by how we live today. This is the freedom and the responsibility that we have not from government but from God.

Then the seventh angel sounded;
and there were loud voices in heaven, saying,
"The kingdom of the world has become the kingdom of our Lord and of His Christ;
and He will reign forever and ever."
Revelation 11:15

Reading

- "Statesmanship and Its Betrayal" by Mark Helprin (*WHTT*, p. 212)

Fourth of July Celebration, Boston, Massachusetts, 2006

Image Credits

Department of Defense: 121 (lower), 122, 135, 137, 139, 142, 143, 147, 151, 153, 154, 157, 171, 174, 183, 186, 207, 221, 213, 224, 240, 242, 244 (upper), 256, 258, 268, 291, 294, 295, 301, 308, 315, 319, 320, 322, 323, 326, 330, 335, 336, 340, 346, 367, 377, 378
Department of Education: 166
Department of Housing and Urban Development: 162, 165
Executive Office of the President of the United States: 126
Federal Emergency Management Agency News Photo: 266, 269, 271, 272, 273, 314
Images of American Political History: 89
JupiterImages (© 2008 JupiterImages): 1, 4, 5, 6, 7, 9, 10, 17, 18, 20 (lower), 22, 23, 24, 25, 26, 27, 28, 30, 33, 36, 37, 39, 40, 41, 43, 45, 46, 49, 52, 54, 56, 58, 59, 60, 61, 62, 63, 64, 65, 66, 69, 71, 77, 81, 84, 96 (lower), 97, 108, 113, 125, 163, 184, 187, 223, 225, 230, 231, 233, 238, 250, 259 (lower), 264, 265, 280, 311, 328, 342, 348, 350, 352, 354, 357
Library of Congress Prints and Photographs Division: 11, 12, 13, 15, 16, 20 (upper), 38, 70, 72, 73, 75, 82, 87, 88, 91, 92, 93, 95, 96 (upper), 100, 111, 115, 117, 118, 119, 121 (upper), 129, 130, 133, 138, 140, 145, 146, 150, 152, 158, 159, 161, 169, 179, 180, 188, 190, 191, 192, 194, 195, 198, 201, 202, 209, 210, 214, 216, 218, 220, 235, 244 (lower), 246, 254, 255, 257, 259 (upper), 290, 296, 299, 300, 302, 329, 331, 333, 337, 343, 344, 358, 369, 372
Lyndon Baines Johnson Presidential Library: 109
National Archives and Records Administration: 292
National Atlas of the United States: 83
Notgrass Family: 361
Notgrass, Mary Evelyn: 35, 228, 239, 247, 249, 253, 263, 266, 270, 298, 347, 371, 374, 375
Office of the Speaker of the U.S. House of Representatives: 98
Ronald Reagan Presidential Library: 245
Strom Thurmond Institute: 107
U.S. Army: 74, 76, 112
U.S. Census Bureau: 261

Quotations from *Democracy in America* by Alexis de Tocqueville and *The Education of Henry Adams* by Henry Adams are used courtesy of the American Studies Collection of Hypertext Documents maintained by the University of Virginia:

http://xroads.virginia.edu/~HYPER/hypertex.html

Select Bibliography

Arctic National Wildlife Refuge, www.anwr.org

Brady Campaign, www.bradycampaign.org

Bureau of TennCare, www.tennessee.gov/tenncare

The Cato Institute, www.cato.org

Center for Health Transformation, www.healthtransformation.net

Central Intelligence Agency, www.cia.gov

City of Spring Hill, www.springhilltn.org

Consumer Products Safety Commission, www.cpsc.gov

Department of Agriculture, www.usda.gov

Department of Commerce, www.commerce.gov

Department of Defense, www.defenselink.mil

Department of Education, www.ed.gov

Department of Energy, www.energy.gov

Department of Health and Human Services, www.hhs.gov

Department of Homeland Security, www.dhs.gov

Department of Housing and Urban Development, www.hud.gov

Department of the Interior, www.doi.gov

Department of Justice, www.usdoj.gov

Department of Labor, www.dol.gov

Department of State, www.state.gov

Department of Transportation, www.dot.gov

Department of the Treasury, www.ustreas.gov

Department of Veterans' Affairs, www.va.gov

Environmental Protection Agency, www.epa.gov

Equal Employment Opportunity Commission, www.eeoc.gov

"A Failure of Initiative," House Select Bipartisan Committee report, available at
    www.house.gov

Farm Credit Administration, www.fca.gov

Federal Communications Commission, www.fcc.gov

Federal Deposit Insurance Corporation, www.fdic.gov

Federal Reserve Board of Governors, www.federalreserve.gov

Federal Trade Commission, www.ftc.gov

General Service Administration, www.gsa.gov

Government Accountability Office, www.gao.gov

Grocke, Vicky. "Compulsory Education, " available at www.nd.edu

Henry J. Kaiser Family Foundation, www.kff.org

The Heritage Foundation, www.heritage.org

Illustrated Bible Dictionary, Wheaton, Illinois: Tyndale, 1980, s.v. "Sanhedrin"

McCullough, David. *John Adams*. New York: Simon and Schuster, 2001.
    Touchstone edition 2002.

Mitchell, Daniel J. "The Impact of Government Spending on Economic Growth," available at
    www.heritage.org

Morgan, Kenneth O., editor. *The Oxford Illustrated History of Britain*. New York:
    Oxford University Press, 1995.

National Aeronautics and Space Administration, www.nasa.gov

National Archives and Records Administration, www.archives.gov

National Association of Counties, www.naco.org

National Association of Towns and Townships, www.natat.org

National Center for Small Communities, www.smallcommunities.org

National Council of State Legislatures, www.ncsl.org

National Governors' Association, www.nga.org

National League of Cities, www.nlc.org

National Rifle Association, www.nra.org

Office of Personnel Management, www.opm.gov

Office of the President, www.whitehouse.gov

"Religion and the Founding of the American Republic,"
    http://www.loc.gov/exhibits/religion/religion.html

Second Amendment Foundation, www.saf.org

Securities and Exchange Commission, www.sec.gov

Small Business Administration, www.sba.gov

Social Security Administration, www.ssa.gov

Tax Policy Center, www.taxpolicycenter.org

The Tennesseean, Nashville, Tennessee newspaper, www.tennessean.com

United States Postal Service, www.usps.com

U.S. Census Bureau, www.census.gov

U.S. Courts, www.insd.uscourts.gov/News/1-05-cv-0813%20Opinion.pdf

Wasem, Ruth Ellen. "U.S. Immigration Policy on Permanent Admissions," available at
    http://fpc.state.gov/documents/organization/31352.pdf

Index

For primary topics, see the Table of Contents.

Also by Ray Notgrass

Exploring World History

This curriculum surveys world history from Creation to modern times. It includes the history narrative, Bible lessons, and reading and writing assignments needed to earn one year's high school credit in Bible, English, and World History.

Exploring America

This curriculum surveys American history from Columbus to the war in Iraq. It includes the history narrative, Bible lessons, and reading and writing assignments needed to earn one year's high school credit in Bible, English, and American History.

For information about these
and other resources available
from the Notgrass Company,
call 1-800-211-8793 or visit
www.notgrass.com.